M000290253

Not to Worry

Jewish Wisdom and Folklore

SUPPORT FOR THE PUBLICATION OF THIS BOOK
IS PROVIDED BY
THE LUCIUS N. LITTAUER FOUNDATION

༄

The Jewish Publication Society is one of the most respected
international Jewish cultural and educational institutions.
In all of its endeavors, JPS seeks to preserve and enrich Jewish heritage.

The Society honors the members of its inaugural Giving Circles,
whose generosity strengthens its ability to achieve its multifaceted mission:

Editor's Circle
SOLOMON AND EDITH FREEDMAN

President's Circle
DR. MOSHE GREENBERG
RONALD P. AND DEBBIE E. SCHILLER

Chairman's Circle
SOL CENTER, M.D.
RABBI ELLEN W. DREYFUS
RABBI MALKA DRUCKER
FRED AND JANE DUBROW
SALLY GOTTESMAN
ESTHER HAUTZIG
DR. AND MRS. REEVAN LEVINE
PHOTOSEARCH, INC.
MRS. HARRIET SOFFA
RABBI STEPHEN WEISS

Not to Worry

Jewish Wisdom and Folklore

Michele Klein

THE JEWISH PUBLICATION SOCIETY

Philadelphia   2003 / 5763

Copyright © 2003 by Michele Klein
First edition. All rights reserved.

No part of this book may be reproduced or transmitted in any form or by any means,
electronic or mechanical, including photocopy, recording, or any information storage or
retrieval system, except for brief passages in connection with a critical review, without
permission in writing from the publisher:
The Jewish Publication Society
2100 Arch St.
Philadelphia, PA 19103

Composition by Book Design Studio
Design by Adrianne Onderdonk Dudden
Manufactured in United States of America
Library of Congress Cataloging-in-Publication Data

Klein, Michele
  Not to worry : Jewish wisdom and folklore / Michele Klein.—1st ed.
    p. cm.
  Includes bibliographical references and index.
   ISBN 0-8276-0753-9
  1. Worry—Religious aspects—Judaism. 2. Bible. O.T.
  Pentateuch—Criticism, interpretation, etc. 3. Legends, Jewish. 4.
  Worry. I. Title.
   BM729.J4 K55 2003
   296.7—dc21

                          2002154015

*For my husband, Jacob,
and my children, Aluma, Allon, Shira, and Tom,
whose worries I have shared and who have often told me not to worry.*

*For my mother, Tsilla,
who has encouraged me not to worry unduly and
to my mother-in-law, Edna,
who has convinced me that worrying is a natural tendency.*

For my father, Peter, as well.

Contents ⚬⚬

Acknowledgments ⌐

I am especially grateful to Helen Eliaspur for many hours of discussion on the intellectual problems that I faced while writing this book. By asking me the right questions, she helped me to worry about what I was writing, clarify my thoughts, and process the mass of research I had undertaken.

I thank Rabbi Reuven P. Bulka for a fruitful discussion of my topic, for his encouragement, and for his comments on some early chapters. Thanks to Professor Morton Ostow and Dr. David Ryde for their comments on individual chapters. Thanks also to Professor Chava Turniansky for discussion about Glückl of Hameln, Susanne Bennewitz for sharing with me some fascinating nineteenth-century women's prayerbooks, and Yaffa Eizen for helping me understand some Yiddish prayers. I am grateful to Hannah Mann for many helpful discussions and to Bill Gross for allowing me to study items in his family collection of Judaica.

I am most grateful to Ms. Rachel Segal for reading my manuscript carefully from end to end, and to my father, Dr. Peter Castle, who willingly reviewed my chapters countless times as I wrote and rewrote them. Their thoughtful remarks were most helpful.

I appreciate having been able to work in the Jewish National University Library, and thank the librarians, especially Gila Flam, the director of the music department. I also found considerable source materials in the Tel Aviv University Sourasky library, as well as in the

Bodleian library in Oxford. I spent many hours working in the quiet upstairs room of the Centre for Jewish Studies at Yarnton, near Oxford.

I am especially grateful to Dr. Ellen Frankel for her professional guidance, trust, and enthusiasm, and to all the wonderful people at the Jewish Publication Society who have helped in the production of this book.

All biblical quotations are from *Tanakh: The Holy Scriptures* (Philadelphia: Jewish Publication Society, 1985) and are reprinted by permission of the Jewish Publication Society.

All references preceded by M. are from the Mishnah. For the Mishnah in English, see translation by J. Neusner (New Haven: Yale University Press, 1991). All talmudic references preceded by B. are from the Talmud Bavli, the Babylonian Talmud, and those preceded by J. are from the Talmud Yerushalmi, the Talmud of the Land of Israel. There are many editions of the Babylonian Talmud, both in Hebrew and in English. See, for example, the translation and edition of I. Epstein (London: Soncino Press, 1935–1938) in thirty-five volumes. For an English translation of the other Talmud, see the translation by J. Neusner (Chicago: University of Chicago Press, 1982–1986) in thirty-three volumes. For the Midrash Rabbah in English, see the translation and edition by H. Freedman and M. Simon (London: Soncino Press, 1951) in ten volumes. And for an English translation of the Zohar, see *The Zohar* (London: Soncino Press, 1931) in five volumes.

The following borrowed material is acknowledged:

Chapter 3: The poem by Abraham Sutskever, from Roskies, D. G., *The Literature of Destruction* (Philadelphia: Jewish Publication Society, 1989), 492–93. Reprinted with permission of The Jewish Publication Society.

Chapter 8: Sholom Aleichem, *Some Laughter, Some Tears*, translated by Curt Leviant (New York: G. P. Putnam's Sons, 1968). Reprinted with permission of Curt Leviant.

Introduction ⌐

"We must not worry. Only one worry is permissible: a person should worry because he is worrying," said the rabbi of Lekhivitz (Lachow-icze, in Polish) in the early twentieth century.[1] Should we do our best not to worry, as the Hasidic rabbi of Lekhivitz taught, or are there situations when worrying is helpful? I sometimes tell myself that the Hasid was correct; I should not be worrying and I try to stop worry-ing. My children often accuse me of being an irrational worrier, al-though they themselves fret over anxieties that I am convinced are the products of their imaginations. Their worries often appear un-necessary to me; they worry over situations that I would never worry about. Their grandmothers are often apprehensive and their father, too, has his own worries. All my friends worry too, about one thing or another. Worrying is not specifically a Jewish trait—most of hu-manity would admit to worrying every now and then. Would the rabbi say that we should all try to control our thoughts and not worry?

Perhaps the Hasid's advice is incorrect, however. Perhaps worry is a healthy, adaptive behavior. By alerting a person to danger, worry can help us to preserve lives, take protective action, or solve a prob-lem. In our worry we may be expressing love and care. Perhaps the Hasid did not think of these aspects of worry.

What is the point of worrying about the fact that we worry, the only permissible worry in the rabbi's teaching? Where will this particular worry lead us?

Worry is a pregnancy. A seed of uncertainty enters the imagination and begins to mature within us. This seed may grow into full-fledged anxiety and drain our strength. For this reason, the rabbi tells us that we should not worry. We could—and perhaps should—prevent it from growing inside us, reject it, abort it. However, there is another possibility; we could nurture this seed until we give birth to a new idea. As we will see in this book, worry can lead us to discovery, insight, and creativity. This is presumably the reason for the Hasid's permission to worry. If we can become aware that we are worrying, we should use our mental turmoil to gain knowledge, wisdom—a new meaning, perhaps, or insight.

I came to the subject of this book through my previous research on childbirth. Jews are fond of using pregnancy and birth metaphorically, but I studied the literal aspects of this process. In the past, the long waiting period from conception through to birth, followed by weeks when mother and newborn were especially fragile, formed a dark tunnel of uncertainty with no guarantees of light at the end. Jews had their own particular ways of perceiving and interpreting the childbirth process and coping with it. What other situations stimulated Jews to worry, I wondered? Have they used similar methods to allay worries in all situations in which the future appears perilous and uncertain? By studying how Jews coped with their worries in the past, can we gain a new perspective on our own worries? Can we find fresh possibilities for finding strength at the end of the worry trip? Can we perhaps also widen our view of Jewish tradition?

Of course, secularization, scientific understanding, and technological advances have considerably changed how people today perceive the world, as well as how people behave. The dangers that we face daily now are not those faced by our grandparents, but aren't we just as anxious as they were, if not more so?

I am neither a psychotherapist nor a religious Jew. I am a secular Jew with a doctorate in psychology. I have no clinical or therapeutic experience. My life has not been marked by any severe trauma and this book does not try to solve any particular problem of my own. My interest lies in positive psychology, not in clinical or abnormal psychology. I am interested in how we can turn our tendency to worry into a positive force. How can our tendency to worry lead us toward meaningful, productive, and fulfilling lives?

In his first speech to the nation on September 11, 2001, President Bush turned to religion to cope with the strong emotion that the day's events had produced in his nation and around the world: "Tonight, I ask for your prayers for all those . . . whose sense of safety and security has been threatened. And I pray they will be comforted by a power greater than any of us." He then quoted Psalm 23: "Though I walk through the valley of the shadow of death, I fear no evil, for You are with me." The next day, he reaffirmed his faith: "In the face of all this evil, we remain strong and united, 'one Nation under God.'" In the aftermath of the terror attacks in the United States of America, churches, synagogues, and mosques all over the world filled with anxious people seeking meaning, comfort, and help in the shelter of religion. Religion provides a feeling of security, community, and care for body and soul, especially when people feel helpless in controlling their futures. The religious community cares for the hungry and poor just as its prayers and rituals address the needs of distressed souls.

The attacks on the Pentagon and the World Trade towers were not the first experiences of terror in Jewish memory; the Jewish people have repeatedly been threatened with massacre, imprisonment, blood libels, and other horrors. A broken spirit is life threatening, not only to oneself, but also to the continuity and strength of the Jewish people. We can learn from the generations of Jews who managed to keep their collective spirit intact in the face of catastrophe. Jews are experts at coping with fear.

Through the ages, religion provided the framework for understanding fear, as well as faith, guilt, and love. It may still interpret phenomena that we do not understand and give meaning to experiences that are beyond our grasp. It may also offer a vision of a better world and a possibility for hope. Jews have long talked of a "world to come," wanting to keep alive the communal striving for a happier future. And messianic movements that spread the belief in an imminent redemption have waxed during eras of terror and waned as anxiety faded.

Psychiatry, the branch of medicine concerned with phobia, chronic apprehension, and excessive worry, was born only when religion was losing its grip on intellectual society, in the mid–nineteenth century. There are now many psychiatric texts on the topic of anxiety and anxiety disorders, as well as popular self-help guides. What does religion offer our contemporary understanding of fear, anxiety, and worry? Judaism has been in existence far longer than psychiatry; what does it offer the worried person?

For at least two thousand years, Torah study has been the ideal Jewish antidote to worry, available mainly to men, not women. Since the period of the Second Temple, however, only a fraction of Jewish men have attained full-time immersion in Torah and spiritual elevation. Women have been exempted from the precept to study and in the past they often had little chance to achieve an elevated spiritual state free from worry. Clearly, the majority of Jewish people have had to find other ways of coping with worry and discovering inner strength. We will see that they found several ways of doing this.

The Scope and Aim of This Book

This book is about worry, the normal everyday worrying that we all do. Whether we label what we all do as worry, anxiety, fear, dread, anguish, or fretting, we are speaking about a multifaceted concept that we have all experienced. We have opted to focus on the word "worry" as this word sounds more normal and less pathological than "anxiety," the clinical word today for a disturbing state of worry.

Psychiatrists today differentiate between the emotion that is a fear of something and the undirected, generalized anxiety state. Similarly, psychologists distinguish between the emotional state of being anxious, and the personality trait of being anxious. In addition, they highlight the interdependent processes of stress, appraisal, emotion, and coping that contribute to our experience of worrying. But here we concern ourselves with worry in general and use words such as anxiety, anguish, fear, and apprehension synonymously, just as Jews have done since antiquity.

The Jewish sources do not define worry and do not use a single word for the subject that we examine here. They actually use many different words for the problem that we call worry and reveal many different attitudes to it. The more Jewish books we open, the more images we find. The view of one Jewish thinker differs from another's. Judaism cannot guide us to an ideal point on a continuum that begins in a state of no worry at all and extends through moderate anxiety to debilitating terror. Furthermore, it is not obvious that worry, anxiety, and terror exist on the same psychological continuum. The view of worry in Judaism is multidimensional: as we all know, there are different contexts for worry, different intensities, and different durations. Moreover, worry might be appropriate and constructive in a certain situation, at a certain time, but useless or even harmful in another situation or at another time.

Psychologists attempted to define worry only in the late twentieth century. In 1983, a pioneer study of worry defined this term as "a chain of thoughts and images, negatively affect-laden and relatively uncontrollable; it represents an attempt to engage in mental problem-solving on an issue whose outcome is uncertain but contains the possibility of one or more negative outcomes. . . ."[2]

Here in this book, the word "worry" includes the niggling, specific, and even acute fear and dread that something bad might happen as well as the more generalized, diffuse feelings of fretting, apprehension, and anxiety. Each individual has his or her particular stock of worries. We each have different triggers that make us worry, hidden in our own experiences and imagination, as well as in our responsibilities and sense of dignity. Also, we each have different styles of worrying: we may fret over every small thing; or we may worry only in a crisis; alternatively, perhaps only after the crisis is over, we may realize how we felt and how we behaved. In addition, we each have different ways of coping with distress.

This book is not about the fear of God, the religious anxiety that rabbis have promoted throughout the ages as a motivation to love and obey God, and as a guiding principle to ethical behavior. It does, however, look at moral anxiety, the fear of sin and evil, which is an aspect of religious anxiety as well as normal worry for some Jews. It also mentions the common worries of the past concerning the Evil Eye, the Evil Inclination, and other evil forces. Jews have often assumed that their worries stem from such evil forces.

Do men and women worry about different things? Do they express their worries in different ways? Do they have different styles of coping? What is the role of women in the worries of Jewish men and the role of men in women's worries? I kept these questions in mind as I researched the book. Where I use the third person masculine pronoun, this usually means that the sentence does not apply to women. For example, it is unlikely that women used the meditative methods described in chapter 4, and therefore the male pronoun is used freely in that chapter.

I have analyzed a common aspect of human behavior in the context of Judaism's rich tradition. I explore the ways in which Jews have experienced, expressed, and understood their feelings of worry. I reveal their attitudes to particular worries, but do not mention each and every worry that has ever disturbed a Jew. I focus on some of the methods that Jews have used to cope with worry, but do not mention each and every way that a Jew has tried to cope with daily concerns. I have chosen only a few methods, which are used by non-Jews too, but which Jews have adapted in their own characteristic ways to suit their own purposes. Jews have clearly also employed other coping strategies.

I have looked at how Jews have customized universal behaviors to suit their own special needs. Non-Jews all over the world have prayed, meditated, and interpreted and induced dreams. Non-Jews have also fashioned amulets and whispered incantations, and most peoples have sung and joked about their anxieties. Here, however, I have focused on the particular ways that Jews have given their own meanings to these behaviors. I have limited the scope of this book by making no cross-cultural comparisons between Jewish and non-Jewish cultures. I have likewise refrained from exploring the non-Jewish influences on Jewish thinking and behaviors that I describe. I have sometimes highlighted a custom observed in a particular Jewish community, but have tried wherever possible to look for continuities in attitudes and behaviors, both in time (between past and present) and across the globe, in the different Jewish communities.

I have looked with modern eyes, with modern understanding, at the ways in which Jews have worried and coped with worry. I have mentioned some theories of psychology that appear to validate or deepen our understanding of traditional Jewish beliefs in modern times. However this study makes no attempt to cover all the modern theories of psychology, nor the tens of thousands of academic papers written over the past few decades on anxiety, fear, and worry.

My aim in writing this book is to see how Jewish wisdom can give us courage to face a world that often appears uncertain and threatening. In addition, I wanted to discover what Jewish history can teach us about psychological strength, peace of mind, and creative thinking. I hope that the following chapters will help readers (those who are well versed in Jewish tradition as well as those who know little) to understand and cope with their own worrying.

Sources

I have drawn considerably from the aggadah, literally the "narrative," in rabbinic sources. Rabbinic teachings contain much narrative that includes homiletical expositions of the Bible, stories, folklore, and maxims. These often reveal the daily concerns and amazing solutions of past centuries, in the rabbinic academy, the Jewish home, and in the community. The heroes of these tales set examples and provide inspiration. Jewish myths offer explanations of the eternal problems of mankind; they describe the associations of earthly and heavenly beings in primeval times and assume that these continue to influence us. Such legends and myths often reflect both the inner and outer worlds of the Jew, and personal as well as communal worries.

Jewish folktales and folksongs mirror dangers in real life; the community as a whole is brought to the brink of disaster by the whim of evil, or the soul of a Jew is threatened by his or her own misdemeanors. Jewish folklore reflects the intense longing for some assured form of salvation. Tales and songs move easily into the realm of fantasy, providing miraculous deliverance or meting out desired revenge. Such folktales and songs are cathartic; they express emotion and strengthen faith. Their themes, often deriving from worry, remain relevant today.

The Jewish devotional literature, including the synagogue liturgy and personal petitions, is another source for discovering the daily concerns and coping behaviors of ordinary Jews. Prayers relay the concerns of the individual, the community, and the whole Jewish people. They assume that human destiny lies in God's hands and include petitions to God for mercy and attention. They include expressions of repentance and atonement, assuming that tragedy might be a punishment for sins. They also offer hope, affirming faith and linking the Jew's present worries with those of other Jews whom God favored in the past.

The Jewish ethical literature guides Jews on how they should behave and feel toward themselves, others, and God. It teaches that certain worries are healthy not only for a person's well-being and moral integrity, but for society, when these promote ethical behavior, and for the cosmos, when these lead to behavior that promotes divine harmony.

The esoteric Jewish mystical literature recognizes the impulses and emotions that often upset or overwhelm us. This literature reveals how Jews shed their worries in order to find communion with God— via special hymns and songs, esoteric prayers, and meditations. Jewish mystics divested themselves of their impulses and all the clutter of sensory perceptions, including worries, when they sought to enter heavenly palaces to find God and receive prophecies about the future. The joyful Hasidic melodies that are well known today grew out of such mystical search for God.

Another product of the Jewish mystical tradition is the attempt to draw down divine blessing. Jews developed theurgical and magical methods to draw on divine power for protection and healing. The large number of protective amulets preserved today bear witness to their important role in countering specific and general worries in the daily life of ordinary Jews worldwide. The writing on these amulets reveals that Jewish men and women have used them in the hope of eliciting God's protection against a variety of dangers, such as the Evil Eye, illness, and nightmares. Although rabbis forbade the use of amulets for any purpose other than for protection against danger, some Jews have used them to cope with other types of worries, for example, in the hope of success in business and arousing a woman's love.

The rationalist thinker may feel antagonistic toward the mystical, kabbalistic, and Hasidic view of the world. However, historically, normative rabbinic Judaism, dominated by rationalist thinkers, stressed the deed more than the thought and the feeling, the fulfilling of the commandments more than the emotion involved in performing them. The kabbalists and Hasidim, however, confronted emotion. These men were aware of the difficulties of attaining the ideal spiritual experience, the love and fear of God. They knew that worry hampers the attainment of such an experience. They recognized the difficulty of conquering, banishing, or sublimating worry. The mystics wrote new prayers, found new ways of praying, and created new rituals to answer their emotional needs. In researching this book, I found that the mystics offered more practical advice for the worried than did the rationalists.

The Talmud noted that anxiety could delay a woman's menstruation and reduce a man's virility. Maimonides and other Jewish physicians noticed additional physical symptoms of anxiety such as trembling, insomnia, and loss of weight in their patients. Thus Sigmund Freud was not the first Jewish doctor to address anxiety. Yet he not only described the somatic symptoms of chronic worriers in detail, but also developed theories to help us understand their existence and therapeutic techniques to treat those who suffer. Even Freud's many critics would admit that he opened up the psychological study of anxiety.

The literature of Jewish humor is relatively recent, but the tradition of laughing in the face of danger is as old as the hills. Jewish humor acquired definitive characteristics of its own over the past century in the United States, influenced by the way that eastern European Jews coped with worry in the nineteenth century. However, this humor differs notably from the fine oral humor of Sephardic, Iraqi, and Yemenite Jews. Israeli humor, too, has acquired its own characteristics in recent years, drawing on all the different ethnic traditions as well as the classic forms of satire, parody, and comedy.

Communal records, the books of rulings kept by Jewish community councils, address worries that arose from accusations and decrees issued from outside the community, affecting their members. They also reveal business concerns within the community, and worries about maintaining Jewish laws, education, and morality.

Finally, there is a fascinating literature revealing how Jews found strength and courage to survive virulent anti-Semitism. This includes diaries, sermons, tales, and testimonies. Some of this material was written in the darkness of the valleys of death. There are also memoirs written after the nightmarish ordeal and documentary material collected by historians in recent times.

The reader will see that I have consulted mystical, philosophical, and historical Jewish texts. I have drawn from the ethical and spiritual ideals formulated by rabbis, rather than from the Jewish legal doctrine of halakhah. Although I have studied a wide range of sources for this book, I could have studied many more. Specialists in rabbinics, Jewish mysticism, history of medicine, philosophy, Jewish literature, ethics, Jewish antiquity, Holocaust studies, psychoanalysis, and psychology—or other disciplines that I have consulted—will no doubt find examples from their particular field of study that I could have included.

The reader will be aware of the long continuum of Jewish history, reaching from biblical to modern times. Where a specific idea or custom arose at a known point in history, I have tried to supply the relevant name and date. However, beliefs and behaviors relating to Jewish law often date back to antiquity. I have tried to avoid phrases such as "in the past," "throughout the ages," and "over the centuries," as they can become annoyingly frequent when referring to Jewish historical continuities in a wide historical perspective.

There have been several pietist movements in Jewish history. To distinguish between the medieval movements and those that date from the eighteenth century and later, I have used the word "pietists" to refer to the Ashkenazic Hasidim of the twelfth and thirteenth centuries and the pietists in Egypt in the thirteenth and fourteenth centuries. I have used the word "Hasidim" to refer to the Hasidim in Eastern Europe in the eighteenth century and later. By the end of the eighteenth century, eastern European Hasidim had several offshoot movements, whose individual leaders stressed different aspects of pietism. The Holocaust destroyed the Hasidic communities in Eastern Europe, but the eastern European Hasidic movements have revived and flourish today in the United States, Israel, and many other countries.

The Plan of This Book

The first chapter of this book looks at the difficult questions of what is worry and how we worry. It also examines some ideas that Jews have offered for why we worry.

The rest of this book presents a variety of methods that Jews have employed to cope with worry. Chapter 2 discusses the cognitive and behavioral strategies that Jews have used to try to stop worrying. It looks also at acceptance of worry, for better or for worse.

Chapters 3 to 8 focus on some ways in which Jews have applied these coping strategies. Thus, in chapter 3, we show that Jews have sometimes quashed their worries by praying and sometimes faced and shared their worries in their prayers. Chapter 4 reveals that some Jews have banished worry in their efforts to meditate and have meditated in the hope of gaining revealing information. Chapter 5 looks at how some Jews have gained insight from their dreams or diffused emotion in their dreams. They have also found ways to try to prevent and remedy worrying dreams. Chapter 6 discloses that some Jews have used theurgical and magical means to gain information and power that they believe might prevent or remove their worrying. In chapter 7, we see that Jews have banished worries with music and admitted their worries in song, drawing strength to cope. In chapter 8, we show that Jews have laughed at their worries with friends, thereby gaining admiration and sometimes a new perspective on their problems.

Each of these six chapters looks at why, when, and how Jews have used the particular method under consideration (prayer, meditation, dreams, theurgy and magic, melody, and humor) to cope with worry.

The concluding chapter considers the purposes and consequences of worry. It shows that sometimes we worry destructively, but points out how we can worry constructively, for the better.

Not to Worry ⤚

Jewish Wisdom and Folklore

1 ⁓ About Worry

"We are distressed about the past, perturbed about the present, and frightened about the future," observed a Jewish poet, Jedayah Bedersi "Ha-penini," in Provence, in the early fourteenth century, meditating on human nature.[1] He evidently noticed the human tendency to worry. But what is worry? Why do we worry? How do we worry? These are the questions we will try to answer in this chapter.

What Is Worry?

Is worry a feeling, an unpleasant emotion, or a disturbing thought? Is it a vague fear or a specific apprehension? It can come in varying intensities, ranging from a mild bother to extreme distress. We may think of it as a state of the heart, the mind, or the soul.

Worry is perhaps also a natural inclination and, in some people, a personality trait. Sometimes it is a life-preserving impulse; often it is a learned response to bitter experience.

The seventeenth-century philosopher Baruch Spinoza thought that worry is an "inconstant pain" arising from the image or idea that something bad might happen.[2] Worry is essentially future-oriented, as we think about an unpleasant possibility. When we worry about the past or the present, we worry about something that is somehow related to or could affect our future.

Worry may involve a distorted perception, a vivid imagination, or heightened attention to danger signals. It may be merely a pessimistic daydream, or a useful tool for solving problems. It can sometimes be a premonition of what is likely to happen, even a self-fulfilling prophecy. Is worry perhaps also a weakness of mind or a failure of reason?

Could worry, as some have imagined, be an evil spirit gnawing away inside us, punishing us? Or is worry the result of guilt, or even a basic insecurity? Worry can be neurotic, but it can also be healthy and adaptive.

Worry may be self-centered, or it may relate to other people, a situation, a task, or an idea. Worry can be personal, something we experience alone, and it can be communal, a feeling that the whole family or the whole community shares.

We can see ourselves as active agents initiating and terminating worry. Or we may experience our worry passively, as uncontrollable, as it swamps us and we feel unable to stop it. The sensation of worrying is often unpleasant. "Better ten small worries than one big one," advises a Yiddish proverb.

Jews have thought about worry in all these ways—as a physical, an emotional, and a spiritual condition. They have also viewed worry as an ethical issue, a supernatural problem, and a metaphysical question. In addition, some Jews have believed that worry may be an existential concern.

Worry is a complex, multifaceted concept that we all know well and have experienced firsthand. The *New Oxford Dictionary of English* (1998) defines worry as "a state of anxiety and uncertainty over actual or potential problems" and "a source of anxiety." The verb to worry means "to cause to feel anxiety or concern." In addition, when used without a direct object, it denotes "to give way to anxiety or unease; allow one's mind to dwell on difficulty or troubles."

Psychologists today argue that worry is not the same as anxiety, although it is similar. Both nouns relate to a state of psychological distress. Worry, as a verb, refers also to a process of anticipating unpleasantness or danger, a process of preparatory coping that can motivate constructive action. The process of worry can sometimes lead a person into an anxious or depressive pit with no sign of a way out, but it can also lead a person to solve a problem and experience joyful relief. The "work of worry" can lead us either way, into or out of anxiety. We can worry for better or for worse.[3]

In this book, we will sometimes focus on the emotional dimension of worry—the negative mood that often comes with or results from worrying. Sometimes we will notice the cognitive dimension of worry—the thoughts and pictures that flood into our minds when we worry. And, as we look at coping strategies, we will frequently look at the motivational dimension of worry that moves us to put an end to negative emotion and change our perception of the situation. We consider that worry is both a state and a process. It is a cognitive state (a real or imagined perception, or chain of perceptions) and a process of thinking and apprehending; it is also an affective state (concern or distress) and a process of feeling and generating emotion; and worry is also a motivating force that involves the consideration of possibilities and the formation of hypotheses or fictions about an issue whose outcome is uncertain. Worry is certainly a complicated human condition, although the sages suspected that God worries too.[4]

The Vocabulary of Worry in Jewish Sources

Bedersi, in the quotation at the start of this chapter, used *mitatzev* for his emotion about the past, *bahalah* for distress about the present, and *yirah* for trepidation about the future. Elsewhere in his treatise he used also *paḥad, eymah,* and *be'atah*—biblical words for fear and strong anxiety. There is a gamut of more than a dozen Hebrew words in the Jewish sources that express apprehensive emotion, the feeling of worry, the sensation of anxiety, as well as the process of becoming fearful. These words are used in different contexts in the Torah, rabbinic texts, and again in modern Hebrew today. They depict long-term and short-lived anguish, situation-specific and diffuse anxiety, and rational and irrational fear. They refer to moral, social, and existential worrying, also fear of suffering and death. The gamut stretches from mild fretting to panic, from trembling anguish to numbing dread.[5]

The noun, *yirah,* and its verb are used very frequently in the Pentateuch, especially in commands to fear God and fear parents. Such awesome fear is not what we think of today as worry. However, the Pentateuch uses the same word in other contexts, such as to depict Adam's concern about his nakedness and Sarah's dread when she is accused of laughing at God's apparently ridiculous promise that she (an old woman) would soon conceive. The same word is used for Lot's anxiety about living near Sodom and Gomorrah after God had destroyed them. Isaac fears that the Philistines may kill him to take his wife, and Jacob is afraid that his brother Esau may kill him and his family. Joseph's brothers worry (still the same Hebrew word, as a verb) when they return from Egypt and find money in their bags. We too worry about how others see us, if we think we have been disrespectful, if we sense danger, and if we have been accused of a misdeed that we did not knowingly commit.[6]

The Pentateuch and later Jewish texts often use synonymous words together to stress an important point. Therefore the biblical use of two words, such as *yirah* together with *de'agah,* or *haradah* together with *pahad,* may have the purpose of stressing one idea—God's promise that those who obey the commandments will not worry. The different Hebrew words may have had subtly different meanings, but were often used together to convey anxiety.[7]

It is difficult to establish precise differences in meaning between the ancient Hebrew words that are translated variously as fear, worry, anxiety, and dread, or to know why one word was chosen as well as or instead of another. We too use several English words to convey such subjective experience and assume that others understand.

The Sages used biblical words to refer to their daily fretting, such as their apprehension lest something bad happen, worry over ill-health, and concern about earning a living. They noticed that a father worried about his daughter and some people were frightened in the darkness of night. The sages also observed that worry can harm a person's health. They understood that thoughts that weigh on the heart during the day can surface in dreams at night. In addition, they knew that worry can distract the Jew from serving God in prayer.[8]

Medieval and later philosophers and physicians also used the biblical vocabulary for anxiety. However, kabbalists and the eastern European Hasidim focused particularly on the disturbing and "alien" thoughts (*mahshavot tordot, mahshavot zarot*) that prevent a man from turning toward God and concentrating on his prayers.[9]

Some Jews had a special vernacular vocabulary for disturbing emotion that differentiated between various anxiety disorders. Thus, for example, in Moroccan Judeo-Arabic, *shakikah* refers to fear, usually noticed in women with hysterical symptoms, quite different from *hatfa,* the "snatched heart" experienced by men who have been out alone in the dark. Other Judeo-Arabic words refer to a trembling fear caused by an evil spirit, a disease of the imagination (possibly what we now call "paranoia"), and a panic attack. Iraqi and Yemenite Jews use *hofah* for fright; Iraqis also use the word *tarkah,* and Yemenite Jews use the word *fadja,* for different anxiety disorders, each calling for its own folk remedy. Iraqi Jews have compared a constant worrier to a chicken in the hen house, constantly afraid of the jackal and the wolf; "Come the jackal, come the wolf" denotes one who lives in constant dread.[10]

Yiddish speakers draw on both German and Hebrew, using *Zorge, Angst,* and *de'agah* for anxiety and worry, as well as the more general term for distress and anguish, *tzuris.*[11]

Others usually understand the vocabulary that we use to talk about our distressed mood, without our needing to define the words we use.

Why Do We Worry?

We often look for the cause of a problem before we set about remedying it. We worry for all sorts of reasons, for reasons that are common to all humanity, and for reasons that come from our own, individual experiences in life. A situation that is worrying for one person may not be at all worrying for another. But usually we do not stop to think why we are worrying, and if we were to stop to think about this, we may well find it hard to say.

Jewish thinkers have traditionally looked to the Torah to answer difficult questions about human nature. Here worry stems from transgression, our need to master, or our need to be sociable. Some Jews realized that worry may result from natural causes, a strong imagination, or from a bad experience. Others noticed that worry surges forth when our desires lead us into some sort of conflict. At times, the fact that a person is Jewish may give cause for worry.

There may be an external source for worrying, or the reason may come from within us. The cause may be obvious, or hidden. Often, a combination of factors may be at the root of our worrying.

In recent times, psychologists, psychiatrists, and psychoanalysts have postulated innate needs and impulses, cognitive processes, as well as cultural and environmental factors that could cause our worrying. Some scientists have tried to answer the question of why we worry by examining brain chemistry and genes.[12] Searching for answers to the question of why we worry makes us aware of the myriad reasons for our own worrying. We could each add from our own experiences to the limited choice of reasons offered below. We start, of course, with the Torah.

We Worry Because We Have Transgressed

The connection between anxiety and transgression appears in the story of Adam and Eve (Gen. 3). God warned that if Adam tasted the fruit of the Tree of Knowledge, he would die. The couple did not know the meaning of death and did not worry. However, they did not die immediately after biting the forbidden fruit. The first effect of the bite was that "the eyes of both of them were opened"; they could see that they had disobeyed and imagine the consequences of God's wrath. God called out to Adam, "Where are you?" The Omnipotent knew the answer, but wanted to reach into Adam's heart.

The man was afraid and hid. The couple worried and denied responsibility for their transgression.

Adam and Eve are our prototypes. We are each historically and biographically guilty, said Martin Buber in 1957, and bear responsibility for our share in the human order of being. Our existential guilt draws us into the anguish of our conscience, and, like Adam, we often try to hide from this. Sometimes it overwhelms us and sweeps us into the abyss.[13]

The Bible teaches that anyone who fails to obey God's laws will suffer anguish, despondency, and worse, live in "terror, night and day, with no assurance of survival" (Deut. 28:66). God imposes worry, fear, and dread as a punishment for sin. However, those people who love and obey God win divine blessing and protection, and need not worry about anything.[14]

Who is a sinner? A frightened person, says Isaiah. Who is a worrier? One who ignores God, a bad, foul, witless evildoer, says the Psalmist. The sinner worries and the worrier has sinned. "As long as a man does not sin, he is feared; as soon as he sins, he himself fears" (B. *Sanhedrin* 106b). In a similar vein, it is told that Solomon ruled fearlessly over the demons until the day he sinned; after that day he dreaded the demons greatly. Our sins break our courage and our strength.[15]

King Saul battled the Philistines fearlessly until he sinned; after that, "his heart trembled with fear." He had disobeyed God's command and lost divine favor. God removed the divine spirit bestowed on him, and "an evil spirit from the Lord" settled in its place (1 Sam. 28:4, 16:14). Rather than face their own guilty conscience, people have often preferred to believe that evil spirits are bothering them. Many Jews have assumed that "spirits of terror and spirits of dread" can speak inside our minds by day or night, and determine our thoughts and emotions. In the late thirteenth century, the kabbalist Abraham Abulafia warned that Satan, the power of illusion with no real substance or durability, can roam the mind when it is not focused on God and create frightening figments of imagination. Until the twentieth century, many Jews assumed that worrying thoughts might come from a spirit that enters the mind or body, but rabbis stressed that this happens only when divine favor is removed, as in the case of King Saul, and is a punishment for some sin. The rationalization that worry comes from an evil spirit allows the illusion that anxiety is caused by an external agent and is not necessarily our own fault.[16]

We Worry Because We Need to Master

God's blessing in the first chapter of Genesis is for man and woman to fill the earth and master it. (The need for offspring, to fill the earth, has often been a cause of worry for Jews, but that topic is discussed elsewhere.) [17] As we grow up, we desire to master our environment and learn to overcome difficulties. Already in the second century B.C.E., the Hebrew sage and aphorist Ben Sira noticed that our work is a cause of worry. The herdsman worries about fodder for his heifers, the potter worries about the quality and finish of his pots, and the scholar worries about the hidden meaning of the proverbs and the wisdom of the ancients.[18]

The man of faith does not worry about food for tomorrow, but "the more wealth, the more worries," says an ancient Jewish proverb, is as true today as ever before (Avot 2:7). The psychiatrist Alfred Adler (1870–1937), an early disciple of Freud who split away from the psychoanalytic circle, noticed that it is human nature to strive to master our environment to feel powerful. This striving—a divine injunction, an innate need, or a learned behavior (however we choose to see it)—can be a cause of worry.[19]

Another psychiatrist, Viktor Frankl (1905–1997), became convinced that those who have no desire to master anything, who lack a goal in life, also worry. The souls of his anxious patients were "hanging in the air," they were not directed anywhere at all.[20] Thus having a task to master and *not* having a task to master may both be reasons for worrying, just as wealth and penury may both lead to worry.

We Worry Because We Are Sociable

In the second chapter of Genesis, God says "it is not good for man to be alone." We must find a partner and live socially. Hillel, an influential sage who lived at the end of the first century B.C.E., wondered, "If I am not for myself, who will be for me? And if I am only for myself, what am I?" (Avot 1:14). If he did not worry about himself, who would worry for him, he pondered, for no one could be aware of his needs in the way that he was. No one could understand him, stand in his place in front of God, or fulfill his duties. Yet, if he only worried about himself, and did not worry about others too, that would be unacceptable: He lived in a social world, he had to help others, adapt to others' needs, and put their concerns in the forefront. Without others he would be lonely and lost. Hillel realized the inevitability of anxiety in this conflict of interests. In addition, both our insecurity regarding our self-worth and our uncertainty about where we stand in relation to others are potential causes for worry. Hillel knew that we need other people; we need to love and be loved, to help and be helped, to belong and feel part of the family and the community.

In the first book of Samuel, Saul's father became concerned when the young man failed to return in reasonable time from an outing. In just the same way, we worry today when a member of the family does not return home or telephone at the expected hour. Solomon ibn Gabirol, a medieval philosopher, observed that we worry when we miss what we love.[21]

The twentieth-century philosopher Abraham Heschel believed that worry comes from a universal need to be needed. We need to feel that our life has value for other people, for another loved one, for society, as well as for ourselves. People worry when they feel "alone in the wilderness of the self, alone in this silent universe, of which we are a part, and in which we feel at the same time like strangers."[22]

"When the guest coughs, he wants a spoon," says a Yiddish proverb. We are concerned to fulfill our guest's desire so that the guest sees that we care. When we are uncertain of another's thoughts, we interpret gestures, even coughs, in our effort to be sociable. We worry when we suspect that others are not reciprocating care. "Beware of your friends, not your enemies," warns another Yiddish proverb. "What is straight talk to your face is slander behind your back." Also, "mix with the neighbors and you learn what's doing in your own house." These proverbs reveal social reasons for worrying.[23]

Erich Fromm (1900–1980), an Orthodox Jew who became a Marxist and a psychoanalyst, thought that anxiety does not arise from a need to be needed or loved, but from the opposite, from the desire to be free and independent. He believed that this desire results from our evolutionary inheritance. He compared the infant's first secure and harmonious environment to the Garden of Eden before the Fall. The growing child, he said, like Adam and Eve, desires freedom to develop his or her own identity, wants to taste each forbidden fruit, but discovers that the path to freedom and independence involves loneliness and helplessness. Loneliness, helplessness, and insecurity are all causes of anxiety, according to Fromm, yet necessary for our healthy development into creative adults.[24]

We Worry Because of Our Nature

Worry appears to be inherent in human nature, a natural human condition. Ben Sira noticed that from the day a human baby comes out of the womb, it is anxious and apprehensive. He assumed that we are born with a natural tendency to worry. [25]

A medieval Jewish philosopher, Sa'adia Gaon, thought that worry is God-given to help us confront and escape from imminent death. We worry because we naturally desire and value life, and do not want to die. However, he also realized that worry sometimes has no external cause, and arises from our impulsive, irrational faculty.[26]

Medieval Jewish doctors believed that emotion arises from the heat of the blood and an imbalance of humors. Rabbi Moses Maimonides (1186–1237) assumed that anxiety is more likely if a person's soul has a cold, and not a warm, nature. In addition, he realized that a sick body could corrupt the imagination and eventually the intellect. Gershom ben Shlomo of Arles, a late-thirteenth-century Provençal scholar, believed that a predominance of black bile influences the force of fantasy to produce frightening images that make a person anxious. He noticed, too, that the force of fantasy becomes strong when the body is weak, asleep, or ill. The sixteenth-century Italian Jewish physician, Abraham Yagel, not only accepted that humoral imbalance could cause mental distress, but believed that there could be astral influences on emotional well-being. Medieval ideas about the natural causes of worrying emotion featured in Jewish medical writing until the early nineteenth century.[27]

Worry could be nature's way of enabling us to prepare for danger before we find ourselves in danger. Perhaps we are genetically programmed to worry for a biological reason, to promote the survival of our species. Perhaps there is an evolutionary reason for our ability to worry that enables us to prepare ourselves to cope with threatening situations by simulating them in our imagination and rehearsing ways of avoiding and overcoming them.

We Worry Because the Imagination Is Stronger Than Reason

Imagination causes us to worry because it "yields no test for the reality of a thing," as Maimonides observed. This great thinker believed that our imagination derives from our sensations and experiences as well as from the bodily humors. The imagination can reproduce sensations and experiences, and combine these to generate fantasies without using will or reason. If we do not exert our will on the imagination, it roams wherever it chooses and can blind us to reality. As soon as we apply reason, however, we test reality and understand whether the imagination is presenting reality or fantasy; we distinguish the possible from the impossible. The intellect analyzes all that the senses perceive. It generalizes, abstracts, and classifies these perceptions so that we understand and discover the truth. It tells us that our worrying fantasy is not real.[28]

When we are asleep or when our bodies are busy, when we wash dishes, weed the garden, or walk home from work, we allow our imagination to take control of the mind and we daydream or worry. Some fourteenth-century kabbalists imagined that, at such times, the mind roams in an intermediary world, above the material world of the senses and below that of the intellect.[29]

Rabbi Judah Löw of Prague (known as "Maharal," c. 1525–1609) was an influential scholar and moralist who reasoned that fear does not exist in reality, but in the intellectual reflection on reality. Worry develops when we brood about things and accept these thoughts as reality, although they are self-inspired and originate within the mind. In the early twentieth century, Abraham Isaac Kook, who became the first Ashkenazic chief rabbi in Palestine, maintained, however, that to free ourselves from our imagination and find the true view of things is as difficult as escaping from a locked dungeon.[30]

We Worry Because Experience Has Taught Us about Danger

A Jewish proverb dating from the post-talmudic period says that "one who has been bitten by a snake is frightened by a rope."[31] The proverb reveals the interplay between bitter experience and imagination that causes worry. It reveals that worry may be a learned response—a "conditioned" response, in the vocabulary of Russian physiologist Ivan Pavlov. The scary and painful experience of the snake's bite remains in the victim's memory. The old, dirty rope coiled on the ground is reminiscent of the snake and causes the trauma of the bite to be recalled into the imagination. Anticipation of the pain and suffering that could again be experienced generates worry.

We may be born with the propensity to worry, but not everybody acquires the habit of fretting. Maimonides and Solomon ibn Gabirol noticed that some people develop anxiety as a personality trait. This disposition may not be innate but acquired through a learning process as a person matures.[32]

Experience teaches us about many situations that are potentially threatening. When we face a dangerous situation for the first time, we feel fear. Then we remember this and can relive it in our imagination. We can anticipate being in such a situation again. Freud and others after him have distinguished between fear, which they have defined as an unlearned or "unconditioned" response, and anxiety, the product of learning, which involves anticipating and imagining the danger. In 1926, Freud wrote that anxiety is undeniably related to expectation; we feel anxious *about* [in German, *vor,* literally "before"] something. "Anxiety is on the one hand, the expectation of a trauma, and on the other a repetition of it in a mitigated form."[33]

Many of our worries do indeed arise out of learning experiences, and some may stem from earliest infancy. Ethologists have noticed attachment behavior in human infants just as in young animals, as well as the ensuing distress—"separation anxiety"—when the attachment is frustrated. A baby becomes attached to a parent or surrogate parent and naturally cries when this person leaves the room. The toddler cries when the teddy bear or the cuddly blanket is lost, a learned response to separation. Soon, just the thought of losing the loved person or object is enough to trigger worry. Psychoanalysts, in particular Erik H. Erikson (1902–1994), believed that the early love relationships between a baby and its parents dictate a person's sense of security later on in life. Erikson proposed that the small child develops a sense of mistrust from early experiences of abandonment.[34]

We Worry Because of Our Inner Conflict

Worry may arise from conflict in the mind. For example, the inner struggle may take place between our contradictory inclinations to good and evil. It may also emerge from a clash between the needs of the body and the desires of the soul, or between our appetites and the norms of society that limit these.

Some Jews have attributed worry to an unending inner struggle between our inclination to do a good deed and our inclination to sin. The concept of Evil Inclination refers to the human urge to indulge various appetites, especially the sexual appetite, and is derived from a verse of Genesis: "the devisings [inclinations] of man's mind are evil from his youth" (8:21).

The medieval philosopher Bahya ibn Paquda, for example, believed that the hidden power that made him worry was the Evil Inclination; the power of his own impulses could lead him to transgress. The Evil Inclination tries purposefully to fill people's hearts with anxiety, he said. It rules over the darkest, innermost recesses of the heart, causing the fantasies of the imagination. He was convinced that this hidden force is a person's worst enemy. "You may be asleep to it, but it will always be awake to you," he warned. You may not be conscious of it, but it is constantly present and alert. He thought of the Evil Inclination as a great king with armies, allies, and troops who shoot arrows from inside and out to defeat and over-power "a poor sage," human reason.[35]

In the thirteenth century, kabbalists imagined the soul as a battle-field where the holy and the demonic fight for control. According to the medieval Book of Zohar, when a child is conceived, angels pro-vide the fetus with the Good and the Evil Inclination, and from the moment of conception, the two powers remain in constant struggle for dominance within a person.[36]

In the late eighteenth century, eastern European Hasidim taught that we have two souls, the divine soul and the bestial soul. Both are always born at the same time, and constantly strive for dominance within each person. The former gives us wisdom and knowledge, whereas the latter gives us our erroneous imagination. The conflict between the truth perceived by the divine soul and the illusory real-ity perceived by the bestial soul (through our fallacious sensory ex-periences) is the cause of worry. Rabbi Nahman of Bratzlav, for example, believed that the divine soul is the natural ruler, but a "mis-take" occurs at every person's birth, resulting in the animal soul ruling over the divine soul.[37]

Rabbi Israel Lipkin of Salant (1810–1883), the founder of a Jew-ish movement to promote ethical improvement, thought that we worry when our natural or learned inclinations for the pleasurable (appetites, lust) conflict with Jewish law, as they do constantly. He was convinced that no one can live a life of calmness and tranquil-ity in the service of God; everyone worries when facing an ethical trial.[38]

Freud renamed these appetites and inclinations the Id. Freud re-alized, as the talmudic sages had noticed many centuries earlier, that libido is a creative life force, whose power generates worry. He came to believe that anxiety is caused by the repression of high-tension impulses or needs, such as sexual desire and hostile aggression, whose expression is frustrated by the behavioral norms and limits of society. He proposed that the Ego creates anxiety to flee from the demands of these unsatisfied desires.[39]

In 1926, he revised his idea about the origins of anxiety and stated that there are three factors at work when "the forces of the mind are pitted against one another." Freud labeled the first factor "biological," referring to the long time that the growing infant naturally remains dependent and helpless, needing to be loved, a need that remains for all one's life. He labeled the second factor "phylogenetic," relating to the difficult, uneven development of the human sexual drive. The third "psychological" factor lies, he said, in "a defect of our mental apparatus" that makes the Ego guard against instinctual impulses and treat them as dangers.[40]

Joseph Dov Soloveitchik, a twentieth-century rabbi and teacher, studied the biblical story of Adam's creation to understand why it is human nature to be anxious. The opening chapter of Genesis says that God created the first man "in the image of God" at the same time as the first woman, and commanded them to fill the earth and subdue it. These first humans are never alone. They strive to be creative and to master the environment. Their striving gives them responsibility and dignity. However, in the second chapter of Genesis, God created Adam from the dust, breathed life into his nostrils, and placed him in the Garden of Eden to till and tend it. God then realized that "it is not good for man to be alone" and created Eve from his rib to help him. This second man knows that he is little more than dust, must serve God, and has to surrender part of himself for his companion. He is humble. His quest in life is to find his real self, his own identity, while obediently serving God. Soloveitchik concluded that there is a built-in tension between these two prototypes that is internalized in the person who has faith. Human nature is conflicted at its core, he believed, with insolvable, anxiety-producing tensions. In this view, the reason for our worrying lies in our creation, in the nature of human being.[41]

We Worry Because We Are Jewish

"Anxiety is always at the root of the Jewish condition," observed Israeli diplomat Abba Eban in 1984, in a discussion about the state of Jews in the United States at the close of the nineteenth century.[42] At that time, many Jews were living on the margin of a more dominant, powerful society and longed to be accepted and respected among the established, successful, non-Jewish local community. Yet, when their accents and their ways differed from the socially accepted norm, they felt excluded.

A century earlier, many European Jews similarly hankered for social standing in the society of the privileged gentiles. Rahel Levin (1771–1833), the daughter of a Berlin merchant, hated the Jewish world in which she grew up and yearned to be accepted into the aristocratic German society. She felt that, since her birth, her Jewish identity was a dagger in her heart that caused her constant bleeding, the source of "every evil, every misfortune, [and] every worry." She eventually converted to Protestantism and married a Prussian diplomat. A friend of hers, the poet Heinrich Heine, also converted to Christianity (in 1825) to gain "an entrance ticket to European culture," but the door remained closed. Christians distrusted him and Jews considered him a renegade. He himself mocked other Jews who had converted like him. For both Levin and the poet, their position on the margin of society was a cause of worry. The anxiety caused by their marginality has often driven Jews to abandon their tradition in the hope of assimilating into the local dominant culture.[43]

Today, Jewish identity is a source of worry to many parents, educators, and Jewish leaders. Some Jews worry that they or their children may not find a Jewish spouse, or that their grandchildren are not being raised within Jewish tradition. Others worry about who is a Jew.

How Do We Worry?

When we worry, we form a picture in our minds that is an uncertain hypothesis about what might have happened in the past, what is happening in the present, or what could happen in the future. The picture may be fixed on one particular idea, or it may constantly change, in the way of the kaleidoscope, into innumerable possibilities. Thus when we worry we focus our attention—voluntarily or involuntarily—on our imagination of a particular scenario.

We imagine the particular event in our mind's eye. We think about what it means. Its meaning(s) will depend on our earlier experiences and previous encounters. Worry begins with a mental appraisal, a mental perception that is interpreted pessimistically, as distressing or problematic.

However, does worry always begin with such a mental perception? Worry sometimes seems to begin as a state of arousal in the brain when the cerebral cortex is not busy. Worry can certainly be triggered by an outside stimulus—something that we perceive to happen in our environment. But at other times, worry may arise endogenously, from within ourselves, with no obvious external stimulus. The brain needs to maintain a certain level of arousal. Every parent knows that a child constantly seeks stimulation: a bored child seeking arousal can be very irksome. An unoccupied adult may also start to fidget, providing stimulation through bodily movements: alternatively, this person may sit still and let the mind fiddle with worrying thoughts. Worry may begin with our biological need for arousal, with chemicals that are released and reabsorbed in the brain. It may begin as a dream begins when we are asleep, without our conscious control.

When a mental perception is unpleasant, an emotional response is generated in the brain, affecting the arousal system. The emotion of worry affects the release of neurotransmitters and hormones; our pulse increases, our breathing shortens, we might perspire a little and tense our muscles. The unpleasant thought leads us to feel emotion that we interpret as worry. One in three people tend to do something with their bodies while they worry: they bite their nails, pace up and down, or smoke a cigarette. We feel worried and we look worried. We have reached the emotional state of worry.

Worry is a process that usually has a beginning and an end. The process of worrying may be a fleeting experience, coming and going in a flash. More often, we worry for five to ten minutes at any one time. Sometimes we may worry for up to half an hour, although habitual worriers spend much longer worrying. As we worry, we anticipate and prepare for a real or imagined problem. The arousal of worry can be a motivating force, similar to libido, that can, but does not necessarily, lead us to action. To put an end to our worrying, we test the possibilities that we have imagined to see if they are realistic and can solve our problem. Sometimes we find a solution; sometimes we dismiss the problem, or lose interest, perhaps coming back to it later. But, sometimes we cannot put an end to our worrying.

Worry becomes a problem when we do not know how to stop this preoccupation of the mind and it prevents us from living a productive life. Worry becomes a problem when, without the possibility of termination, it becomes more and more unpleasant and leads to depression, debilitating anxiety, misery, or even sickness.

Habitual Worrying

We all have periods when we find it difficult to stop worrying, but we eventually do stop worrying. However, some people become habitual worriers; they literally make a habit of worrying and spend hours every day worrying. These people do not know how to stop worrying. They do not, and apparently cannot, take initiative to stop or control their worrying thoughts.

The process of how they worry may be a little different from the process of worrying among the rest of us. These people may be more sensitive than others to their inner changes and to outer signals. They are quick at focusing their attention on potential dangers or problems, exaggerate these, and interpret them in a catastrophic way.

Habitual worriers have difficulty controlling their thoughts. They feel that their worries intrude on their thoughts, without their having any possibility of controlling this intrusion.

In addition, habitual worriers are unable to solve the problems that pop into their minds. Their worrying does not lead to effective solutions, or to their taking any action that ends their worry. So they go on and on worrying. They become more and more concerned with the pessimistic possibilities that they can think of, exaggerate these, and catastrophize (that is to say, they pump up what another may see as a small worry into a possible catastrophe).

As worry is unpleasant, why do these people continue to worry? Something may serve to reinforce the act of worry in those who make a habit of worrying. For example, the act of worrying may win attention for the worrier and therefore give social reinforcement for worrying. Or the pleasant relief that comes when the worry turns out to be unfounded may provide the positive reinforcement for indulging in this behavior. Alternatively, the habitual worrier may derive some gain from the arousal that comes with worry. Worry might be an effective distraction to boredom.

Gender

We have seen that some people are better at imagining danger than others; Jewish men have often thought that women have a greater ability to fantasize and therefore worry more. Jews have noticed that men and women have different natures. Until the eighteenth century, it was generally accepted that a man's nature was hot and strong, whereas a woman's was cold and weak and thus more susceptible to emotion. Men could apparently exert their intelligence and reason to control their imaginations, to prevent their worrying, while women were generally thought to have lighter minds, which were easily disturbed by flights of the imagination and unnecessary worry.[44]

While working on this book, I realized that gender differences remain apparent today. Women reacted immediately to the topic of my study with the remark, "This book is for me, I am such a worrier!" In contrast, men responded with a joke, an anecdote, or a comment that this book will be the ideal gift for their wives or their mothers. Women are not usually ashamed to confess their worrying, whereas men are less likely to admit to being anxious. Many more women seek help for anxiety than men.

These observations do not mean, of course, that women naturally worry more than men. The gender difference in worrying may be that women tend to accept that they worry, whereas men (except, for example, Woody Allen) may prefer to hide theirs. Thus the difference—if there is such a difference—may be a result of social learning and not the result of different nature or temperament. Men and women may be equally desirous of and possess the innate mechanisms for preserving life, mastering the environment, and being loved. Nevertheless, we cannot rule out the possibility that there are biological differences between men and women in how, when, and why they worry, just as there are biological differences between the sexes in libido. One day, molecular biochemists may be able to tell us whether gender differences in worrying are learned or innate, but it is likely that, as with most human behavior, the answer lies in the complex, ongoing interaction between nature and nurture.[45]

Age

We learn from experience to become sensitive to inner bodily changes and external signals, and therefore we may reason that worry increases with experience. The writer of Ecclesiastes depicted worry as a characteristic of old age and Sa'adia Gaon noticed that "the longer a person lives, the greater are his cares and worries and troubles." He wrote this toward the end of his life. Perhaps he noticed that he was no longer able to curb his worrying in the way he used to. Has the elderly person learned from experience to become more sensitive or has the chemical balance in the brain's arousal system changed over the years? Or is it just that older people worry about different things as they age, no more, no less?[46]

Maimonides, however, believed that men worry less as they grow old and wise, eventually ceasing to worry as death approaches; he did not think about women. He reasoned that the bodily humors of young men are hot and therefore the young are emotional. He thought that with increasing age, the bodily forces weaken, causing the emotions to dull, and enabling the intellect to gain strength. As the old man approaches the time of his death, his knowledge of God and his joy in that knowledge allow his soul to separate happily from the body and death "is nothing but a kiss." Yet Maimonides admitted that most people follow their emotions and do not acquire wisdom: most people worry in old age as they did when they were younger.[47]

Recent epidemiological surveys show that about one in five elderly people suffer from intense anxiety symptoms. However, anxiety is more prevalent in the forty-five- to sixty-four-year-old age group than among the elderly. In addition, college students were found to worry more than the elderly about finances and social relations. Students and pensioners were equally concerned about their health. Thus there is no strong evidence that we are likely to worry more as we go through life. There will always be some people who worry more than others—the habitual worriers—but there is no reason to believe that we will all become chronic worriers as we grow old. Sa'adia may have been an anxious old man, whereas Maimonides perhaps suffered less from worry as he grew old.[48]

Sa'adia and Maimonides apparently did not notice that children worry and that a child's anxiety can be particularly disturbing. Infants are frightened by loud noises and strange people. Every parent is familiar with a child's fear of being alone in the dark and all the other anxieties that prevent children from falling asleep at night, that surface in their nightmares, or cut their appetites. Freud proposed that adult anxieties can be traced back to infantile fears that never leave us as we grow up.[49]

However, as children grow into teenagers, their early fears are replaced by worries related to school, social relationships, and self-image. The young adult may begin to worry, in addition, about environmental and social issues. As we grow older, the focus of our worries and the situations that trigger them certainly change. As we grow older, those of us who do not become habitual worriers may acquire new coping strategies to limit the act of worrying. We are still far from understanding the individual differences, gender differences, and developmental changes from infancy through to old age, in the process of worrying.

There are times when we want to worry in the hope of solving a quandary or finding a way out of a difficult situation. On the other hand, when we worry out loud we may exasperate others, especially when we cannot stop fretting. Worry becomes a problem when it interferes with our daily lives and prevents us from fulfilling our goals.

2 ᲐᲒ Coping Strategies

"Do not worry about tomorrow because you don't even know what may happen to you today," advises the Talmud (B. *Yevamot* 63b). This teaching assumes that we can stop ourselves worrying and should do so.

Toward the end of the fourteenth century, the son of a certain Shmuel Levi wrote his autobiography. Aged thirty-three and apparently sensing that his life was ending, the Ashkenazic Jew began his account when he was sent as a boy from his home in Dürren to study in Mainz in 1370. Three months after arriving in Mainz, he received the news that his father was seriously ill and about to die. After three days of travel on his long trip home, some highwaymen captured him. A wealthy relative living in the vicinity paid a redemption fee for the boy's release, but by the time he reached home, his father had died. A year later, the boy joined the army of a duke who was at war with another noble. When he returned, he enraged his mother for some reason, and left home again. Although only fifteen, he soon asked to marry a girl whom he had chosen, but the local community did not approve, and he left to study in another town. He later married another girl and settled in a town near Dürren with his new wife. In 1378, the wealthy cousin who had redeemed him as a teenager was arrested and killed. The following day, the young husband was arrested, together with his mother and two sisters, and all their possessions were confiscated. They were eventually released from prison, and his sisters died three years later. For a while, he gained a meager income from his community responsibilities, but he frequently changed residence, moving from one town to another. In 1390, he was arrested after an argument with another Jew. He was fined and released. Soon after, a Christian viciously attacked him and left him for dead. The autobiography ends with the hope that he will be allowed the merit of going to Jerusalem and becoming one of the builders of the new Temple.[1]

This man apparently lived by the talmudic motto not to worry about tomorrow. The manuscript does not tell us why the author wrote his little autobiography. This Jew, who was not a scholar, a leader, or a wealthy man, but just an ordinary person, looked ahead without trepidation to the world-to-come and apparently believed that the blows of the past were also not worth worrying about. Did this man choose to omit his feelings about his life as he recorded it? Or had he truly banished all emotion in the course of his short but difficult days on Earth? We have no evidence that he was a pietist or particularly saintly, but he apparently knew how to find his path in life every time he was thrown from it. He does not waste words on emotion, but just tells us what he did. He went home, left home, moved house, again and again, doing what he thought he needed to do after each mishap. He did something to bring about change.

Why Have Jews Wanted to Stop Worrying?

Worry is a problem when it disturbs the fulfillment of our goals and when it makes us ill. Most of us try to limit or stop worrying when it becomes disruptive, unpleasant, and depressing. Religious Jews want to stop worrying when this prevents them from performing their duties and serving God. Mystics and Hasidim have wanted to keep out thoughts that hinder their cleaving to God. Doctors want patients to stop worrying in the hope that this will remove distressing symptoms. Children want parents to stop worrying and allow them to get on freely with life. Each of us wants to stop worrying when it becomes unbearable and out of control. Few

Jews have merely accepted worry without trying to do something about it.

How Have Jews Tried to Stop Worrying?

Our strategies for trying to stop unpleasant worrying may be quite similar to those of our ancestors. The oldest therapeutic advice is found in the Bible: "If there is anxiety in a man's mind let him quash it, and turn it into joy with a good word" (Prov. 12:25). We have already seen that, in biblical times, worry was associated with sin and was unacceptable. Anyone who worried had to do something about it. Toward the end of the third century, two sages in Tiberias discussed this issue. One, Rabbi Ammi, recommended banishing worry from the mind, whereas the other, Rabbi Assi, advocated talking it over with other people.[2] Sometimes Jews have transmuted unwanted worries into useful, positive thoughts. Sometimes they have tried to limit excessive worry to a tolerable, intermediate level. Banishing, transmuting, or limiting worries involves making a mental effort that will affect the act of worrying.

We can stop worrying if we can identify and solve the problem at the root of our distress. We may try to think of a practical way out, sometimes alone, and sometimes by talking about the relevant concern with others. We may seek information, in the hope that new knowledge will reduce or remove the worry. In addition, we may seek to influence or exert control over the source of distress. Such thinking, talking, and seeking also involve mental effort.

Sometimes a worrier escapes into another, happier world by indulging in wishful dreaming or meditating. Many Jews have told stories to escape from worry.

By Banishing Worry

We have already seen that Rabbi Ammi recommended quashing worry. This sage studied under Rabbi Yohanan ben Nappaha, an unusual man, a healer, and a mystic, who lost all of his ten sons. This unfortunate man showed the tooth of his last son to distressed people to encourage in them a spirit of resignation like his own. As he buried one son after the next, we would have expected him to worry about those who were still alive, but the Talmud reveals that he radiated light and set an example to others.[3]

How does one quash worry? The Talmud advises engaging in religious activity. It proposes three antidotes of progressive strength: Torah study, reciting the *Shema* prayer, and contemplating the day of one's death.[4] Jews have tried to banish worry by focusing their minds on the Torah and on God, putting heart and soul into studying biblical verses and calling out to the one and only God who might hear their voice. If this did not help, some contemplated their own mortality.

Maimonides similarly advocated religious activity to overcome upsetting emotion, but advised also listening to good music and taking walks among flowers and trees. An Italian doctor and rabbi, Jacob Zahalon (1630–1693), encouraged his anxious patients to change their environment (also the way of coping of Shmuel Levi's son in the late fourteenth century) and use their intellect to overcome upsetting thoughts.[5]

Legend tells that one day Dov Baer, the Hasidic Maggid of Mezhirech was approached by a new disciple who complained that ever since he had joined the master's circle, his business had failed and he had become poor. The Hasid quoted the sages: "He who wants to grow wise, let him go south, and he who wants to grow rich, let him go north." Then he explained that by thinking of himself as if he is nothing, he frees his spirit so that it no longer occupies space and can be both in the north and in the south at the same time.[6] The eighteenth-century Hasid taught meditative techniques to banish worry and gain such spirituality, but such techniques are not easy to use, as we will see in chapter 4.

Shneur Zalman of Liadi, the Hasidic rabbi who founded the Chabad movement, may have believed that we cannot truly banish worry, but we can repress it. "We should pretend not to know or hear the alien thoughts [including worries]," he taught.[7]

We will see in subsequent chapters of this book that Jews have rid themselves of worry by focusing their minds on Torah and the liturgy. They have quashed worry by listening to good music and by laughing at good jokes. Instead of brooding, they have engaged in "stringing pearls for the delight of Heaven."[8] In addition, Jews have also tried to banish worry with magical rituals, incantations, and amulets.

By Transmuting Worry

One day, a Hasid lost all his money. He had been a wealthy man, but suddenly he was reduced to poverty. His dismayed wife asked why he did not show any anxiety at all about their predicament. "The worrying that another would do in a year," he said, "I have done in a moment." He was now free to continue living his life joyfully.[9]

The Hasid admitted that he did worry, but only for a moment. In that moment, as soon as he became aware that a worry was surging into his head, he managed to convert it into a positive thought. Knowing the Hasidic ideals, we assume that he converted his worry into love of God, as only this wonderful feeling would enable him to continue living his life joyfully. Converting worry into love of God involves a concentrated mental and emotional effort, a combination of willpower, intellect, and desire.

Not many people have the strength to do this. Jews have found historical paradigms that help them convert worry into positive thinking. Some have managed to adopt an optimistic approach to a worrying situation, and some have transformed worry into a more acceptable activity. These methods require a mental effort. However, it is also possible to displace worry without mental effort, as we will soon see.

Historical Paradigms The classical stories of the sacrifice of Isaac (*Akedah*), the Exodus, and the destruction of the Temple (*ḥurban*) were retold and embroidered into legend, to serve as paradigms in worrying situations. When Jews found their lives threatened, they often thought of these examples. "God makes us remember our past so as to break our solitude," according to the teaching of the Ba'al Shem Tov, the founder of eastern European Hasidism.[10]

A mother and her seven sons, who were tortured by Antiochus IV because they refused to eat pork, is another ancient story that has helped some Jews to find strength. As each son faced torture, he thought of God. "Most remarkable was the mother," says the second book of Maccabees. "Filled with noble resolution, she took her womanly thoughts and fired them with a manly spirit." She directed her thoughts to God and told her last remaining son that God would restore his life (2 Macc. 7). Similarly, the Talmud relates that while Rabbi Akiva was tortured to death by the Romans (in 135 c.e.), "he directed his mind to accepting the kingship of heaven with love" (B. Berakhot 61b).[11]

By thinking of such stories, Jews have converted their worries into hope and faith, finding psychological strength in the grand lessons of history. The Jews who witnessed the massacres of the Crusaders thought of martyrdom as a self-sacrifice, an *akedah,* whereas mass martyrdom was a *ḥurban.* In 1596, a young man named Luis de Carvajal was imprisoned by the Spanish Inquisition in New Spain (now Mexico). Determined to face his trials in a saintly fashion, like the great men of antiquity, he wrote without a trace of worry to his family to "remember the sacrifice of the saintly Isaac" as well as the faith of saintly Abraham, the dangers confronting Moses, and other biblical precedents. Similarly, childless women have found company with biblical Hannah and followed her example by converting worry over barrenness into prayer. The sublimation of worry through biblical stories became ritualized in prayer—in the prayers recited today in the synagogue as well as in private supplications.[12]

Optimism In worrying situations, Rabbi Akiva would say "whatever the Merciful One does is for good" (B. *Berakhot* 60b). Legend tells us that whenever misfortune befell Akiva or his colleague, Nahum of Gamzu, they both retorted with *"gam zu le-tovah"*—"this, too, is for the good." The psychiatrist Viktor Frankl referred to such rationalization (that whatever happens must have some good in it) as "tragic optimism." His tragic optimist turns suffering into a human achievement and converts worry into a desire for responsible action. Frankl believed that we can become optimistic when we can find a meaning for our predicament. Akiva's psychological strength was based, like Abraham's, on faith. Faith fired their optimism and gave their lives meaning.[13]

In the sixth century B.C.E., Ezekiel found a way of converting worry into an optimistic vision that helped many Jews later on. In his day, the Jews exiled in Babylon were uncertain of their future. Ezekiel prophesied that a Temple flowing with restorative waters would follow a great bloodbath. Many Jews followed Ezekiel's example of converting worries into messianic thoughts of redemption. Like Ezekiel, they sought a prophecy that would give them hope. Some calculated the exact day of the coming of the Messiah. Some believed their own suffering would hasten the coming of the Messiah. For example, in fifteenth-century Spain, some Jews believed that as soon as they had suffered their fill of torments, the Messiah would appear. In 1648, in Poland, as the murderous Cossacks approached his town, Rabbi Samson of Ostropol assured himself that his struggle with the forces of evil would redeem the whole of Israel. In recent years, the Bratzlav and Lubavitch Hasidim have given new life to the messianic movement. They attract many worried, alienated Jews, offering them a new direction and a new meaning to their lives.[14]

Transformation   Commitment to Torah and trust in God presume a mental struggle against worry, reasoned Maharal (in sixteenth-century Prague), and demanded that we sublimate worry into fear of heaven, to fulfill a worthwhile goal (in his view, one that serves God). The eighteenth-century Hasid, Rabbi Menahem Mendel of Vitebsk, similarly taught that we must transform every self-serving, egocentric thought that alienates us from God (that is, prevents us from cleaving to God) into thoughts that serve God.[15]

The nineteenth-century founder of the Lithuanian Musar (ethical) movement, Rabbi Israel Lipkin of Salant, taught Jews to transform their undesirable inclinations into good ones that suit the Torah commandments. We can conquer and quash our disagreeable tendencies with an unrelenting effort of self-analysis, willpower, and self-correction, he taught. However, these "dark" impulses will remain hidden in the (unconscious) depths of the soul and can suddenly break out at any time. He believed that only an intense emotional excitement can bring about their desired transformation into virtues.[16]

Jews from Libya told a tale of healing, in which a destructive worry is transformed into a harmless worry without a mental effort on the part of the worrier. There was once a nasty king who fought a battle with the Jews. Some dirt entered his eye in the heat of that battle. He withdrew to his palace, rubbing the sore eye, and his pain increased. Each doctor who came to treat him failed to relieve his trouble and was put to death. The king continually worried about his eye and rubbed it, which only made it worse. Finally a Jewish peasant visited the palace and promised he could heal the king's eye. The peasant told the king to undress. He felt the royal belly with his rough hand and pronounced that he could feel a tapeworm that was eating away the inside of his stomach and growing bigger every day. He told the king that the tapeworm was a much more serious problem than the eye and gave him a bottle of medicine to rub on his stomach each day for a week. On the eighth day, the peasant promised, the tapeworm would die and he would feel better. The king became so worried about his tapeworm that he forgot to rub his eye. The eye quickly improved and of course the imaginary tapeworm soon disappeared as well. The happy king rewarded the Jew and allowed the Jews to live peacefully in his land forever after.[17] Yiddish-speaking Jews have summed up the same wisdom in a proverb: "If you want to forget all your troubles, put on a shoe that is too tight."[18]

By Limiting Worry

Not all Jews have advocated banishing or transmuting worry. Some have recognized that worry can be beneficial, and only excessive worry needs to be limited. Ben Sira (the second century B.C.E. Hebrew sage and aphorist), for example, pointed out that the working man must worry in order to reach perfection in his work, just as the student of Torah must worry about what is evil and repent for transgressions. Yet he demanded that we control our every thought, to prevent our developing a cowardly heart full of foolish imaginings.

"A mind established on well-considered thought will not be afraid in an emergency," he taught.[19]

The medieval Babylonian philosopher Sa'adia Gaon believed that all human impulses, including the natural impulse to worry, are God-given for human survival, but should be used in appropriate situations only, to fulfill God's intentions for the world. He warned against indulging impulses that serve no purpose. If we indulge these impulses, he said, it is a sign that we lack cognitive discipline. We must use our intelligence and reason to control worry, just as we control our appetites. When there is no legitimate reason to worry (that is, no physical or ethical danger) our cognitive faculty should advise us to stop worrying. Sa'adia Gaon's life was riddled with public quarrels; we wonder if he always managed to use his intelligence to limit his worrying.[20]

Maimonides similarly believed that we can conquer the worries that surge into the imagination by using our full intellectual faculties, although some people find this task difficult. He was convinced that we can harness all the powers of our soul—the senses, imagination, and intellect—to improve our attributes and find the perfect middle way of serving God. He favored seeking the "golden mean" in our personality traits, as well as in our bodily humors.[21]

Maimonides thought that we must train ourselves away from the extreme of any trait, toward the middle. He advised practicing "again and again the actions prompted by those dispositions that are the mean between the extremes and repeat them continually until they become easy and are no longer irksome." In the twentieth century, behaviorist psychologists discovered they could train people to do this. Behavior therapy is used today to help people overcome specific phobias, including fear of flying, fear of failing a driving test, and fear of spiders.[22]

Maimonides believed that a mature person uses reason to overcome emotion, but he realized that only the pious, saintly man could banish all emotion in his quest for God. The thirteenth-century kabbalist, Abraham Abulafia, similarly believed that it is necessary to control the mind, like a rider controlling his horse. We should be able to control our fantasies and emotions just as a horseman controls his steed, spurring it forward or reining it in as we please. At all times the imagination must similarly remain subject to our will, "not straying from its authority, even by a hair's breadth." Five centuries later, Nahman of Bratzlav (now in the Ukraine) used the same imagery. Worry is like a horse that has strayed from the correct path and taken the wrong road, said Rabbi Nahman; the rider takes the reins and compels the horse to return to the correct path. Our minds must act like this rider.[23]

A Hasidic version of Hillel's paradox (see chapter 1) favors a limited amount of worry. It tells us that every person should have two pockets to dip into, according to the need of the moment: "For my sake the world was created" is inscribed on one, and on the other, "I am earth and ashes." The Hasid reminds us of our majesty and supreme worth, on the one hand, and our humility and nothingness, on the other. The Hasid taught that a little worry in life is desirable, even necessary, to make us dip into these pockets. Yet he warned against the extremes of wanton joy, which might come if we live with our hand in the first pocket only, and miserable despair if we choose the other pocket.[24]

In the early twentieth century, Abraham Isaac Kook similarly taught that a little care, to prevent mishap and harm to oneself or another, is beneficial and a natural human caution. A little worry inspires love for life, vitality, and joyfulness. To remove this worry, he warned, is to weaken the soul. But when worry disturbs our spiritual pursuits and prevents us from fulfilling our goals, we must limit it. His poetry reveals his own very evident struggle with anxiety.[25]

Psychiatrists today often prescribe drugs to reduce anxiety to a manageable level, for those who cannot limit their worrying by mental effort alone. They may combine this treatment, however, with another form of therapy, such as behavior therapy or psychotherapy.[26]

By Thinking Creatively and Positively

Once upon a time, a king decided to take a stroll outside his palace, among his townspeople, and observe the atmosphere. For this, he took off his royal garments and donned a pauper's rags, to make sure he would not be recognized. He wandered among the houses of the rich and the shacks of the poor, peering through windows and listening to conversations. One Jewish couple, in the poorest neighborhood, caught his attention. This couple seemed happier than any other people he had seen. They were eating fruit, drinking wine, and singing praises to God. The king (in disguise) knocked on the door, anxious to discover the source of this couple's happiness. The couple invited him in without hesitation, invited him to share their fare, and continued their song. After a while, the king asked the poor Jew how he earned his living.

"I mend shoes, and the few coins I earn each day are all we need," replied the Jew.

"What will you do when you are old and cannot work?" asked the king.

"I don't have to worry, because God will look after me," said the Jew, reassuringly.

The king laughed and went home. The next day, he issued a decree forbidding the mending of any shoes in his kingdom, to test the faith of this strange Jew. The Jew soon discovered the decree, but did not worry, because he noticed a water carrier selling water and decided that he could earn a living in this way too. He bought a huge jug, filled it at the well and then carried it around the city, selling water. In the evening, he returned home, ate and drank with his wife, and sang praises to God. Again, there was a knock at the door, and the visitor of the previous evening reappeared. Again, the couple happily shared their meager fare with him. The disguised king asked the Jew how he now earned his living, in view of the recent decree against cobblers.

"Just because the king closes one door to me, the Holy One does not abandon me," he explained. "God opens another door for me."

The visitor soon left, and the next day the Jew discovered a new decree, this time against selling water. The Jew was not upset. He noticed some woodcutters walking past and asked to join them. He spent the day in the forest, sold the wood he had cut, and with the coins he earned, he bought the daily meal that he shared with his dear wife. Sure enough, the disguised king returned a third time, and found the Jew happy as usual.

On the fourth day, the king ordered his soldiers to capture all the woodcutters on their way to the forest and force them to become palace guards. Each woodcutter was given a uniform and a sword, but was told they would be paid only at the end of the month. The penniless Jew, however, wanted to buy his daily meal and knew he and his wife would not last the entire month without food. He went home and made himself a wooden copy of the beautiful new metallic sword and then took the real sword to the market and sold it for a good price. Once again, the disguised king knocked on the door, amazed at the continued serenity and happiness of the Jewish couple. The visitor inquired how today the Jew had earned his dinner and discovered what he had done with the king's sword. The visitor then asked what the Jew would do if the king discovered the sale.

"Why worry about tomorrow?" answered the Jew with equanimity. "I simply place my trust in God with all my heart."

On the fifth day, the king ordered all his guards to report to the town square for an execution of a criminal. The king and all his people came to watch the event. The crime, apparently, was the robbery of a melon from the palace garden. The ruthless king declared the death sentence and ordered our Jew to carry it out with his sword, or be killed himself if he refused.

Fully composed, the Jew announced, "Please allow me first to pray to my God for strength and then I will fulfill the king's order."

The Jew spoke to God in a voice that all could hear. "Lord of the Universe, you know that I have never killed even a fly and that I would never kill any living creature, let alone a human being, but now I am commanded to do so or lose my own life. May it be Your will, O Holy One, that if this man is guilty, I shall cut off his head with my sword with a single blow. But if this man is innocent, let my sword turn to wood, and all the people gathered here will know he is not guilty."

With bated breath, the whole kingdom saw him pull out his sword and raise it high over his head, and everyone could see that it was wooden. At that moment, the king realized the great wisdom of the Jew and asked him to become his permanent, trusted adviser.

The poor Jew in this folktale, which was told by Jews in Afghanistan, places his faith in God and does not succumb to worry, or to bitter thoughts about his fate. Instead he shows remarkable resourcefulness, as each day he finds a new solution. He combines faith with positive thinking. He actually takes full responsibility for his fate. Instead of wasting his energy and imagination on anxiety, he uses these forces constructively to solve the problem of the moment.[27]

The poor Jew would not have read the treatises of the seventeenth-century Dutch philosopher Baruch Spinoza, yet he knew (like the great thinker) that emotion that only serves to cause misery is better transformed into a more useful activity.[28] Yet worry often seems to come naturally, without an effort, slipping into our minds without our noticing. It is more difficult to think positively and creatively than to worry.

The Talmud tells us that one day Rabbi Eliezer fell sick and his disciples came to visit him. Eliezer told them that God must be very angry with him to have afflicted him so badly. His friends were terribly upset and cried in despair. Only Rabbi Akiva laughed. The friends were surprised at this outbreak of mirth. "Why do you laugh?" they asked.

"Why do you weep?" retorted Akiva.

His friends pointed out that Eliezer was suffering and they were weeping at his distress.

"For that very reason I rejoice," explained Akiva. "As long as I saw that my master's wine had not soured, his flax was not spoiled, his oil had not putrefied, and his honey had not turned rancid, I thought, God forbid, that he may have received all his reward (prosperity) in this world, leaving nothing for the next. Now that I see him lying in pain, I rejoice, knowing that his reward has been treasured up for him in the Next World."[29]

Akiva laughed because he suddenly saw the situation differently from his friends. As we will see in chapter 8, humor can sometimes reveal an unexpected way of looking at a situation and in this way help us change our perspective. It can sometimes help us convert worrying thoughts into positive thoughts.

Worry can lead us to think differently and creatively about a problem. We may cope with worry, as Akiva did, by widening our perspective, by increasing the breadth and depth of our field of vision so that we become less egocentric. We may also cope with worry, as Akiva did, by choosing to perceive a situation optimistically instead of pessimistically. Thus a patient who has agreed to undergo major surgery probably worries about pain and the possibility of dying from the forthcoming operation, but copes with the worry by looking beyond the operation to a means for recovery. And the highway motorist who glances anxiously at the gas gauge when shooting past a gas station worries that the tank is already half empty, unless he or she realizes that the needle actually shows that the tank is still half full.

Some psychologists and rabbis today are teaching people to transmute pessimistic worry into positive ideas. Some have adopted Viktor Frankl's therapeutic search for that which is meaningful in life to help convert disturbing worries into positive thoughts. Similarly, modern "positive" psychologists, such as Martin Seligman, focus on a client's strengths in order to guide him or her toward happiness and self-fulfillment.[30]

By Talking about Worry: Facing and Sharing Worry

"Better pour out your troubles to a stone—but don't carry them within yourself."[31] Jews have usually turned to God with their worries and not to a stone, as this proverb implies. By pouring out their worries and sharing them, especially with God, they have tried to reduce their anxious burden. They have shared their worries with God through prayer and by reading Psalms. They have also shared their worries with a rabbi, often hoping that the rabbi would somehow remove them with practical advice, a prayer, or good deeds. In addition, they have of course shared their worries with family, friends, and even strangers—often just anyone willing to listen.

The talmudic Rabbi Assi may have been a worrier. Perhaps he disagreed with Rabbi Ammi about the best way of coping with worry because sharing his concerns with his rabbinic colleagues helped him personally. Alternatively, Assi may have realized that only a sage had the intellectual tools to banish worry, and most people in his day lacked these. Thus he may have been speaking for the men who did not devote their lives to study as well as for women and children when he argued with his colleague. It is possible that this sage, who refused the positions of leadership offered him, was sensitive to the psychological differences between the rabbinic elite and all other Jews. Maybe he noticed that when a child awoke from a nightmare or was frightened to go into the street, a mother asked her child to talk about the worry causing his or her distress.[32]

The eighteenth-century Hasidim especially encouraged Jews to talk about their worries. Their leaders were in tune with the psychological needs of the whole community, not just those of the rabbinic elite. They developed their own doctrine of the *tzaddik*, the righteous rabbi, who listens to other people's troubles and tries to help. Jews who could not banish their worries alone could talk to the *tzaddik*. There is a story about a Hasid who went one day to see a *tzaddik*, Shalom Roke'ah of Belz, because he was troubled by frightening visions and evil thoughts, and hoped that the rabbi could heal his soul. The *tzaddik* closed his eyes as he concentrated on the many worries that the suffering man confided in him. The worrier noticed that, behind his closed eyes, the rabbi labored to return all the troubling thoughts to their divine source, a technique that will be described in the next chapter. When the Hasid finished his confession, the *tzaddik* opened his eyes and assured him that God would now help to keep him free of concern. He was right, apparently, because we are told that the Hasid was never troubled again by a single disturbing thought.[33]

The talking over and sharing of worries does not necessarily require action or an answer. "When one person speaks to another and tells what is in the heart . . . then the very speaking works salvation," noticed the Hasid Menahem Mendel of Vitebsk. Sharing worries involves admitting them. This rabbi knew that sometimes merely expressing and admitting them helps. "We need to share our joys with other people, and we need even more to share our fears," wrote Rabbi Harold Kushner recently, after his child died tragically of a rare disease.[34]

"The Lord becomes attentive to the man who sings in the midst of his troubles and accepts them good-naturedly and with laughter," according to a Hasidic leader, Yakov Itzhak ("the Seer") of Lublin (1745–1815).[35] Jews have expressed their worries in wedding songs and lullabies and laughed at their worries with friends. Since the Middle Ages and increasingly in modern times, Jews have faced their worries in satire and parody, sharing their worries in humor.

Talking over worry with another person or other people, Rabbi Assi's approach, is used in psychotherapy—in the one-to-one therapeutic meeting and in group sessions. Talking over worry has often involved exploring the origins of the worry to understand the problem fully. Freud and later psychoanalysts adopted this approach. However, talking over worry can also focus merely on the present moment: the Gestalt therapist Fritz Perls and his followers pointed out that it is not necessary to know why we worry, if we focus on how we worry and what we can do with it. In addition, talking over worry can help a person to look ahead, to find a direction in life, to want to do something: Viktor Frankl developed this therapeutic approach.[36]

By Seeking Knowledge and Gaining Wisdom

Wisdom is the quality of having knowledge, experience, and good judgment. We prefer to know and understand what is going on, to gain experience in a worrying situation, and assess it correctly, rather than to remain confused and uncertain. We seek meaning in what we do and for what happens to us. We try to understand our relationships with other people. Knowledge of our own selves and of the world within which we live sometimes helps us to dispel uncertainty.

We want to know what will be even though sometimes we cannot know, and sometimes the knowledge we gain may aggravate worry.

Long ago, the Proverbist understood the desire to gain wisdom and knowledge: "Happy is the man who finds wisdom, the man who attains understanding. . . . The Lord founded the earth by wisdom; He established the heavens by understanding. . . . They will give life to your spirit. . . . Then you will go your way safely. . . . When you lie down you will be unafraid. . . . You will not fear sudden terror or the disaster that comes upon the wicked . . ." (Prov. 3:13–25).

One of the early rabbis stressed the importance of knowledge a little differently. He taught that we must always know from where we came—from a putrid drop; where we are going—to a place of dust, worms, and maggots; and before whom we are destined to give an account and reckoning—the King of Kings (Avot 3:1). This sage's perspective was wide; some of us nowadays live in the here and now and have difficulty thinking ahead or stepping back to see how far we have come on our life's journey. Some of us spend our lives worrying about uncertainty instead of seeking knowledge of where we are going. But for many Jews, the knowledge (of where they come from, where they are going, and to whom they will have to render account) has given meaning to their lives. Viktor Frankl noticed that people are anxious when they find no meaning in their lives. The search for knowledge, wisdom, and meaning is a way of coping with worry.[37]

The Talmud depicts a man walking in the dead of night, in pitch darkness, fearing brambles, snares, wild animals, and bandits. He has no idea where he is going. When he comes upon a lamp, he can now see the brambles, the briars, and the pits. He no longer worries about falling and hurting himself, yet he is still afraid of wild animals and bandits; he still does not know where he is going. When dawn comes, he is saved from both the animals and the bandits (who hide in daylight), but he remains lost in the wilderness. When he comes to a junction, he is saved from every danger. Why at the junction, asked Rabbi Hisda? Because, the Talmud concludes, here he meets both the learned man and the day of death (B. *Sotah* 21a). Rashi explained that the lamp represents the commandments, which save him from some trouble but do not remove his fear; the dawn symbolizes the Torah, which saves him from sin and suffering; and at the junction, he discovers where he is going—to the day of his death. This story teaches that whatever the dangers we meet or imagine, only knowledge of Torah and of our own mortality will lead us to understand the course of our lives and thus relieve us of our fretting. However, the characters in this tale may represent different aspects of our selves. The brambles, snares, wild animals, and bandits may be allegorical, representing harmful qualities within our selves, such as sadness, evil desires, worries, and pride. The more we understand about ourselves, the more likely we are to be able to cope in worrying situations.[38]

Medieval philosophers also praised the desire for knowledge. Solomon ibn Gabirol, for example, whose life was beset with misfortunes, thought that he could free his soul from its dark distress by applying reason and pursuing knowledge. Maimonides, too, believed that the road to happiness lies in acquiring true knowledge. The knowledge that these men sought was of course Torah and divine knowledge, which they deemed the highest and truest form of knowledge.[39]

However, when worried, people have often sought specific knowledge to give meaning to something they do not understand. Sometimes they have sought information that would help them decide what to do. When scientific, objective knowledge has been unavailable, people have sometimes tried to gain supernatural information. Some worried Jews have sought this by inducing divine revelation, interpreting dreams, and invoking angels or spirits. However, what one person considers supernatural knowledge, another may consider fantasy or delusion.

It is human nature to search for knowledge in times of worry. If we have a pain, a rash, or a lump, we will probably consult a doctor for a cure. We want information that will tell us that there is nothing seriously wrong and that the problem will respond to treatment and disappear. When the doctor cannot offer a cure, we may continue to worry and seek a second opinion. When the doctor diagnoses a serious problem, our worry increases and we seek further information or another way of coping.

Much effort and money is invested today in the search for knowledge, in making predictions about the future as well as discovering the answers to problems that arise in our environment. The intention to make life safer and reduce our worries is a motivating force (although perhaps not the only one) in this expenditure. For example, meteorological stations predict the weather, and the information they provide enables pilots of airplanes and boats to plan a safe route and gives people time to shelter from an oncoming hurricane. Another example—and there are many more that we could choose—is the enormous sum of money that is spent on medical research, in the attempt to avoid and cure terrible illnesses.

Knowledge is often not enough to help us cope with worry. We have to be able to apply the knowledge we have found to reduce uncertainty or to provide meaning. We have to use the knowledge and act upon it. Action and a feeling of being in control, as we will now see, are also important in coping with worry.

By Seeking Control

We often feel helpless and worried when we sense we have no control over our destiny. If we could control our future, we imagine, we might be able to steer it in a happy direction, away from worry. The effort of coping often involves an attempt to grasp control, either through our own action, or by calling on someone else or others who may be able to exert control.

One of the fundamental paradoxes of religion concerns divine providence and free will: The ancient sages taught that "everything is foreseen, yet freedom of choice is given" (Avot 3:19). There is clearly no reason for worrying if everything is foreseen. Most Jews have believed that their lives are somehow determined by the Creator. We "cannot foresee the actions of God, who causes all things to happen," said the writer of Ecclesiastes (Eccles. 11:5).

Paradoxically, Jews have also believed that we can choose our own actions and thoughts ("freedom of choice is given,") and therefore we have some control over our own future and must take responsibility for our behavior. As soon as we see ourselves as active agents, we think that there might be something that we could do to solve a problem, remedy a situation, or reduce uncertainty or danger.[40]

Maimonides and Baruch Spinoza believed that we can choose and control our actions and thoughts. The seventeenth-century philosopher observed that most people make no effort to do this, being ignorant, superstitious, and slaves to their feelings. He taught that we should not suppress, repress, or suffer emotion passively, but instead transform it into a feeling of activity that we can cause and control.[41]

Nietzsche observed the human "will to power," and Alfred Adler believed that the driving force behind our behavior is our striving for power. Both noticed that we like to feel in control of our lives. One way of coping with worry is to find a way of gaining the upper hand.[42]

Some Israeli mothers recently gave us an example of how to convert worry into responsible action. These were mothers of soldiers serving in southern Lebanon in 1997. They were worried that their sons might be killed or maimed in the daily exchange of fire. When two Israeli helicopters crashed over northern Israel, killing seventy-three young men who were being ferried into southern Lebanon, the worried women waited to hear that their own sons were alive and then met to decide on a plan of action. "That evening transformed us from people resigned to the idea that there is no other choice, to those determined to find a solution," said one of the mothers. They decided to form a pressure group, Four Mothers, to pressure the government to withdraw from Lebanon. (The name of their group was purposefully reminiscent of the four biblical matriarchs.) They mobilized many mothers from all over the country—those with sons on the front as well as those without—and became a vociferous force that the government could not ignore, demonstrating, and meeting with politicians to make their demands. These demonstrations and meetings enabled them to talk about their worry, share it with others, and take action. Their activity and their specific worry for their sons' safety finished in May 2000 when Israel withdrew all its soldiers from southern Lebanon.

External Authority   There are times, however, when we feel helpless, unable to control or change anything ourselves. When this happens we often look for someone who might help, an authority with more power or knowledge who can exert this control for us. For example, a person who worries about preserving the value of a sum of money may consult with a bank manager or stockbroker.

Many Jews—men and women—have believed and continue to believe that the ultimate, divine power might help them. They have talked to God in their prayers and pleaded to God for mercy, protection, and guidance. In the past, some worried Jews called on angels or spirits, which they believed had access to the divine realm, to intercede with God and bring help or advice. Often, Jews have turned to a rabbi for help, or to a faith healer with a reputation for working miracles who, they imagine, has more power than an ordinary person.

Freud noticed that many people have turned to God when they are worried and lost, just as the growing child looks to a parent for help in such moments. He believed that mankind has "a powerful need for an authority who can be admired, before whom one bows down, by whom one is ruled and perhaps even ill-treated."[43] Freud was no feminist; he depicted the God of the Jews, the Supreme Being whom he could not accept, as an authoritarian father figure. (But he had his own powerful need for authority; he wanted to rule and have others bow to him. He had no interest in either accepting a higher authority or, apparently, in praying.)

Freud also noticed that people often project their worries onto an external source. It is often easier to take precautions against an external danger than against a human weakness. Frightened travelers who imagined evil spirits lurking in every dark shadow took an amulet and recited powerful incantations to protect themselves from danger. Jews not only imagined evil spirits and protective angels, but also gave them names so that they could protect themselves against the harmful ones and invoke the help of the angels.

Some psychological studies have shown that those who external-ize problems by blaming the environment and not accepting respon-sibility for their own behavior and experiences are more anxious than those who take responsibility and seek to control worrying situations themselves. In laboratory experiments, Martin Seligman and his col-leagues showed that when rewards and punishments are out of a per-son's control, that person feels helpless and becomes depressed and anxious. We may learn, already in childhood, in the family environ-ment, to take an active approach to coping with worry by taking re-sponsibility for our own feelings. Alternatively, we may learn to become passive toward our worry and blame our unpleasant feelings on the environment or nature.[44]

In contrast to what might be expected from Seligman's studies, Michael White has found that helping people to externalize their problems in order to talk about them enables them to cope better with a specific worry. Non-psychoanalytic, narrative therapy, which White pioneered in the 1980s, helps worried people, especially chil-dren and their parents, to externalize their worry. By separating the problem from the suffering person in an externalizing conversation, a distance is established, and the problem can then be discussed and played with humorously, without worry. For example, a child who has a problem of regularly soiling his or her pants may be labeled as suffering from encopresis and feel ashamed and worried: White re-defines the situation for the child by saying "you can outsneak Sneaky Poo and stop it from sneaking out on you." The child can then think of and discuss ways of outsneaking Sneaky Poo through storytelling and playing games without feeling guilty or worried.[45]

Jews who have uttered incantations and obtained protective amulets knew what White discovered in recent times, that we can gain a feeling of control by externalizing the problem. What is im-portant is the feeling of doing something in the face of worry; pas-sivity does not promote coping.

Assertiveness: Warnings and Rulings Before the Israelites crossed the Jordan and entered the Promised Land, Moses and the elders were concerned that these people should behave themselves and live according to the commandments. They charged the people to obey all of God's laws. They warned them of the curses that would befall those who disobeyed and the blessings that would sweeten the lives of the faithful. Later, the prophets who worried about the iniquities of the people similarly issued warnings and rulings. The rabbis continued this pattern. They coped with their worries, for example, about the moral fiber of Jewish society, relations with non-Jews, and assimilation by issuing warnings and rulings. Local record books preserve rulings that reflect leaders' worries concerning the behavior of people in the community. Thus, for example, Jewish councils ruled to limit ostentatious dress when Jews went into the street and to limit the size of a wedding or other family celebration for fear that fancy clothes and large gatherings would aggravate relations with non-Jewish neighbors. Similarly, worried leaders sometimes ruled against employing non-Jewish servants and against gambling, as they were well aware of the disastrous effects such behaviors might have on a family.[46]

In a similar way, when a young boy sets off alone on his bicycle, his mother calls after him her set of warnings and rulings that stem directly from her own worries: "Do not speak to strangers, be careful on the road, be back before dark!" When we worry about other people, we want to control their lives, to make them behave in a way that will keep them out of the dangers that we foresee. We boss them around, attempting to organize their lives. Parents do this to their children and spouses do this to each other, out of love and concern.

By Escaping into Fantasy

After Adam and Eve had tasted the forbidden fruit, God called out to them. The worried couple chose to hide, hoping to avoid divine wrath; they would have liked to escape, but they could not escape from God.

Houdini, the famous magician, perfected the art of escape. His remarkable escapes out of the most challenging situations imaginable may have been symptomatic of the worrying specter of failure that he had witnessed in his father, an unsuccessful rabbi who died when Houdini was a child. His escapes succeeded in making him famous and wealthy, but physical escape from worry is not always possible, and we sometimes seek to escape mentally instead.[47]

When we find ourselves in a worrying situation, we often wish we were somewhere else. Sometimes we wish that a fairy godmother would suddenly appear and, with a shake of her wand, transform the worrying reality into a happy scene. Jews have been especially fond of fairy tales, legends, and miracle tales in which worries are solved and dreams come true, evil is punished and good wins out.

Sometimes we escape from worrying reality by running away from a danger as we sleep, changing fact into fantasy. For example, Ida Bauer (named "Dora" in Freud's publications) related such a dream to Freud in 1900, when her father brought her for a cure. The eighteen-year-old girl's relations with her parents were bad, and her relationship with her father, who was having an affair with Ida's closest friend, was particularly bad. She dreamed that she received a letter from her mother telling her that her father was dead. She journeyed home (in her dream) through a thick wood and found her mother and others at the cemetery. Her dream was wishful fantasy. Ida had thought about suicide but her dream solved her problem in an easier way, with her father's death.[48]

Sometimes we escape into fantasy by daydreaming optimistically. Some Jews have reached a different state of consciousness, detached from this world, by listening to music or meditating. But usually such escape involves only a temporary flight from unpleasantness, and we have to return to face reality. Escape from worry through fantasy or meditation can be dangerous if it leads a person to abandon the return to reality, as we will see in chapter 4. Such a person dissociates completely from reality and no longer distinguishes the real world from the fantasy world. Some of the Jewish false messiahs were men who escaped from worry into delusion.

Whereas the dream and other altered states of consciousness are personal ways of escaping from worry, the folktale is a collective way of escaping into fantasy. As family members or community members shared the same worries, they enjoyed together the communal telling of a story that allowed their wishes to come true.

Jews have told and retold biblical tales and later legends, as well as miracle tales in which anxiety disappears as wishes come true, to strengthen their faith and help them cope with difficult emotion. Such tales, with universal motifs, helped people to face anxiety through the world of fantasy Rabbis have often used a narrative approach in sermons and in private consultation with worried people. However, Jews also told tales within the home; elderly family members told traditional stories to the younger members, transmitting through these their faith that a solution can always be found, perhaps first in fantasy and then, as the listener becomes optimistic, also in reality.[49]

As the storyteller narrated a well-known tale, he or she adapted and improvised details to suit the emotional needs of the moment. The hero could turn into a heroine, or into the local rabbi. The enemy currently threatening the community could turn into a demon. Jewish folktales provide happy solutions, for example, to a spouse's infidelity, a terrible sickness, or an evil decree.

In Jewish folklore, Elijah the Prophet brings good tidings, restores health to the sick, and reveals divine information. Elijah is often a guardian angel who helps the weak and poor. For many worried Jews in the past, Elijah was not a mythic figure of folklore, but a real angel, and Jews hoped he would come and help them in their hour of need. Many saw Elijah in their dreams or received encouraging messages from him in their sleep. Some met him in the marketplace or on a lonely road. The second-century sage Shimon Bar Yohai had been hiding in a cave for twelve years and must have worried about the safety of leaving it. Akiva wanted to study but must have worried about leaving his young wife. Elijah's guidance allegedly changed the lives of these two men. Some of the Provençal kabbalists of the twelfth and thirteenth centuries allegedly received divine revelations from Elijah that legitimized their new, controversial kabbalistic interpretations. The Safed kabbalists reported revelations from Elijah during mystical contemplation as well as in their dreams. In Podolia, which is now in the Ukraine, Elijah told an elderly childless man, Eliezer, that soon his wife would bear him a son. Elijah also appeared to that son, Israel (who became the Ba'al Shem Tov), when his horse collapsed on a steep mountain path and he despaired of delivering his load of kosher flour for the Passover matzot. Also in North Africa, the Ottoman Empire, Yemen, and lands farther to the east, worried Jews found relief and hope in the belief that they had encountered Elijah.[50]

Often, instead of Elijah, the spirit of a certain dead person has revealed itself to a worrier, either in a dream, or when summoned by someone through magical or meditative techniques. Many Jews have experienced the revelatory visit of Elijah or of the spirit of a dead person as a true reality and not as a product of the imagination. However, these visions and auditory experiences may well be an escape from unpleasant truth into the comforting world of fantasy.

Television put an end to the popularity of telling folktales as entertainment at family gatherings, although parents and children still enjoy the classic tales. A recent study of Moroccan Jewish folk narratives revealed that women preferred to tell the fairy-tale genre that allows them to overcome their trials and win out. Men, however, prefer telling sacred legends, venerating their saintly ancestors and idealizing the holy man. The gender difference in the telling of folktales reflects a difference in the traditional concerns of the two sexes: in Moroccan Jewish families, women worried more about domestic problems whereas their husbands worried more about religious problems.[51]

A reason for the continuing popularity of Jewish tales and legends is that we continue to find meaning in them. Many traditional stories can be interpreted to reveal truths about ourselves, as Nahman of Bratzlav certainly understood two hundred years ago, and as some psychoanalysts have spelled out for us in recent times. Alfred Adler appreciated that fantasy can be a good way of coping with worry because we can formulate a fictional goal and fabricate a story that allows us to strive to fulfill this goal. More recently, the child psychoanalyst Bruno Bettelheim followed Adler in pointing out that fairy tales serve an important educational purpose by allowing children to experience anxiety through fantasy and having the tension solved for them in a happy ending. Folktales teach that conflict, evil, and worry are universal and unavoidable but can be mastered optimistically. Jewish fairy tales and miracle tales teach that it is permissible to wish for a happy solution and that sometimes, with divine help, wishes come true.[52]

In the postmodern era, movies replaced the telling of such tales. A generation grew up experiencing anxiety at the movie theater or on the television screen in their own homes, knowing that the evil that took place before their eyes was mere fiction. However horrific the movie, it was just fantasy. As the world watched the towers collapse on September 11, many of us wanted to believe that what we watched was just another screen fantasy and that soon the good guys would save everyone, and life would go on normally, as before. The psychoanalysts were wrong; the fantasies that we grew up on did not prepare anybody to cope with this terror. Fantasy is useful only if it helps us to cope with reality, gives meaning to our difficult experience, or gives us strength.

Accepting Worry

If we cannot put a stop to our worrying, should we just accept that this is our nature? The Proverbist teaches, "Happy is the man who is anxious always, but he who hardens his heart falls into misfortune" (Prov. 28:14). He condemns excessive tranquility and complacency, believing that we should constantly judge ourselves and check that we are living righteously. The Proverbist is not thinking of worry, however, but of religious anxiety (which, we have said, is not the topic of this study, but must nevertheless be recognized here). He wants us to fear God always and worry about taking the right path in life.

Some rabbis have recognized that worry that is useful (because it promotes survival and morality) must be accepted and encouraged. For example, we have already seen that Sa'adia Gaon accepted as necessary all worry that helps us to avoid danger and ensure survival. Moreover, we will see (in chapter 3) that some rabbis have taught that we must worry in order to repent. Fretting about what we have done or said may teach us a lesson that may help us in the future, in which case it is desirable and beneficial. We may learn from our worrying how to improve ourselves or how to prevent something bad from happening again. Most rabbis in the past and still today have taught that we must constantly evaluate what we have done in our lives in order to repent and perfect ourselves.[53]

Glückl of Hameln, in the early seventeenth century, hid her worrying from other people because she thought it was unacceptable, but we all know people who do not hide theirs.[54] Some are almost proud of their worrying and accept it as their nature without struggling. Many Jewish men and women have admitted their worries in their private prayers and letters as well as in their songs and jokes. At the moment of admission, they accept their worry. This is a way of coping with worry, although it does not put an end to worrying.

As self-acceptance enables us to value ourselves as human beings in spite of our shortcomings, the encouragement of self-acceptance may be an important element in psychotherapy, for example with homosexual people.[55] Traditional Judaism does not teach that we should strive for self-acceptance, however. It tries instead to promote the search for self-improvement and self-perfection.

Worriers today may still use the same coping strategies that Jews have used through the ages. Some people may have their own favored way of coping. However, most of us use several different techniques, according to the specific situation: Sometimes we banish worry or transmute it into a constructive thought; sometimes we talk about it, sharing it with others. Often we seek information to understand better the cause of our worry. At times, we turn to someone stronger or better informed than ourselves who can put an end to our worry. On occasion we may escape from it into fantasy, or just accept it as natural and not try to stop worrying. In the next six chapters we will examine some of the different situations in which Jews have applied these strategies.

3 ⤳ Prayer

A Hasid consulted Rabbi Menahem Mendel of Kotzk about his anxiety.

"Don't worry," advised the rabbi. "Pray to God with all your heart, and the good Lord will have mercy on you."

"But I don't know how to pray," protested the distraught Hasid.

Pity surged into the heart of the rabbi as he told the poor man: "Then you have indeed a great deal to worry about."[1]

Another Hasidic rabbi, Simha Bunim of Pshiskhe, used to say that if your heart is full of worry, you can lighten it through ardent prayer and gain faith in God's mercies.[2]

These rabbis, who lived around 1800 in an area that is now Poland, might have counseled the worried man to attend the synagogue when the congregation gathered to pray, and concentrate on the prayer ritual wholeheartedly. Such concentration would leave no room for worry. They knew that by praying three times a day, the Jew would have regular "time-out" from his worries, and would thus limit his worrying and prevent it from taking over his life.

Alternatively, these eastern European rabbis might have advised the Hasid to share his worries with God in a personal confession, admitting all that weighed down his heart. They could have assumed that such a prayer would have a cathartic effect; it would release tension and uplift him. We will see that Jews have often talked about their worries to God in their private prayers. They have also shared their worries with others while they pray. Prayer often connects the person praying with God and also with others who share or have shared the same concerns.

The Jew who confessed that he did not know how to pray had perhaps become convinced of his inability to pray because he sensed no relief from his worry after trying to pray. Perhaps he hoped the rabbi would pray for him, with good effect. He probably confided in the rabbi in the hope that the holy man would do something to help. However, even though Hasidic rabbis have customarily prayed for others, neither of the two rabbis offered to pray for the worrier.

Another Hasidic rabbi, as we will see below, may have tried to show the worrier that it is possible to transmute the worry, through prayer, into full faith in God's mercies. This, though, is more difficult than the other forms of prayer that help Jews to cope with worry.

For these rabbis, and many others through the ages, prayer was the accepted way of coping with worry. Clearly, prayer has other functions as well, but the focus of this chapter is to look at why, when, and how Jewish men and women have used prayer to cope with worry. But first, what is prayer?

What Is Prayer?

According to the *Encyclopedia Judaica*, prayer is an "offering of petition, confession, adoration, or thanksgiving to God." Prayer is a way of seeking contact with God; it is a communication with the Almighty from the heart. It assumes that God exists, listens, and might answer.[3]

Prayer can be a personal plea for help and guidance, an attempt to influence fate, and determine an uncertain future. When it takes the form of supplication or confession, it can be a channel for facing worries, for sharing them with God and sometimes with other people too. But when personal prayer turns to praising God and giving thanks for divine grace, it can lead beyond self-concern to become an escape from worry and a path to enlightenment.

Prayer can also be a group communication, recited with the congregation in fixed phrases—the liturgy. The liturgy also enables Jews to praise and thank God, ask for mercy, and repent with other Jews at fixed times of the day and year. It teaches the worried person what to pray for.

Prayer can be a communication with God for another person or for the people as a whole—an intercession. Abraham and Moses prayed for the sake of their people, setting the example to Jewish leaders, including kings, prophets, and holy men. Many of the Psalms are prayers asking for God's mercy for the people.

The Hebrew word for a person who prays, *mitpallel,* is the reflexive form of the word meaning "to judge" and "to hope." Thus the person who prays is one who engages in self-judgment and finds hope. The early sages taught that God wants us to judge our behavior. We must admit and redress the wrongs we have committed, refrain from repeating our sins, and affirm our faith in God and Torah. Jews have done this by praying.[4]

Prayer can also take the form of repentance. The Hebrew word for this is *teshuvah,* meaning "going back, returning" to God and the Jewish faith. *Teshuvah* also means "response": The person praying expects a divine response. Formed from the root *shuv,* "to turn," repentance involves a "turning about," or "turning to," to overcome the past and reach a different, more ethical orientation or direction in life. It is a process of searching, often a series of small turnings, in an effort also to find the divine spark. This introspective process may first promote some worrying as we face and admit our shortcomings to ourselves.[5]

"Service in the heart" is prayer, says the Talmud (B. *Ta'anit* 2a). According to Jewish tradition, prayer is a way of serving God that entails directing our hearts to heaven with vigor. Prayer involves concentration, intention, and devotion.

For some Jews, prayer can also be a way of cleaving and uniting with God. This chapter, however, looks at prayer as a heartfelt communication and as a means of self-judgment; prayer that takes the Jew on a journey to the divine realm is discussed in the next chapter.

The halakhic aspects of prayer are irrelevant to this study.

Why Do Jews Pray to Cope with Worry?

Jews pray to let God into their lives. They also repent and supplicate God in the hope of climbing out of the muddy rut in which they
worry along the path of life. They may pray hoping for the fulfillment of their wishes and a change for the better in their predicament.
Sometimes, by praying, they broaden their view of the world and
change their understanding of their own problems.

To Find God and Reap Benefit

Traditionally, Jews pray in order to elevate their souls to connect
with God. They pray to make God immanent. The benedictory
prayers of the Jewish liturgy heighten awareness of the Divine, induce joy, and eliminate troubling concerns. Through prayer, Jews oc-
cupy and fill their minds with thoughts of God, they feel God's
presence, and free themselves temporarily from daily concerns.

The medieval philosopher Judah Halevi taught that we pray for
the sake of our souls just as we eat for the sake of our bodies; whereas
the body needs some food three times a day, so too the soul needs
refreshment and sustenance after periods of anxiety. If we neglect to
nourish the divine spark within us, our spirit grows weak and we feel
worried. Prayer can raise us beyond the here and now and carry us
toward our ideals.[6]

Rabbi Soloveitchik (the twentieth-century philosopher mentioned in chapter 1) prayed regularly; but he also prayed when his
wife was dying of cancer and all hope was gone. He could not find
God in the whitewashed hospital. In black despair, he prayed fervently at home, in his room, on his knees and soon felt that God
"was right there in the dark room; I felt His warm hand, *ki-veyakhol*
(as it were), on my shoulder, I hugged His knees, *ki-veyakhol*. He
was with me in the narrow confines of a small room, taking up no
space at all."[7]

In his first speech to the nation after the horror of September 11,
2001, President Bush recited a verse from the Twenty-third Psalm;

he prayed and he asked his people to pray. Prayer may have been his gut reaction to his intense emotion, but it may also have been his way of gaining strength for the uncertain future in the face of world terrorism. He must have believed that prayer is helpful in conquering fear. We can imagine that he found courage in the knowledge that God is present.

In the following days, prayer houses filled up with worried people looking for comfort and hope. Communal prayer engendered a feeling of community, of not being alone in the world, and confirmed that love exists. For these reasons, many people who did not usually attend religious services did so in those anxious days.

To Seek Help

Since earliest times, men and women have prayed because they wanted help in facing the uncertain future. For example, Abraham and Moses remonstrated with God for the sake of others in danger; Jacob prayed when he was worried about his forthcoming meeting with Esau; and Hannah prayed when she despaired of having a son. During the Babylonian exile, the worried Israelites longed for communication with God and listened to the prophet who communicated with God for them. Biblical stories teach that it is worthwhile praying as God does sometimes help.[8]

Worried Jews have often felt strengthened by these biblical stories and have invoked them while praying, hoping that God would answer them too. Those afflicted by drought or floods, pestilence or war, or personal distress have called for God's help, recalling the incidents recorded in the Bible when God listened and showed mercy: "May He that answered Abraham our father on Mount Moriah answer and hearken to the voice of crying this day. . . ." The prayer of the afflicted continues, naming six other precedents: May He that answered our fathers at the Red Sea, Joshua at Gilgal, Samuel at Mitzpah, Elijah at Carmel, Jonah in the belly of the whale, and David and Solomon in Jerusalem answer the cry of the afflicted.[9]

A husband's prayer that his wife give birth easily similarly pleads:

> May the One who answered Sarah, answer [now]; may the One
> who answered Rebekah when she went to plead the Lord, answer
> [now]; may the One who answered Rachel when she gave birth
> to Joseph, answer [now]; may the One who answered Hannah
> when she gave birth to Samuel, answer [now]; may the One who
> remembered all the barren women and the birthing women an-
> swer [now] and remove and save [my wife] from the decree im-
> posed on Eve.[10]

This and many other supplicatory prayers make use of the ancient
doctrine, traditionally referred to as the "merit of the Patriarchs," that
God will help the Jews because of the covenant with the Patriarchs
and the good deeds of ancestral figures.

Jews have often prayed because they want help, but their rabbis
have sometimes warned them not to be optimistic about seeing results. The talmudic sages warned that if we expect our prayers to be
fulfilled, we may end up frustrated and upset. In medieval times, the
Ashkenazic pietists taught that "prayer depends on the heart" and
that if we pray wholeheartedly, our prayers are accepted. However, a
Spanish kabbalist warned that the pleas of the righteous are sometimes rejected. The influential fifteenth-century philosopher Joseph
Albo taught that a prayer is sometimes not answered because God is
unwilling to answer it. In contrast, the Ba'al Shem Tov, the founder of
the eastern European Hasidic movement, taught that prayers are always answered, but sometimes in a way that is hidden from us.[11]

Most people who pour out their hearts to God in distress probably
hope that their prayers will be fulfilled by some sort of divine intervention and do not think about how they themselves might be instrumental in bringing about this fulfillment. The person who is
certain that God hears and will answer may be tempted to disclaim
responsibility for the future. However, the Jew who is aware that God
might not answer has to face the possibility of climbing out of the
muddy rut alone. This person must take responsibility for finding
the new road and solving the worrying problem.

To Bring about Change

Bahya ibn Paquda, the eleventh-century pietist philosopher, believed that Jews are duty-bound to introspect and judge themselves. "Choose what is good for your soul, son," he warned, "before you come to vain regret and endless anxiety." He taught that we should think about our relationship with God and our obligations to God and evaluate what we have done in our lives. We must also think about what we still have to do, before it is too late, and in this way we can change ourselves for the better as well as improve the world we live in. Bahya promised that, if you introspect and repent, "the Creator will do away with your sadness, alleviate your fears . . . and guide and manage you." In addition, he assured his readers that such behavior purges worry, enlightens the mind, and leads to good traits and unending happiness. He detailed thirty forms of introspection that will "whisk away the darkness of doubt from your heart."[12]

In a nineteenth-century prayer beginning "Lord of the Universe, how I suffer with worry and anxiety about my little children who are ill," a worried mother recalls that Abraham was willing to sacrifice his son, had God not sent an angel to save him. She thinks of the children who would have been killed by Haman, had they not prayed with Mordecai the Jew. She remembers the babies who were cast into the Nile following Pharaoh's cruel decree. She calls on God to show mercy to her, just as God showed mercy to others. She supplicates God to let her children recover and grant them strength to study Torah. In addition, she hopes and pleads that they will grow up to have children themselves, and grandchildren.[13]

The woman praying realized that she was not the only mother to suffer for her children, nor would she be the only mother whose children had died, if this were to be their fate. The mother realized that others survived terrible grief in previous generations and this gave her a sense of perspective. In addition, she allowed herself to think ahead and wished that her children would survive and grow up to bear offspring themselves. As she widened her view, she moved in her prayer from pessimistic worry to optimistic hope. Her prayer did not change her children's predicament; the change occurred in her.

The prayer helped her to convert worry into hope and she came to see the situation differently.

Dr. Rachel Remen, an American physician and spiritual teacher, has pointed out that prayer helps, not when we ask for things we want, but when it takes us beyond fear and hope to humility and the recognition of grace. "Prayer is a movement from mastery to mystery," she writes. It enables a person to relinquish the desire to control life and accept that "there may be many reasons beyond reason." Prayer can be a means of facing a predicament and seeking change. It can bring about change in how we see our situation.[14]

When Have Jews Prayed to Cope with Worry?

The early rabbis ruled that Jews must pray three times a day—morning, afternoon, and night—and not only when in need of help. However, these sages allowed private prayers, encouraged repentance (especially in times of danger), and arranged extra public prayers in times of communal distress.[15]

"Repent one day before your death," advised Rabbi Eliezer, in the early second century. He meant that we should repent every day, because tomorrow we may die. Another sage, Rabbi Eleazar, recommended praying before misfortune comes. In addition, the Talmud teaches that reciting the *Shema* keeps troubles away. Each day, religious Jews confirm in their prayers their intention to return to observe God's laws: "Return us to You, O Lord, and we shall return, renew our days as of old. . . ."[16] Those who could return fully to God would rid themselves of their worries and reach a spiritual goal that many pietist Jews have sought.

The Talmud stresses the importance of prayer at any time; Jews do not have to wait for the hour of congregational prayer to turn their thoughts to God. They should pray in the synagogue, it is taught, but if they cannot do this, they may pray in the field; if they cannot pray there, they can pray on their beds; if that too does not work out, then they should meditate in their hearts and be still.[17]

One rabbi, Samuel bar Nahman, said that repentance is like the sea, in which nothing hinders you from purifying yourself at any time, whereas prayer is like a bath, which you may not be able to enter when you want, for various reasons. Two rabbis argued over whether repentance or prayer is more effective: one said that repentance accomplishes all, and prayer only half; the other chose the reverse position. Clearly the two concepts are intertwined.[18]

Jews have prayed in times of danger, in the face of worry that is not life-threatening (such as in the hope of success in a business deal), and in times of moral and social anxiety. Some pray every day, some only on particular days of the year, and some only in times of crisis, when they are worried.[19]

When in Distress

Why is Israel like an olive? The Talmud tells that just as an olive does not yield its oil until pressed, so Jews do not repent until afflicted. However, the Mishnah teaches that if we find ourselves in a situation that might be dangerous, we should address God in prayer. Indeed, many worried people do not pray until they discover that they have no hope of helping themselves in any other way. The childless woman who cannot conceive, the cancer patient whom the doctors can no longer help, and the distressed American fearing an anthrax attack may pray for divine assistance, even though they have never prayed in their lives before, when they see no other way of helping themselves. Jews have prayed when in personal distress, for another in distress, and when the community is in distress.[20]

Maimonides thought of repentance as a lifelong process that should be taking place constantly in our hearts. In addition, he assumed that human troubles are not mere accidents, but are experienced by God's decree, and therefore Jews are commanded to cry to God in times of trouble, to pray and repent.[21]

Jews have sometimes added a special prayer to their private prayers or gathered together for joint prayer at times of particular danger to the Jewish community, such as during a drought, anti-Semitic violence, or an epidemic. In the thirteenth century, Nahmanides, Rabbi

Moses ben Nahman, an influential Spanish philosopher and kabbal-ist, taught that whenever the community is distressed, it is a mitzvah for Jews to plead fervently with God "to affirm in moments of dis-tress our belief that the Holy One listens to prayers and intervenes to grant aid."[22]

In 1648, the Jews of Polnoye heard that the Cossacks were rav-aging Jewish communities nearby. They gathered in the synagogue to pray and repent with the hope of averting a massacre in their own town. Soon the news came that the Cossacks were approaching. Spreading their prayer shawls over their heads, the Jews prayed with great fervor to sanctify the Name, as Rabbi Akiva had done when the Romans tortured him many centuries earlier. But the Cossacks massa-cred them all in the synagogue, "on holy soil. May God avenge their blood!"[23]

The kabbalist Nathan Neta Hannover (d. 1683), from whom we have just quoted, was a friend of the rabbi who encouraged the Jews to repent and pray in the fearful days that preceded the massacre. Be-fore Hannover himself died a martyr in a later pogrom, he recorded his friend's prayer, expressing the fear of apostasy and ending with sanctification of the Name. Hannover advised its daily recitation. We do not know to what extent these seventeenth-century Polish Jews believed that God would answer their prayers and avert massacre, but they certainly believed that by dying as martyrs sanctifying the Name of God the Messiah's coming would be hastened for the good of all Jews.[24]

In 1784, the Mantua community formulated a prayer for the Jews—and non-Jews—of Spalatro who were stricken with plague. "Look down, O God, from Heaven, from your holy habitation. Bless the Jewish people and also have compassion and mercy upon all the peoples of the world, particularly the people of the city of Spalatro. Do not permit Satan to enter their homes to plague them, but order the angel who is wreaking havoc among the people: 'Enough, now, stop, for they are all the work of My hand.'" Similarly, when yellow fever ravaged New York City in 1803, the Sephardic community composed a special prayer for the Day of Atonement that addressed their fear of this fever. It is likely that their praying together gave them strength.[25]

Jews have prayed, too, when worried about private matters. We have already noted the worry of childlessness that features in some personal prayers. Another example is the apprehension that a parent feels when a daughter or son marries. Thus a mother's prayer on the wedding day of her daughter, dating from the mid–nineteenth century, admits how often she has wished for the day when her daughter would enter into "the proper sphere of woman." And yet now that the day has come, it is not only joy that she feels in her heart—fear and anxiety disturb her glowing wishes. She prays fervently for her daughter's future happiness in her new life as wife and mother. When her son gets married, though, she is more specific about her worry. She prays to God that not the smallest cloud darken the horizon of the young couple's marital happiness. She expresses her egotistical hope that filial love will never leave his heart, that his love for his wife will not weaken or deaden his feelings for his parents so that he will continue to love and revere them and give them joy. The worry expressed here is the fear of loneliness, of losing her son's love, perhaps even the fear of helplessness in old age. Marriage is a time when relationships change and a mother has a hard time "letting go" of her son. This prayer was written by a woman, but it admits any parent's desire that a child become a happy and independent adult, as well as the natural worry of separating from the child who has been nurtured for so long, who no longer wants or needs parenting. By admitting these conflicting emotions in a prayer, a parent faces them, and takes the first step toward solving the conflict.[26]

Would the Jews of Mantua have supplicated for the people of Spalatro had they discovered an inoculation against the plague? If the Jews of Polnoye had obtained firearms to repel the Cossacks, would they have prayed in the synagogue? Religious Jews still pray for a safe birth and for a safe journey, just as they pray for recovery from a serious illness, and for other Jews in distress. But a secular parent has no tool or medicine other than strength of character to fight anxiety about a child's marriage or trek to the Far East. A secular Jew is unlikely to pray today, unless severely pressed, like the olive.

When Worried for Moral Reasons

Jews have prayed and repented when worried about their own behavior, especially about thoughts or acts that they consider morally reprehensible. The Talmud records prayers that reveal this sort of worry, one for reciting every night at bedtime, and another for the early morning. At bedtime, the supplication follows the *Shema:* "May it be thy will, O Lord . . . do not accustom me to transgression; and bring me not into sin, or into iniquity, or into temptation, or into contempt. And may the Good Inclination have sway over me and let not the Evil Inclination have sway over me." And upon awaking: "Do not bring me into sin, or into iniquity, or into temptation, or into contempt, and bend my inclination to be subservient unto Thee. Remove me far from a bad man and a bad companion, and make me cleave to the Good Inclination and to a good companion in Thy world . . ." (B. *Berakhot* 60b).

At the end of the day and before starting work the next day, the traditional Jew worries about transgressing: Moral anxiety has been ritualized in Judaism. These prayers can be found in the daily prayer book and are part of a religious Jew's daily life.

How Have Jews Used Prayer to Cope with Worry?

We can pray alone or in a group. We can pray out loud, or in silent contemplation. Prayer can be sung or muttered under the breath. It can be ecstatic or tearful, benedictory or petitionary, ritualized or spontaneous. It may start out in one of these modes and change to another. There are many different ways of praying. Jews have prayed in their own words in private pleas, devotions, and repentance. Some have prayed for others who worry. And as we have seen, sometimes the whole community in the synagogue recites a special prayer that addresses a communal worry.

There is the traditional Jewish liturgy for fixed times of the day, month, and year. At such times, alone or with a congregation, Jews have reached up to God in prayer. In addition to serving God in this way, some have tried to unite their souls with God and some, as we will see in chapters 4, 5, and 6, have developed special prayer techniques in their efforts to draw down divine blessings and receive revelations.

The prayer ritual and the benedictory prayers help Jews to quash worries. In these prayers, the Jew tries to concentrate on divine worship and prevent daily concerns from distracting this worship. In contrast, repentance allows Jews to talk with God about their worries. Petitionary prayers often address personal concerns and allow Jews to share and talk about their worries.

By Quashing Worry for Prayer

Since worry affects the heart and prevents wholehearted service to God, it must be quashed. This was the view of Rabbi Ammi (as we saw in the last chapter). The early sages taught that we should never give up prayer in despair, even if a sharp sword is laid at our throats, or a snake winds itself around our heels. Rabbi Akiva set the example. It is told that even the iron combs that ripped him to death did not prevent him from praying the *Shema* with all his heart and soul. The fourth-century mystical *Sefer Yetzirah,* advised: "Lock your heart that it may not brood."[27]

The prayer schedule of the religious Jew divides up the day and structures time into morning, afternoon, and evening, just as it structures the week into working days and the Sabbath, and marks out the months according to the new moon and the Jewish festivals scattered through the year. There is therefore never a long period when a person can allow worry to take its grip for any length of time. Worry concerns and fills time, but the Jewish daily prayer book, the *siddur* (literally, "order"), orders time in a person's life. The order of the prayers limits the time that a Jew can spend worrying, allowing regular spiritual refreshment between bouts of worrying. The prayer ritual, at fixed times, with fixed formulas, is a fence to worry. Jews have built physical and imaginary fences around themselves to protect what is within from outside threats as well as to prevent what is within from going out. Prayer limits worry and prevents it growing too large and taking over the heart.[28]

The ideal that we must concentrate fully in order to pray wholeheartedly led to much rabbinic discussion about the problem of distracting thoughts, as we will see. If they cannot be banished by an act of will or through a surge of faith, can we not somehow transform them to serve God?

Full Concentration in Prayer: Devekut   The word used in the Bible for cleaving to God (*d-v-k*) is the same as that used to describe how the tongue cleaves to the mouth and how a man cleaves to a woman. There is no room for anything between the two, between the person cleaving and God, not even a single worry. Deuteronomy commands us to love and cleave to God (Deut. 11:22). The Talmud teaches that we can cleave to God as one sticky date cleaves to another, or by desiring and delighting in God as a man desires and delights in the woman he loves, or by attaching ourselves to God.[29]

Since medieval times, Jews have used the word *devekut* to refer to the process of cleaving to God, the process of binding one's soul to God, for example, by concentrating only on the Divine in their prayers. This mental and emotional cleaving precludes worrying in the heart or the mind. Thus, a Jew who aspires to cleave fully to God—and this has been the goal of mystic and pietist Jews—must quash worry, exclude it completely. Some nine hundred years ago, Bahya ibn Paquda wrote that to recite a prayer with the tongue, while the mind is elsewhere, is like a body without a soul, or a peel without its fruit. He taught that we must remove all distracting thoughts while praying and direct our full attention to God. We must still the body, stop worrying, and concentrate fully on praying in order to surrender the soul to God. He pointed out that the sages prepared prayer texts for Jews to recite because they recognized the problem of distracting thoughts. They knew that without a prepared text we would find it difficult to pray.[30]

Maimonides thought that if we do not empty our minds of every thought and imagine that we are standing in front of God's glory, we are not really praying. He assumed that an intellectual effort is necessary to banish worry and think of God during prayer.[31]

According to the medieval kabbalists, prayer must be without a blemish—without distracting thoughts—just as the beast sacrificed in antiquity had to be without blemish. Sacrifice, korban, means to draw near (root k-r-b) to God. Until the destruction of the Second Temple, sacrifice was the Jew's offering to God and a form of service to God. In the synagogue, prayer completely replaced sacrifice. The kabbalists taught that prayer stirs the fire in our hearts instead of the fire on the sacrificial altar, so that the pure thought of the prayer ascends and unifies with "the Source of the endlessly sublime flame." In the thirteenth century, Rabbi Azriel of Gerona prayed by fixing his thought on God, directing his words toward the Divine, "like the flame that is attached to the glowing coal." He and other medieval kabbalists believed that through will and intention, it is possible to overcome all concerns and surrender the soul in prayer to God.[32]

The Safed kabbalist, Rabbi Eleazar Azikri, believed that he had to remove all thoughts so that his soul could cleave to the Divine "as a magnet to iron," and liked to pray alone. "Since the hearts of Jews are His house," he explained, "we should sweep from them all the rubble and dust of sinful thoughts." These "sinful thoughts" refer to thoughts that disrupt intimate communion with God, and thus include worry.[33]

The Ba'al Shem Tov taught that prayer should focus on the divine source and not on personal worries. By praying merely for our own physical advantage, we cause a dividing curtain to fall between us and God, he explained, because we thereby introduce material matter into the spiritual realm, and God cannot answer the prayer at all. Ideally, we should be totally divorced from the physical world when praying, unaware of our existence in the world. The Ba'al Shem Tov and his disciple, Dov Baer, the Maggid of Mezhirech (d. 1772), taught that when we pray we should have nothing in mind or heart other than God. But they were both fully aware of the difficulty of maintaining this ideal state.[34]

The Problem of Distracting Thoughts   Mundane thoughts—
especially worries—often disturb our concentration, however hard
we try to avoid them. Some Jews have believed that it is possible to
banish worry with an intellectual effort, by exerting reason and
willpower. Others have believed that faith banishes worry and that
only someone with perfect faith can be free of disturbing thoughts.
Abraham and Noah are the exemplary men of faith who did not fret
when others would have worried.[35]

Most of us can dismiss worry from our minds at times, in order to
concentrate fully, but at other times, worry wins out and prevents us
from concentrating on anything serious. The talmudic Rabbi Eleazar
realized that people do not always have the mental power to banish
their worries and taught that we should first test ourselves to see if we
can concentrate our attention for proper prayer. If so, we should
pray; but if not, he said, we should not pray. On one occasion at least,
his student prayed twice, probably because the first time, he was not
concentrating properly.[36]

As we noted in the last chapter, Maimonides believed that only
the pious, saintly man can banish all disturbing thoughts in his quest
for God, and most people (who are not saintly) find this difficult. The
medieval Ashkenazic rabbi, Samuel the Pious, pointed out that
women and men who lack the ability to concentrate fully might find
it easier to focus their minds if they pray in their mother tongue instead of Hebrew, the language of the liturgy. His son, Judah the Pious
of Regensburg, taught that if a worry breaks our devotion during
prayer, we should stop awhile to regain concentration and then continue to pray. He developed a special technique to cope with the
problem of distracting thoughts in prayer. This involved concentrating on the Hebrew letters in the words of the prayers. His prayer was
long and drawn out, requiring considerable mental discipline to
maintain full concentration on the task. He closed his eyes or covered his head with a prayer shawl to keep out distractions, and directed his mind to heaven.[37]

The Book of Zohar sharply criticized those who pray without full
concentration. It taught that we must direct our thoughts and hearts

with willpower in order to pray. Nevertheless, the Zohar offered practical advice to those who want to pray but whose minds are distressed: first praise God and then say a prayer, even if the prayer lacks concentration. This prayer can address the worry.[38]

When Rabbi Joseph Karo prayed, he sought to unite his soul with God, but worries and mundane thoughts often disturbed him. This sixteenth-century Safed kabbalist and author of the Shulḥan Arukh code of Jewish law recited verses of Jewish law (Mishnah) to suppress all thoughts that might distract his divine service.[39]

An Ashkenazic Jew, Pinhas Katzenellenbogen of Mehrin (1691–1765), recited his own little prayer every day declaring his trust and faith in God, and calling on God to keep anxiety and fear well away from him. He recorded in his memoirs, "Truly it is not in my nature . . . to be fearful of anything because I have trusted in the Lord and put my faith in Him." Yet every day he called on God, declared his trust and faith out loud, and then pronounced some mystical devotions—permutations of special names—silently, three times. Finally he vocalized his desire to be protected from anger, evil impulses, anxiety and fear, and all bad things that can happen. Pinhas probably found that the kabbalistic meditations helped to quash his worries and promote his concentration on cleaving to God. (He may have believed that they added power to his prayer, as we will see in chapters 4 and 6).[40]

The Ba'al Shem Tov's great-grandson, Nahman of Bratzlav, found that the act of praying brought him before the King, and in his wonder at the King's splendor, he forgot his own existence. His fervent worship enabled him to banish thoughts that pinned him to the material world. He taught that prayer is a Jew's weapon; with this weapon Jews can fight all their battles against their impulses. He advised that even if we feel really upset when we begin to pray, we should use our mental powers to pray joyfully and guide our thoughts in the direction of God. He suggested that a joyful melody might help, as we will see in chapter 7.[41]

Religious Jews today often read psalms for the whole of an intercity bus journey, a train ride, and a plane trip, a time-tested method for removing distracting thoughts and turning the heart and mind to God. This way their minds are not free to worry about a possible tragedy, a family problem, or a business deal. The Twenty-third Psalm ("The Lord is my shepherd"), in particular, is a prayer for banishing worry: "Though I walk through a valley of deepest darkness, I fear no harm, for You are with me." This psalm reminds the worried person that however uncertain the path may appear, God is nearby and therefore there is no need to worry.

Transmuting Worry through Prayer Those who cannot banish all distracting thoughts can perhaps transmute them into divine service. For example, Rabbi Eliezer's prayer for times of danger avoids any mention of danger and simply pleads, "May your will be done in heaven above, grant relief to those who revere You, and do that which is good in Your sight" (B. *Berakhot* .29b). The Talmud teaches that worry can be sublimated through prayer and benedictions: Undesirable thoughts are channeled into a socially acceptable activity—prayer.[42]

In a popular guide to Jewish ethical living, Rabbi Isaiah Horowitz (d. 1630) offered a prayer that expresses the desire to find joy in serving God whatever the danger: "Be near me [God] so that the pain not confuse me and my thoughts continue to cleave to you, joyful in the hour of suffering."[43]

The Ba'al Shem Tov developed his own technique to convert distracting thoughts to holy thoughts when they disturbed his prayer. He believed that every action and thought has an external form and an inner "root," a divine spark that comes from God. Using a meditative method (see chapter 4), he raised the divine spark that he believed to be hidden in his disturbing thought and returned it to its divine source. For example, he could raise a thought that involves lust to the Universe of Love (*Ḥesed*), the divine root of lust, and he could raise a fearful thought to the Universe of Courage (*Gevurah*). Some Hasidim used this meditation technique to maintain the holiness of the prayer when worry disrupted their concentration.[44]

As we will see in the next chapter, elevating and sublimating distracting thoughts in this way is no simple task. Some of the Ba'al

Shem Tov's disciples realized that not everyone can do this. They therefore developed the doctrine of the *tzaddik*, the saintly man who undertakes this effort for worried Jews. But some later Hasidim believed that even the *tzaddik* cannot succeed at this task and the idea of elevating undesirable thoughts was eventually abandoned.[45]

The nineteenth-century Lithuanian, Rabbi Israel Lipkin of Salant, was not a Hasid and developed a very different technique that includes ethical study and group prayer to sublimate dark thoughts. This method of study and prayer involves a special melody, rhythm, and much repetition to arouse in the participants both maximum concentration and emotion—an intense fear of divine retribution—that will transform the soul for the better. [46]

In 1859, far from the eastern European Hasidim and the ethical classes of Israel of Salant, Rachel Simon, a British Liberal Jew, counseled, "Turn every trial to account; however trifling in its character, make use of it as the polishing instrument that will change the roughest stone into the jeweler's prize." This profoundly spiritual woman believed that prayer could help a person transmute even a small vexation into awareness of God's love. [47]

By Talking about Worry in Prayer

For the many people who cannot banish worry while praying, there is the possibility of talking about it in prayer. A Jew may want to speak to God from the heart, in private, in his or her own words. However, rabbis have written formulas for private supplications and the special prayers of a worried community. Today, some Jews are writing new prayers to help us cope with specific worries.[48]

A person may talk about a worry to God in a private prayer and even take responsibility to seek a solution. Alternatively, the worried Jew might blame God for the current predicament and beg God to cause a change for the better. The sad and angry outburst may be cathartic and release emotional tension, so that the person makes contact with God and feels redeemed.[49]

A supplication to God often includes a natural outpouring of wishful thoughts. Rabbis warned, however, that there are certain wishful thoughts that we should not pray for. For example, we should not pray for an overabundance of good to be taken away from us, for death to descend on the wicked, or for the impossible, because these wishes must not or cannot be fulfilled. Even though the expression of wishes promotes hope and positive thinking, we should not expect a miracle: we have to remain aware that some hopes and wishes cannot be fulfilled. As the American Rabbi Jack Riemer has said, we can pray "for strength, determination, and willpower, to do, to become, instead of merely to wish."[50]

A Jew may be able to talk to God privately in prayer in a way that would not be possible when talking to another person. We can express socially unacceptable feelings in prayer, knowing that God will not respond, "Shame on you for thinking that," or "Don't be silly!" For example, the prayer mentioned earlier by a woman on her son's wedding day allowed her to express her worry at a time when happiness was expected. Some worried Jews journey to the grave of a holy person in order to confide their distress and to ask the departed soul to pray for God's blessing. We will see, though, that many do also share their worries with other people and they pray together or for each other.

Introspective Prayer   Medieval philosophers (such as Bahya ibn Paquda and Jonah ben Abraham of Gerona) and pietist rabbis (such as Judah of Regensburg and Eleazar of Worms) demanded that Jews judge themselves. They recommended a process of repentance that involves much prayer as well as other penitential behaviors, such as fasting and giving to charity. The process has many steps to lead the Jew to change his or her ways and return to God's laws.[51]

An introspective prayer, in German, of an educated Jewish woman who was worried about her unhappy marriage was published in a Jewish prayer book in Sulzbach in 1832. In it, the distressed woman first admits to God that her marriage is sadly not the source of great happiness that it should be, and this causes her great suffering. She tells God that she wants to examine herself, to see if she is responsible for her sad state of affairs. God blessed women with softness and patience, she notes, and then asks herself if she is always soft and patient in her relations with her husband. Furthermore, she asks herself if perhaps her irritability, selfishness, resentment, suspicion, and touchiness have led to her husband's distancing from her and to his perception that she is lacking in love. She promises God in her prayer that she will change her ways and treat her husband with kindness, patience, goodness, and care, in the hope of winning back his heart and retrieving marital happiness. She hopes her distressed sighs will turn to cries of joy. The prayer ends with a declaration of her dependence on God and some verses from the Fifth Psalm ("Give ear to my speech, O Lord . . .").[52]

The woman was clearly worried about her marriage. She knew something was wrong but she did not merely supplicate God for mercy and compassion. She thought through her problem by talking to God, in a prayer. She thought introspectively and judged herself. She took responsibility. By the end of the prayer she found energy to change her ways and determined to try to be kinder to her husband. She found hope and strengthened faith in God's mercies.

Although the liturgy includes a short prayer for old age, a personal prayer printed in Yiddish in the early twentieth century expresses the worry of aging parents who find they have become dependent on their adult children and cannot manage to live without their support. The elderly person first asks introspectively: Did I myself behave properly toward my parents? Perhaps I caused them grief or disgrace. Then the prayer admits the worry of having become a burden, dependent on the younger generation, and the fear that the young may not treat the old person honorably and kindly. "May I never become burdensome and superfluous at their table, as they never were at mine. . . . May I not be grieved by them, nor them by me. . . . " Finally, the old person praying asks for punishment, should things go badly, that the young people be spared. By looking inward and admitting these worries in a prayer, the elderly person faces them and can take action.[53]

Emotional Prayer from the Heart   The Bible relates that Hannah prayed to God in her despair at her childlessness, weeping all the time. Elijah prayed to God in earnest for a sign to prove God's supremacy to the prophets of Baal.[54] The Psalmist, too, prayed in times of trouble: "Out of the depths I call you, O Lord. O Lord, listen to my cry" (Ps. 130:1–2); "In my time of trouble I call You, for You will answer me" (86:7). Jeremiah pleaded, "O Lord, you know—remember me and take thought of me," as he poured out all his miseries to God (Jer. 15:15). Job, too, cried out to God in his affliction: "I cry out to You, but You do not answer me. . . . With Your powerful hand You harass me" (Job 30:20–21).

The early rabbis encouraged private petitions and the insertion of "something fresh" into one's prayers, to ensure that supplication is genuine, from the heart, and not just a recitation by rote. Jews added their personal pleas, according to their specific worries, to their regular prayers. Some of the private prayers of pious men entered the *siddur*. For example, an early prayer for going on a journey begins with the supplication, "May it be your will, O Lord my God, to lead me forth in peace, direct my steps in peace, and uphold me in peace." Jews have often added heartfelt supplications to this talmudic formula, as well as biblical verses and meditations with many repetitions as the worry on a journey can last a long time.[55]

In contrast to Maimonides, who ruled that we should not pray if we cannot banish distress from our hearts, the Zohar taught that tears from the heart, tears of entreaty and penitence, break through the gates and doors of heaven. The Zohar promises that "he who prays and weeps and cries so much that there is no feeling left in his lips— that is perfect prayer, prayer in the heart, and it never returns empty." However, sullen tears or tears for vengeance are useless, according to this source. Whereas petitionary prayer must be tearful, the Zohar teaches that prayer praising God must be joyful, joy springing from the love of communion. All prayers must be heartfelt and directed to heaven.[56]

According to the Ba'al Shem Tov, we can arouse divine compassion by praying with a great cry, a melody, or a deep sigh that comes from the depths of the heart. We can pray in a field or a side street as well as the home or synagogue; however, our prayers do not always rise up to God. He taught that prayers rise up only if they are said with the heart lifted to heaven. We should cry out to God as we would if we were hanging by a hair and a tempest raged to the very heart of heaven. We should cry out to God as if we do not know what to do and there is hardly time to cry out. As we pray, we should feel that we have no refuge, but must remain in our loneliness and lift our eyes and hearts up to God: "And this should be done at all times, for in the world a man is in great danger."[57]

Some European Jewish women, in the nineteenth century, and possibly in the preceding century too, formulated prayers that would answer their particular spiritual needs. In 1859, in Britain, Rachel Simon suggested a little prayer for reciting in times of trouble: "Oh God! let not little things vex me and disturb my spirit, nor let me be disheartened by my own shortcomings, but help me to overcome my deficiencies. Strengthen me with a fervent faith in you. . . ." She was convinced that God gives strength, and to trust in God is to receive God's blessing.[58]

Rachel's contemporaries on the European continent published prayer books in the languages that they could read. These included prayers for all the different occasions in a woman's life when she ought or might want to pray, focusing especially on the worries related to marital life, childbirth, and sickness that were predominant in their lives.[59]

Unconventional Prayer An eighteenth-century Hasid, Rabbi Levi-Itzhak of Berditchev (a town now in the Ukraine), had shown concern about the well-being of others, but one day he withdrew to his room and lay on his bed, reading from a little book or gazing blankly around him. After a year, his heart remained broken but he pulled himself together and began to roar at God, in Yiddish, in the middle of his prayers or after a long silence, on Yom Kippur and on Passover. "If You refuse to answer our prayers," he threatened God, "then I shall refuse to go on saying them." And, another time: "Know that if Your reign does not bring grace and mercy, Your throne will not be a throne of truth." During the Holocaust, in the death camps, Elie Wiesel gained strength and courage from the legends he had heard about Levi-Itzhak, the rabbi who dared to remonstrate with

God, the rabbi who was a fighter, asked questions, and gave brave answers when God remained silent.[60]

Levi-Itzhak was not the only Hasid to abandon the formal style of Hebrew statutory prayer when seriously worried. Nahman of Bratzlav did this too. Nahman poured out his thoughts before God in a field, conversing with God from the depth of his heart, as Isaac had done in antiquity. The Bible tells that Isaac went out to meditate (la-su'ah) in the field toward the evening. Lasu'ah, according to the Talmud, refers to some form of prayer, actually "conversation with one's own heart," according to Rabbi Abraham ibn Ezra (1089–1164). Nahman taught that we should all set aside a certain time each day for outdoor solitude, when we can pour out before God our most intimate desires, worries, and frustrations, for this is the way that the ancients prayed. We should do this aloud, not necessarily in Hebrew, but in whatever language allows us to express ourselves directly from the heart. Nahman knew that there are times when it can be very difficult to express our deepest feelings in this way. He suggested that at such times we merely call out, "Oh God, help!" or "Lord of the World!" We should keep trying though, he said, even if we find that for days we just repeat this single phrase over and over again, because finally, after regular attempts, patience, and faith, speech does emerge directly from the heart.[61]

Worried Jews have often supplicated God in their mother tongue, the language in which they could best express their heartfelt distress, and not in the Hebrew of the liturgy. They have occasionally addressed God unconventionally when praying, with "Dear Friend," or "Healer of Broken Hearts."[62]

Abraham Sutzkever (b. 1913) tried to pray, on January 17, 1942, while he was imprisoned in the Vilna Ghetto, after the Nazis had murdered thirty-three thousand Vilna Jews in six months, including his mother and his newborn son:

> I think I just thought of a prayer,
> But I can't imagine who might be there.
> Sealed in a steel womb,

How can I pray? To whom? . . .
Still, someone in me insists: pray!
Tormenting me in my soul: pray!
Prayer, oh wildest surmise,
I still babble you till sunrise.[63]

Unlike the Hasidim who knew that God was listening, Sutzkever had no idea if God was there; could God be present, watching what he himself had seen the Nazis do to the Jews? Could God be present and allow such horror and terror? If God is not there, he wondered, could he still pray, was there any point in praying? Clearly he thought that praying might help him and in his predicament he felt the need to try. His prayer was only babble, the only form of communication he could manage at that point.

Graveside Prayers   The Talmud tells us that Caleb, one of the spies sent by Moses to reconnoiter the land of Canaan, visited the graves of the patriarchs at Hebron, as he feared the evil intentions of the other spies. He prostrated himself and prayed "My fathers, pray on my behalf that I may be delivered from the plot of the spies" (B. *Sotah* 34b).

Medieval Jews who were unable to travel to Hebron sometimes asked a traveling friend to go and pray there on their behalf, to convey their supplications to God. A medieval prayer for reciting at the sacred cave in Hebron addresses the souls of the dead ancestors: "Oh! Fathers of the World, beloved of God, how can you rest in your graves when we, your children's children, ever in hope, have tried so hard and yet have not been granted rest? Plead with God, I beg you! Wake up Moses, the faithful shepherd. . . ." The prayer goes on to ask for nothing less than the final redemption that has long been a Jewish dream and, of course, would end all worries.[64]

Hebron is not the only burial site where Jews ask the dead to pray on their behalf. Rachel's tomb south of Jerusalem, Rabbi Shimon Bar Yohai's on Mount Meron, and Elijah's cave near Haifa remain age-old prayer sites for worried Jews. Similarly, in Europe, the graves of Maharal in Prague and Rabbi Moses Isserles in Cracow, for example, became favorite sites. In Yemen, the grave of Rabbi Shalom Shabazi was a popular site for supplication. In Iraq, Jews visited the tombs of the prophets Ezekiel (near Hilla) and Jonah (Nineveh) and of Ezra the Scribe (near Basra) as well as the graves where some of the talmudic Sages were said to have been buried. In other countries, too, Jews have visited graves of holy men when they were particularly worried—there are too many to mention here.[65]

At Rachel's tomb, Jews ask that their prayers be fulfilled for the sake of the good deeds that Rachel performed in antiquity. Sometimes they ask for redemption, for the good of all, but often the person praying mentions a personal worry too. This is a favorite site for the prayer of childless women who recall that "God remembered Rachel; God heeded her and opened her womb" (Gen. 30:22) and pray that God will now similarly remember them.[66]

In the early seventeenth century, Ashkenazic Jews printed books with prayers for reciting by the grave of a holy person in the hope of remedying the sick and dying. These prayer books bore titles such as "The Book of Medicine for the Soul," "The Book of Words of Truth," and "The Book of Life." Sometimes these prayers were written out in the local spoken language as well as or instead of Hebrew, for those who had difficulty praying in the holy language. In recent years, graveside prayers have become an increasingly popular method of coping with worry in Israel.[67]

By Praying with Others

The Rabbi of Kotzk, mentioned at the start of this chapter, pointed out that when people eat, they do so to fill only their own stomachs. When Jews pray, however, even alone at home, they bind themselves to all other Jews, and their prayers gain strength and ascend for the benefit and good of all.[68]

Jewish petitionary prayers are often in the plural, "grant us," rather than in the singular. Praying together with other people increases the power of prayer.[69]

The Zohar explained that congregational prayer is more effective "for it ascends with many hues, comprises many facets, and . . .

becomes a crown," whereas the prayer of the individual is of only one hue and is less likely to be accepted. When Jews pray together, their prayers unite and God does not judge each one on its own. The prayers of individuals, however, are each judged for their purity, and God rejects those that are blemished.[70]

The sixteenth-century Safed kabbalist Rabbi Isaac Luria saw a further advantage in praying with others. He believed that by sharing our prayers with others, we might promote harmony in the world and hasten the redemption. Thus when the soul of one Jew praying is distressed—"whether it has to do with some illness or with his children"—all the other Jews praying must pray on behalf of that person.[71]

The kabbalists innovated prayers for personal use, incorporating such ideas, and these gained considerable popularity. For example, in a prayer written for a pregnant woman, she requests that God fulfill her personal petitions together with all the other petitions of all other Jews who bid God's mercy. The woman praying realizes that she is not the only person in need and is not alone—other people have worries too. She widens her perceptual horizon, thinks ahead, and dares to hope. The prayer admits her faith in God and hopes that her wishes might be fulfilled.[72]

In 1975, two Holocaust survivors recalled a winter evening in Bergen-Belsen. One was a rabbi; the other was a secular socialist. On that day there had been a "selection." Hundreds of sick and helpless Jews were kicked and beaten to death. That night was the first night of Hanukkah. The rabbi improvised a *hanukkiyyah* (candelabra) by filling a clog with boot polish and placing in it some threads from the rags they wore to serve as wicks. The rabbi recited the blessings as he lit the wicks, but at the third blessing, which thanks God for keeping us alive and enabling us to reach this day, he hesitated. He looked around for a short moment, and then recited the blessing in a strong, reassuring voice. The secular Jew protested, "How can you possibly thank God for keeping us alive on such a day?" The rabbi admitted that he had asked himself the same question when he had paused. He had even searched the room to consult with another rabbi. However, as he looked up, he caught the intense look of those who had gathered to hear the blessings and find momentary happiness in the light of the flickering wicks, and he knew immediately that he had to go ahead and finish the blessing, to maintain their faith. At that moment the secular Jew understood the power of the prayer. Later he often found himself consoled by that prayer.[73]

The short prayer ritual allowed the participants to let God into their hearts, even for a very short moment, and sense the spirit that was still alive within them. In addition, it allowed them to feel their togetherness and gave them some strength.

By Praying for Others

According to the sages, "a sick person's prayers on his own behalf are more efficacious than those of anyone else," yet Jews often preferred to replace the first person singular in petitionary prayers with the first person plural, for the benefit of all. The Talmud teaches that if we pray for others when we ourselves are in need of the same help, our prayer will be answered first. We have seen that traditionally a Jew must worry about others, not only about himself or herself. But in moments of stress and dread it is often difficult to think beyond ourselves and to raise ourselves above our personal needs. Raising ourselves out of our own egocentricity helps us to cope with our personal worries.[74]

Jews supplicate for God's blessing with the traditional *mi she-berakh* blessing during the Sabbath morning service: "May He who blessed our fathers, Abraham, Isaac, and Jacob, bless . . ." this congregation or a certain sick person, those in captivity, or those in danger. This blessing is recited for the well-being of the whole congregation, as well as for individual people. On the Sabbath, a Jew must rejoice and not worry; therefore the cantor or the leader of the prayer in the synagogue utters the blessing that the worried person requests.[75]

The Bible makes clear that some people are better than others at having their prayers answered. Worried Jews have often traveled long distances in search of such a person—an intercessor—in the hope that he will pray on their behalf.

The Intercessor's Prayer   Moses told his people at Sinai, "Fear no man, for judgment is God's. And any matter that is too difficult for you, you shall bring to me and I will hear it" (Deut. 1:17). The message was clear: They should turn to Moses with their worries. The Israelites cried and complained as they crossed the desert after leaving Egypt and Moses indeed prayed and remonstrated with God for the sake of his people. Not only Moses, but also Abraham, Joshua, Solomon, the Psalmist, and the prophets prayed for the benefit of their people. They set the example of intercession, in which a holy person communes with God on behalf of another person.[76]

The Talmud tells that once a rabbi's son was dangerously ill. He sent messengers to Rabbi Hanina ben Dosa (a sage who lived in the Galilee in the first century) to ask him to pray for the son's recovery. Hanina went up to his chamber on the roof and prayed. When he came down, he told the messengers that the fever had left the boy. He knew this because he had felt his prayer flow freely. When the men arrived at their master's, they found that the fever had indeed disappeared.[77]

The Talmud tells, too, that when fear of drought was in everyone's hearts after a dry winter in the land of Israel, some rabbis prayed for rain, without success. Those who managed to induce the rain were simple people who performed good deeds, rabbis who humbled themselves, and Rabbi Akiva with his prayer "Our Father, our King" (*Avinu Malkenu*). These men were able to intercede with God through their prayers, on behalf of the people.[78]

Worried Jews have sought out a holy person—a *tzaddik*—to intercede with God on their behalf. They could perhaps stop worrying if such a person would agree to pray for them. The biblical word, *tzaddik,* literally means "a righteous man." The Talmud assumes that the *tzaddik* has high moral standards, is capable of creative acts similar to God's, and can annul divine decrees. Moreover, God desires to hear the prayers of these righteous men.[79]

Since antiquity, Jews have told tales of righteous people who have removed people's worries by performing wonders. We will see in chapters 4 and 6 that some Jews have sought to acquire the special powers of the *tzaddik* of antiquity for the benefit of others. Some have believed they were chosen by God to be a channel for the flow of blessings.[80]

It is told that on the eve of Passover, some Arabs were sailing their merchandise up the River Tigris, from Basra to Baghdad. Just before reaching the port of their destination, a large crack appeared in the bottom of the boat, the dirty water flooded in, and it was clear that the boat would sink within minutes. One man on board, a Jew, sat unflustered watching the others panic. When the Arabs accosted him, he offered to pray for their safety, on the condition that they said "Amen" to his prayer and reward him if he saved them. The Jew stood up, raised his eyes to heaven, and prayed in a loud voice, "Samuel Adoni, stand up in prayer on our behalf before your Creator. Perhaps God will have mercy upon us for your sake and will save us from this imminent death!" As soon as the men said "Amen" the crack in the boat was filled in and the water in the boat evaporated. They landed safely, and a few weeks later they brought their many gifts of thanks to Rabbi Samuel Barzani. Barzani lived in the early seventeenth century, but his "natural force was not abated" after his death and Kurdistan Jews visited his tomb in Amadiya and called on him, in the hope that he would intercede on their behalf.[81]

In the eighteenth century, the eastern European Hasidim used the word *maggid,* usually meaning a preacher, to refer to a few righteous men who prayed to draw down divine blessings for their communities. The Hasidic *maggidim* knew how to pray in a special way. It is told that worried Jews came from far and wide to ask for the help of Israel, the Maggid of Koznitz (1733–1814). If the request was simple, he merely closed his eyes and whispered his prayer. If the request was really difficult, he waited until the time for his midnight prayers. When these opened the gates of heaven, he slipped his difficult petition between the tearful verses of the midnight ritual, and his pleas were granted. It is also told that Rabbi Yehiel Mikhal, the Maggid of Zlotchov (d. c. 1786) raised the limp prayers of the spiritually feeble, by joining his own prayers with theirs and enabling God to hear.

He, in turn, connected his thoughts to those spiritually superior to himself for the same elevating purpose.[82]

North African, Sephardic, and Oriental Jews have also visited the holy men of their own communities and often still do so today in the hope of an intercessory prayer. The custom of visiting a holy man for this purpose also continues in Hasidic communities.[83]

The Intercessor's Problem   In the Book of Exodus, the father-in-law of Moses warns Moses that he would wear himself out trying to cope with the worries of all his people. This task is emotionally exhausting.

But according to Hasidic doctrine, the *tzaddik* is a man who has conquered his emotion completely so that he has full control over it and is no longer disturbed by anything. The true *tzaddik* must connect himself to his people, listen to and feel their worries in order to channel them upward, but not be disturbed by what he hears and feels.[84]

Apparently, some of these men could not always live up to the ideal. These men stretched themselves, sometimes to the breaking point. Thus, for example, Rabbi Shneur Zalman of Liadi (1745–1813), the founder of Chabad Hasidism, implored his followers to refrain from pouring out their worries to him as these made him unbearably miserable. His plea was ignored, however, and he continued to try to resolve every personal problem presented to him. His contemporary, Rabbi Naftali of Ropshitz, grew exhausted. He began to pray each morning that all those in need of help would find it themselves, and not come to him with the delusion that he could help them. One day, he stopped receiving the worried and withdrew from the world until he died. A generation later, Isaac Meir (d. 1866), the rabbi of Gur (Poland), also tired of listening to his people's worries and requests to pray for them. He knew that some Jews granted him magical powers and assumed he could right all wrongs, without their needing to strain their souls. He announced that he would only see those who thought their worries were preventing them from serving God, but no one who wanted him to solve a material problem.[85]

In 1917, Freud noticed that patients transfer emotions to the psychoanalyst. Freud taught that the analyst must neither yield to these emotions nor reject them, but reflect them back at the patient. This is more difficult for the worrier than consulting a *tzaddik*. Later psychoanalysts, like the rabbis just mentioned, have admitted, however, that they do react emotionally to their patients' "transference."[86]

Prayer has become a fashionable tool in spiritual psychology in recent years for helping the worried, the depressed, and the confused. Therapeutic prayer groups may draw on existing prayers to cope with particular worries and add "something fresh" from their own hearts, in their own words, as so many Jews have done in the past. When a solution miraculously comes about following prayer, the relieved person may believe that this is a divine blessing. But sometimes the prayer just gives a person psychological strength to find a new way of looking at life or a new way of responding to life, and this is the solution. Prayer can help us to help ourselves if it widens our perspective, for example, as we realize that others worry too and want to assist us. Prayer can help us if it can keep our hope and faith alive and prevent us from being engulfed by distressing emotion. In addition, prayer is useful if it stimulates a turning around, a positive change in our thinking or behavior. Viewing relief as a divine response or as a result of our own actions are two sides of the same coin, the currency of prayer.[87]

4 ⁓ Meditation

The Talmud tells a well-known tale about four second-century Jewish sages who entered a "garden" (*pardes,* literally "orchard" or "paradise"). The story is short and peculiar. It begins cryptically, with Rabbi Akiva warning his three companions that when they reach stones of pure marble, they must not say "Water, water" because "He who speaks untruth shall not stand before my eyes" (Ps. 101:7). The story continues, telling that only Akiva entered the "garden" safely and left in peace, because he was worthy. Ben Azzai saw and died. Ben Zoma saw and became afflicted. And the "Other" (Elisha ben Avuya) "cut the shoots" (B. *Hagigah* 14b).

The earliest versions of this enigmatic tale omit Rabbi Akiva's warning and may have been a parable that taught about the fate of the soul after death. However, the later versions assume that these four men undertook a meditative journey, a mystical quest, which ended in a wonderful divine vision only for Rabbi Akiva, whose soul and intentions were pure. It ended badly for the other three, who were not worthy of the divine vision. One lost his life, one lost his mind, and the third lost his faith.[1]

Versions of this story, dating from the fifth or sixth century, detail the men's path to the divine realm. The mystics required esoteric knowledge of hymns and adjurations to pass through seven heavily guarded gates to reach the divine figure on the throne of glory and gain revelation. From the late talmudic period onward, mystics set out on this dangerous meditative path to the supernal realm because they were worried, desired divine knowledge, and sought power.

Some of Judaism's most brilliant and influential men used meditative techniques to banish their worries and concentrate on cleaving to God. They gained insight and strength in this way, but they all knew and warned that the meditative methods are dangerous and not suitable for everyone.

When we worry, our mind is wrapped up in itself. We become "narrow-minded," aware of our problem and little else. Mystics have believed that the meditation process expands the mind beyond the narrow self to the spiritual, beyond thought as we know it to a higher, happier, enlightened consciousness. Meditation can lead to a state of heightened attention, intense perception, apparently outside time and space, where reality appears eternal. This peak experience can bring about a change in attitude, a new way of seeing the world without conflict or chaos.

What is meditation? Why have some Jews meditated to cope with worry? When have they chosen to do this? And how have Jews focused their minds to keep out disturbing worries? Let us explore all these questions and also look at the dangers involved in undertaking the meditative journey.

What Is Meditation?

Meditation, according to the *Oxford Dictionary,* is the action or practice of focusing one's mind for a period of time for spiritual purposes or as a method of relaxation. In Judaism, meditation has always involved an awareness of God and has had a spiritual purpose.

For some pious Jews in the past, meditation was a way of life, a form of contemplative prayer, and their means of wholeheartedly cleaving to God. These Jews learned how to control their stream of consciousness, ignore their distracting thoughts, and strengthen their powers of concentration and devotion as they reached up to God.

Jews have often claimed that their meditative techniques are a revival of those that the ancients used to draw down prophecy and divine blessings. This claim gives their methods the flavor of tradition. In the early third century, Jewish mystics developed a secret doctrine about the divine world based on a mystical exegesis of a verse of Ezekiel. This doctrine involves the *merkavah,* a spiritual chariot, a "Chariot of Light." Jews came to refer to the mystical journey to the divine realm, undertaken using meditative techniques, as *ma'aseh merkavah.* Those who undertook the *ma'aseh merkavah* aspired to achieve a vision similar to the visions of God that Ezekiel attained by the Chebar Canal (Ezekiel, chapter 1).[2]

The Jewish practice of meditation has involved preliminary preparation. Traditionally, the mystic is a man—not a woman—who is pious, learned, mature in mind and body, and has acquired humility, equanimity, and self-discipline. The mystic purifies himself and isolates his senses in order to undertake his meditative journey and attain his spiritual experience. Today, however, some women also engage in Jewish meditation by picking and choosing elements in the long tradition that Jewish men developed through the ages, so that they too can reach their spiritual goals.[3]

The journey involves contemplation—concentrating the mind in certain ways. The Hebrew word often used for meditative contemplation is *hitbonenut,* formed from the reflexive word whose root is *b-y-n,* "understanding," "knowledge." The Jewish mystics believed that meditative contemplation is the process of acquiring understanding, of acquiring pure, divine knowledge. The insight acquired at the end of the meditative path is a peak experience that mystics have often believed to be a divine vision or revelation.

The final stage involves the mystic's return to his fellow Jews. We have already seen that of the four men who entered the "garden," only Rabbi Akiva returned safely. Not everyone can undertake the meditative journey and return safe and sound. Some people may return deluded or damaged.

There are many different kinds of meditation, but all attempt to alter or train a person's attention, increasing concentration and decreasing susceptibility to distraction. Meditation can involve the mind's zooming into concentration, restricting and sharpening focus while cutting out distracting thoughts. However, meditation can also expand awareness and lead to wide-angled perception.[4]

Why Meditate to Cope with Worry?

Worried Jews have meditated to free their minds from all their disturbing thoughts, to become closer to God, and to attain religious ecstasy. Some have meditated in the hope of seeing or hearing God, or in an effort to draw down divine favor.

In late antiquity, pious men used meditative techniques to prepare for prayer, to banish their worries, and to awaken their spirituality in readiness for prayer. Philo Judaeus of Alexandria (c. 20 B.C.E.–50 C.E.), an early philosopher, admitted that he meditated in order to cleave to God in purity, without distraction. Jews have often used meditative techniques to strengthen their concentration and devotion in prayer, when worry has interfered with their ability to pray.[5]

Some Jews may have meditated, as Philo did, to escape from the confines of the material world and free their souls. The psychoanalyst Mortimer Ostow has recently suggested that Akiva's companions chose the meditative path in order to escape from unpleasant reality into the world of illusion. These men were social misfits. When they could no longer adjust themselves to a society that did not accept them, they chose to escape from it. When their anxiety—sexual, social, or ideological—was too much for them, they isolated themselves and sought refuge in another world.[6]

Professor D. J. Halperin, a scholar of early *merkavah* mysticism, has argued that the mystics in the fifth or sixth centuries undertook the meditative path to the spiritual realm in the hope of gaining knowledge that would give them power and status. He points out that the mystics were the underdogs of a society ruled by the highborn rabbinic intelligentsia and he suggests that they drew a feeling of strength from their spiritual journeys. The mystics' heroes were Rabbi

Akiva, a man of the people; Rabbi Eliezer ben Hyrcanus, a farmer's son; and Rabbi Ishmael ben Elisha, who allegedly learned his Torah with the aid of magic. They related their visions in the synagogue, in spite of rabbinic opposition. The rabbis saw this behavior as threatening "to the collective sanity of their religious [rabbinic] culture and responded with suppression and dread." [7]

While in captivity in Babylon, Ezekiel gained apocalyptic revelations of a cataclysmic destruction, as well as instruction about what should be done to achieve salvation. Some worried Jews meditated with the hope that they, too, would receive a divine revelation—a prophecy telling them what to do and promising better days.

In later times of communal crisis, such as during the Spanish Inquisition and during the pogroms in Eastern Europe, some men undertook the meditative path in the hope of gaining a fast lane to information and power, or even to hasten the arrival of the Messiah. These men apparently meditated for the good of the Jewish community, not for their own peace of mind, and sometimes in the grand hope of redeeming their people from their suffering. In late fifteenth-century Jerusalem, the kabbalist Rabbi Judah Albotini reasoned that, in antiquity, Moses saved his people by meditating on Divine Names. Albotini believed that the sages could have done the same to prevent the destruction of Jerusalem by the Babylonians and the Romans. They refrained, he explained, because they assumed the destruction was God's decree. Albotini may have similarly refrained from attempting to hasten the Messiah, but some other kabbalists thought it was worth trying in the hope of putting an end to Jewish suffering. [8]

Albotini prepared a question before meditating, in the expectation of inducing a divine revelation that could be directly useful. He taught that one's question should always be on the subject of religious worship and not about a mundane worry, but his warning tells us that perhaps he knew people who did in fact use this method to cope with a specific worry. [9]

Albotini was not the only kabbalist to model himself on Moses. Rabbi Yohanan Alemanno, an Italian kabbalist who was his contemporary, believed that Moses prayed, uttered Divine Names, and meditated until the divine blessings descended into the world. The Book of Deuteronomy (chapters 9 and 10) tells us that Moses ascended the mountain and received the tablets of stone after forty days and forty nights without eating or drinking. Moses may literally have climbed the mountain, fasted, and received the tablets, but kabbalists believed that the words of the Bible carry hidden meaning, and that this prophet actually engaged in a meditative journey that culminated in divine revelation. Moses delivered wonderful blessings to his suffering people; the kabbalists, and later the Hasidim, yearned to do the same, especially during times of anti-Semitic pogroms.[10]

Rabbi Isaac Yehudah Yehiel Safrin, a Hasid who lived in the mid–nineteenth century, was convinced that Moses' ascent to receive the Torah was an ascent of the soul. He viewed Moses as the master of the meditative journey. The Hasid confessed in his diary that he wanted to achieve greatness and attempted the ascent.[11]

Some kabbalists explained that meditation should be undertaken only for communal good and for the purpose of sanctifying God, and not for one's self. The story of the demise of Akiva's three companions, which is related at the beginning of this chapter, cautions those whose motives are self-serving. Yet some men certainly meditated in search of knowledge that would relieve their own personal anxieties. For example, the sixteenth-century Safed kabbalist rabbis Joseph Karo and Hayyim Vital kept written records of their meditations that reveal answers to their personal concerns.[12]

While meditation may involve an active search for spirituality, for a sensation of the divine or of eternity, Jews today rarely see it as a path to divine revelation, prophecy, or supernatural power. They now engage in meditation for relaxation, as a means of banishing worry and finding peace of mind. They meditate because they find this activity spiritually enriching and physically restorative. Recent psychological studies show that meditation techniques can be beneficial in treating anxiety; they can control pulse and respiratory rates as well as promote relaxation and the feeling of refreshment.[13]

When Have Jews Meditated to Cope with Worry?

Some pious Jews have meditated regularly in preparation for daily contemplative prayer, to remove worries, focus the mind, and improve concentration. Some have meditated regularly during contemplative prayer in an attempt to expand their consciousness and merge their souls with God. And some have meditated when, being particularly worried about the future, they wanted to gain special knowledge and power that would enable them to bring a comforting message to the people.[14]

The Bible tells us that prophets were granted divine knowledge, especially in periods of impending doom, when people were worried. We can imagine that such information may have convinced some people to change their ways for the better and reassured them of a better future. When the age of prophecy passed, some anxious Jews sought the prophetic experience for themselves, using meditative techniques.

Worried people have often welcomed the promise of better times when this promise comes from someone with special knowledge. When people lived in constant fear and uncertainty, as Jews did during the Roman rule, the Spanish Inquisition, and the Cossack pogroms, they wanted information. They probably wanted to know why they had to suffer so and that an end to their suffering was in sight. When optimistic, objective knowledge was unavailable, Jews sometimes used meditative methods to attain divine revelation. After meditating, Rabbi Ishmael (late first–early second century) allegedly came to believe that the formidable enemy power was about to be destroyed, and he shared this insight with other Jews to give them hope. The Portuguese kabbalist Rabbi Shlomo Molcho (1501–1532) and the Polish Rabbi Samson of Ostropol (d. 1648) both engaged in meditative techniques to obtain useful angelic revelations during the waves of terrible attacks on Jews that occurred in their times.

Rabbi Ishmael had been taken captive by the Romans and was redeemed by another Jew. It is told that when he heard that the Romans were about to kill ten Jewish sages, he meditated to find out if this was the whim of the emperor or a divine decree. The angel revealed that God gave permission to Samael, the archangel of Rome, to kill the ten sages because Joseph's brothers had sinned in antiquity. Samael agreed to kill them only on the condition that Rome would be completely destroyed and the Jews would be freed of their persecutors. Ishmael was able to tell his colleagues that the ten martyrs were the price the Jews were paying for the destruction of their enemy. He offered them a vision of a better life afterward and so, we assume, reduced both his and their worries.[15]

Shlomo Molcho was born in Lisbon soon after all the Jews had been expelled from Spain. The Jews in Lisbon were unsafe and fearful. Molcho used meditative techniques to achieve prophetic visions. He prophesied that the Kingdom of Esau (Christianity) was about to fall and the Messiah would soon appear. He foresaw an earthquake that would herald the beginning of the End of Days. He gained added confidence in his prophecies when major floods occurred in Europe, an earthquake shook Lisbon and neighboring towns, and a "fiery, wondrous sun" (in fact, Halley's Comet) was seen above Rome. Whereas the pope had been impressed by the clairvoyant, Emperor Charles V was offended by the man's manner and condemned him to burn at the stake.[16]

When Rabbi Samson in Ostropol heard rumors that Chmielnicki's hateful Cossacks were approaching, massacring and plundering the Jews, he meditated on a biblical verse. An angel revealed that an evil decree was upon the Jews and the Jews must perform sincere repentance to avert it. Samson shared this insight with his community and begged everyone to repent wholeheartedly to avert the decree. One account claims that "all [the people] repented greatly . . . but it did not help." Another account said that the people did not listen to his words. Both accounts reported that the Cossacks massacred everyone.[17]

Anti-Semitic pogroms were still frighteningly common in Poland a century after Chmielnicki's men had decimated the Ostropol community. On the New Year in 1746 (Rosh Hashanah 5507), the Ba'al Shem Tov meditated. He wrote to his brother-in-law that on this occasion he entered the palace of the Messiah and asked him when the Messiah would come to redeem the Jews on Earth. The Messiah replied that this would happen only when the Ba'al Shem Tov's teaching had become famous and revealed to all, when other people could also make the spiritual ascent. This experience encouraged him to teach the esoteric meditative methods to others and disseminate them as widely as possible.

In 1747, five Jews were killed in Izyaslav (a city in eastern Volhynia, now Ukraine) as a result of a blood libel, even though they tried to escape death by converting to Christianity. The Ba'al Shem Tov was clearly very worried for the Jews as he learned of more reports of blood libels. Just as Ishmael had allegedly queried an angel about the fate of the Jews, the Hasidic master now meditated again, in order to seek enlightenment. He asked, why was there such anger in heaven that even those who apostatized were killed? Samael (in the eighteenth century, this name no longer merely designated the archangel of Rome, but was a term for the angel of death and for the ruler of the domain of demonic powers) explained to him that he killed the Jews "for the sake of heaven"—for the sins of the Jews. In the later blood libels, Jews did not apostatize, but died as martyrs, "sanctifying the Name." By the merit of these martyrs, taught the Ba'al Shem Tov, the Messiah would come.

On New Year 1749, the Ba'al Shem Tov meditated another time, clearly still worried about Jewish destiny. This time he requested of God, "Let us fall into the hands of the Lord but let us not fall into the hands of man." He was indeed shown in a vision that there would be a great epidemic in Poland and adjacent lands so that Jews would not be killed by the hands of man.[18]

It may be difficult for us nowadays to see these visions as comforting or stress reducing, but we must understand that the Ba'al Shem Tov (and Ishmael, Molcho, and Samson of Ostropol) lived in dangerous, threatening times. The knowledge gained through meditation—the promise of the destruction of the enemy that terrorized the Jews and the coming of the Messiah—was a consolation, even if Jews had to sacrifice their own lives and the lives of others to reach this end.

How Have Jews Meditated?

Like the path of mystics in other religions, the path that Jews have traditionally followed in order to meditate takes time and preparation. The preparation includes purification, solitude (shutting out both external and internal stimulation), and gaining full control over human inclinations, including the banishment of each and every worry. Only then can the mystic engage in contemplative techniques—mental exercises that guide his heart and mind toward the peak spiritual experience. The heart, the seat of spiritual experience, is like a pool of water that must be cleaned before the water of pure knowledge can be poured into it, according to a medieval pietist in Egypt.[19] Many mystically inclined Jews learned how to focus and purify their thoughts to reach the point where they received a divine flow, like a flow of water, spreading in all directions through their souls. During the peak experience, the mystic enters an unusual state of consciousness—perhaps ecstasy, enlightenment, a vision—and reaps the benefits of the flow as he regains peaceful sensation of the earthly world. Ideally, at the conclusion of his meditative journey, the Jewish mystic uses whatever he has received for the good of the community and not merely for his own benefit.

Preliminary Rituals

The *merkavah* mystic indulged in ascetic practices for some time before meditating; he fasted for some days, abstained from sexual activity, washed and cleansed himself, and (if he lived before the fifth century) purified himself with the ashes of the Red Heifer. (The ashes of the unblemished Red Heifer were used in a biblical purification ritual, but the last of these ashes were used up in the fifth century.) The adept then sat on the ground with his head between his knees, probably covered by a prayer shawl, and whispered the songs and praises of God that he had learned from his teacher.[20]

Some mystics wore clean white clothing for meditation and some meditated in their prayer shawls. The Jewish prayer shawl with its blue thread helped them to think of God, since the blue thread in the tassel of the prayer shawl resembles the sea, the sea resembles the firmament, and the firmament resembles the Throne of Glory. This idea symbolizes the ascent they were about to undertake.[21]

We will see in chapter 7 that Jews have often used music to calm a worried soul, escape from worries, and sometimes also to induce divine revelation. Some mystics sang or played music as they meditated. For example, the Spanish kabbalist Abraham Abulafia (1240–after 1291) thought that the vowel points in the Hebrew sacred text are notes that can be sung, and indeed he sang them while he contemplated the letters of the Divine Name to induce an ecstatic state. Rabbi Judah Albotini, who had studied Abulafia's method, explained in his meditation manual that, after the preliminary rituals and seclusion, one should "advance to playing music on all kinds of instruments," if he knows how to play them, "in order to give pleasure to the vital soul." He added that a person who cannot play an instrument can sing, instead, of his desire for Torah. [22]

Psalm 119 appears to have had particular significance for Jewish meditation. It is arranged alphabetically, with eight verses for each letter of the Hebrew alphabet, and uses the vocabulary of meditation. Maharal of Prague pointed out that the eightfold repetition of each letter raises the reader to the spiritual realm, just as the circumcision of the eight-day-old infant boy and the eight garments worn by the High Priest while serving in the Temple denote spirituality. And the Ba'al Shem Tov was allegedly taught that if he recited Psalm 119 every day, he would be able to maintain his cleaving to God even while speaking with people. Still today, many religious Jews quietly recite Psalms to keep worries out of their minds, especially when traveling and at the bedside of a sick person or a birthing woman.[23]

Equanimity

For almost two thousand years, Jewish pietists have disciplined themselves to banish distracting thoughts in order to cleave to God.

The Talmud praises those who know how to "overcome their tendencies," those who can rise above their emotions, "those who are insulted but do not insult, who hear themselves scorned, but do not respond, who serve God with love and rejoice in suffering."[24]

Judah Albotini advised the student of meditation to convince himself that no one can harm or help him. The meditator should be in control of everything and feel that he is lacking nothing. In this way he trains himself to remove all the worry and emotion that prevents him from becoming close to God.[25]

The mystic's mind should be so full of God and so free from worries that even if he were to touch a naked woman, he would not feel any emotion whatsoever, according to the diary of Joseph Karo, who meditated regularly.[26]

The Hebrew word for equanimity, *hishtavvut*, has the same root as the word *shiviti*, which appears in Ps. 16:8, *shiviti Ha-shem le-negdi tamid* (traditionally translated as "I have set the Lord always before me"). According to the Safed kabbalist Rabbi Eleazar Azikri (1533–1600), this verse actually means that the Psalmist made everything and everyone equal before him, including those who praise him and those who condemn him, for he is a worm. The Ba'al Shem Tov understood this verse to mean "I have been stoic; God is before me at all times." His disciples taught that we should pay no attention to worldly matters, only to spiritual matters. They believed, though, that only a *tzaddik* can achieve equanimity and meditate, and not the common Jew, as no ordinary man or woman can really gain full control over emotion.[27]

Solitude

Pietists, kabbalists, and Hasidim stressed the need to be alone in order to reach their meditative goal. These men meditated in a quiet room or attic, a lonely place out of town, or a quiet garden, where there was vegetation and a good fragrance, but usually isolation of the mind was more important than physical seclusion.

The biblical prophets sometimes gained enlightenment in the company of others, and moreover, it could be dangerous to meditate alone. Some kabbalists supposed that the pietists of the Mishnah prepared an hour before praying by isolating their minds from all sensation of the material world in their effort to merge with the Divine Nothing, and gain divine blessing and enlightenment. [28]

Bahya ibn Paquda, the medieval philosopher, valued both physical and spiritual solitude for meditative prayer. A century later, Moses Maimonides allowed that only pious men should seek seclusion for concentrating all their thoughts on the Divine, to deliver themselves up totally to God. He evidently thought that most people should not try this. [29]

Medieval pietists in Germany and in Egypt sought "solitude within the multitude," living within the Jewish community, but praying in their own synagogues, where they could lengthen their prayers and meditate without disruption. These Jews sought to isolate their minds even when they were among other people, sometimes shutting their eyes to ease this process.[30]

In southern France, the philosopher Rabbi Levi ben Gershon (Gershonides, 1288–1344), wrote about isolating the consciousness, so that worries, reveries, fantasies, and all input from the senses are cut off from the mind in order to reach the peak spiritual experience. Similarly, his kabbalist contemporary Rabbi Isaac of Acre sought to nullify his senses and divorce his thought from all perception for the same reason.[31]

In Safed, Eleazar Azikri secluded himself to meditate, rising at midnight when the house was totally quiet and deserted. Only the most advanced adept, he believed, could isolate his mind from the material world and have his whole mind on God when other people are around. [32]

The Ba'al Shem Tov, who spent much of his youth isolated from society, knew how to direct his whole mind and imagination toward God, so that his soul no longer felt its body and seemed no longer to exist at all. His disciple, Dov Baer the Maggid of Mezhirech knew how to dissolve his soul into nothingness, to "cast off corporeality" and annihilate thought in order to reach the spiritual realm. [33]

Nahman of Bratzlav walked and conversed with God alone in the fields as Isaac had done before meeting Rebekah. When physically alone, Nahman sought to isolate his soul by banishing all concerns, so that all of his being became like nothing, nonexistent. Solitude, in an open field on a summer evening, was his way of ridding himself of worry in order to commune with God. [34]

The feeling of being alone in the world, however, is a different sort of solitude. Unlike the detached solitude of the pietists, the feeling of being lonely can cause worry instead of banishing it. The mystics knew that solitude can sometimes be a threatening experience, even terrifying; they repeatedly warned that this path is dangerous and not suitable for everyone.[35]

Contemplation

In Jewish meditation, contemplation involves an intense, pro-longed mental activity during which all worries are removed from the mind. For example, Rabbi Ishmael, who was born not long before the destruction of the Second Temple (70 C.E.), allegedly sang certain hymns to empty his mind of his worries and focus on his spiritual journey. Then, by reciting twelve Divine Names exactly 112 times, he reached the highest heavenly chamber, where he adjured an angel to reveal the information he sought.[36]

In the early thirteenth century, Rabbi Eleazar of Worms knew about the ancient technique of repeating Divine Names and said it was known to Abraham, who kept it secret. In sixteenth-century Safed, Joseph Karo and Hayyim Vital repeated verses of Mishnah, in-stead of Divine Names, to gain access to the divine world. Karo did so at night, sometimes reciting forty chapters before an angel began to speak to him through his own mouth. He considered himself one of the "chosen few" who could attain angelic visitations and enlighten-ment when he meditated.[37]

At the time of the afternoon prayer, Hayyim Vital repeated a pas-sage of Mishnah three times to isolate his soul and enter a "slumber of solitude," which was not sleep, during which he could ask questions and receive inspiration. Wrapped in his prayer shawl, alone, with eyes closed, he focused his mind on the ancient sage mentioned in the Mishnah passage he had chosen to recite and repeat. In this way, he found he could merge his soul with that of the ancient sage, ask him questions, and receive the reply from his own mouth. Sometimes the message was explicit; sometimes it was veiled and required interpretation.[38]

In seventeenth-century Poland, Samson of Ostropol repeated a biblical verse to induce an angel to reveal divine secrets to him. He repeated the thirty-eighth verse of Psalm 78 (a verse often used by Jews for purification and atonement of sin) as well as a special name derived from the first verses of Deuteronomy 32 (in which Moses requests that words should come out of his mouth "as the rain").[39]

In the middle of the nineteenth century, in Lithuania, Israel Lipkin of Salant developed the meditative method that came to be used in all the Musar yeshivot, the yeshivot devoted to ethical improvement. The Musar students were not mystics but mostly mature householders who had studied Torah and had accepted community responsibilities. They met daily for about an hour before the evening prayer. After some ethical study, one of the group read aloud a verse or rabbinic saying expressing a moral teaching, and the others repeated it after him aloud, trying to see in their minds the dire consequences of unethical behavior. The students repeated the verse or rabbinic saying in a special melody. This opened each person's heart, filled it with "the waters of understanding . . . to bring blessing into the heart of man." The Salant rabbi realized that merely exerting the mind to banish worries is insufficient because there will always be more worries waiting to surge forth.[40]

Concentration on Permutation and Combination   The mystical *Sefer Yetzirah*, written in the talmudic period, explains how to permute Hebrew letters in order to elevate the soul. The letters of a word or biblical verse are permuted systematically, using a method of rotation. This text explains also that "when Abraham gazed, he looked, saw, probed, and understood. He graved, hewed, and combined (*tzaraf*)," and gained divine revelation. Mystics wanted to do whatever Abraham did to gain divine revelation. Some mystics meditated by gazing at the letters, permuting them first in writing and then in the mind, in the hope of divine revelations. Eleazar of Worms, for example, contemplated permutations and combinations of the Hebrew letter *alef* with the Tetragrammaton, systematically altering the vowel combinations. His older relation, Judah the Pious of Regensburg, contemplated the Hebrew letters in each prayer, counting the *alefs,* the *beits,* and the other letters too, to help him banish all distracting thoughts while praying.[41]

Abraham Abulafia reasoned that the ancient prophets had combined (*tzaraf*) letters, words, and Divine Names in the way described by the *Sefer Yetzirah,* and he tried to do likewise, to achieve prophecy. He overcame his distracting thoughts by focusing on Hebrew letters that he wrote down in circles, nine letters in each circle, permuting the letters and manipulating them to make groups with equal numerical value. He permuted the letters and the vowels of the letters of the Divine Name with a pen, until his heart became "extremely warm," and the pen dropped out of his hand. He then vocalized his letter combinations, permuting the vowels on each letter, singing them as he did so, regulating his breathing to the rhythm of the permutations, and moving his head in time in the way that musicians combine notes. He learned to meditate in this way on the Tetragrammaton and on the seventy-two-letter Divine Name (derived from Exod. 14:19–21). This contemplation gained him enlightenment and visions of the future.[42]

Rabbi Isaac of Acre and other mystics in the Holy Land also combined and permuted Hebrew letters to meditate, believing they were engaging in an activity that was performed in antiquity. These intellectual exercises could clear the mind of all disturbing thoughts, but, much more importantly, they could also prepare the soul to receive the Holy Spirit.[43]

Concentration on an Imaginary Image A thirteenth-century kabbalistic text explains that the early pietists of the Mishnah, who meditated in the hour before their prayer, concentrated on imaginary light to dispel distracting thoughts and make their spiritual ascent. "Imagine that you yourself are light, and that all of your surroundings, on every side, are also light," this text explains. In the middle of this light is a throne of light, and facing this is another throne with a light above it. To the right is also a light and to the left, yet another light. Above these two is a light, around that is a light, and above this is the Crown (*Keter*, the highest divine emanation in kabbalistic terminology), "the light that crowns the desires of the mind and illuminates the paths of the imagination, enhancing the radiance of the vision." All the lights are named with words that have kabbalistic meanings. The pietist concentrated on these lights until all disturbing thoughts disappeared and the whole mind reached the highest level of the Godhead, the Divine Nothing. Then the pietist prayed and drew down divine blessings according to his will.[44]

The Spanish kabbalist Rabbi Joseph Taitatzak fled the Spanish Inquisition and settled in Salonika, where he remained worried about the demonic force of Christianity. By thinking of the four letters of the Tetragrammaton, so that they float up and down in the air in different shades of color—white, red, green, and pale blue—he induced an angel to reveal divine knowledge, which he wrote down as the revelations came to him.[45]

Another kabbalist, Joseph Tzayyah (1505–1573), may have meditated by contemplating the palm of his hand; he associated the creases of the joints of the three middle fingers with nine divine emanations and the area at the base of the fourth finger with the tenth divine emanation. However, this Jerusalem-born rabbi is best known for his meditation of magic squares. Each horizontal row of the square is a "house," and each number in this row is a "room." Each room represents a "thousand myriad parasangs" (that is, 30–40 million miles, as a "parasang" is thought to equal three or four miles) and a thousand myriad colored lights. The magic square of the highest divine emanation (*Keter*) has ten by ten "rooms." Tzayyah sat in solitude to meditate, with his head between his knees, and allowed his mind to travel from imaginary room to imaginary room. He contemplated the immense numbers and colored lights in each room until he saw the Divine Light as a true vision.[46]

In Safed, Moshe Cordovero (1522–1570), who had studied early Jewish meditative methods, recorded the way that he himself succeeded in achieving the peak experience. This influential rabbi meditated only on the Tetragrammaton, using the vowel points and colors to represent the divine emanations. He assigned particular vowel combinations and a particular color to each emanation. He chose to dress in an appropriate color for meditation so that the color would be visible to his eyes, but he also contemplated the color in his mind, seeing it in his imagination. Before contemplating the Tetragrammaton, he first imagined that he unified all the levels of his soul. He then contemplated the Holy Name to unify all the divine emanations into a powerful unity, like a strong knot. In this way he believed his soul could become a channel for the divine flow of blessings.[47]

Also in Safed, Eleazar Azikri used the visual force of his imagination to meditate. He isolated himself and meditated by mentally uniting Divine Names "in a brilliant flame." A kabbalistic manuscript, compiled in Damascus in the mid–sixteenth century, instructed the reader: "You may picture the Ineffable Name as the white flame of the candle, in absolute whiteness" and contemplate its pure white light.[48]

Another Safed kabbalist, Elijah De Vidas (d. c. 1593), related a parable which he attributed to Isaac of Acre, although the story has not been found in any of the latter's manuscripts. There once was an idle man, it is told, who noticed a beautiful princess leaving the bathhouse. He sighed, and said in a voice that she could hear, "Oh, if only I could do with her just what I want!" Unexpectedly, she answered him, "That will happen in the cemetery, not here."

The man took this as an invitation to meet her in the graveyard. He went there and waited, his mind full of lusty thoughts. Day and night he sat and waited, hoping that soon she would come as promised. He longed for her, and in his immense longing, he thought about her beauty. He stayed in the graveyard, waiting and thinking only of the princess. As time went by and she failed to appear, his intense contemplation on his memory of the princess's beauty made him forget about her physicality and his own libido; in fact, he forgot about the whole physical world in which he lived. His contemplation caused his thoughts to become sublimated and purified. This contemplation on her beauty elevated his soul until it merged with the Divine. He became a holy man of God and all passersby sought his blessing.[49]

The princess may have intended that the promised meeting would come about in the world to come, when the man died and he became fully spiritual. Alternatively, her reply may have been intended to make him sublimate his sinful lust, which is what eventually happened. In the view of the Safed kabbalist, however, the princess probably represented the *Shekhinah,* the exiled, feminine element of the Holy One, who yearns to be reunited with the Divine Godhead. According to Safed Kabbalah, the end of her exile—her ultimate joy— depends on the actions and thoughts of the Jews. As long as men's thoughts are impure, the *Shekhinah* will remain in exile.[50] The story therefore teaches that we have to sublimate our inclinations in order to fulfill our religious goals and that we can do this by focusing the mind in contemplation. In this story, the sexual impulse is transmuted into a spiritual experience. Worry, too, can be transmuted, as we have already seen in chapters 2 and 3.

The End of the Meditative Journey

We can learn to follow the meditative path and gain a spiritual experience. We may even see a vision or hear a voice at the height of the meditative path, but that is not the end of the road. The next step is to return safely. However, the Jewish mystic usually had yet a final task at the end of his journey. He wanted to deliver his message—an explanation, a course of action, or a prophecy—to others, a message that would help his people cope with worry. Moses ascended the mountain and received the tablets from God, but when he descended and saw that his people had made the Golden Calf, he saw that there was no point in delivering his divine revelation to such a people. It was only after his second trip up the mountain that the people were ready to receive the revelation (Deut. 9 and 10). A person who sees a vision or hears a voice may help others only when the audience believes that the reported revelation is indeed a divine blessing.

Nowadays, if someone talks of receiving a divine revelation, we may well think that person is deluded.

The Peak Experience

Jews have meditated in the hope of reaching the divine realm and gaining a divine vision or blessing. Many have been content to hear an angel's voice at the peak of their meditative trip, or the voice of a sage who died long ago. Is this a spiritual experience, an inspired insight, or actually a divine revelation? Some religious Jews believe that a divine revelation is possible, although they acknowledge that sometimes a vision may be a delusion.[51]

The peak experience can sometimes bring about a reconciliation and acceptance of death, so that the person who meditated no longer worries about death, and anxiety disappears. Some people who have achieved the altered state of awareness that comes at the end of the meditative path have reported a sensation of being near death, of seeing the "sweetness" of death, and felt they could willingly die. The Jewish mystics knew that a person might find the meditative state wonderful and prefer not to regain contact with the physical world.

The Arabic, Sanskrit, and Japanese languages have words (*wusul, samadhi, satori* respectively) for the enlightened, awakened state at the end of the meditative path. In Buddhist and Hindu texts, the peak experience encountered on the meditative journey is viewed as an altered state of consciousness, a super-conscious state. This is not the same as the hypnotically induced trance, in which attention is dulled. Far Eastern meditation leads the mind to a state of super-awareness where the mystic sees, notices, and realizes what he had not perceived before. In this heightened state of consciousness the self appears to exist no longer as an entity that is separate from the world but is merged into the universe. This is apparently the state that Jewish mystics reached in the past when they felt their souls merging with the Divine Nothing or Divine Light.

The American psychologist Abraham Maslow (1908–1970) explored the nature of transcendent experiences and discovered that many people have peak experiences without undertaking the meditative path. People who have experienced moments of intense joy and ecstasy have related the same sensation of heightened awareness, detachment from time and space, and feeling of unity and eternity. Maslow pointed out that some lonely people who experienced this sensation interpreted it as a divine revelation and felt the need to communicate it to a mass of people. Most people, though, do not interpret these experiences as religious revelations, but merely as self-actualizing, self-validating experiences that reduce worrying and promote the feeling that life is worthwhile.[52]

Some users of psychedelic (consciousness-expanding) drugs have reported the feeling of losing one's separateness of being while melding with the universe, similar to the state that religious mystics sometimes attain. The possibility that a drug can induce a psychological state akin to religious ecstasy suggests that the mystic's meditation somehow enables him to bring about changes in his own brain chemistry. Indeed, the EEGs of Zen masters have been found to be significantly different to those of controls.[53]

The meditative procedures that Jews have used to banish their worries and induce a peak experience have certain elements in common with the methods that have been used by hypnotists for more than a century. Hypnotists use an induction procedure that leads the subject into relaxation and eventually into a trance, or altered state of consciousness, in which he or she becomes "as if" asleep while remaining receptive to ideas that may or may not be recalled upon "waking." In the examples cited above, it looks as though the Jewish mystic may have hypnotized himself using a meditative method to induce a trance. In this unusual state of awareness, he sometimes vocalized or wrote. Jews who have reached this state have believed that their souls reached the spiritual realm and an angel or God put the words in their mouths or ears, or moved their hands in writing. Such vocalization and writing, performed in a trance, is now called "automatic" speech and writing, as it occurs without conscious involvement.

Some people cannot be hypnotized, whereas others are extremely susceptible to hypnosis. Hypnotists have estimated that 10–15 percent of the population cannot be hypnotized while only 5–10 percent can easily achieve this altered state of consciousness. Some of those who are extremely susceptible, like the Jewish mystics in this chapter and Yehudit in chapter 6, can induce an altered state of consciousness by themselves, and sometimes they can bring on a trance by mere autosuggestion, without the induction ritual. It is clear, however, that only a small percentage of people can use the Jewish meditation methods to cope with worry. The mystic rabbis obviously knew this, but believed that it was only the learned, righteous, and pure who could succeed. Today we have no better idea about why one person is more suggestible than another, but few people now would accept that achieving a peak experience through meditation depends on righteousness and purity.

Scientists today have found that brain imaging during a hypnotically induced trance, which may admittedly not be the same as a super-conscious state, reveals increased blood flow to certain areas of the brain. Some think that the brain can "turn in on itself" and treat products of the imagination as real and believable, cutting out the sensations of the external world. These scientists think that the subject relaxes the frontal lobe circuits that usually monitor thoughts and behavior and evaluate sensory perceptions so that the imagination takes over. Others reject the possibility of an altered state of consciousness and believe that some people use their imagination much better than others, and can even use it to control fear, pain, perception of color, or whatever else they choose.[54]

The Danger of Delusion

The story at the beginning of this chapter is a cautionary tale. The meditative journey is dangerous. Of the four men who sought to enter the "garden," only one returned safely. Why did the others fail so catastrophically? Ben Azzai was unusual because he never married. He was known as a saintly man but he was never ordained, which is also unusual in view of his great learning and love for Torah. He was especially interested in the physical appearance of God and man. Ben Zoma did not stand up when etiquette demanded this show of respect. His behavior differed from the social norms of his day, and he too was never ordained, despite his great learning. Elisha ben Avuya was also a great scholar, but he sang Greek songs and read heretical books. All three men were probably misfits before they meditated and did not return safely from their journey. Their motives for undertaking the journey were self-serving and not for the communal good. According to tradition, these men were not worthy of divine revelation; only Akiva was worthy and could return from the journey successfully—with divine knowledge.

A hypnotist knows how to terminate the trance in the person who has been hypnotized, but someone who has meditated to attain an altered state of consciousness may have great difficulty in terminating the meditative journey. When Ishmael meditated, his teacher sat with him and touched him with an unclean cloth when it was time for him to return to daily life. The cloth was not merely a dusty rag; it was a cloth that had been rendered impure by contact with a menstrual woman. As menstrual blood was considered revolting in ancient times (and long after, too), this cloth would have been sure to jolt Ishmael's consciousness back to the material world. Judah Albotini, who meditated alone, recommended adjuring the soul by a terrible oath not to return to God, but to stay in the body as before. The Ba'al Shem Tov, however, warned his disciples not to undertake the mystic journey alone for fear that the isolated soul cannot come back and would suffer the fate of any one of Akiva's three companions.[55]

In the Second Book of Kings, Jehu says that the prophet's disciple who anointed him was a madman (meshuga), one who converses or meditates. A fifteenth-century philosopher and exegete explained that the prophet's disciple who anointed Jehu was deemed mad because he meditated: he appeared demented, not paying attention to mundane affairs—he was in another world. The madman-prophet link occurs also in the Book of Jeremiah.[56]

The mystic rabbis were aware of the problem of knowing whether a vision or voice obtained during meditation was truly a divine revelation or a mere fantasy or delusion. They believed that a vision might be mere fantasy if for some reason the mystic did not deserve divine revelation. Abraham Abulafia admitted that until he was thirty-one years old his visions were not divine revelations but mere fantasies. He recognized the danger of inducing semi-conscious raving and uncontrolled ecstasy instead of true prophetic vision. However, when he became convinced that he was attaining true divine revelations, he portrayed himself as a prophet with a special mission. The rabbi of Barcelona denounced him, and he was shunned by the rabbinic establishment of his day and also denounced by later rabbinic leaders. But he nevertheless gained followers and over the years his meditative methods became popular.[57]

Samson of Ostropol's writings reveal that he confused reality with fantasy and could not differentiate between the two. Also in the seventeenth century, Shabbetai Zevi, the infamous false messiah, used meditative methods to induce divine revelations that we know were delusions concerning his being the redeemer of Israel. Zevi was able to convince many Jews that his visions were divine revelations, that he was the Messiah, and that all their troubles would soon be over forever. One night he rose at midnight, ritually immersed himself in the sea (a purification ritual to prepare for meditation), and appeared at the synagogue at dawn dressed in a gold-braided robe, inviting those in the house of prayer to come and kiss the hand of the king. Most of those present did. On another occasion, he bought a large fish, dressed it as a baby, and announced that the redemption would occur under the astrological sign of Pisces. He was publicly lashed and driven out of Constantinople, where this event occurred. The prophecies of Zevi and his followers led to heresy and moreover encouraged widespread religious anarchism. Shabbetai Zevi managed to persuade hundreds of thousands of people in the Holy Land and the Diaspora that he was the Messiah, although many other people realized that he was only deluded.[58]

Nahman of Bratzlav was acutely aware of the danger of lonely meditation and the link between prophecy and madness, leaving society to decide who is a prophet and who is mad. He knew that meditating alone, as he did, made him vulnerable. "A person who sits alone in the forest [where he liked to meditate] can sometimes go mad," he said. He believed that the end of the meditative journey is a question of faith: with a strong faith, the experience is inspiring, but without this, dark forces, fantasies, and delusions take over the mind. He thought of himself as a messianic figure who bore the soul of the biblical Moses, the soul that would belong to the Messiah in the last generation. Nahman saw the worrying events in the early years of the nineteenth century (such as the oppression of the Jews under Alexander I, the growth of heresy in the form of the spreading Enlightenment, Haskalah, and the Napoleonic wars) as signs of the coming of the End of Days and felt he had personal responsibility for bringing about national redemption. However, he and his entourage knew that, in the wake of Shabbetai Zevi, messianism was a socially sensitive issue, too sensitive to discuss with outsiders. He knew the danger of being thought deluded and his only chance of succeeding at his messianic task was to be very careful.[59]

The Jews who meditated in the past believed that what they saw or heard came from a source far beyond the confines of the bodily senses—from God directly, an angel, or from the soul of someone who was dead. These were men whose culture was their religion, whose personal life was steeped in religious behavior. It was natural for them to seek a solution to their deepest worries using religious tools that had religious meaning. The main concerns of their society and era shaped their visions. In worrying times of religious persecution, their visions reflected their hopes for the coming of the Messiah to redeem them from their suffering. Samuel C. Heilman and Eliezer Witztum have worked as therapists in the ultra-Orthodox community with some distressed young men who similarly report revelations from personal angels. These therapists believe that the men are suffering from severe psychotic disorders, but that Jewish mysticism gives their hallucinations a religious context within which they can be understood.[60]

Today clinical psychologists and psychiatrists recognize delusions as a form of neurosis or psychosis, in which the psychotic—but not the neurotic—has lost touch with reality. Delusions are organized according to the patients' individual beliefs and are comparatively logical, stemming from an original personal premise that society views as erroneous. Delusions may be elaborated into a complicated world scheme, a plan for the world that solves all problems as the person sees them. Sometimes the deluded person attempts to disseminate this plan through publications, speeches, and nowadays electronic means. Some people may not see the original premise as erroneous and are persuaded by the "prophet."

Delusions and hallucinations are now considered symptoms of mental illness, but they are also a known result of sensory deprivation and sleep loss. Sensory deprivation and prolonged sleep deficit both induce hallucinations, the hearing of voices as well as visions. People in isolation from external sensory input, such as prisoners in solitary confinement in a bare cell, start to hallucinate and have difficulty thinking logically.[61]

We have seen that the Jewish mystics commonly isolated themselves as part of their preparation for meditation. They reduced external stimulation to a minimum and created a state of sensory deprivation. In addition, they often fasted before setting out on the meditative path. As already mentioned, Moses fasted for forty days and forty nights before receiving the Tablets. Did he receive his divine revelation in a state of sensory deprivation? The Safed mystics and many Hasidic masters deprived themselves of sleep regularly in order to study and pray, and then meditated at midnight. At this dark hour, a man who had not had enough sleep over an extended period could easily induce a hallucination. Joseph Karo's little angel and the voices heard by so many other mystics can be understood as hallucinations.

The meditation that Jews have engaged in is not a simple way of coping with worry and, as the rabbis realized, is not suitable for everyone to use. We do not need to recite or permute Hebrew verses to break out of our narrow-minded worrying and achieve a happier state of consciousness. We can find other ways to escape from the familiar world and attain an experience that expands and heightens our awareness, energizes us, and validates our existence. We also do not need to search for psychedelic mushrooms or the local hypnotist.

By stepping out into nature—for a jog in the woods, a hike in the stillness of the desert, or a stretch on an unspoiled beach—we may heighten our awareness of eternity and find that the world and our specific problems look different. We must remember that familiarization dulls perception, especially when we are anxious. We can cope with worry by stepping aside, seeking new horizons—on this earth, not necessarily in the spiritual realm—and doing something that makes us widen our perception, reorient our look at our world, and find new strength.

The recent popularity and proliferation of books on Jewish meditation, the blossoming of Internet sites promoting Jewish meditation, the budding of new centers for Jewish meditation, and the organizing of retreats on the subject show that there is a growing interest in this ancient tradition. At the same time, there is a renewal of awareness that meditation can be dangerous for some people, when it may trigger a psychiatric breakdown.[62]

5 ⁓ Dreams

It is told that, one night, a Jewish merchant from Prague walked close to a ruin on his way home. A black dog ran up to him and circled around him, barking fiercely. The man was certain that the ferocious beast would tear him to bits with its vicious fangs. Somehow, the man managed to reach home alive and went straight to bed, traumatized and exhausted. Later that night a barking noise woke up his family. His wife noticed that her husband was barking in a dream and was bathed in sweat. The terror of his experience that evening had returned in his dream. Upon waking, he told his family that he had dreamed that he was riding a black dog in a column of dogs and riders, and he had barked like the others so that he would not be eaten alive. The dream recurred the next night and on subsequent nights, and the distressed man soon became too ill to fulfill his daily duties. His family realized that they had to find help.

They turned to Maharal, the great rabbi Judah ben Bezalel. The rabbi took the initial precaution of checking the man's prayer shawl and phylacteries. He found them flawed and explained that the man was threatened by the black dog because the ritual objects no longer protected him. He ordered the man to replace the flawed objects with new kosher ones and immerse himself in a *mikveh*, the ritual bath, for ritual purification. He sent him home with an amulet for extra protection and specific instructions to sleep in the house of study, not at home, for the next seven nights.

On his first night on the study house bench, the merchant again dreamed that he was riding a black dog in a column of dogs and riders, but he did not bark and the dogs did not eat him alive. On the second night, he dreamed he was riding his dog away from the column, and the other animals did not follow him. On the third night, he dreamed that he dismounted his dog and it did not attack him. On the fourth, he dreamed that he returned to the ruin where he had passed that fateful night, but this time no dog appeared. On the fifth, he dreamed that he lit a torch and approached the ruin and nothing happened. On the sixth night, he dreamed that he set fire to the ruin and it burned to the ground. The next day, he discovered that the ruin had indeed just burned down. On his last night on the study house bench he slept sweetly and soundly and rose in the morning with his full strength completely recovered.[1]

This story reveals that dreams may throw back to us what preoccupied us before we went to sleep. They can admit and express our worries. They can also diffuse them and sometimes solve our problems. In addition, the story reveals that we do not necessarily have to interpret a dream in order to work through the worry expressed in it. The rabbi did not look for symbolism in the content of the dream. The behavior therapy that cured the man of his anxiety did not require an understanding of the meaning of the dream. The man changed his bed and his prayer accessories, dipped into the *mikveh,* and worked through his worry stage by stage in his dreams, reducing the elements that caused him fear until nothing fearful remained.

Unlike Joseph's famous dreams, which are mentioned below, this man's recurring dream was not obviously future-oriented or prophetic. Nor was it clearly an expression of a wish. We may wonder if the cause of the man's persistent nocturnal terror was merely the fact that he had temporarily felt his life to be threatened by a dog. We could think of the black dog as symbolical or allegorical. Admittedly, the rabbi did not interpret this canine image, although he could have declared it, for example, symbolic of evil, a demon sent by God, or a representation of the man's sins. Nor did the rabbi reveal that the black dog might be a projection of the man's guilt. Yet he recommended proper prayer (by demanding replacement of the prayer shawl and phylacteries), ritual purification, and a week in the house of Torah study, which are all acts of repentance. The rabbi understood that the dream had significance and was apparently stimulated by some past action or actions that made the man feel anxious. He showed the (sinful?) dreamer the path back to righteousness and good health by making him change his ways and improve his religious observance. The rabbi's advice was a program of behavior therapy, not psychoanalysis. The dreamer slowly worked through all the worry-causing behaviors that arose in the dream, without analysis of their meaning. The dreamer overcame the feelings of helplessness and insecurity that had expressed themselves so powerfully and made him ill.

Most people today experience anxiety dreams. Frequently or infrequently, we wake up frightened and sweating and sense relief as we discover that the experience was only a dream. Sometimes we realize why we dreamed a particularly worrying dream, but at other times we have no idea why it appeared. Most of us dismiss a worrying dream and start the day, but when it recurs and disturbs us night after night, as the dog dream bothered the man in the story, we might want to tell someone about it. This tale reminds us that a dream may recur until we pay attention to it and take some action.

Some dreams express our worry, some remove it, and others create it. So, what are dreams? Why, when, and how have dreams helped Jews cope with their worries? How have Jews prevented anxiety from rearing its ugly head in the dark of night? And what is to be done if, after all, anxiety lingers after a disturbing nightmare?

What Are Dreams?

We all know that a dream is a series of thoughts, images, and sensations that occur in the mind during sleep. Scientists know from the electrical activity in our brains that we dream during sleep, even if we are convinced that we rarely or never dream.

A dream is a unique state of awareness that occurs during sleep. This state of awareness is different from our waking awareness. We can dream that we are flying and yet wake to find that our limbs are lying heavily on the bed. We can also daydream, letting the mind roam into fantasy.

Ever since antiquity, Jews have taken dreams seriously. They have believed that a dream could be a residue of past experiences and thoughts, a true revelation, or mere stuff and nonsense. Today, some people think that dreams are just the natural activity of the imagination during sleep, fed by worries, wishes, memories, sensations, and expectations.[2]

Residues of Past Experiences and Thoughts

Ecclesiastes observes that dreams come from much brooding. The Talmud says, "One is shown in one's dream only what sits in the heart (hirhurei libo)" (B. Berakhot 55b). And a Yiddish proverb repeats this ancient folk wisdom: "What we talk of by day, we dream of at night."[3]

The Talmud illustrates this principle. It tells us that Emperor Trajan of Rome once asked a rabbi, "You Jews profess to be very clever, so tell me, what shall I see in my dream?" The rabbi told him that he would see the Parthians robbing him, and forcing him to feed unclean animals with a golden crook. The emperor thought about this all day and at night indeed saw this distressing vision in his dream.[4]

"Do not sleep in a deep ravine, and you will not have bad dreams," says a Kurdistani Jewish proverb, warning against involvement in worrying matters. Kurdistani Jews have assumed that worrying situations bring on bad dreams.[5]

Some medieval thinkers believed that dreams are shaped by our morality. Thus, for example, the Ashkenazic pietist Eleazar of Worms taught that if our thoughts are good, our dreams will be good and will prophesy good things, but if our thoughts are bad, our dreams will be bad and their solutions will be bad. In Spain, the author of the Zohar similarly concluded that the righteous can receive divine messages, but the sinful receive deceiving, even distressing messages, although the dreams of both may contain a mixture of truth and falsehood. But Yiddish-speaking Jews have preferred to shake off responsibility for their dreams, with characteristic humor: One of their proverbs says, "In dreams it is not the dreamer who sins but his dreams."[6]

Divine Messages

Like other ancient peoples, Jews have believed that a dream may bear a supernatural message, even a message directly from God. In the Bible, God speaks to the prophets in a dream, sometimes in riddles, but makes sure that the divine message is understood, if necessary, with the help of an angel.[7]

While the Bible teaches that dreams may convey divine messages, it also warns against false prophets who believe their dreams bear divine revelations, even though they are not divinely inspired.[8] Jews have long been aware that a dream may not be a true revelation, but only nonsense. According to a second century sage, Rabbi Meir, "Dreams are of no consequence" (B. Yoma 83b). His contemporary, Rabbi Shimon bar Yohai, compromises: "Just as wheat cannot be without straw, so there cannot be a dream without some nonsense" (B. Berakhot 55a). The Talmud explains that "dreams are one-sixtieth of prophecy" (B. Berakhot 57b). In other words, a dream contains a grain of truth and much meaningless falsehood.

Jews in the past believed that the soul of a sleeping person is free to roam around outside the body. The common experiences of flying, floating in space, and falling in dreams probably confirmed their belief in the freeing of the soul from the body during sleep. Jews have often imagined that dreams are the real experiences of the traveling soul as it meets with angels, demons, or departed souls, or receives messages directly from God. They thought that angels convey truth, but that demons convey the falsehood manifested in our dreams.[9]

People have sometimes noticed that a dream premonition was later fulfilled, and concluded that their dream did indeed contain a true prophecy. For example, Rabbi Israel Isserlein, who lived in the fifteenth century in what is now Germany, once dreamed a bad dream about his friend and realized that it was prophetic when the friend was hit in the eye during a brawl at the *mikveh* the following day. The rabbi of the Portuguese community in Amsterdam, Manasseh ben Israel (1604–1657), also experienced a prophetic dream. When his mother was clearly dying, he dreamed that someone who was alive and well was buried next to her grave. Later, as he sat mourning his mother's death, he was most surprised when a visitor reported the unexpected death of the man he had dreamed about and told him that he was buried next to his mother.[10]

The wife of a Hasidic rabbi once had an ominous dream and insisted that her husband should move out of his study. He ignored her warning and the following night there was a fire in his room and all his books were burned. Another worried woman, whose husband did not come home one night, dreamed that he had been killed and indeed he had been killed just as she had seen in her dream. Such reports confirmed the popular belief that dreams should be taken seriously. Of course, dreams that produce false premonitions are not worth reporting.[11]

Expressions of Unconscious Wishes

"To a good person bad dreams are shown and to a bad person good dreams are shown" (B. *Berakhot* 55b). Perhaps the sage who made this observation realized that dreams are expressions of wishes: the good man wakes up worried from dreams about improper wishes that he succeeds in banishing during waking hours, whereas the bad man enjoys fulfilling his wishes during sleep.[12]

Freud believed that all dreams express our wishes, especially hidden wishes that are threatening or dangerous. Wishes that arise in dreams, in disguise or plainly, can come from daytime thoughts that have been unsatisfied or suppressed. In addition, they can arise from gastric needs, as Isaiah pointed out in biblical times, and especially from the sexual appetite. Freud proposed that dreams in fact fulfill unconscious wishes that are infantile in origin, often sexual in nature, and are disguised in symbolism to protect sleep.[13]

Why Does Dreaming Help Us Cope with Worry?

A dream can help us cope with worry by making us face whatever is disturbing our peace of mind. It can throw our worry back at us in our sleep, twist it, and solve it in surprising ways. It allows us to simulate threatening events and practice ways of avoiding danger. A dream may give us insight, motivate us to take action, and can diffuse emotion. It might offer hope and change a person's mood for the better. Of course it may also provide an ominous insight that generates more worry, a situation that we will explore later in this chapter.

Because Dreaming Can Offer Insight

The Bible reveals that some people who were especially worried about something could have the future revealed in a dream.[14] A dream, whether or not we believe it has divine provenance, sometimes provides an insight that calms worry. Sometimes it reveals a solution to a problem that bothers us before we fall asleep. Sometimes it reveals a new option for action or points us in a new direction.

Two rabbis had been disrespectful to the head of the rabbinic academy. Both men had the incident on their consciences before falling asleep that night and both dreamed that the following day they should apologize and make peace with their senior. In another instance, the head of a rabbinic academy in Babylonia had been reading a rabbinic text and was unsure of the meaning of an Aramaic word he found there. That night his dream directed him to another book, where he found the solution to his problem. A medieval rabbi made a halakhic ruling about wine, but worried about whether he had ruled correctly. That night two biblical verses came to him in a dream (one about drinking from wine bowls and the other about unclean things) and he understood that he had made the wrong ruling. Another medieval halakhist allegedly delayed ruling on a point of law until he saw in his dream what he should rule.[15]

Because Dreaming Can Have a Cathartic Effect

Rabbi Hisda, a third-century Babylonian, taught that the emotion in a dream may be sufficient to make the dreamer feel better. Similarly, Rabbi Pinhas of Koretz, an eighteenth-century Hasidic sage, taught that "dreams are a secretion of our thoughts and, through them, our thought is purified."[16]

As mentioned above, Freud believed that dreams distort repressed wishes to prevent anxiety from disturbing our sleep. As long as we do not wake up, dreams help us cope with anxiety. However, when we have an anxiety dream, he reasoned, it is because our psychic censor has been overpowered.[17]

Alfred Adler, who had been an early disciple of Freud but soon went his own way, believed that a dream uses emotion and mood to propel us forward toward our goal. A dream often comes true, he taught, because the dreamer trains and prepares in the dream for the goal to come true in waking life. In addition, the dream fantasy may help motivate us to solve the problems confronting us so that we can achieve our goal.[18]

After studying many patients' dreams, Ernest Hartmann has concluded that dreams express the emotional state of the dreamer and serve to "calm the storm," reducing the disturbance of the emotion by diffusing it. The dream provides a metaphor for the anxiety, he says, allowing the dreamer to work on the emotion by expressing and experimenting with it in different ways. Hartmann believes, as Rabbi Hisda also believed, that it is not important to remember our dreams, as the dream-work takes place even if we are unaware of what we dreamed and slowly diffuses the emotion. Even when the dream is forgotten, the dream has a therapeutic function.[19]

Antti Revensuo proposes an evolutionary theory concerning the ancient biological function of dreaming in helping human beings to survive and spread. He argues that dreaming is a defense mechanism, comparable to other bodily defense mechanisms, such as the immune system, that automatically elicit a response to potentially dangerous situations. In this theory, our innate ability to dream exists specifically to help us develop and maintain skills to avoid threatening situations. Dreams sometimes simulate such situations, although not always. When we are exposed to danger we will probably dream about the situation, experience fear, and rehearse in the dream some ways of escaping from the danger. Dreams search for and process emotional memories, allowing us to rehearse worrying situations. They help us cope with worry by allowing us to practice handling emotion and solving conflicts.[20]

When Have Dreams Helped Jews Cope with Worry?

As we have already seen above, dreams are helpful when they provide insight that we can use creatively to remove worry, but sometimes we are unable to find meaning in our dreams. Well aware of this, Jews have often told their dreams to a friend or a person known for successful dream interpretation in the hope of gaining insight that would be therapeutic. The man who dreamed that he was being attacked by a troupe of man-eating dogs did not find that his dream helped him cope with his worry; his dream only made him feel worse. It was the rabbi who helped him to find therapy through his dreaming. Dreams also help us cope with worry when they offer a happy solution to a disturbing situation or when they prepare us to reach our goal.

When Interpreted

Often we dismiss a whole dream as mere nonsense, just as Rabbi Meir would have done in late antiquity. However, Rabbi Hisda encouraged Jews to look for meaning in their dreams: "A dream that is not interpreted is like a letter that is not read." One of his colleagues warned, moreover, "Part of the dream may be fulfilled, but not all of it can be fulfilled" (B. *Berakhot* 55a). Sometimes a dream carries an obvious message concerning a particular worry that has been bothering us and we can use this knowledge therapeutically. Sometimes we may suspect that a dream bears a hidden message and we seek help to understand it. But clearly it is not always easy to know what we can learn from a dream and what we should ignore as nonsense. Many Jews who were puzzled by their dreams consulted a sage, a doctor, or an elderly woman—whoever had a reputation for insight and interpretative skills. Clever dream interpreters have never been short of business. Freud's interest in the interpretation of dreams followed a long and well-established Jewish tradition.

A dream can be interpreted in any number of ways. Joseph and Daniel may have had the benefit of divine inspiration to guide their interpretations of the dreams of Pharaoh and Nebuchadnezzar, respectively, but without such inspiration how can a person know that a particular interpretation is correct? The Talmud tells us that, during the period of the Second Temple, there were twenty-four dream interpreters in Jerusalem; each interpreted the same dream in different ways and all interpretations were fulfilled. This tale teaches that there may be many meanings to a single dream. One interpretation does not necessarily exhaust the full meaning of a dream.[21]

The Talmud offers an example of interpretations fulfilled: Two men approached a dream interpreter, Bar Hedya, and related dreaming about the same verse. One offered to pay the man for his interpretation, and indeed did pay him. The other did not. The interpreter foretold happy outcomes for the dreams of the man who paid him and predicted all sorts of disasters for the dreamer who wanted his service free of charge. In both cases the interpretations proved correct. The unhappy man eventually decided to pay Bar Hedya, just as his happy friend had done. The subsequent interpretations were all favorable. One day these two men were traveling in the same boat. As they disembarked, the dream interpreter dropped a book he was carrying. His companion picked it up and saw written in it "all dreams follow the mouth." He then understood that Bar Hedya was to blame for all his former misfortunes. (Bar Hedya fled from the furious man, but refused to change his ways, and died gruesomely).[22]

According to the Talmud, "all dreams follow the mouth"; that is, they follow the interpretation given to them (B. *Berakhot* 55b). This is a warning: We have to be careful when interpreting a dream because the interpretation can determine its effect. A woman once dreamed that the attic of her house had split open. She told this unusual dream to Rabbi Eleazar, who interpreted it as a sign that she would conceive a son. She went home and indeed conceived a son. One day, she dreamed the same dream and again she told it to the rabbi. He interpreted it the same way as before, and she soon conceived another son. The third time that she dreamed the same dream, she could not find the rabbi and told his students instead. Their interpretation was that she would bury her husband. This too came to pass. When Rabbi Eleazar heard her wailing, he asked what had happened. When he discovered what his students had said, he accused them of murder.[23]

The rabbi may well have understood that the woman's dream was mere nonsense, but if she was worried enough to come to see him about it, it was his responsibility to help her overcome her anxiety and think positively about life. His interpretation made her feel better and she looked forward to bearing a child. This story teaches that we should be careful when we interpret a dream and seek to understand how a dream can help us to change our ways for the better. And the dream interpreter has a duty to interpret a person's dream in a way that reduces worry, as long as this is moral.

A favorite Sephardic ballad, "The King of France," legitimizes the expression of a mother's and a daughter's worry about the girl's future—about her finding a husband and being accepted into his family. The dream at the center of this ballad fulfills their eager wish for a happy outcome to this common worry: The singer tells in rhymed verse that one of the king's three daughters reports her dream to her mother and expects a good and happy interpretation. The girl dreamed that she was standing next to a door and saw the full moon. She looked out of a window and saw a deer. Finally, she leaned over a well and saw a golden post and three birds pecking at it. The mother interprets the dream. The full moon is your mother-in-law, she explains; the deer is your older sister-in-law, and the three birds are your younger sisters-in-law. The golden post is your husband, the king. The last verse of the song announces, "The carriages waited by the gates to take her away to other lands." The girl will evidently soon leave home and become the wife of a king. This is the dream that almost every young Jewish girl's mother wants to come true.

The mother interpreted her daughter's dreams as good omens. However, she skipped over one element of the dream in her interpretation in fear that "dreams follow the mouth." The birds pecking at the golden post in the girl's dream hint at strife that may well be expected between the young bride and her sisters-in-law, as each seeks the attention of the "king." The mother ignored the dream's indication of family strife, hoping to avoid its occurrence. She interpreted the dream so that only good could be expected to result from it.[24]

Some Jews wrote manuals for those who wanted to find meaning in dreams. The imagery of these manuals is very much linked to the daily life of the observant Jew and has nothing in common with the sexual and archetypal imagery that interested Freud and Jung. For example, Solomon Almoli, a Spanish Jew who became a physician to the sultan in Constantinople in the early sixteenth century, wrote his *Interpretation of Dreams* based on traditional Jewish dream interpretations gleaned from the Book of Daniel, the Talmud, and medieval Jewish thinkers. This book was first published in Salonika, c. 1515, and became immensely popular; it was reproduced later in other books, republished, and translated into Judeo-Persian (1901) and Yiddish (1902). Almoli pointed out that if a scholar dreams he manages to ride his horse across a dangerously turbulent stream, the horse is a symbol of wisdom and the dream indicates that his learning will help him through difficult situations. However, if the dreamer is not a scholar, the horse represents strength and the dream reveals that he will overcome a difficult physical struggle. Here again, the interpreter seeks a meaning that can help the dreamer to feel optimistic.[25]

Some Jews have believed that certain dreams, such as those that involve immoral behavior, are best not revealed, let alone interpreted, lest they "follow the mouth" and come true. Some rabbis warned Jews to be wary about telling a dream—good or bad—to any other person, even to a spouse. By the same reasoning, we should clearly not tell a dream to someone who does not like us, as that person may interpret it in a harmful way. Jews have often preferred to banish a worrying dream, as described below, rather than to have it interpreted.[26]

Freud believed that dreams can help people cope with anxiety when they are interpreted to reveal the forbidden wishes that caused them. He used this principle in the psychoanalytical therapy of his patients.[27]

When Dreams Offer a Happy Solution

In the Bible, Isaiah notices that a man who goes to sleep hungry dreams that he is eating, whereas one who goes to sleep thirsty dreams he is drinking. A Yiddish proverb warns, "Dumplings in a dream are not dumplings, but a dream!"[28] Dreaming about food or about sex may be the body's response to an unfulfilled need or wish. Similarly, a sinner's dream of redemption, a childless woman's dream of bearing a child, and a poor man's dream of finding money are wish-fulfilling dreams. The fantasy gives pleasure, although short-lived, as it dissipates when we wake up to reality. Such a dream may briefly improve our mood and, at best, foster hope and optimism. Often, Jews have interpreted such dreams as divine revelation, and the happy dreamer finds renewed faith and psychological strength.

Wishful dreams were one way that some people managed to escape, albeit temporarily, from the Nazi hell. Miriam Lesser remembered a recurring dream that she had when she was ten years old and worked endless days on almost no food as a slave laborer in a German workshop during the Second World War. She stood on a box hidden under her long skirt to make herself look taller, so that the Germans would not notice her true, diminutive size and remove her from the workplace that she shared with her mother. Every night she curled up into a tiny corner of the overcrowded room and fell asleep immediately. In her sleep she found herself in a sunny orange grove in Palestine, picking oranges with her friends, and she was the only one who could reach the high branches without standing on a box. She alone was tall enough.[29]

A woman in Bergen-Belsen dreamed at the end of March 1945 that her father came to visit her, brought her food, and told her not to worry; she should prepare for a journey on April 7 and must not lose faith. This dream came at a time when the death camp was inundated with a massive number of prisoners who had been marched from other camps farther east as the Germans retreated. The conditions were worse than ever and people were dying all around her. The dream gave her hope and helped her to convince others to keep hoping for the end of the war and liberation. Liberation in fact came on April 15, eight days after the dream had predicted, and she survived, perhaps partly owing to the hope that the dream had aroused in her.[30]

Similarly, while Arab and Jewish Israeli children living in conflict zones often dream about violence and death, a few have reported wishful, utopian dreams about peace. Those who dream violent dreams sometimes solve them heroically. For example, an Arab girl dreamed that an Israeli soldier asked her for bread and she poisoned him, stole his weapon, and killed the Israeli occupiers. A Jewish child living in a conflict zone often dreamed of a Palestinian attack on a bus, school, or shop, and not only escaped alive but also acted heroically, killing the attacker, saving others, or doing something that gained the dreamer praise. A Jewish woman living in the West Bank during the El Aqsa Intifada in 2001 reported a recurrent dream in which she is ambushed by armed Palestinians, but the dream always ends happily when she shouts that she is a midwife.[31]

Daydreams, like night dreams, can offer imaginary solutions to an ongoing concern. Daydreams are more likely than night dreams to offer happy solutions. While wishful daydreaming is one way of escaping from worry, it may, however, be maladaptive to overindulge in it, just as it may be unwise to overeat or overindulge in other behaviors. Overindulgence in wishful fantasy may lead to the inability to distinguish the real world from the fantasy world.

Jews all over the world have told well-loved folktales that strengthen people's hopes of having a happy dream that puts an end to their worrying. Such tales are healing tales that have given hope in worrying times.

A well-loved tale of the dream of a chief of police begins with a miserably poor man who decided to go to Baghdad to see if he could improve his lot in life. He arrived in the city, tired from his long journey and decided to sleep on the floor of a mosque. He was awakened suddenly by a kick from the chief of police. "Where are you from?" he asked gruffly. The poor man told him that he had come from far away because he dreamed he would improve his luck in the big city. "Stupid fellow!" snickered the policeman. "You came all the way here because of a dream? I too dreamed that under a date tree by the canal in the public gardens there is a jar full of gold coins. Do you think I was foolish enough to go there and start digging? Dreams are stuff and nonsense!" The poor man said nothing and turned over on the mat to go back to sleep. In the morning he went down to the public gardens and looked for a date tree. He dug beneath it and there, sure enough, he found the treasure. With the gold coins he was able to buy a big house and open a shop.[32]

In a Hasidic version of the tale, the policeman dreams that the treasure is buried in the poor man's home far away. The poor man goes home and finds the treasure buried under his stove. The Hasidic version teaches that not only should we take our dreams seriously, but that another person's dream can become our own reality. In addition, this story is interpreted metaphorically; we can find the treasure that we are looking for—knowledge of truth—at home, that is, within ourselves.[33]

Nahman of Bratzlav wanted to become a true *tzaddik* who could repair the wrongs of this world, but worried that his "utterly repulsive" sexuality would be the cause of his failure. In one anxiety dream that occurred in December 1809, he found himself alone in the house of study, only to discover that outside lots of people, including his disciples, were mocking him for having committed a terrible sin. Nahman escapes to a far-off country, but there he also finds people whispering about him and mocking him. He goes into the woods, hoping that the matter will calm down in his absence. Eventually an old man calls for him, but he, too, berates the Bratzlav rabbi, shaming him and telling him not to expect paradise in the next world. Nahman dismisses him and continues to live in the forest with a few disciples. However, soon he begins to fear that he will forget all his learning and asks one of his men to fetch him a book. The man returns without the book and Nahman panics that he will forget all his learning. Then the old man reappears with a book. When the Bratzlav rabbi opens it and finds it is in a foreign language that he can neither read nor understand, he becomes utterly miserable. The dream ends happily, however, as the old man reveals that he is a messenger from the upper world and that all those who had rejected him for his terrible sin (whose nature is not revealed) forgive him.[34]

When Dreams Reveal What to Do

Worried Jews have often paid close attention to dreams that reveal the path to a desired goal. Sometimes a worried person dreamed of a remedy, tried it out the next day, and found that it worked. In Morocco, a blind Jew allegedly regained vision after dreaming of a certain cure, and a cripple stood up and walked after being told to do so in a dream.[35]

Some years ago, a Moroccan-born Jewish woman recalled that when she was young and newly married, she expected to conceive. When there were no signs of pregnancy, she began to worry. She consulted the midwife and doctor but nothing they suggested helped. One night she dreamed that she met a *tzaddik* who told her that she must give him some bread, or he would not cure her. Puzzled, she related her dream to her mother. (In North African, Sephardic, and Oriental Jewish communities, the aging mother, the woman of experience in the household, is traditionally the interpreter of dreams.) Her mother realized that the spirit of the *tzaddik* had appeared in the dream to help her daughter conceive and told the young couple to visit the *tzaddik*'s grave. A whole party accompanied them on the pilgrimage to the grave, bringing food and candles. They prayed and sang. Soon after returning home, the young woman conceived. The family believes that the dream was responsible for the birth of their daughter.[36]

Sefer Hasidim, the book about the lives of the medieval Ashkenazic pietists, cites an instance where a Jew was uncertain whether his dream contained a true revelation that he should follow, or whether it was deceptive nonsense. He had dreamed that he should marry a certain woman, but when he sought her out afterward she refused his proposal. He then dreamed again that he would be committing a sin if he did not marry her. Unsure of whether he should act according to his dream or ignore the dream's message, he consulted a sage. The sage ruled that had the woman been decreed to marry him, she would have accepted his offer, but as she had refused him, she was apparently not the right woman for him. The sage told him to stop worrying about marrying this woman and to find another wife.[37]

Hayyim Vital confessed that one Sabbath eve, in 1566, he said *Kiddush* and sat down to eat but was too worried to swallow anything. He wept, sighed, and grieved because he felt cursed and because he had neglected his Torah for two years. Because of his worry, he left his meal untouched, lay facedown on his bed, and wept. He fell asleep and then dreamed a wondrous dream. The dream was very vivid and he described in great detail his meeting with Elijah the prophet, who took him to the Garden of Eden where he saw geese, an omen that he would gain wisdom, and met God on the holy throne. God promised the kabbalist a place on the right side of the divine throne. Vital asked to remain in heaven and to not be returned to the world below, but God pointed out that Vital was still young and must return to fulfill commandments, learn Torah, and improve his soul. His statement that this was a wondrous dream reveals that it made him happy. The dream evidently gave him renewed energy and motivation to return to a religious way of life, in the hope that he would one day sit at God's right side in the Garden of Eden.

Vital reported another dream that followed a state of anxiety. One Friday night, in the spring of 1577, he woke up most upset when he found that he had a nocturnal emission. He went back to sleep, however, and the departed soul of his old teacher appeared to him in a dream and told him that the time had not yet come for Vital to go and live in Jerusalem. The dream instructed Vital to go with his old teacher to a cave, a burial tomb of one of the earliest sages in the land of Israel. There he found a splendid building of antiquity made of huge stones, and he noticed the name Samael engraved on one of these stones, as well as other names that he did not recall. Then his old teacher told him that the time had come for Vital to go and live in Jerusalem. The kabbalist woke up and moved to Jerusalem.[38]

The dream appears to have no connection to the distress that preceded it, except that the name Samael represents defilement and the Evil Inclination. The upsetting incident earlier in the night had made him realize that he did not deserve to make his planned move to head the yeshiva in Jerusalem. Indeed, at the start of his dream, his teacher tells him that he is not yet permitted to go. However, as the dream progresses, his wish is fulfilled and he wakes up happy with the knowledge that he may now make the desired move.

How Have Jews Used Their Dreams to Cope with Worry?

Let us turn to the story of Joseph's dreams to see how they helped him cope with worry. We remember that Joseph was the young, favored son of Jacob, the patriarch. The Bible tells us that when Joseph was seventeen he tended the flocks with his brothers and complained about his older siblings to their father. Their father loved Joseph best of all his sons and gave him a coat of many colors that was more beautiful than any that his brothers owned. When his brothers saw that their father loved Joseph more than them,

> they hated him so that they could not speak a friendly word to him. Once Joseph had a dream which he told to his brothers; and they hated him even more. He said to them, "Hear this dream which I have dreamed: There we were binding sheaves in the field, when suddenly my sheaf stood up and remained upright; then your sheaves gathered around and bowed low to my sheaf." His brothers answered, "Do you mean to reign over

us? Do you mean to rule over us?" And they hated him even more for his talk about his dreams. He dreamed another dream and told it to his brothers, saying, "Look, I have had another dream: And this time, the sun, the moon, and eleven stars were bowing down to me." And when he told it to his father and brothers, his father berated him. "What," he said to him, "is this dream you have dreamed? Are we to come, I and your mother and your brothers and bow low to you to the ground?" So his brothers were wrought up at him, and his father kept the matter in mind." (Gen. 37:2–11)

Joseph and his family believed that an image in a dream could represent an idea, but they also believed that the message of the dream was prophetic. The dreams, which used different images to convey the same message, confirmed the boy's feeling that he was specially favored. Joseph wanted to believe that, some day, his family would bow low to him, like the sheaves and the stars in his dreams. He was younger than his brothers and subservient to them. His dream admitted his wish to make his brothers subservient to him. By telling his family the dreams, Joseph wanted to make his wish come true. His belief that his wish would eventually be realized gave him the strength to face his older brothers. It gave him courage, determination, and a goal in life. But his telling his dreams almost cost him his life. His brothers' hatred swelled and they conspired to kill him. Suspecting that Joseph's dreams were prophetic, they hoped to prevent them from coming true: "They said to one another, 'Here comes that dreamer! Come now, let us kill him and throw him into one of the pits; and we can say, "A savage beast devoured him." We shall see what comes of his dreams!'" (Gen. 37:18–20). Not only did Joseph survive, but many years later his brothers indeed bowed low to him.

The brothers understood the meaning of Joseph's dreams and became worried. But Joseph's anxiety concerning his father's favoritism and his brothers' hatred was dissipated by his dreams. They allowed him to hope for the happy situation when they would serve him. His road was long and dangerous, but he found his way eventually, strengthened by his hopeful dreams.

Joseph's dreams helped him to cope with worry. However, not everyone has such useful dreams. Some Jews in the past were not content to wait endlessly until a helpful dream chanced to appear. Jews who were worried about a decision they had to make, the choice of a spouse, or even the coming of the Messiah, sometimes engaged in special behaviors in the hope of inducing a dream that would answer a question that they posed before falling asleep. On occasion the dream needed interpreting before the message was understood.

Dream Questions   Weeping, fasting, and praying have sometimes induced a dream revelation. In addition, some worried Jews have asked a specific question before going to sleep, in the hope of receiving an answer in a dream. The process of inducing dreams to answer such a question is referred to as *she'elat ḥalom* in Jewish sources, literally "dream question."

Some Jews strengthened their prayer for a specific dream with meditative techniques, divinatory magic, or a combination of these methods before falling asleep. The preparations that Jewish men undertook to induce nighttime dreams are not dissimilar to those (described in chapter 4) that induce dreamlike states of consciousness where the mind reaches a state conducive to receiving a vision, insight, or inspiration. In the past, dream induction usually involved purification, fasting, and isolating oneself, the same preparations undertaken by the mystics who engaged in meditation. The goal of both the mystics and the worried man wanting to induce a dream was the same—to gain knowledge that would reduce uncertainty. The dream was an easier and safer way to achieve the revelation, however.

When a Babylonian sage did not know the correct solution to a problem concerning the payment of certain tithes, he prayed, "May it be the will of God that I behold [the answer to my question] in a dream" (B. *Menaḥot* 67a). The sage expected to learn the answer in his dream so that he could issue a ruling on the matter under discussion. He probably assumed that his soul could free itself from his body during sleep and roam the heavens to access true information in the divine realm. Some Jews imagined that there is an angel, a "Prince of Dreams" or "Master of Dreams," whose job it is to convey dreams to the soul of the sleeper. Many Jews have dreamed that the prophet Elijah, a *tzaddik,* or another familiar departed soul came to them with a revelation in a dream. Many have also believed that on occasion the dreamer's soul could receive a message directly from God.[39]

In the early eleventh century, someone wrote to Hai Gaon, who was the head of an important rabbinic academy on the banks of the River Euphrates, to ask if some pietist men, who fasted for several days, stayed in a pure place, and recited chosen biblical verses before falling asleep, could genuinely see prophetic visions. Hai Gaon replied that he had indeed heard of the custom of asking dream questions. He had heard that one person saw proven answers in his dream, while others looked for signs of an answer in their dreams, received no answer, and worried. He knew that formulas for asking dream questions existed and that some people had tried to use them, but he confessed that he had not seen the "Master of Dreams" in his own dreams.[40]

In the thirteenth century, Jacob of Marvège asked questions before going to sleep to gain in his dreams divine answers to problems of Jewish law. We do not know if he fasted, wept, or prayed before asking his questions. He did, however, ask God to tell the holy angels to respond to his request before the Throne of Glory "with a true and valid answer, well ordered, with complete clarity and without any ambiguity." He also worried about whether the reply he might receive would be genuinely divine—it could come to him through an evil spirit rather than an angel—and whether he could reveal the reply to other sages. It appears that one dream question elicited further dream questions, and the process of extracting all the desired information took more than just one night. Jacob of Marvège wrote down the divine replies that he received. Dream revelations became a popular literary genre in medieval France and Spain, and later in other countries too.[41]

Jews who worried about the punishments that awaited their souls after death often asked dream questions about the world to come and their expected places there. The medieval Ashkenazic pietists, the

Safed kabbalists, and some Italians, such as Abraham Yagel and his contemporar, Rabbi Leone of Modena tried to find out in their dreams about the world to come. There are several versions of the tale of the pious man who asks a dream question to discover who will sit next to him in heaven. Judah of Regensburg, the medieval pietist, was fond of this tale and related his own version:

A pietist (similar to Judah himself) was worried about whom he would sit next to in paradise. He sought the answer in a dream question and discovered the man's identity. He found his future neighbor in a far-off place. The future neighbor proved coarse and insulted his visitor, but nevertheless allowed him to enter his home. That night all the local prostitutes came to the house. The coarse man gave them plenty to drink and danced until the wine made the women drowsy and they fell asleep. Then he left. The pious man was shocked and deeply distressed. The next day, as he prepared to leave, he met the sinner, for this was clearly what he was, and asked what good deed he had done to deserve to be his companion in paradise. The sinner revealed then that by gathering the prostitutes and giving them drink he kept all the other Jews away from sinning. He himself never laid with any of them, but went home to his mother as soon as the women had fallen asleep.[42]

Some Jews induced dreams to discover more mundane information, such as the whereabouts of a stash of money or which woman to marry. Hayyim Vital often asked a dream question before going to sleep. Like the talmudic sage, he prayed "let it be Your Will . . ." but he also recited a Divine Name that he had written down for this purpose and directed his whole mind to the relevant divine emanation, a Jewish meditative technique. Then he voiced his question and fell asleep. In 1564, he asked a dream question about his prospective bride. A year later, he was engaged to be married but quarreled with his fiancée. He asked a dream question to see if he should nevertheless marry her. As he matured, he asked more intellectual dream questions, for example, to gain kabbalistic knowledge.[43]

Leone of Modena confessed that after his mother had proposed day after day that he should marry his cousin Esther, he engaged in dream divination by saying a prayer to find out whom he would marry: "In my dream, an old man held my hand and led me to a certain wall upon which was drawn a portrait covered with a curtain. When he drew aside the veil I saw a portrait of my cousin Esther, as well as the color of her garment. While I was still gazing at the image, it changed, and another one, which I could not clearly make out, replaced it." In the morning he told his dream to his parents, who dismissed it as insignificant. When he eventually met Esther at the signing of the marriage agreement, she was in fact wearing a dress exactly the color that he had dreamed. She was beautiful and wise, but died of a sickness before her wedding day. Eventually Leone married another woman, presumably the one he had been unable to identify in his dream.[44]

Another rabbi in Modena, the kabbalist Abraham Rovigo, could not receive answers in his own dreams to the questions that worried him, so he gave his questions to his student, Mordecai, who addressed them to the angel that visited him in his sleep. Mordecai wrote down the content of his dreams in a little book, and Rovigo read them and sometimes interpreted them for him. Rovigo was concerned about his poor relations with his brother, their arguments over the shop that they owned, and its sale that would enable his planned journey to the Holy Land. He was also concerned about choosing a husband for his daughter, and about his son, whose behavior caused him great distress.

Mordecai also gained dream revelations that enlightened his own worries. In the spring of 1695, he received a very distressing letter from his wife, who had remained with their son in Zolkiew, Poland, where the son had married. His wife wanted a lot of money, having none left at all. She reminded him of his promise not to be away for more than a year—he had been absent already for two years. She accused him of leaving them to die in the ongoing attacks of the "Ishmaelites" (Cossacks), who had taken some women and children hostage, burned down houses, and destroyed their food supplies. But Mordecai had no money to send her, and he had a religious mission to fulfill in Modena. Worried and not knowing what to do, he asked a dream question. The angel that appeared in his dream proposed that he send for his family to join him in Italy, so that he could continue his mission. But, if after all, he chose to travel, the angel continued, he should go as far as Cracow and send for them to join him there, where he could also pursue his goal.[45]

Formulas for Inducing Dream Revelations An ancient formula for inducing a dream revelation, apparently used by Jewish men in fifth- or sixth-century Babylonia, and possibly earlier by Palestinian mystics, is preserved in several manuscripts. It requires fasting for three days prior to the night of the desired dream. One must recite chosen verses from a number of Psalms each night. On the third night, after repeating the verses from Psalms yet again and mouthing some esoteric Names, one prays to God to reveal "a certain matter." One supplicates the Prince of Dreams to come peacefully and speedily, that his words be clear and remembered upon awakening. The prayer goes on at length, repeating praises of God, adjurations, magical names, and supplications.

The man desiring a revelation must not speak much with a woman on the night of the expected dream. This directive, after the three-day preparation, reminds the Jew of the revelation on Mount Sinai, when Moses said to the people, "Be ready for the third day: do not go near a woman" (Exod. 19:15). The ancient formula for inducing a dream revelation continues: "Direct your heart toward heaven and be careful," for if the Prince warns the dreamer not to reveal what is told in the dream, or does not reveal anything in the dream, the content of the dream must remain secret. But if the angel of the dream answers the dream question and does not command the dreamer to keep this secret, then the dreamer can tell others all that was revealed. Finally, the text warns the dreamer to be careful not to tell more than was actually dreamed, for if he lies, the Prince of Dreams will never appear to him again. If he reports his dream faithfully, however, the Prince will come whenever summoned.[46]

A popular handbook of Jewish magic, *Shimmush Tehillim* (The Use of Psalms), dating from the gaonic period, recommends first purifying oneself and then reciting Psalm 23 ("The Lord is my shepherd") seven times before falling asleep. An eleventh-century manuscript advises dressing in pure clothes after fasting for three days. Before falling asleep, the dreamer must recite Psalm 23 seven times and then adjure the angels to show him what he wants to see. The dreamer must not sleep in a house where there is a woman. The text promises that the dreamer will see a wondrous dream that will tell him what the dreamer wanted to know. This formula, the manuscript assures, is "good, fitting, tested and true." The instructions are for a man's use, not a woman's.[47]

Similar formulas for inducing dream revelations have been preserved in other medieval and later mystical and magical manuscripts, and these eventually made their way into printed books. Clearly, even a tested and proved formula did not always produce the desired results, because these "remedy books" usually suggest trying several different methods for inducing a dream. If one method did not work, a person could try another the next night, and a third the subsequent night, in the hope of receiving the desired dream sooner or later.

In the twelfth century, Abraham ibn Ezra wrote that *Sefer Razi'el* recommends reciting the first verse of Ezekiel, which contains seventy-two letters (of magical significance) in order to query the heavenly powers in a dream. In the first published edition of *Sefer Razi'el* (1701), a book of kabbalistic cosmology that contains some magical remedies for common worries, we are offered several other suggestions. One involves adjuring the Prince of the Dream and focusing on the vowels of the Tetragrammaton (a Jewish meditative technique described in chapter 4).[48]

A book of remedies "from Jerusalem," collected in the late nineteenth century, when there was a booming market for such literature, contains a "proven" method for asking a dream question, which has shadows of the medieval formulas cited above. This one is more user-friendly, since it does not require a three-day preparation of fasting and purification, but instructs merely not to eat much and abstain from wine on the night of the desired dream. The worried person must recite Psalm 23 seven times (as above) after reciting the evening *Shema* prayer. He must then write on a thin parchment the Names

"Itzhak Aman Taltarah" (meaning unknown) with crowns on the Hebrew letters. (This ornate lettering is known as "Assyrian" lettering and is often used in holy texts and on amulets.) He must put this parchment in his left ear and go to sleep on his left side without speaking to anyone, while thinking about this with full concentration. If the dreamer is unable to recall the dream, he must turn his nightdress inside out and go back to sleep and the dream will come again. (This last recommendation appears also in a Yiddish manuscript of magical remedies written in 1474).[49]

Another remedy book, also compiled in the late nineteenth century, offers three more suggestions, all "tested and tried" and bearing the impossible pedigree of coming from Sa'adia Gaon, Hai Gaon, and Moses Maimonides, among others. They all involve purification, especially a ritual bath and refraining from putting one's hand below one's belt, a clean bed and a clean room, abstinence from meat and wine, and meditation on certain Hebrew letters and vowel points.[50]

Necromancy The Talmud explains that the phrase "one who inquires of the dead" (Deut. 18:11) refers to one who fasts and then spends the night in the cemetery, so that a spirit may rest on that person and reveal desired information. Moreover, the Talmud tells that Rav, a third-century Babylonian sage, "went to the cemetery and did what he did." The sage probably fasted and spent the night by or on a grave to commune with a spirit of the dead and learn what he desired to know. The Talmud does not specify, however, whether the necromancer fell asleep and saw the spirit in a dream.[51]

A pietist Jew in medieval Germany stretched himself out on the grave of a departed Hasid and whispered his dream request into the tombstone. He was worried about whether his ascetic practices were acceptable to God. The worried person lying on the gravestone asked whether his behavior would be rewarded in heaven. He assumed that the departed soul of the Hasid would have access to divine information and would be able to communicate this to the dreamer's soul during his sleep. He was delighted when he dreamed he was in paradise.[52]

The induction of dreams is a form of divination. Biblical law forbids divination, including necromancy, and Maimonides reminded

Jews of this law. His Ashkenazic pietist contemporary, Judah of Regensburg, specifically forbade the asking of dream questions, fully aware that Jews were engaging in this behavior. Some continued to do so, as we have seen. Nowadays, those who want to induce a dream relax or meditate and then say a short prayer or think about the desired dream just before falling asleep. However, weeping, fasting, and praying, the traditional Jewish behaviors for inducing dreams, may stimulate emotional arousal before sleep and thus influence the nature of dreams experienced.[53]

How Have Jews Coped with Dreams That Cause Worry?

Preventing worries from arising may sometimes be better than trying to cope with them once they have flooded in on us, so Jews have sometimes made a specific request in their prayers before falling asleep at night. Others have, on occasion, obtained a protective amulet if they or their children were specially troubled by evil dreams. Jews developed their own characteristic ways of coping with a nightmare that generates worry, by fasting to avert disaster and converting it into a good omen with a special prayer.

Preventing Anxiety Dreams

The talmudic prayer to recite before going to bed at night includes a plea: "Let not my thoughts trouble me, nor evil dreams, nor evil fancies, but let my rest be perfect before thee." Rabbis later copied this prayer into the daily prayer book.[54] Interestingly, prayer books written especially for women do not include any prayers that refer to anxiety dreams, let alone forestall or banish them. Jewish liturgy was written by men, and predominantly for men. Whereas men's dreams could be prophetic, a woman's bodily impurity and her lack of spirituality ruled out any possibility of her having a revelatory dream. A man's anxiety-provoking dream was therefore taken seriously for the truth it might portend, whereas a woman's could be dismissed as nonsense. Nevertheless, we have already seen evidence that women themselves have taken their dreams seriously. Mothers presumably practiced intuitive wisdom on their own anxiety dreams and those of their children and did not feel the need for a prayer formula.

Some Jews living in Babylonia between the sixth and eighth centuries fashioned amuletic bowls, inscribed with incantations against demons believed to bring anxiety dreams. Men, women, and children in Mediterranean lands in the Middle Ages, and in European countries until the early twentieth century, used similar protective items bearing incantations against evil demons that convey worrying dreams. A protective stone, *ahlamah*, translated as amethyst—the third stone in the third row of the High Priest's breastplate—may have been used to keep away anxiety dreams in medieval times. In the twelfth century, Abraham ibn Ezra reasoned that the word *ahlamah* is derived from the same word as dream, *halom*. He wrote, "Whoever wears this stone on his finger never fears dreams" for it has a magical power that influences dreams. This tradition, if it was ever a tradition, must soon have fallen into disuse as there is no trace of it in the most common Jewish remedy books.[55]

A remedy book offering alternative advice for preventing bad dreams, also attributed to Abraham ibn Ezra, suggested putting saffron-colored alum under one's head when going to sleep. If this did not have the desired effect, one should replace the alum with a stem of rosemary that had been pulled out of the ground with its root. A portulaca plant placed under the headboard was supposed to ensure pleasant dreams.[56]

A medieval Judeo-Arabic text on sexual medicine offers a prescription to counter wet dreams—a source of worry for Jewish men. The recipe involves making a cooling pomade from sorrel and lotus leaves and applying this to the pubic region before going to sleep.[57]

Remedies for Anxiety Dreams

We have seen that Jews have often prayed in the hope of averting disaster. Since ancient times, Jews have also fasted for the same reason: Fasting is an accepted method of repenting and of expiating sins (as on the Day of Atonement) and can be a first step in changing one's behavior and attitude. Some Jews have fasted and prayed when severely worried by a bad dream.

A Dream Fast   The Sages reasoned that when a dream foretells disaster, a person may still have a chance to repent while fasting and may succeed in averting tragedy. They ruled that a dream fast must be performed on the day of the dream and not delayed. They allowed fasting even on Shabbat—which should be a day of joy—in the special case of a bad dream.[58]

Maimonides advocated the dream fast, not only as a means of protection from danger or to abolish harmful decrees, but as an obligation so that the dreamer may reexamine personal actions and repent. However, some rabbis advised against fasting after a bad dream on any day, reasoning that this might reduce a person's strength.[59]

In the seventeenth century, Manasseh ben Israel fasted and repented with all his heart when he realized that his dream was an evil omen for the fate of his friend who had been traveling by boat from Danzig. When the friend failed to appear at the Dutch port at the appointed time, the rabbi dreamed of a certain biblical verse and understood it to indicate that a tragedy had occurred at sea. Manasseh fasted and repented in the hope of nullifying his bad dream and his friend indeed appeared safe and sound a few days later, reporting that there had been a terrible storm at sea and that his life had been saved by a miracle. As Manasseh recorded this incident, it appears that he believed his fasting and repentance had saved his friend's life.[60]

The necessity of undertaking a dream fast on the Sabbath was controversial. On the one hand, Rabbi Jacob Segal Moellin (d. 1427, known as "Maharil") wrote, "It is better that a man fast on Shabbat because of a dream, than that his heart be troubled; he will derive more pleasure from the fast than from his food." On the other hand, Isaiah Horowitz, an influential sixteenth-century Polish rabbi, usually advised people not to fast on Shabbat, but admitted that he knew many people who did so whenever they were worried by a dream.[61]

Joseph Karo, in his Shulḥan Arukh, allowed dream fasting on Shabbat following a dream that had recurred three times, and following the gravest dreams. "According to old books," he notes, these are a Torah scroll being burned, the concluding service of Yom Kippur (which he himself actually dreamed), and the beams of one's house or one's teeth falling out. (Freud interpreted a man's dream of his teeth falling out as a fear of castration.) Karo added that some people said that dreams about reading from a Torah scroll or marrying should also be classified as grave dreams.[62]

A Special Prayer   According to the Talmud written in Israel, a man who has had an anxiety dream must recite a special prayer during the morning liturgy, like this:

> May it be Thy will that all the dreams I have dreamed during this past night or other nights, if they be for good, may they come to pass and bring me joy and happiness, blessing and life. But if they be otherwise then, just as you changed the bitter waters at Marah to sweet waters through the work of Elisha, and just as you changed the curse of Balaam to a blessing, so I pray may you change all of my own bad dreams, and all other bad dreams concerning me, to bring me good, blessing, health, life, happiness, joy, and peace.[63]

But the rabbis in Babylon developed a sort of magical ritual to help a person convert a worrying dream into a good outcome and share it with friends at the same time. The dreamer shares distress without needing to reveal the content of the dream. (As we have seen, some rabbis warned Jews to be wary about telling a dream to any other person, even to a spouse.) This *hatavat ḥalom* ("turning a dream to good") ritual has all the characteristics of a magical ritual, even though it was inserted into the Jewish liturgy and recited in the synagogue during morning prayer.

The ritual requires the presence of three friends. The dreamer asserts that the dream was a good dream, when in fact it was a bad dream; this is a form of contagious magic, where the effect of pronouncing the dream "good" is expected to make it good. The dreamer repeats seven times the declaration "I dreamed a good dream" and is answered seven times by his three friends, who confirm that the dream was good in a set of phrases that include the word "good" seven times. The ritual continues with biblical verses that include threefold repetitions of three significant words: three verses contain the word "overturn," three have the word "redeem," and the last three refer seven times to the word *shalom,* "peace." In this way unwanted emotion is replaced by repetitions of words that refer to converting the bad dream, redeeming, and peace.[64]

Three- and sevenfold repetitions are common magical practices. There was an effort at some point (attributed to a twelfth-century rabbi) to reduce the initial repetitions about a good dream from seven to three—"the usual number of times an incantation is recited"—an act that confirms that this ritual was indeed a magical practice.[65]

The clearly magical nature of the *hatavat halom* ritual probably led Maimonides to exclude it from his Code of Jewish Law. But the Spanish kabbalist who wrote the Zohar in the late thirteenth century favored the ritual: "a man's friends should affirm the good solution and so all will be well."[66]

Eleazar of Worms suggested abrogating an evil omen by acting out the dream, in addition to the traditional measures, thereby ensuring the dream was fulfilled in a way that was not harmful. For example, when a married man dreamed that he was carrying a bird and it flew away, this was a bad omen. The medieval pietist recommended that, in addition to fasting and giving charity, he should catch a hen (or cock) and then let it fly away, as he had seen in his dream.[67]

Before Hitler destroyed Jewish life in Salonika, in northern Greece, Jews who wanted to avert evil that was forecast in a dream took part in a special ceremony, presided over by a rabbi. The unhappy dreamer gave the rabbi 160 small coins and placed the head and feet of a slaughtered fowl on the tombstone of one of Salonika's righteous dead, hoping that the soul of the departed *tzaddik* would intercede to avert the evil dream omen. The unhappy person might make an extra effort to cancel the dream prediction by sponsoring a scholar's learned lecture on Jewish law.[68]

The Babylonian ritual features in the prayer books of Italian and Ashkenazic Jews, sometimes in a shortened form, whereas the prayer of the sages of Israel appears in some Sephardic prayer books, sometimes in a lengthened form. Some prayer books include both of the ancient formulas to transmute a worrying dream.[69]

6 ～ Theurgy and Magic

It once happened that there was a dry winter in the land of Israel. The people were worried that, should rain not come soon, there would be famine and death. The rabbis prayed to God, but the skies stayed blue. So they asked a man named Honi to pray for rain. He prayed and all the people watched the sky hopefully, but it remained blue. Honi then drew a circle in the dust and stood inside it, turned his face upward, and cried out in a loud voice "Master of the World! I swear by Your Great Name that I shall not move from here until You have mercy on Your children!"

The people rejoiced as the sky clouded over and the first drops splattered onto their parched land. But the drops soon stopped and the people turned again to Honi: "Those drops were sent only to release you from your vow. They will not fill our empty cisterns nor give our crops strength to grow."

So Honi asked God for rain to fill the cisterns and water the fields. The rain soon fell in torrents. It drenched and flooded the land and the people became worried again. They complained to Honi that the rains would destroy the world.

Yet again, Honi turned to God: "Master of the Universe! The people whom You brought out of Egypt do not like misfortune, but they also do not want too much of a good thing. May it be Your will to cease the rains now." A wind immediately swept away the clouds and the sky turned blue again.

One of the sages sent him a message: "If you were not Honi, I would excommunicate you, but what can I do to you if God grants your plea as a father grants the request of a son?" (*Ta'anit* 3:8, B. *Ta'anit* 23a).

When worried Jews saw that their prayers remained unanswered, they sometimes tried a more powerful technique of prayer, or, as we have seen in chapter 3, they turned to someone with a reputation for having prayers answered and working wonders. Honi was a miracle worker who lived in the first century B.C.E. We see from his vow that he expected God to answer his prayer. He expected that his actions would draw down divine blessing for the good of all the people. In the eyes of the sage, however, Honi had done something that was forbidden. He stood inside an apparently magic circle to adjure God. His behavior looked like sorcery or witchcraft. As the Bible forbids magic, he deserved excommunication.

The Bible rules, "Let no one be found among you . . . who is an augur, a soothsayer, a diviner, a sorcerer, one who casts spells, or one who consults ghosts or familiar spirits, or one who inquires of the dead." Such behavior, the Bible continues, is abhorrent to the Lord (Deut. 18:10–12).

What was the key to Honi's success? Was it the vow showing his faith that influenced God to send a blessing? Or was it the magical circle, which was not an act of faith? Did he perhaps purify himself first and prepare in some special way that would increase the power of his prayer? Did he swear by an esoteric Divine Name that was purposely omitted when the story was written down? If we draw a circle and stand in it to call on God when we are worried, we are unlikely to cause the weather to change or to bring about any other blessing. What was Honi's secret?

The sage's comment teaches us that only Honi can be allowed such behavior, and we should not try to emulate him. The editors of the Talmud may have purposely withheld information about the secret to his success so that other worried Jews would not be able to practice magic. Alternatively, perhaps the talmudic story is a folktale, a mixture of fact and fantasy. Perhaps the editors wrote down the tale to teach a different lesson, the lesson that miracles do happen. The story appears in a text full of legends of miracles wrought for worthy people, where the miracle is a testimony of religion. Miracles strengthen hope and faith.

This chapter does not examine recent efforts to prove or disprove the existence of spiritual forces, for example, through scientific experiments on the paranormal. We accept that some people perceive the world differently from others; some believe that a supernatural world exists, others don't. Some people have tried to influence the supernatural world in their favor, just as others have tried to control the natural world. A very ill person may consult a specialized physician who knows how to manipulate sophisticated medical technology in the hope of a cure. That person may also consult a faith healer known for an unusual ability to manipulate supernatural forces to produce beneficial results. The use of one method does not negate the use of the other. Those who are sure that there are no angels and demons will probably not use a protective amulet. Those who are sure that God cannot reveal information or send down divine blessings will probably not seek the help of a *tzaddik*. But some worried Jews today do believe in supernatural power and in the possibility of drawing down divine help. Some consult a *tzaddik* or a Jewish faith healer following a recommendation that this person worked wonders for other people.

Rational-minded Jews have denounced all the magical behaviors described here. For example, the medieval philosopher, Judah Halevi, derided Jews who conjured spirits, used Divine Names in magical ways, and made amulets. Maimonides, too, denounced all forms of magic. Today the head of a kabbalistic yeshivah in Jerusalem, supported by the leading Jerusalem rabbis, has denounced magical behaviors. Yet worried Jews continue to try them.[1]

We have already seen that Jews have tried to induce divine revelation and draw down blessing by praying and meditating. We have also looked at magical methods for banishing worrisome dreams. This chapter focuses on yet other ways that Jews have sought knowledge and power to cope with worry. We will first look at the meaning of the word "theurgy" and the concept of Jewish magic. We will then examine why, when, and how Jews have used theurgy and magic to cope with anxiety. Finally, we will see that these methods have been reinforced by success stories and stories of miracles. Worried people often find comfort in hoping for a miracle that will solve their problem and remove their anxiety. They are willing to try a variety of remedies in the hope of a miracle.

What Is Theurgy, What Is Jewish Magic?

"Theurgy," according to the *Oxford Dictionary*, means "the operation or effect of a supernatural or divine agency in human affairs." It can also refer to "the power possessed by a human being to secure or prevent such divine action, especially the magical power which . . . might be acquired by long training, self-purification and esoteric learning practices." Theurgy includes the effort by the kabbalist or Hasidic master to induce a flow of blessings. The holy man who purifies himself and meditates in order to turn himself into a channel for divine flow is performing an act of theurgy. Especially since the seventeenth century, the theurgic adept was often called *Ba'al Shem*, Master of the Name, because he knew how to use esoteric names to gain divine action.[2]

The expert in Jewish theurgy is God-fearing, righteous, and—usually—educated in the esoteric lore of Jewish mysticism. He undergoes various purification rituals, such as fasting and immersing in a ritual bath, and recites certain blessings or Divine Names before attempting to secure divine action for the benefit of another person or other people. The *tzaddik's* intercessory prayer and the meditative journey to draw down blessings, behaviors that we have discussed in previous chapters, are forms of theurgy. In this chapter, we will look at some other Jewish theurgical techniques.

"Magic," according to the same dictionary, is "the power of apparently influencing the course of events by using mysterious or supernatural forces." These forces are the forces of the spiritual world, the world of angels and demons, good and evil spirits, which cannot be proven or quantified, but which many people have believed to exist.

Women, especially (mostly elderly midwives whose names have not survived), used magical methods in the hope of preserving life within the home.[3] They were often well respected and well versed in women's prayers, in the Jewish laws relevant to their lives, and in folk remedies. They had their own folk remedies for curing fear and protecting their families against illness and death—mainly incantations, often including biblical verses, and potions based on sympathetic and contagious magic.

Many Jews have believed that the words of Torah, even the letters from which they are written carry divine power, and moreover, that Jews can profit from their spiritual force.[4] We will see below that they have used biblical verses, Divine Names, and adjurations as their main tools in theurgy and magic. In addition, Jewish men and women have often drawn on non-Jewish magical techniques, such as the magic circle or a divining cup, in the hope of enhancing the possibility of beneficial results.

Traditionally, Jewish theurgy and magic involve the use of natural means to gain beneficial results. Most Jews who practiced theurgy and magic were not sorcerers who called on the powers of evil: biblical law dictates that sorcery deserves the punishment of death.[5]

The dividing line between theurgy and magic is often not clearcut. An act that one *tzaddik* thinks is theurgy, another may think is magic. What one Jew believes is an act of faith or a powerful prayer, another may dismiss as an act of magic. Honi may have believed that his prayer was an act of faith that God responded to, whereas the sage apparently suspected that a forbidden act of magic may have produced the desired results.

There are significant gender differences in the practices of theurgy and magic. Women could not attain the esoteric knowledge and necessary purification for theurgy and therefore their attempts to manipulate spirits have always been considered magic. Women sometimes conjured spirits in glass mirrors to find answers to worry-ing issues, and used magical cures in the home. In contrast, men engaged in theurgy; they manipulated Divine Names, drew down an-gels for divine revelations, and issued amulets. Some worried Jewish men also engaged in contagious and divinatory magic, and a few have also uttered curses to inflict harm on a fearful enemy.[6]

Jews sometimes suspected that a lonely old woman who brewed healing potions, uttered protective charms, and cast the Evil Eye en-gaged in sorcery. (Those who cast the Evil Eye inflict harm on an-other by casting their gaze on that person.) In contrast, the miracles performed by saintly men, including their casting of the Eye, were often seen as wondrous acts wrought with divine help.[7]

In early twentieth-century Sana'a (Yemen) and Baghdad, some rabbis tried hard to curtail women's magical practices by forbidding Jews to consult them, but to little avail. Rabbi Yehudah Petayah (1859–1942), for example, tried to curb women's magic and offered instead to cure people of the fear syndrome and other sicknesses using traditions accepted by Jewish law—amulets and incantations.[8]

Why Use Magic or Theurgy to Cope with Worry?

Whereas the Jewish religion advocates faith, righteousness, atone-ment, and prayer as guiding principles for life, it offers no certainty that tragedy will not strike, no certainty of remedy or relief from mis-fortune. When people are severely worried, and other advice has not helped or is unavailable, they are often prepared to follow uncon-ventional, even irrational advice. They may also seek special knowl-edge about the future in the hope of discovering a comforting solution.

Jews who believe that their anxiety may derive from a power out-side themselves have often tried a magical or theurgical method on the assumption that only a supernatural or divine force can affect such a power. Jews have often tried such a method because they have heard it recommended. In addition, it can do no harm and is usually cheap. A worried, helpless person may choose such a method because it gives that person a feeling of control and a sense of security.

Furthermore, the social interaction between the powerful, authoritarian adept and the weak and worried sufferer is usually a single, short encounter that may reduce anxiety quickly. The intense look in the eyes of the wonder-worker reveals a divine spark. He promises a prayer or provides an amulet, giving immediate proof of his willingness to help, and perhaps even promises that the worrier will return in a year, happy. The expert, just like any specialist, assesses quickly whether the worrier might be receptive to his or her particular advice and may decline to help if the chances of this appear small. Thus if the expert agrees to help, the worrier hopes for success.

To Discover the Future

It is, of course, human nature to seek information when we are worried, and, when objective knowledge is unavailable, Jews have sought knowledge in the supernatural realm. The Bible tells us that when King Saul faced the Philistines at Gilboa, he felt very worried. He turned to God, but received no answer, not even in his dreams. The *urim* (explained below) and the prophets also provided no hint of the future. So, under cover of night, King Saul consulted a woman who could conjure up spirits and tell him what he sought to know. At first she refused because the king had ordered the death of all those who conjure spirits, but the king promised she would not be harmed. Soon, the spirit of Samuel arose in the dark, terrifying both the woman and the king. It confirmed his worst fears; he had lost God's favor and he would die in battle the next day.[9]

Saul hoped that the spirit's revelation would reduce his worry, but knowledge of his forthcoming demise may have increased his fear instead and reduced his efficiency in battle. The woman who conjured up Samuel's spirit performed divinatory magic. We have already seen in previous chapters that some Jews have engaged in divination to gain information that might reduce their uncertainties about the future.

The Bible refers also to the *urim* and *thummim*, a priestly "instrument of decision," a device for obtaining prophecy that was used until David's time. Some biblical commentators assumed that this instrument was the Ineffable Name, or the esoteric seventy-two-letter Divine Name, which enlightens understanding, casting light like a crystal or mirror.[10]

To Treat the Perceived Cause of the Problem

Until modern medicine offered alternative explanations, many Jews believed that evil spirits were responsible for the unpleasant experiences of the imagination, such as nightmares and daytime fears. They imagined that spirits could visit or enter a person and cause severe symptoms. Theurgy and magic might banish or nullify such supernatural forces, which were unlikely to be influenced by scientific methods.

For most of human history, there was little or no differentiation between rational and irrational approaches to the causes of human distress, or between the scientific and the magical approaches to healing and protection from danger. Many people believed that a medicinal potion or a surgical procedure might cure a physical problem, whereas a magical remedy might protect against and cure a problem caused by the Evil Eye or demons. But often it was impossible to know the true cause of a problem. As healing magic gained status during the Renaissance, some Jewish physicians, such as Abraham Portaleone (1542–1612), Abraham Yagel (1553–c. 1623), and Hayyim Vital (1542–1620), did not hesitate to use healing methods that clearly had a magical provenance when they suspected that patients' symptoms had a demonic origin.[11]

In the days when doctors had few certain remedies, many patients probably preferred to try a cheap and painless magical cure first, before trying a painful and unpleasant physical cure. A person may have placed as much faith in the success of an amulet that was recommended as in a medicinal or surgical procedure. In addition, a magical method was often more easily available and applicable to a wider range of worries.

Because a Method Has Been Recommended

Even though the Bible condemns magic, as we have seen, Jewish magical handbooks have often proffered advice bearing the recommendation that it has been "tried and proved" successful. Such advice includes practical remedies, formulas to avoid danger and to obtain power over evil forces, and methods to gain information about the future.

When Jews wrote down magical advice, they often took care to note who had used or recommended it to supply it with a pedigree and credibility to offer it as an accepted tradition. Magical knowledge was often attributed to a biblical figure or a well-known rabbi. For example, a medieval magical text declared that Divine Names derived from verses of Torah were revealed to Moses at Mount Sinai; Moses then conveyed them to a certain priestly family, who passed them from father to son. A mystical book, *Sefer Razi'el* (mentioned in chapter 5), depicts magical figures "as drawn by Adam" for protection against demonic danger. A seventeenth-century magical guide attributes a magic square to protect against the plague to the twelfth-century physician and philosopher Abraham ibn Ezra. Other books attribute formulas for protective amulets and remedies to the medieval Ashkenazic pietists Judah the Pious of Regensburg and Eleazar of Worms, and Spanish kabbalists Nahmanides and Joseph Gikatilla. Some magical advice allegedly comes from the sixteenth-century Safed kabbalists Isaac Luria and Hayyim Vital. However, a given method may be attributed to one rabbi in one book and to a different rabbi in another.[12]

To Gain the Feeling of Control

When our doctor cannot remedy our illness, we often seek out a specialist, someone with special understanding or skill. So too, when a worrier cannot remedy a serious concern, she or he may choose to consult someone known to have special power who might be able to bring about a desired change. The Jewish worrier may turn to a learned *tzaddik* who is known to pray particularly effectively, or who has a reputation for seeing what others cannot. Alternatively, the worrier may seek a recommended faith healer, who could be a charismatic man or woman with little formal education and a lot of folk wisdom. The worrier consults a person with a reputation for working wonders in the expectation that this person can take control of the situation and bring about a change for the better. (We do not know if Honi was a holy, learned man or a charismatic, perhaps illiterate, man who had performed at least one good deed, but those who asked him to pray for rain hoped that he had the power to take control of the situation, as indeed he did.)

We will see below that some worried Jews in the past used magic or theurgy to gain a sense of control over circumstances in which they felt helpless—to calm the sea during a tempest, to prevent their house from catching fire, or to escape from prison. Some preferred to project their anxiety onto a demon rather than admit that worry comes from inside the mind: it is easier to gain a feeling of control by using magical methods to banish an evil spirit than by dealing with one's own inner weakness and conflict.

For Reassurance and a Sense of Security

The Talmud tells us that Rabbi Eliezer ben Hyrcanus (late first through early second century C.E.) invoked heavenly support for his views in a rabbinic dispute. "If my ruling is correct," he said, "let the carob tree be torn from its place." And it was torn from its place—some said one hundred cubits, others said four hundred. If his halakhah was correct, he asserted, then let the stream of water flow backward. And it did. If his pronouncement was correct, he insisted a third time, then let the study house walls slant. And indeed they slanted. He manipulated supernatural forces in his favor because he wanted reassurance for his views, but his colleagues excommunicated him for his actions.[13]

Jews have often recited biblical verses when worried. Maimonides' experience as a physician taught him to recognize the value of soothing and reassuring verses in healing the soul. At the same time, he firmly objected to their recitation for curing bodily ills or any magical purposes.[14]

In addition to reciting biblical verses, Jews have adjured angels and carried an amulet to gain courage—to face an enemy, walk home in the dark, or deliver a baby. A person who wears an amulet may feel safe in the face of uncertainty, protected by its esoteric Hebrew formulas and its symbols, especially if it was made and given by a pious man who promised that it would help. The amulet symbolizes the bond between the worrier and the saintly man who issued it. Psychoanalysts have called such an object a "transitional object," similar to the infant's comfort blanket or cuddly toy that symbolizes the mother's breast. The amulet gives a sense of security to its bearer.[15]

Nowadays the mobile phone (in Hebrew, significantly, *pelefon*, "wonder-phone") has an almost magical role in coping with everyday worry. The cellular phone enables us to call our loved ones and our business associates day or night, at the slightest worry, to check that everything is fine and that there is really no need to worry. It allows us to seek reassuring information at almost any time.

The wonder-working rabbis, mystic physicians, and aging midwives who have used theurgical and magical methods have traditionally radiated competence, care, and wisdom. The worrier transfers concern to the expert, who reassures the worrier that the problem is now in expert hands. This improves the morale and relaxes the worried person, who, as a consequence, gains a feeling of security.

Because Such Methods Can Do No Harm

Jews have engaged in little anti-demonic rituals, like throwing salt and spitting (*tfou, tfou, tfou*), that are so engrained in Jewish folklore that we do not think about the fact that they originated in magical beliefs. The Book of Kings relates that Elisha threw salt into a spring near Jericho to neutralize harmful effects (2 Kings 2:19–21). The pollution in the water was surely demonic; throwing salt was an ancient protection against evil spirits. Spitting is recorded in the Talmud as a practice associated with "whispering" over a wound, reciting biblical verses or incantations for remedial purposes. Today, instead of actually spitting to keep bad luck well away from us, we just say "*tfou, tfou, tfou*," the sound of spitting. The threefold repetition also points to the magical origin of this custom.[16]

Many of us say "*tfou, tfou, tfou*," or use phrases such as "*keine horah*" or "*beli ayin ha-ra*" (Yiddish and Hebrew expressions meaning "without the Evil Eye") without thinking, knowing that they can do no harm. We use them because they are embedded in the linguistic tradition of our culture, not because we believe in demonic powers or believe for a moment that they help or protect us. When a grandmother receives a compliment about her grandchildren, she may respond automatically with "*tfou, tfou, tfou*," or an expression to keep away the Evil Eye, showing that she is aware that her good luck in having such wonderful family could suddenly turn. In the past, most Jews feared that good luck could raise the Evil Eye, which could take the form of other people's jealousy or some other type of harm. The modern Jewish grandmother is unlikely to think about the Evil Eye in particular, but she may nevertheless use such phrases in her daily vocabulary because she grew up with them.

The magic circle is similarly engrained in Jewish folklore. The protective custom of circling the room of a newborn baby with an iron blade has just about died out now, but wedding guests still sometimes circle the newly married couple, and participants at a burial sometimes circle the dead body.[17]

Many Jews display an amulet in their home, business, or baby's crib, without necessarily believing that the amulet is really protective. They continue a tradition that can do no harm.

When Have Jews Used Theurgy or Magic to Cope with Worry?

Worried Jews usually use magical or theurgical practices in the hope of doing good and only rarely to harm those whom they fear. Mostly, they have used them to protect people in dangerous situations, especially in situations of long-lasting worry, such as when on a journey, in the event of severe illness, and during childbirth.

They have also employed magical methods to protect themselves from harm when all is well, even when they felt unusually happy, as a preventive against their luck turning. For example, Jews traditionally increased their protective precautions on a wedding night and during the week after the birth of a baby so that the happy bride and groom and the healthy newborn baby would not be harmed by the Evil Eye. Today, as mentioned above, many continue to decorate their premises and vehicles with protective amulets in the hope of protecting themselves from any misfortune.

The Talmud relates that several of the sages in late antiquity used the force of their powerful gaze to hurt and kill people who threatened their authority.[18] These men acted in this way because they were worried. Jews have occasionally cast a curse to harm a dangerous person, as we will see below.

On occasion, worried Jews attempted theurgy or magic when they wanted to hasten redemption. For example, the Italian kabbalist Moshe Hayyim Luzzatto, author of a popular ethical treatise, believed that he was the reincarnation of Moses and would redeem his people from their exile. In 1735, he was forced to leave Italy on account of his alleged messianic and magical activity. In 1814, Yakov Itzhak, the "Seer of Lublin," together with two other Hasidim, engaged in a theurgical effort to bring about the coming of the Messiah. Their effort failed and they all died within a year of their attempt.[19]

Some Jews secured an amulet for other worries too, such as to gain "grace and favor," that is, social acceptance with a certain family, or among business associates, or government officials. Others have whispered Psalms and magical incantations, for example, in the hope of freeing a man from prison, winning a court case, or harming an unpleasant neighbor.[20]

How Have Jews Used Theurgy and Magic to Cope with Worry?

We will now look at the most common tools of Jewish magic and theurgy—the biblical verses, Divine Names, and adjurations that Jews have recited to cope with worry. We will also look at their practice of inscribing these on protective amulets, often inside magical circles, squares, and stars for extra power. We will focus on the most common ways that Jews have used these tools to prevent or cope with worry, but not on the less popular behaviors of astrological divination, geomancy, or chiromancy, although on occasion some Jews used these techniques too. Necromancy has been discussed in earlier chapters and will not be repeated here, although it is, of course, a form of divinatory magic. This is a sampling, and not a comprehensive review of Jewish magic and theurgy.

By Using Biblical Verses and Divine Names

In antiquity, Near Eastern peoples bound protective devices on their arms and foreheads and inscribed their door lintels with protective signs. Jews inscribed biblical verses instead of pagan magical markings. Deuteronomy instructs men to bind the *Shema* prayer and the subsequent words about love for God on their hands and foreheads and, in addition, to inscribe these words on their doorposts and gateposts (*mezuzzot beitekha ve-sha'areikha*) (Deut. 6:4–9, 11:13–21). Archaeologists who excavated the Dead Sea Scrolls found ancient tefillin (phylacteries)—small leather boxes containing biblical verses on parchment—that date from the first century of the Christian era. The parchments in these boxes are inscribed with a variety of biblical verses, rather than identical biblical passages, suggesting that these objects may have served personal needs, for protection from harm, or for remedying a specific worry.[21]

In addition to writing such verses on parchment, Jews have often recited certain verses and Divine Names when they are worried, in the belief that they bear spiritual power. Divine Names are taken from biblical references to God, or are formed by permuting or combining letters in one or more biblical verses.

Mezuzzot and Tefillin   Jews have followed the injunction of Deuteronomy literally. The mezuzzah and tefillin are ritual objects, not amulets, that provide a permanent symbol of God's presence and the Jew's faith in God, reminding Jews of their personal bond with God. Yet Jews have long assumed that the words of Torah carry divine power, and that by binding them on themselves and putting them on their doorposts, they would be protected from harm by the spiritual force of the words.[22]

Jews have made sure that these objects are expertly made. Only a pious man with special training can make them flawlessly, on kosher parchment, in purity. Any flaw renders them useless for religious ritual and for protection. The skilled scribe writes out the designated biblical verses on a carefully prepared parchment, which is then rolled up and inserted into a tube, forming the mezuzzah that is fixed to the doorpost.[23]

The Talmud tells us that the head of the rabbinic academy of Sura sent a mezuzzah as a gift more precious than any jewel to the friendly Parthian king, promising that it would protect him. The Talmud also says that children will die in Jewish homes that do not have a mezuzzah on the doorpost. Furthermore, the Talmud states that a man who puts a mezuzzah on his doorpost and tefillin on his arms and head will be fortified against sinning. Such statements may well be a means of reinforcing Jewish law, but Jews have also understood them literally, as testimonials of the protective qualities of these items.[24]

The Babylonian Talmud remarks that Michal, daughter of King Saul, wore tefillin and the sages did not object. She was a luckless woman with reasons for worrying. David, the man she loved, had endangered his life to pay her father's bride-price of one hundred Philistine foreskins, but later, in David's absence, Saul gave her to another man. Reunited with David, she jeered at him and aroused his anger. She died childless. We wonder why the Babylonian sages assumed that this woman of antiquity wore tefillin. Did they perhaps believe that she wore them to profit from their special, spiritual power, to fortify her and help her gain protection from sin? (However, the Jerusalem Talmud does cite an objection to Michal's wearing tefillin.)[25]

Toward the end of the gaonic period, mezuzzah parchments began to acquire clear amuletic features. Three letters, forming the word *Shaddai,* were written on the back of the parchment. The letters form the initials of *shomer delatot Israel,* "guardian of the doors of Israel," although the word itself is a name for the Almighty. Jews have considered this word especially potent for keeping demons away and have frequently inscribed it on amulets. Some medieval Jews in France and Germany added also a magical three-word name, made by permuting the opening text of the mezuzzah verses, and even decorated the whole of the reverse side of the parchment with magic pentagrams, hexagrams, and the names of angels. Instructions for making a mezuzzah resembled those for making amulets: scribes took into account planetary influences, believing that certain hours were more auspicious than others.[26]

Rashi, the leading commentator on the Bible and Talmud who lived in the eleventh century, warned that the mezuzzah had to be properly attached to the doorpost for a house to be protected from demons. And in the thirteenth century, Rabbi Meir of Rothenburg, who boasted some twenty-four *mezuzzot* in his house, observed that some Jews who were slack in observing the biblical injunction were perhaps unaware of its effectiveness in keeping demonic harm out of the home. It is told that an evil spirit tormented this rabbi during his midday nap, until he fixed a mezuzzah on the doorpost of the room in which he rested. From then on, he was no longer disturbed.[27]

In the late fourteenth century, the bishop of Salzburg asked for a mezuzzah to put on the gate of his castle, hoping to enjoy its protective qualities. The rabbi refused.[28]

Maimonides sanctioned only the word *Shaddai* on the reverse of the parchment, vigorously condemned the magical additions that transformed a biblical commandment into an amulet, and forbade the giving of a mezuzzah to non-Jews. By the fifteenth century, his condemnation of magical additions to *mezuzzot* had won out; only the word *Shaddai* remained on the reverse side of the parchment.[29]

Jews nevertheless continued to believe in the protective powers of the mezuzzah. Thus, for example, in the sixteenth century, when an Ashkenazic community was decimated by the plague, its leaders inspected the *mezuzzot* on the doorposts to discover those that were improperly written or damaged and therefore responsible for the harmful visitation. Legend tells that a person in Safed who repeatedly suffered from demonic possession became well when a mezuzzah was fixed to the doorpost.[30]

Kurdistani Jews tell that a midwife once saw a demon attempting to harm a birthing woman. When the new father heard of this, he suspected that the *mezuzzot* in the house were imperfect and had lost their power to keep out demons. He checked them all and indeed found some that needed replacing. Worried Jews regularly checked the *mezuzzot* in the villages of Eastern Europe to make sure that evil spirits would not enter their homes. During the First World War, some Jewish soldiers carried a mezuzzah in their pockets to protect against harm from the enemy. A few years ago, a well-meaning Israeli lady suggested that a friend check the *mezuzzot* on his house after a nasty car crash.[31]

For most Jews today, there is nothing magical or theurgical in their tefillin and *mezuzzot*. These ritual objects now serve only as a daily reminder of their faith.

Divine Names   The Torah uses many names when referring to God in addition to the Tetragrammaton, the four lettered Divine Name. As Jewish law proscribes pronunciation of these four letters, Jews enunciate other Divine Names, such as *Shaddai, Adonai,* and *Elohim.* There are also esoteric Divine Names. The forty-two-letter Divine Name was created by permuting and combining the letters of the Tetragrammaton. Other Names were formed from certain biblical verses, for example, the twenty-two-letter Name (numerically equivalent to Num. 6:24–25) and the seventy-two-letter Name (by permuting certain letters in Exod. 14:19–21).[32]

In the first century B.C.E., Hillel warned of the mortal danger of making use of the "Crown," probably a Divine Name. This warning was soon interpreted as relating to the danger of using a Divine Name for personal purposes instead of for the good of the community.[33]

A favorite protective prayer, *anna be-kho'ah,* asking for God's support and protection, is based on the forty-two-letter Divine Name. Often used in protective incantations and on amulets, this prayer was attributed to a first-century sage, Nehunya ben Ha-Kanah, the teacher of Rabbi Ishmael (mentioned in chapter 4), but was probably composed only in the thirteenth century by a Spanish kabbalist.[34]

According to Jewish legend, Joseph della Reina, who may have been a late fifteenth-century Spanish kabbalist, uttered the Divine Name in an attempt to overthrow the demonic powers of Christianity—the Spanish Inquisition—and bring about redemption. This legend acknowledged the strong desire of many worried Jews to destroy the power of the church. In 1519, Della Reina's effort was reported to have failed because he burned incense—an idolatrous practice—during his magical act. A few decades later, a sage in Safed was said to have recognized Della Reina's soul in the body of a black dog and knew this reincarnation was the punishment for his sin. These additions to the legend were cautions for those who might be tempted to emulate the magician.[35]

In 1648, Samson of Ostropol manipulated Divine Names to try to stop the Cossack pogroms in the Ukraine and save the Jews. This is fact and not a legend. This Polish rabbi believed that the Divine Names that were numerically equivalent to the names of evil forces had the power to annul the evil forces. He apparently wrote down his magical secrets in case others after him would need to use them to conquer the demonic force of Christianity. He believed that 1648 was the year predicted by the Zohar for the coming of the Messiah, and that he himself could help to bring this about with his theurgical acts, even if he died in the process. He was said to have conjured the demon in charge of the forces of evil, with the intention of overwhelming him and his forces with the power of the Holy Names—but he failed.[36]

Some doctors who were well read in Kabbalah, such as Hayyim Vital and Joseph ben Tirshom, who both practiced in Damascus in the sixteenth century, combined and permuted Divine Names and biblical verses to treat their worried patients. Few reliable facts are known about Eastern European masters of the Divine Name, such as Eliyahu of Chelm (d. 1583), Joel of Zamosc (d. 1703), and Binyamin Binesh of Krotoszyn (d. early eighteenth century). Kabbalists in North Africa and all over the Middle East wrote combinations and permutations of Divine Names and biblical verses on protective amulets.[37]

Biblical Verses   The discovery of the Priestly Blessing (Num. 6:24–26) inscribed on two silver amulets in a burial cave near Jerusalem, dating from the sixth century B.C.E., suggests that these verses were used as a protective formula. Jews have recited this special blessing in incantations and inscribed it on amulets for protection in times of worry.[38]

Before electricity was invented, going out in the dark of night was especially scary. Jews recited the *Shema* prayer and Psalm 91, sometimes with added protective magical formulas, to banish their fears. For example, a ninth-century prayer book recommends that the worried traveler invoke angels for divine protection after his prayer: "On my right, El, on my left, Uziel, in front of me, Nemuel, and behind me, Shashiel; the *Shekhinah* above my head, save me, Lord, from evil affliction and from satanic harm."[39]

Psalm 91 (known as the "song of afflictions," or the "song of plagues" from verses 7 and 10) protects against evil spirits, according to the Talmud. Similarly, Gen. 49:22 ("Joseph is a fruitful bough . . ."), combined with a certain rude gesture of the hand, and Gen. 48:16 ("And may they be teeming multitudes upon the earth") protect against the Evil Eye. When reciting these verses of Genesis, which were part of Jacob's blessing, a Jew invoked Joseph's immunity from the Eye, which was handed down to his descendants.[40]

Jewish women have repeated Exod. 11:8 (". . . 'Depart, you and all the people who follow you!' After that I will depart . . .") as a "tried and proved" birth incantation for easing delivery, and eventually incorporated this verse into the texts of prayers recited by birth helpers. This could be a plain request to God to enable a quick departure of the baby from the womb, just as the Jews made their exodus from Egypt. It could also be an address to the evil spirits: Once all these had left the area, the baby could be delivered safely. *Sefer Razi'el* similarly noted as "tried and proved" the recommendation to write an adjuration on deer parchment, including permutations of the Aramaic word *puk*, meaning "get out" or "come out," and tying it to the birthing woman's navel while whispering the verse of Exod. 11:8.[41]

Psalm 67 ("May God be gracious to us and bless us . . .") is a favorite for promoting spiritual strength. Isaac Arama, a fifteenth-century Spanish rabbi, assumed that King David's shield, *Magen David*, was not the hexagram that we think of today, but Psalm 67 written in the shape of a menorah (a candelabra). The warrior allegedly meditated on the mystery of this psalm before going into battle and conquering the enemy. Jews have attributed great protective power to this "menorah psalm," which often decorates protective amulets.[42]

By Using Amulets and Other Objects Bearing Magical Power

The Mishnah forbids the use of pagan amulets, but allows Jews to use amulets made by an "expert," a man with specialized knowledge and experience in making approved amulets. The Talmud explains that a Jew is permitted to go out of the house wearing an amulet that has been issued by such an expert and has proved effective at least three times, an amulet that has been "tried and proved to work" (Shabbat 6:2; B. *Shabbat* 61a–61b). Many Jewish amulets are undoubtedly the work of an expert, made on kosher parchment, fresh pottery, clean metal, stone, or cloth, and carefully inscribed with Divine Names, biblical verses, and supplications, according to ancient formulas that are known to have been proved successful. However, Jews have also used amulets that are non-expert copies and, sometimes, charms culled from local, pagan magic. Instead of relying solely on the power of Hebrew letters, these rely on magical powers attributed to the animal, vegetable, or mineral substance from which they are made.

Amuletic bowls, which people may have drunk from, hoping to imbibe the power of the words inscribed on them, were excavated in Iraq at the site of Nippur, in ancient Mesopotamia, and date from the sixth to the eighth centuries C.E. Biblical verses, the forty-two-letter Divine Name, and adjurations inscribed in the Aramaic of Babylonian Jews demand protection against the Evil Eye, child-killing female demons, and evil spirits that bring nightmares and sickness. The names of the person(s) requiring protection and sometimes a legend about the feared evil power are written concentrically around the inside of the bowl. The long text on one bowl restrains all demons by pronouncing them "bound," preventing them from taking evil action. This text ends with a quotation from Song of Songs: "Encircled by sixty warriors of the warriors of Israel, all of them trained in warfare, skilled in battle, each with sword on thigh, because of terror by night" (3:7–8). This biblical verse suggests that this particular amuletic bowl served to protect against demonic danger in the dark of night. Jews who feared demons believed that they were most dangerous at night, when they could not be seen.[43]

An amulet dating from the Middle Ages, preserved in the Cairo Genizah, was made for a man named Yehudah ben Simhah, apparently as an antidote to anxiety. It starts with the formulaic "May it be your will, O Lord" followed by a Divine Name, *Ehyeh-Asher-Ehyeh* ("I am that I am," Exod. 3:14). It requests that God guard and sustain this man "from the Evil Eye, from evil spirits, from every enemy and adversary, and from fear, trembling, terror, shaking, anguish, and from pain, discomfort, headache, faintheartedness, and pains of the heart." The amulet continues with invocations of the forty-two-letter and twenty-two-letter Divine Names, protective angels, a protective hexagram with magical inscriptions within it, and repeated requests for protection against the woes already mentioned. Like the bowls, it calls on a large repertoire of Jewish magic in the hope that the combined power of the Divine Names, the verses, invocations, and adjurations will indeed prevent Yehudah from worrying.[44]

A Jewish man worried about being physically attacked could find a formula for making a protective amulet against the harm of any weapon in a popular kabbalistic book, *Sefer Razi'el*. Here he is told to copy on a kosher deer parchment the names of certain angels, specific Divine Names and biblical verses, angel script (letter-like figures whose meaning is unknown today), and hexagrams with the Tetragrammaton inscribed within. He should carry this parchment on him (folded or rolled into a small casing) hanging on a necklace.[45]

Toldot Adam, a remedy book first published in Zolkiew in Galicia, in 1720, offers advice for making an amulet to use on board ship, for those anxious about a maritime journey. The advice is attributed to Nahmanides, a thirteenth-century rabbi, philosopher, and kabbalist, and promises that when the amulet is tied to the boat's mast, the vessel will sail quickly, without mishap, in the desired direction. However, the book insists that the amulet be prepared in great holiness; the expert must first purify himself with many immersions in the ritual bath. *Toldot Adam* notes a report by Tzvi Hirsch, a seventeenth-century Polish kabbalist that claims that Joel Ba'al Shem used the amulet in 1648, when many Jews fled the Chmielnicki massacres by boat and were chased over the water by the Cossacks. The boat with the amulet went wondrously fast and escaped the enemy. The evidence that this advice has been tried and proved to work was important in influencing other worried people to make use of this amulet on a sea voyage.[46]

Since the eighteenth century, and still today, some amulets have invoked Meir, "the miracle worker." Rabbi Meir was a second-century halakhist who studied with Rabbi Akiva, Rabbi Ishmael, and Elisha ben Avuyah (mentioned in chapter 4). Legend tells that Meir once threw some stones at some man-eating dogs. When they charged at him he merely called out, "O God of Meir, answer me!" and they turned away. Some amulets carry a final pleading inscription: "Answer me, God of Rabbi Meir, the miracle worker. Answer me!" Another inscription at the end of some amulets pleads, "For the merit of the holy Rabbi Meir 'the miracle worker,' may this person be protected from now and forever more."[47]

Legend tells that one day a rabbi accused the Ba'al Shem Tov, literally the "Master of the Good Name," of making improper use of

God's Name. He denied the accusation and promised that he only used his own name when making amulets. A personalized amulet, given by a trusted *tzaddik,* was a permanent symbol of the holy man's pledge to help the worried person, a personal bond between himself and that person.[48]

In the nineteenth and early twentieth centuries, many amulets used in the Diaspora were made in Jerusalem, which had remained a center of kabbalistic activity for several hundred years. Many Jews believed that an amulet from there carried the added spiritual power of the holy city and the Holy Land, even when it was printed on a press and not handmade by a ritually pure expert. Thus, for example, amulets from the Holy Land to promote love and peace within the home (and avoid marital tension) were especially popular in Morocco.[49]

An amulet to protect a home from fire, found recently in the Republic of Georgia, but made in Jerusalem in 1874, tells that a Jew named Joseph Eligoulashvili had been saved by its power at the time of a fire in his town. Such an amulet, that had been tried and proved effective, was copied and used by others who feared fire, which was common where houses were built of wood and their inhabitants went to bed by candlelight. The amulet adjures the angels guarding the divine realm to protect Eligoulashvili's house. It names at least two hundred angels. It also includes four stars of David enclosed in magical circles containing the initial letters of protective biblical verses and is decorated with *menorot,* trees, and pictures of holy sites in the Holy Land.[50]

A parchment amulet was made sometime in the first half of the twentieth century, in Italy, specifically for an anxious Jewish woman, Carolina, daughter of Hannah. It was made to protect her from illness, pain, distress, sorrow, and harm. In addition, it ensured that she would always have a clear mind and not be disturbed by bad thoughts or confused by distressing dreams and fantasies. It cited verses from the Priestly Blessing, invoked the Tetragrammaton, *Shaddai,* and the protective angels Michael, Gabriel, Raphael, and Nuriel. It was decorated with a drawing of the menorah and the hexagram.

Another twentieth-century parchment amulet was made for an anxious man to protect him against all that he feared, requesting that the Good Inclination (and never the Evil Inclination) should always rule over him and that he might find an income. This amulet carries the *Shema* prayer and an adjuration to banish bad thoughts and protect the bearer's heart from distress.[51]

Many Judaica collections contain such amulets. While these examples are handmade and personalized, Jews have also mass-produced amulets, hoping that their magical inscriptions would offer protection and believing that they would in any case do no harm.

Magical Circles, Stars, and Squares   Just as Honi stood in a circle to increase the power of his prayer, Jews sometimes inscribed biblical verses or Divine Names inside a circle for extra power, as in some of the amulets just described. Sometimes they created a protective circle to ward off demonic harm.[52]

Jews have often used the hexagram, too, in their protective magic. The magical seal in the form of a hexagram was known as the "seal of Solomon." In Jewish magic, as in early Christian and Arab magic, it was associated with the ancient king whose wisdom was legendary. Sometimes it is created out of a Divine Name, or with such a Name written within its lines. Jews in Arab lands, especially, have used this symbol for extra power on their amulets. For example, a remedy book used by Moroccan Jews promises that whoever carries this seal will be protected from harm and distress. Sometimes the seal of Ashmedai (Asmodeus) is drawn on the amulet, since according to talmudic legend, it was this demon king who taught Solomon his knowledge of magic.[53]

In twelfth-century Germany, the *Magen David,* the "shield of David," was a magical shield created out of the seventy-two-letter Divine Name with four Hebrew letters in the center. In the fourteenth century, the *Magen David* took the form of a hexagram, inscribed with a Name. Since then, protective amulets have often carried an inscribed hexagram.[54]

In addition, Jews have inscribed the Hebrew letters of Divine Names and biblical verses in magical squares, again in the hope of extra power. For example, amulets sometimes carry a three-by-three square with the Hebrew letters of the Name *Shaddai* in all their per-mutations and combinations. Alternatively, the square might contain the letters that represent the numbers one to nine, with number five, *he* (a symbol for God's Name), in the center. Each row, column, and diagonal adds up to fifteen, and the Hebrew letters, *yod, he,* form a Divine Name. An amulet to protect a person from nightmares, for example, might have a four-by-four magic square with the four initial letters of Psalm 91:5 ("You need not fear the terror by night") written into each row and column. In the mid–eighteenth century, Rabbi Jonathan Eybeschutz allegedly created a sort of magic square using the initial letters of the Hebrew phrase that says "the people of Israel lives forever and ever." He wrote this special square on a parchment the size of a mezuzzah and, it is told, thereby averted an anti-Semitic decree to excommunicate all the Jews in his city.[55]

Ritual Articles   In November 1827, Sir Moses Montefiore, the British philanthropist, was on a ship on his way home from Jerusalem. He wrote in his diary that for some days there had been gales and a heavy sea, and particularly dark clouds continued to threaten the ship's safety. "A little before noon, I threw into the sea a small piece of my last year's Passover cake, laid by on the evening of the Haggadah, supplicating the Almighty to protect us and to avert the coming tempest, likewise to tranquilize the still troubled ocean." He noted in the evening that "it is with the warmest gratitude I humbly acknowledge the Almighty's kind interposition on our be-half. The clouds which appeared to everyone on board so dreadfully threatening during the morning have, as it were by a miracle, dis-persed and, instead of their pouring their fury upon us, the sea also became every hour more and more tranquil."[56]

Montefiore apparently believed that the spiritual power of the Passover *afikoman* transferred to the sea with the help of his prayer. Montefiore was not original in employing a small piece of the Passover bread to calm the sea. This must have been a well-known charm in his day among those who traveled to and from the Holy Land, as it is writ-ten down in remedy books together with the details of the particular verses of Psalms that should be recited in the prayer to calm the sea.[57]

Jews have also employed other ritual objects in times of danger to gain spiritual power. The Torah cover, *parokhet,* for example, could be laid over someone in serious danger. Sometimes a person drank water from the cup-shaped Torah finials, the *rimonim* that crown the staves of the scroll, to gain strength. And some women who feared dying in childbirth kept the *etrog,* the citron used ritually during Sukkot, the Festival of the Tabernacles, to use as a charm for easing delivery.[58]

Afghanistani Jews keep a beautifully carved walking stick for when the Prophet Elijah should visit. As long as the Prophet has not come, they use this stick for protecting and healing the weak, believing it to have special spiritual properties. Similarly, Moroccan Jews have preserved the belt of an eighteenth-century *tzaddik,* which is also used by worriers for added spiritual strength.[59]

In Israel today, we often see a person wearing a red thread tied around the wrist. This thread, called a *bendel* (the Yiddish word for a little ribbon), is a good luck charm that can be purchased from religious hawkers by the Wailing Wall, Rachel's tomb, and near the Safed cemetery where the great sixteenth-century kabbalists are buried. A century ago it was customary for a Jewish woman to take a red thread and measure it around Rachel's tomb, so that it could absorb some of the holiness of the site. In Eastern Europe, Jews visited the grave of a *tzaddik* and measured the tombstone with a special string that they tore up afterward to serve as wicks for candles that they lit in the synagogue. Both customs assume that the spiritual power of the holy person buried in the tomb transfers to the thread or string as it touches the tomb. The person wearing the *bendel* hopes to benefit from the good deeds of the holy person buried in the tomb. The Jew who burned the wicks in synagogue in Eastern Europe made use of the same principle to gain spiritual strength in the face of a particular worry.[60]

By Adjuring Spirits

Since earliest times, Jews have believed in spirits—pure spirits and demonic spirits—that are free to move and convey information between the human world on Earth and the divine world above. We have already mentioned the biblical story in which the worried Saul persuades a woman to conjure up spirits to discover his future. Jews have sometimes engaged in conjuring spirits when worried, even though the Bible prohibits this behavior. The Bible also says that an evil spirit entered Saul and his heart trembled with fear. Jews have often assumed that an expert can exorcise such an evil spirit that causes anxiety, as we will see below. Also, some Jews have adjured angels of destruction to harm an enemy.

The "Princes" and the "Sword"   The Bible tells us that Joseph hid a silver cup in his brother's bag, a cup that could be used for divination as well as for drinking. Was Joseph a skilled diviner who conjured an angel in his cup? The Bible leads us to understand, rather, that his wisdom was a divine gift. Talmudic lore tells us that the angel Gabriel, God's messenger, taught Joseph seventy languages so that he could rule Egypt. A medieval Jewish amulet depicts Joseph adjuring this angel to reveal magical secrets, including the seventy languages and the seventy Names of God.[61]

Whether or not Joseph engaged in conjuring an angel in a cup to reveal desired information, this behavior was very common in ancient Egypt, Babylonia, and classical Greece. This divination requires a polished or reflective surface, such as a cup of water with a layer of oil on top, a piece of glasslike crystal, or a mirror. Alternatively, a knife, a polished fingernail, or the palm of the hand smeared with soot and oil would serve the same purpose. A child, usually about nine years old, would look intensely at the polished surface reflecting the sunlight until something appeared to be visible in it. An adult would hold the child and whisper the names of angels repetitively into first one ear and then the other until the child gained a vision of the "princes" in the mirror-like surface. The adult, who could not see the vision, would then tell the child what to ask the "princes." The child would focus intensely on the vision and report the "princes'" message to the adult. Finally, the adult would tell the child to dismiss the vision so that it disappears.[62]

The talmudic sages ruled that "it is permitted to inquire of the 'princes of oil' and the 'princes of eggs,' but [one does not do so because] they give false answers" (B. *Sanhedrin* 101a). The Hebrew word for "princes," *sarim,* is possibly a misreading of *shedim,* meaning "demons," as the words look very similar in Hebrew. However, the fact that the "princes" might give false answers did not deter worried Jews from summoning them.

We have seen (in chapters 4 and 5) that mystics adjured angels to do as they wanted. The *sar ha-panim* ("Prince of the Divine Presence") adjuration, which Rabbi Akiva allegedly learned from Rabbi Eliezer, is the most famous. It entails an invocation ("I call on you [angel] . . . "), a statement of the mystic's goal, an adjuration ("I adjure you . . . "), a list of secret names, and concludes with a formula for dismissing the angel that performed the mystic's will. Two other formulas, the "Great Seal" and the "Terrible Crown," were attributed to Nehunya ben Ha-Kanah, Rabbi Ishmael's teacher. The association of these formulas with Rabbi Eliezer and Rabbi Nehunya gave them a tradition and legitimacy.[63]

Legends about angels that conveyed desired information to the ancients legitimized attempts to induce and adjure angels and spirits. For example, legend tells us that the angel Raphael (the angel of healing) gave medical secrets to Noah, and the angel Razi'el (*raz,* "secret," *-el,* "divine") supposedly revealed secrets about the universe to Adam. A magical text, probably of Babylonian origin and dating from the talmudic period, explains that angels revealed esoteric information to Moses, including the "Sword." This Sword is mentioned in the patriarch's last words: "O happy Israel! . . . A people delivered by the Lord, Your protecting Shield, your Sword triumphant" (Deut. 33:29). The magical text promises that this Sword can be used to fulfill every wish, reveal every secret, and perform every miracle. A man who wants to use this Sword, the text insists, must first undergo ritual purification, secretly retire from the world so that no one knows his intentions, pray, and recite a special blessing. The text then explains how to conjure up various angels using magical Names. The adept who masters this technique can use the Sword in many worrying situations: for protection, to remedy an ill, for divination, and to harm an enemy, by following advice in the text.[64]

Jews summoned the "princes" to find out the identity of a thief or the whereabouts of stolen property or to learn about the coming of the Messiah—an event that would put an end to all worries—as well as to gain information for other reasons. In the Middle Ages, Rashi explained that a black-handled knife is necessary to invoke the "princes of the thumbnail." The Ashkenazic pietists summoned spirits in the reflection of a cup or a thumb. Hayyim Vital consulted a woman who used this method to verify a dream that predicted that Vital would lead the Jews to redemption from Islam and Christianity. In 1730, a glass mirror in a black casing, as well as a black-handled knife, a black candle, and a book of incantations were allegedly found among the belongings of the messianic kabbalist, Moshe Hayyim Luzzatto. In addition, Yemenite, North African, Italian, and Sephardic remedy books, dating from the fifteenth century onward, advised summoning spirits to appear in the reflection of a cup or oily surface and reveal information related to their worries. Elderly Jews who immigrated to Israel from southern Morocco in the mid–twentieth century continued to practice this form of divination in Israel for some years.[65]

Ritual Banishment of Evil Spirits We have already seen that some Jews assumed that a pure spirit from a divine source can enter the soul of a righteous person and reveal divine secrets. By the same reasoning, a demonic spirit can enter anyone who is not righteous, and cause anxiety and severe disturbances of the imagination. The treatment for such demonic possession traditionally requires that an adept adjure the harmful spirit to leave the body of the afflicted person.

In late antiquity, Josephus Flavius wrote that an exorcist named Eleazar had cured men possessed by demons by putting under their noses a ring whose seal hid certain names prescribed by Solomon. The "Sword of Moses" could also be written on an amulet for use against a spirit that had entered a person's body. Similarly, an amulet from post-talmudic Palestine invokes the ring of Solomon and the rod of Moses to expel an evil spirit; both the ring and rod would have been engraved with the Divine Name.[66]

Medieval Ashkenazic Jews believed that evil spirits follow God's decrees and therefore there is no human protection or remedy for demonic harm. Nevertheless, from the sixteenth century onward, some rabbis uttered powerful prayers and blew on a shofar to expel a harmful demon from a miserable person. According to the Zohar, blowing the shofar overpowers the forces of evil.[67]

In Safed, in 1571, a rabbi reported a frightening eyewitness account of the plight of a poor woman who was possessed by the soul of a sinful Jew, which had turned into a demon. In front of some one hundred spectators, including rabbis and heads of communities, two men familiar with incantations addressed the demon, demanding to know its name and provenance. The voice told them who he had been and that he had sinned many sins. When he died, his soul was not admitted to heaven or Gehenna, and had wandered restlessly from place to place ever since. The voice said that he had visited this woman before, but she had then adorned herself with protective amulets that prevented him from returning to her. But one day she did not wear the amulets and he entered her again. In a loud, stormy voice the demon assured them that he wanted to be freed from the woman by the men's prayers and the blowing of the shofar, but he could not. The two men exhorted the demon to leave through one of the woman's big toes and then prove to those present that he had in fact left by extinguishing the light of a candle burning in the room. However, the demon did not leave, and the woman remained possessed until her death eight days later. According to the report, the demon had strangled her and departed with her soul.[68]

Hayyim Vital, who was living in Safed at the time, reported that he once interrogated a demon who had invaded a woman's soul and who revealed that he entered her as a punishment for her evil thoughts; she had lost her faith in Providence and in God's miracles. Tearfully, the woman promised to do whatever Vital ordered. He exorcised the demon, who escaped through her big toenail.[69]

Most Jewish reports of demonic possession presumed that the sick person was a sinner. Eastern European Jews used the Yiddish word *dybbuk* for a sinful soul destined, after the sinner had died, to transmigrate from body to body instead of reposing in heaven. Demonic possession became the popular diagnosis for anxiety-related illnesses such as hysteria and what we now call schizophrenia, as well as epilepsy.[70]

The Vilna kabbalist, Pinhas Elijah (c. 1742–1821) wrote that it was customary (in his time) to attribute mental problems to a *dybbuk* and call on a *ba'al shem* for a cure. This scholar maintained, however, that many patients apparently possessed by demons in fact suffered from disturbances of the imagination owing to physical causes that could be treated by conventional medicine.[71]

From the eighteenth to the early twentieth century, some wonder-working rabbis published accounts of their casting out of demons that had invaded the bodies of unfortunate people. Thus, for example, there is a story that the Ba'al Shem Tov released the *dybbuk* of an irreverent Hasid who possessed a woman, speaking with a male voice through her mouth. Another story tells that the Hasidic "Seer of Lublin" released a *dybbuk* that was putting words in the mouth of a poor, anguished Jew. The possessed man collapsed, the little toe of his left foot swelled up, and, with a puff, the *dybbuk* escaped through the open window.[72]

Holy men in Iraq, North Africa, and Yemen similarly gained reputations for exorcising demons in the nineteenth and early twentieth centuries. They uttered incantations and wrote protective amulets for worried Jews. In Baghdad, Rabbi Yehudah Petayah gained a reputation for curing people from fear caused by demons. He wrote Hebrew letters on a very thin and tiny slip of paper that the sufferer could swallow by drinking from a glass of water. Iraqi Jews had a special name for fear caused by a demonic attack—*tarkah*. (*Matruk* refers to someone who is in a state of shock from such an attack). North African Jews, too, had a special name for demonic possession—*tesayera*.[73]

From the early nineteenth century onward, some enlightened, rationalist Ashkenazic Jews ridiculed the concept of the *dybbuk* and tried to put an end to exorcism. In the early twentieth century, S. An-ski, a Russian and Yiddish author and ethnographer, dramatized the exorcism of a *dybbuk* for the stage, annoying some Hasidic rabbis who remained convinced of the real danger of demonic possession.[74]

In 1913, Freud drew a parallel between the belief that a dearly loved relative changes into a harmful demon and the neurosis that he noticed in a wife who had lost her husband and in a daughter who had lost a parent. He reasoned that demons, like such neurosis, are only creations of the human mind, projections of people's unconscious hostile wishes and emotional impulses. He believed that the woman's neurosis and the complaint of demonic possession are both acts of self-defense to hostile emotion, their unconscious wish for the death of a recently departed loved one.[75]

A Recent Case   In Jerusalem, on April 22, 1999, Rabbi David Batzri, the grandson of Rabbi Petayah of Baghdad, exorcised a *dybbuk* from an Indian-born Jewish woman named Yehudit. Batzri studied Kabbalah, became interested in mental health, and often visits patients in psychiatric hospitals. He has specialized in performing *tikkunim,* reparations for repentant sinners desiring to "return" to the religious way of life (*teshuvah,* see chapter 3). He has worked with homosexuals, adulterers, barren women, and anorexics.

Yehudit lives in Dimona, Israel. At the age of eighteen she married Pinhas and in the following years bore him six children. Pinhas was unemployed and spent all the money she earned from cleaning jobs on drink. Sometimes he forced her to give him even her housekeeping money. When her husband lay dying in the hospital, Yehudit found religion helpful. She began to attend meetings for the newly Orthodox and traveled to rabbis to receive blessings, comfort, and help. She learned about spiritual life after death and that those souls that are too sinful to enter heaven or Gehenna are cast about between the worlds by the slings of destructive angels. After her husband died, Yehudit began to have fainting spells, during which the voice of a man came out of her throat, identifying itself as Pinhas.

On one occasion, frightened witnesses called Yehudit's sister. The sister, who had not believed the reports of what was happening to Yehudit, found her sister lying in a faint. Yehudit's sister touched Yehudit and asked her to wake up, but she lashed violently at her and a man's voice issued from her saying he wanted to take her, and demanding a *tikkun* for his soul and his son's recitation of the *Kaddish* prayer for the repose of his soul. Soon some yeshivah students heard about Yehudit's plight, became convinced that a demon had possessed her, and arranged for her transfer to Rabbi Batzri in Jerusalem.

In Jerusalem, she was put on a mattress in a room where there were some twenty rabbis. She was given a book of Psalms and told to read from it. Soon she trembled and appeared to faint and the male voice began to talk from within her. After a good hour, she "woke up" and was told that the *dybbuk* had left her through her little toe. In that hour, the rabbi talked to the voice and he and his colleagues recited prayers and blew on shofars. Finally the rabbi commanded the *dybbuk* to leave Yehudit (through her toe, of course).

Batzri later explained that her husband's soul had been slung about between the worlds since his death and decided to enter her body to allow her to perform a *tikkun* for his many sins. Finding refuge in his wife's body, he begged, through her mouth, for this reparation, so that his soul could rest in peace. The rabbi performed the mitzvah of granting *tikkun* to the miserable soul, thereby freeing Yehudit from the demonic possession. Now she could be free of worry about her husband's plight.

Batzri's exorcism was purposefully recorded by a video camera. The film was distributed and heavily advertised to warn the sinful about the fate of the soul after death and to teach that it is never too late to repent. (The tale of the Safed *dybbuk* was disseminated in the late sixteenth century for the same reasons.) However, Batzri did not foresee the consequences for poor Yehudit of the media exposure and the massive press response. She became too ashamed to show her face in public and went into hiding, with new worries in her mind.

By reciting psalms, Yehudit found she could alter her state of consciousness, just as Jewish mystics have done for many centuries (see chapter 4). They too recited or sang psalms until an angel or the soul of a deceased person spoke through their mouths. As Yehudit was constantly thinking of her dead husband, and not of angels, it was he who spoke through her mouth.

Yehudit was despairing, weak, perhaps also ashamed, isolated and confused. One psychologist commenting on her behavior diagnosed her—without meeting her, from journalistic reports only—as suffering from a "disturbed associative identity" reminiscent of a "multiple personality disorder," a hysterical syndrome produced by the "repression of part of her personality" or "some unfinished problem." Another psychologist pointed out that Yehudit was in great distress and found a way to attract attention and help: "She felt exceptional, unworthy, miserable, and poor." She missed her husband, but his unpleasant personality prevented her family from offering her sympathy for her grief at her loss. She wanted him to regret his sins and change. Consciously or unconsciously, she summoned him forth and secured his repentance in a socially accepted fashion.[76]

Had Yehudit asked for help from either of these psychologists, they would certainly have safeguarded her privacy. She would not have been treated for merely one session, however. She would have had to agree to many sessions of therapy to sort out her "unfinished problem" and "personality disorder." No psychologist would claim to cure her in one hour. In contrast, at the end of her session with the rabbi, he told her that the *dybbuk* had left.

Not only was the rabbi able to treat Yehudit in just one hour, his treatment was free, in contrast to most psychological treatment. Furthermore, Yehudit was told that she stood to gain from it financially, with the distribution of the videotapes.

Incapable of self-help, Yehudit needed someone powerful, with a reputation for success in helping those who suffer. She accepted the rabbi's proffered solution and hoped that it would relieve her suffering. Unfortunately, the attention paid to her story by the media overwhelmed her. Meanwhile, Batzri became famous and a religious party used the videotape for political gain in the national elections. Disillusioned by the rabbi's exploitation of her plight and the need to fight a legal battle to gain her share of the income from the videotapes, she now claims she is merely a good actress who knows how to reproduce her husband's voice at will.[77]

A Curse Just as Jews pray for and seek to draw down divine blessings for the good of another person, so too, on occasion, Jews have cursed in the hope of harming a dangerous person. In biblical times, cursing was a weapon of the oppressed; a slandered man may curse his slanderer. The Talmud mentions a case in which a father cursed his son, uttering the Divine Name, and the boy died. It warns that the curse of an ordinary person, as well as a sage's curse, should not be taken lightly and that an undeserved curse may fall back on whoever utters it.[78]

Just two days after Yom Kippur, 1995, some religious Jews gathered outside the home of Prime Minister Itzhak Rabin. Wrapped in prayer shawls, they uttered a curse, *pulsa de-nura* (in talmudic Aramaic, a "fiery lash"). The curse adjured the angels of destruction to kill the wicked Itzhak, son of Rosa. These religious Jews were severely worried by Rabin's peace agreement in Oslo. They thought that the only way of stopping the return of land to the Arabs was to kill the man who engineered the return. They believed that the curse would work within thirty days. After Rabin's murder, one month later, the leader of the group who had uttered the curse boasted of his prowess on Israeli television. The man who shot Rabin was jailed, but not the men in the prayer shawls.[79]

No rationalist person believes that Rabin died as a direct result of this curse, although those who uttered it certainly believe that they managed to influence supernatural forces to work in their favor. Because many Jews have believed in the destructive power of a curse, some rabbis wrote out a special formula for recitation in the synagogue, in front of the congregation, to release a person from a curse and cancel its power. It declares God's consent to consider the curse null and void.[80]

The Story of the Theurgical/Magical Act

There is no doubt that by wearing an amulet, reciting biblical verses, or consulting a *tzaddik* or a faith healer many Jews have found at least temporary relief from worry. The rationalist, of course, believes that the reason for this beneficial result is not the manipulation of supernatural forces, but a change in faith, perspective, or morale. The special act has to be performed so that the good result can take place, but the act itself may not be the cause of the benefit. If theurgy or magic works, the rationalist thinks, it is due to the fact that the worrier has been told that it works and expects it to do so. Thus the beneficial effect may be due to the confidence instilled by the adept or to the report of the feat, or both together.

Those who have practiced magic and theurgy have often made sure that their successes are publicized so that worriers would believe that these methods do really work. Just as the haters of Rabin boasted of their successful curse on television, so too those who have consulted tzaddikim and faith healers have boasted of their successes. Tales of wonder-working travel fast. It is probably not by mere chance that Honi's story has survived the ages. People like stories that end happily, stories with extraordinary, magical endings, Cinderella-like stories. Worried people want to believe that miracles can happen.

The Talmud tells many miracle tales, not only Honi's story, and there are wondrous legends about certain kabbalists. So, too, in the eighteenth century, Rabbi Jonathan Eybeschutz and his disciple, Samuel Essingen, spread tales of their amulets and miracle cures to enhance their reputations. Their contemporary, the Ba'al Shem Tov, allegedly instructed his disciples to disseminate tales about the miracles that he himself worked. However, one story in which Eybeschutz is the miracle worker is similar in theme and message to a story about the Ba'al Shem Tov. Existing miracle tales were adapted and retold to suit the rabbi in question. Moroccan and Iraqi Jews, too, enhanced the reputations of their tzaddikim with tales of wonders they performed for worried people. Jews have mixed memories, dreams, fantasy, and fact into miracle tales that give temporary happiness and psychological strength.[81]

A Hasid, Israel of Ruzhin (d. 1850), observed that his people no longer knew the place in the woods where the wonder-working Ba'al

Shem Tov found solitude (a prerequisite for drawing down divine power). They also no longer knew how he created a fiery spark, nor the special prayer he recited when he saw misfortune threatening. Yet the Ruzhin rabbi hoped that by merely telling the stories of the Ba'al Shem Tov's miracles, he too could help worried people.[82] Perhaps he realized that these stories raise hope and morale and that this is the first step in coping with worry. Did he realize that it is the story that precedes the wonder-worker's act that brings about the emotional change?

Elie Wiesel, however, has observed sadly that it is no longer sufficient to tell the story. In the shadow of mass destruction, certainly, a story is insufficient to relieve anxiety.[83] But if we can distance ourselves from this shadow, a miracle story, say at bedtime, may well change our mood for the better. Until modern times, miracle stories have been a part of every Jewish family's folklore, enjoyed by adults and children alike. We can still enjoy these stories today and use them to raise morale and inspire hope.

Rabbis who have realized that stories are now not enough to help worried people have used modern technology to publicize their special power. Printed photographic portraits of Menahem Mendel Schneersohn, who led the Lubavitcher-Chabad Hasidim from his home in Crown Heights, Brooklyn from 1950 until his death in 1995; the Baba Sali, a Moroccan Jewish wonder-working rabbi; and Rav Kadouri, an aged Jerusalem kabbalist, hang in many homes, shops, and vehicles. Those people who display the portrait may hope that the amuletic reproduction carries a little of the rabbi's spiritual power. Or they may find comfort in the reminder, which these portraits provide, that miracles can still happen.

Schneersohn's face beams today from massive billboards and over the Internet.[84] The Baba Sali's photo and blessing can be bought for a few shekels at every post office in Israel. In 1996, Rabbi Kadouri's amuletic medallions were mass produced for Benjamin Netanyahu's election propaganda, and in 1999, Rabbi Batzri's videotaped exorcism enjoyed record sales, promoting his fame as well as benefiting a religious political party. As the power of these men is publicized, some age-old traditions are maintained. One is the tradition of keeping alive the belief in miracles to promote religious faith. Another is the tradition of telling stories, the tradition of the "tried and proved," which is essential to the success of theurgy and magic. Still today, the story about the success of a particular method may be the most important element in its ability to help a person cope with worry. In addition, by publicizing their successes, these men increase the likelihood that weak and worried people will turn to them for help, thereby widening their power base and boosting their status in the community.

As long as science and medicine cannot adequately explain and remedy worry, there will always be an interest in alternatives; there will always be those who can confidently supply the alternatives as well as those willing to try them.

7 — A Moving Melody

The courtiers of King Saul knew that music could be therapeutic for a troubled mind. The Bible tells us that "whenever the [evil] spirit of God came upon Saul, David would take the lyre and play it; Saul would find relief and feel better, and the evil spirit would leave him" (1 Sam. 16:23)

Why did David's music make Saul feel better? The Talmud merely notes that beautiful sounds restore the spirits, without being more specific.[1] Could the harmony of the sounds have caused chemical releases in his brain that pacified him? Did the melody perhaps inspire him with its beauty and elevate his thoughts away from his distress? Or was its rhythm contagious, exciting him to tap his feet with joy? Music has many ways of affecting us, and we can only imagine why and how it helped Saul to change his mood.

We do not know whether David also sang to Saul as he played the lyre; in antiquity, instrumental music was often an accompaniment to song. We may wonder whether David played a well-known song, perhaps a dance tune or a drinking ballad. Or perhaps he played the sort of music that helped a prophet to receive divine inspiration. Alternatively, David may have chosen a soothing tune.

Music moves us in many different ways. A melody, an important element of music, is a relation between tones, actually more than a series of tones strung together. We can hum a melody, sing it, play it on one instrument or on many, vary its rhythm, and add harmony, but it remains the same melody. A melody is a pattern, a distinct, organized whole that is more than the sum of its parts. The progression of tones in a melody gives us the impression of movement, but the music does not move. Yet it *is* moving—it moves us, our feelings, our emotions. Music is emotive; the words "emotion" and "emotive" are formed from the Latin "e" (out) + "movere" (to move). Melody arouses feeling, it moves us, and can move us out of and away from the feeling of worry to another sensation.

Only certain music helps us cope with worry, not just any music, and the same melody may have a different effect at different times. The effect of music on our mood, on our understanding and on our perception of a situation is personal, and depends partly on our state of mind when we hear or create music. The effect that music has on us is determined also by our environment, culture, and experiences. As adolescents and their parents well know, the music that cheers or relieves one may disturb and upset another. The tunes and rhythms that an adolescent strums on a guitar or chooses to listen to alone or with friends are usually different from those that a middle-aged adult chooses. Music that moves us at a protest demonstration may not move us the same way when we are at home. A song that calmed us as a small child may no longer have the same effect a few years later.

We will now look briefly at the complex nature of music and then go on to examine why, when, and how music can help us to cope with worry. How have Jews used music therapeutically, without a modern diploma in music therapy?

What Is Music?

Music is a complex product made of many attributes of sound, combined together in an ever-changing temporal relationship. The *Oxford Dictionary* defines music as the "art or science of combining vocal or instrumental sounds (or both) to produce beauty of form, harmony, and expression of emotion." Of course, beauty of form is subjective and what one person finds beautiful may leave another unmoved. Harmony is the combination of simultaneously sounded notes to produce chords and chord progressions that are pleasing. However, the chords and chord progressions that please one person may appear as no more than noise to another. Music enables us to express emotion and can itself be expressive of emotion. In addition, music represents emotion, puts us in touch with emotion, and arouses us to feel emotion. Moreover, this oversimplified dictionary definition omits any mention of the divine, which has often been an important element in the way that Jews have employed music to cope with worry.

Song (one of the many elements of music) is the breath of the whole universe, according to Rabbi Yohanan in the Talmud. In medieval times, the kabbalistic Book of Zohar taught that vocal music influences the angels and the stars, in fact the whole divine world, so that God showers mercy on the living. The eighteenth-century founder of eastern European Hasidism explained that a song is "an angel which bears us above the spheres and puts us to sleep in the lap of God." It is "the diamond bridge which leads upward out of the valley of depravity into the heart of God." George Steiner, who has not steeped himself in Jewish mysticism but is nevertheless deeply moved by certain music, believes that music is "the soliloquy of being, of the original *fiat* echoing itself." Jews, like many peoples of the world, have believed that there is a divine element in music.[2]

Music is the means of communication between souls, wrote the French author Marcel Proust in the early twentieth century. However, music is a language for communicating between souls only if the souls share the same culture and respond to the same kind of music. Music may nevertheless also be a language to communicate with the divine, to reach up to God, to open the gates of heaven and to draw down blessing, as the poet Moses ibn Ezra discovered some eight hundred years ago. "Music is the only language . . . at once intelligible and untranslatable," wrote anthropologist Claude Lévi-Strauss. Music achieves more than words; it mirrors, represents, organizes, and arouses feelings.[3]

Why Does Music Help Us Cope with Worry?

The eastern European Hasid, Nahman of Bratzlav, teaches us the ways in which music helps us cope with worry, in a long and involved fable about two men who were lost in a forest at night. Anyone lost in a forest at night would probably feel worried, and would listen carefully for signs of salvation or danger.

The men in the dark forest heard the sounds of wild beasts roaring and howling in strange voices. All the animals and birds were roaring, whistling, and shrieking and there was a terrific noise. The men became very frightened. But when they listened carefully, they realized that there was a melody in the sounds, and that the animals were in fact singing a very wonderful song. As they listened carefully, they grew extremely happy. They believed that there was no happiness in the world comparable to that elicited by the exquisite beauty of the music and they wanted to stay forever in the forest with the lovely music.

The spirit of the forest then explains that this music, which had made them forget their fear and feel happy, was sung by the animals who are grateful to the moon for lighting up the night. The spirit offered one of the men an instrument made of leaves and colored things, which would play the same wonderful melody they had heard if placed on any bird or beast. This man used the instrument to restore harmony to the land and its people and he became king.[4]

Rabbi Nahman wanted Jews to interpret his tales just as they interpret Torah, to discover their deeper meaning. The music in the forest, heard only at night, is the song of the animals and the angels, which ceases when Jews begin their morning prayer. Just like human prayer, the song of these creatures is a communication with the divine. It ceases at dawn to allow God to hear the morning prayer of the Jews. For Nahman, music was a way of communicating with

God. Music indeed enables us to transcend our own selves, our own little world of worries, and find God, goodness, and beauty.

As long as the animalistic tones were fragmented and disordered, they remained frightening, but as soon as the men perceived the harmony in the sounds and understood the combination and progression of tones, these turned into music in their ears. Our world, too, sometimes appears threatening when we cannot understand it. As soon as we perceive some order, our uncertainty diminishes, and we feel less worried. Nahman understood that music can help us to cope with worry because it can enable us to focus our minds, find order, and understand our environment.

The future king discovered that just as he could unite the animal songs into an experience of harmony, so too, the new instrument, made up of the fragments of the forest, could help him find harmony in his fragmented world. This instrument, *tevah* in Hebrew, is like the ark (*tevah*) of the covenant. The man who has this instrument, like the man who has Torah, can create a harmony that will lead him out of anxiety and confusion to do great things. The rabbi's story teaches that music reveals to the man (the Jewish soul) lost in the forest (exiled—exile is an archetype of Jewish anxiety) how to overcome the worry of uncertainty (end the exile) and become king (bring about redemption, the end of all worry). Nahman believed that the Messiah will come with the ultimate restoration of harmony. The story teaches that music can help not only the individual worried soul, but also the whole Jewish people, as music can restore harmony to the world.

The musical instrument is like Noah's ark (again, *tevah*) as it ensured the survival of the chosen man, the man destined to look after the community. The musical instrument leads this man out of the forest to his land and gives him the power to become king. Nahman knew that music transports us away from worry and gives us strength to live and to help others.[5]

The music assured the men that they were not alone in the forest. If the birds and the beasts were singing, their plight must not be too bad. Music can promote a relationship between people listening to or creating music together. In the Second World War, the marching songs of prisoners and the entertainment music of the ghettos provided participants with a sense of togetherness, in the same way that the singing of a congregation in prayer strengthens participants' feelings of belonging and of not being alone in the world. In the company of others, we hear our voice blend with other voices, and our identity merges with the group. Music reduces worry when it makes us realize that we are not alone.

The Bratzlav rabbi told another tale in which a handless beggar announces that he can heal—with ten kinds of music—an imprisoned princess who is mortally ill. The beggar is clearly Nahman in disguise, whereas the princess represents every man or woman dragged by anxiety into the prison of his or her mind. The ten kinds of music refer to the ten composition modes of David's psalms or to the ten voices of the shofar, the ram's horn that Jews have used since antiquity to stir their hearts with awe and reverence, to remind themselves of God's sovereignty. These ten kinds of music help the princess to transform worry into happiness because they draw her near to God. Nahman assumed that if we can draw near to God, we will stop worrying—an assumption that we have met in previous chapters of this book. The piercing notes of a shofar, the singing of psalms, or even a musical work of art performed in a concert hall or reproduced on a compact disk may help us to do this. Nahman was both an inveterate worrier and a deeply musical person. He was fully convinced of the healing power of music and he used his wonderful voice to cheer himself and others in moments of worry.[6]

The rabbi of Bratzlav believed that melodies and songs are born in the effort to turn worry and despair into happiness. "The worried will allay their fears with songs of joy," he promised, and "by means of their song will achieve joy and ecstasy." To sum up, we learn from Nahman that music can help us cope with worry by promoting joy. It can help us to focus our minds and promote our understanding. It can make us feel strong, put us in touch with God, and transport us into another realm, far away from worry. It can also put us in touch with other people and make us realize that we are not alone. In addition, and most important in the Hasid's mind, music is able to restore harmony and thereby terminate worry.[7]

When Have Jews Used Music to Cope with Worry?

Jews have used music to cope with worry in threatening and distressing situations, and during rituals, celebrations, and other social gatherings. They have also used music in an attempt to attain prophecy, as we saw in chapter 4.

In Threatening and Distressing Situations

Worried Jews have sometimes sung or played music in threatening situations. A story is told about Israel Najara (c. 1600), who gained fame as the author of the Sabbath song *Yah ribbon olam*. Najara could play a soft sweet melody on his flute that could transport his listeners from the world of worry all the way to heaven. Legend tells that when he was young, Najara left his parents' home in Safed for Damascus to indulge his penchant for Arab tavern music. One day, he decided to return to Safed and on his way he was taken prisoner by some Bedouin who wanted to kill him and keep his possessions. The young man asked to pray before he died and they granted his request. He took out his flute and piped his prayer to God. Some camels nearby heard his music and came toward him, thumping their feet in time to the music. When the Bedouin came to their prisoner, they found him surrounded by a circle of dancing camels and were terrified at the Jew's amazing power. Najara was oblivious; he went on communing with God on his little flute, walking in the direction of Safed. He arrived safely in his hometown with his group of dancing camels.[8]

Najara was a prisoner when he played his flute and escaped. His melody literally carried him away, all the way home. Of course, we can usually escape only mentally (not physically) in response to music. Jews have often sung in life-threatening situations and in times of oppression to sense and declare their intellectual and spiritual freedom.

Jews have sounded the shofar to add power to their prayers in times of distress, such as in times of drought, pestilence, and war. We saw in the last chapter that rabbis have used the shofar for extra power when exorcising a demon.[9]

During Rituals and Secular Gatherings

Jews, like all other peoples, sing or play music during rituals, celebrations, and other social occasions, when they want to banish distracting thoughts and focus their minds in a particular way. For example, the traditional tunes of the repentance prayers on the Day of Atonement help Jews to feel penitent and focus their thoughts on searching their souls, whereas the fast beat of the wedding musicians encourages guests to dance, forget their worries, and rejoice with the newly married couple. Women have improvised tunes and the words of songs to express or banish their worries while performing their daily chores, such as when grinding grain, kneading dough, and scrubbing laundry, as well as at social occasions before a wedding or a circumcision.

Already in late antiquity, Jews were aware that, like sexual love, music can arouse the body and lead to a transcendent experience and happiness. But, like sexual love, music has the power to arouse inappropriate emotion, such as lewdness, and even immoral behavior. For this reason some rabbis disapproved of singing and music making, and especially forbade women from engaging in these activities in the presence of men. Some felt that music was out of place among a people mourning the destruction of their Temple and banned entertainment music and emotional singing in the synagogue and sometimes also at Jewish social gatherings. Others allowed the liturgical chant that focuses the mind and promotes religious understanding, but no free melody that arouses sensual feelings. Of course, they could not stop a woman singing to herself as she scrubbed her laundry, a farmer singing as he plowed his field, or prisoners singing as they marched, as their tunes eased the burden of their existence.[10]

In the early seventeenth century, Rabbi Leone of Modena collaborated with the most illustrious Jewish composer of his day, Salomone de Rossi, to revive the Jewish musical tradition that had existed in the ancient Temple, but their attempts to introduce art music (as opposed to music created with a religious purpose or any other purpose) into the synagogue met with considerable controversy. Italian rabbis soon began to complain also about the singing and dancing that went on in Jewish homes. In 1726, some of these rabbis enacted laws to permit only the singing of Hebrew songs, without the accompaniment of musicians, on the tense night before a circumcision, when a baby's life was thought to be most vulnerable to harmful powers. These laws were part of a concerted effort by rabbis all over Italy to curb secular entertainment and promote religion instead. However, their lenience regarding women's singing on the night before a circumcision may reveal that these men understood its psychological purpose—to banish worries at a time of heightened danger.[11]

How Has Music Helped Jews Cope with Worry?

How has music helped Jews cope with worry? We could answer this question at a scientific level and look for changes in brain chemistry—the excitement of the arousal system or the endocrine system. We could answer it also at a psychological level and assess changes in behavior, cognition, and mood. Alternatively, we could follow the example of the biblical story of Saul and answer the question at a spiritual level. We could suppose, as Jews have supposed, that music removes evil spirits and opens the gates of heaven so that blessing descends upon us. Or we could presume, as Jews have also presumed, that music elevates our souls, raising our spirits.

We could also study separately the effects of creating music and those of listening to music when we are worried. We could even examine the different effects of instrumental and vocal music, or of experiencing music alone or with others, or with another. However, such a study is beyond the scope of this book. We will limit our answer to what some Jews have chosen to tell us, to heighten our awareness of how we ourselves could benefit from music to cope with worry. We will look first at the belief that music can affect the body and the soul. We will see that music can focus thoughts, effectively banishing worry. It also allows us to talk about and face worry. In addition, music can elevate the soul to an awareness of beauty, joy, and (sometimes) God. Finally, we will look at how Jews have gained strength, power, and understanding through music, which can also help us cope with worry.

By Affecting the Body and Soul

Jews have sometimes used music as a form of medicine for a troubled soul. We have already noted that David played his lyre to relieve Saul's suffering. The Babylonian philosopher Sa'adia Gaon (882–942) believed that we should create music that helps to balance our humors, to achieve what Aristotle termed the "golden mean." Sa'adia Gaon identified eight distinctive rhythmic modes that stimulate the four humors (the blood, phlegm, yellow bile, and black bile) to arouse basic impulses, such as the impulse to rule, to be courageous, joyous, or sorrowful. He believed that music affects the equilibrium of our bodily secretions (the humors), changing our thoughts and moods for better or for worse.[12]

In medieval Spain, music was a well-recognized antidote for the suffering soul. The poet Moses ibn Ezra (c. 1055–after 1135) thought that the four strings of the lute, or other convex-bodied string instruments, stimulate the four humors and thus affect the soul. He explained that the first string is subtle and stimulates yellow bile, the humor that arouses courage and boldness; the second stimulates the blood, which enhances happiness; the third stimulates phlegm, the cool and moist humor that makes the eyes weep and the soul feel sad; and the fourth, the thickest, heaviest string, stimulates black bile and melancholy. He believed that music came into being at the beginning of creation to promote equilibrium and harmony among the four humors and among the elements of the cosmos.[13]

Moses ibn Ezra gained temporary relief from his mental distress by listening to a lute player. He explained how the music helped him:

His heart pulsed to the rhythm, responding also to the harmony of the strings and to the melody of the musician's singing voice. The music closed "the gates of darkness" and opened "the heights of heaven," purifying the poet's thoughts so that he almost felt "the spirit of the angels of God." The music aroused the poet physically, banished his worry, and enabled him to sense God's blessing reaching down to him.[14]

Some other medieval Spanish Jews, for example the philosopher Joseph ben Judah Aknin (c. 1150–1220), taught that physicians could learn to use the art of music to cure the soul. In 1403, such a physician, Profiat Duran, explained the therapeutic effects of Jewish music on men's souls: Musical chanting of biblical texts strengthens their powers of understanding, whereas the free melody sung in supplicatory prayers and by righteous men rouses their feelings for God.[15]

In the thirteenth century, Abraham Abulafia noticed that several strings played harmoniously at the same time give a sweet flavor to the ears, which, he thought, then passes to the heart and on to the spleen, reviving a person's sense of happiness. He could achieve the same effect by singing in a special way. He created tunes out of the Divine Names, by singing each letter with awe and reverence according to the tune he believed to be associated with each vowel point, and found that this special singing created joy in his soul. Abulafia also noticed that music affects the intellect and can sharpen understanding, as we will see later in this chapter.[16]

In 1492, during the Inquisition, a priest watched Jews who had been expelled from Castile leave by road and through fields "with much labor and ill-fortune." They could not have known what was in store for them at the end of their journey and must have been worried. They eased their journey with singing and by beating a rhythm on drums and tambourines. The rhythm of the instruments stimulated their muscles, helping them walk and giving them strength.[17]

The forced marches of the Jews under the Nazi terror were different; they led to a horrific form of captivity and, usually, death. A Hasidic follower of the grand rabbi of Bobov was a slave laborer at Mauthausen in December 1944. One day, delousing day, all the prisoners were sent to the showers. In the middle of their wash they were ordered out to the compound for a roll call. Naked, wet, emaciated skeletons stood to attention in the icy wind. One person appeared to be missing, so the count began again, only to confirm that one person really was missing. The prisoners had to stay put while a search began. Their bodies turned white with a frosty glaze. They dropped, one by one, as the last ounce of warm air inside them froze. The young Hasid knew his feet had stuck to the icy ground, which was pulling him down forever. But suddenly he remembered his rabbi's advice, "A Hasid must sing, a Hasid must dance; it is the secret of our survival!" The rabbi's tune welled up inside him, melted his heart, and revived his soul. His lips slowly began to move with the tune, then his body, and his feet. Burning tears streamed down his face as he realized that the Bobov melody was helping him to survive. The roll call was over and the compound was strewn with bodies, but the Hasid was alive, thanks to the Bobov melody.[18]

A late eighteenth-century Hasid, Naftali of Ropshitz, had taught the Hasidim to sing the *niggun,* the song of joy. This song is "a precious key, a key that opens all the doors, even those that God keeps closed. . . . [It] makes our hearts beat faster. The *niggun* opens the gates of heaven." The Hasid at Mauthausen had remembered the song that would make his heart beat faster, pump his warm blood to his frozen limbs, and keep him alive.[19]

Today, without thinking for a moment, a person might automatically sing a lullaby to calm a crying baby. We all know instinctively that a tender song can relax an infant, affecting the baby bodily so that it goes to sleep. Small children soon learn to sing by themselves—keeping worries away—and some may hum themselves to sleep.

Paradoxically, although certain music will tend to send a baby to sleep, it can also arouse the body in a particular way. The human arousal system is complicated and cannot be explained here. We may find that music calms or irritates, soothes or excites, rouses us to ecstasy or reduces us to tears. The arousal generated by a particular air may be pleasant one day but annoying the next. Clearly, the way that music affects us depends not only on bodily arousal, but also on social and psychological factors, such as the situation we are in and our state of mind.

By Focusing Thoughts

Rabbis and cantors have developed chants for reading Torah and reciting prayers that help Jews to focus their thoughts on God. They have sounded the special notes of the shofar to inspire awe and love of God. Such organized sharing of music during a ritual, celebration, or other social gathering intentionally orders people's thoughts and feelings. It promotes a certain mood and, in doing so, it banishes worry. Filmmakers employ the same wisdom to dictate mood and emotion in an audience. They choose carefully the music for their soundtracks, to promote distress, suspense, or relaxation at the appropriate moment, so that viewers become emotionally involved in the film's story.

The medieval Ashkenazic pietists sang a long, extended tune on individual words during their prayers to focus their minds on God and promote devotion. ". . . Search for a tune that you find pleasant and sweet. Say your prayer in this tune. It will be full of intention and concentration. . . . There is nothing that brings a man to love his creator and to rejoice in his love more than the voice raised in an extended tune."[20] With these words, Judah the Pious taught that a tune helps a person to attain the desired mental state to focus on God as well as to overcome distracting worries and other secular thoughts. This custom soon became popular in central Europe, and later mystics encouraged joyous, passionate singing to God, expressed from the heart, with full devotion and intention. The sweetness of the voice and the beauty of the tune were unimportant. The song channels the emotions of those praying so that they all share the same desired thoughts and feelings of devotion in the synagogue. The same effect occurs when musicians play at a wedding to promote feelings of joy, and at a memorial service, where the desired mood is one of sadness.

Ritual music can help Jews to eliminate their worries and focus their thoughts. For example, the familiar strains of the repentance prayers affect people in different ways. For many Jews the opening Kol Nidrei chant of Yom Kippur Eve may be the key that opens their dialogue with God. However, for other Jews, the somber tune may promote a comfortable feeling of belonging to the group, a sense of continuity with all those other Jews in the world singing the same tune, or with their own ancestors who sang the same words on the same day. Worries usually disappear as a singer becomes enveloped in a familiar tune.

Rabbi Leone of Modena was unusually musical and was convinced that music could rid the listener of all that weighs on the heart. Believing that "the greatest possible beauty of voice" should be used for praising the Lord and creating "a joyous mood for the Torah," he introduced polyphonic renditions of Sabbath hymns in his synagogue to help Jews banish their worries and become joyous when they came to pray.[21]

In Lithuania, in the middle of the nineteenth century, Rabbi Israel Lipkin of Salant taught his many students to contemplate an ethical teaching (a carefully chosen verse from a Jewish source) in a rhythmic, melodious, emotional recitation. He chose vocal music that would focus the mind, promote concentration, and also move his students emotionally. He favored the group situation, where people chant or sing together as the sharing of rhythm and melody increases the emotional effect.[22] However, the ability of music to improve our concentration is qualified and specific; it is untrue that any music will focus our minds and banish our worries. Israel of Salant chose tunes that he believed would help his students.

A tune can help us fill empty time and keep worries out of mind. When our mind is not focused, we often fill it, without noticing, with a tune that we hum, whistle, or hear as it goes round and round inside our head. We often do this in the shower or when out walking. Children do this while they play alone, when lying in bed before going to sleep, and when dressing in the morning. Although some of us may have forgotten how to sing, most of us find ourselves humming or whistling or singing out loud at some time or other. As we do so, our mind relaxes and, unconsciously, we start thinking about something that pops up, thinking around it, reorganizing our thoughts with the aid of the tune until we understand them better and gain inspiration. Then we suddenly stop humming or whistling and take notice of the idea and of where we are. We should be able to discover and repeat the pieces of music that have a beneficial effect on ourselves and call on them in moments of worry.

By Enabling the Expression of Worry

Song is both a privilege and a blessing. Often in the past, singing may have been the only way some people could express their true feelings. Jews have given vent to their worries in tune, rhythm, and verse, sometimes singing the traditional words of a song and sometimes improvising their own words to a well-known tune. They have also hummed a song to convey emotion without words. Songs can declare feelings that we are reluctant to talk about, with calming and relaxing effect. Jews have expressed their feelings for God in religious songs and their other feelings in secular folksongs. They have faced worry in some wedding songs, lullabies, and dirges, at worrying times during the life cycle.

Wedding Songs Hired musicians may succeed in inducing joy at a wedding party, but already in talmudic times rabbis recognized other emotions simmering before a wedding. For centuries, Jewish parents arranged the weddings of their daughters, and the girls had little chance to get to know their future husbands. Girls lived sheltered lives, attached to home, but after their weddings would likely live with their husbands and their husbands' families whom the girls did not know. During the period between engagement and marriage, songs were one way of expressing the bride's worries and helping her to face the uncertain future.

The parents of both bride and groom have worried about their child's wedding. Would the girl make a faithful wife? Would the groom provide for her and make her happy? Today, too, some parents feel anxious as the day of their child's wedding approaches. Until recent times, families admitted their worries in traditional songs when they met at prenuptial gatherings. They often improvised according to the worries of the moment, to reduce the tension in the air. For example, on the Sabbath following an engagement in Bukhara, Jewish women of the couple's families played a game called "the singer and the drink" in which a full glass was passed from one woman to the next. If she could not sing a song, she had to drink all the contents of the glass. Judeo-Spanish speakers in Morocco and in the Balkans sang traditional songs about the worry over a dowry for a daughter and the bickering that sometimes ensued when a groom's family considered the dowry too small.[23]

Sephardic Jews also sang of the worry that a spouse was being unfaithful; sometimes the unfaithful partner is cursed in the song, but sometimes the song brings a happy end and the fear turns out to be unfounded. Sephardic women have sung such traditional songs, some of which date back to medieval Spain, at social gatherings before weddings and also privately, according to their moods, as lullabies, or while doing their daily chores.[24]

Iraqi Jewish mothers have faced their worries about a forthcoming marriage in a traditional song at the henna ceremony, the night before the wedding. The groom's mother sings to the bride's mother a well-known blessing for strength, but soon continues to admit her feeling that her son is being taken away by the other's daughter and slips into improvised verses about whatever else is upsetting her.[25]

Love songs sung by the women of Sana'a, in Yemen, sometimes to the rhythm of drums, at any time of day or night, and at prenuptial ceremonies and weddings, reveal the full gamut of human emotion. They express the romance of love, separation anxiety over the loss of a beloved, or the fear that love may be unrequited. Yemenite women have also sung about a young girl's desire to escape from her father to her loved one. Disappointment in love and other people's gossip about a young girl are yet further worries aired in Yemenite song. A woman who was worried, angry, or feeling romantic might sing one of these songs while doing the laundry or cooking.[26]

One theme that appears in Yiddish wedding songs is the worry that a planned marriage will suddenly be called off for some reason. The families involved spend much time and money preparing for the occasion; the sudden cancellation of the wedding could be a nightmare come true. Alternatively, perhaps someone is not entirely happy about the marriage and hopes that it might be cancelled after all. The songs involve scenarios wherein a wedding is called off owing to the bride's sudden death, or the groom's, or the tragic deaths of both. A song in which the bride dies when the Angel of Death comes for her tells of her pleading for her life and her taking leave of the groom and her family. In another song, the bride, who becomes pregnant before her marriage—another worry—dies of sorrow in her groom's arms. In yet another song, the young man refuses to marry the girl he seduced, she poisons herself, and he then drowns himself. Eastern European Jews who sang of the groom's death often favored a tragic, watery demise.

The angry groom who murders his bride because her parents objected to the match or because she did not return his love is yet another subject of Yiddish folk songs. Suicide following a family fight is also a subject of these songs; for example when a mother does not approve of her son's choice of bride, or a young bride has a tiff with her parents. Emotions heat up as the wedding approaches, and worries can become destructive. The theme of the cancelled wedding may be a worry or a desire. Today Jews celebrate weddings by hiring musicians to create a happy atmosphere, one that is conducive to dancing and general enjoyment, and the expressive, therapeutic songs have disappeared.[27]

Lullabies   Today, as always, it is natural for a woman whose baby is crying to sing about her worries. Lullabies have soothing melodies and relax the singer while calming the baby. Women have often sung to soothe their own shattered nerves. Jewish women usually sang lullabies in the language they spoke in their daily lives. (In contrast, pious and literary Jewish men sang mainly religious songs, in Hebrew.) The medieval *Sefer Hasidim* advised parents not to sing the songs or tunes of the gentiles or verses of the Bible to calm a baby's crying, but instead to intone verses of the Talmud set to music that would help the parent to remember them. Women would not have known the talmudic verses or tunes, and therefore it is likely that this ruling applied to fathers rather than mothers. A woman would have sung whatever song came into her head in order to calm her crying infant, probably improvising to suit her mood. A woman was completely free to express her worries in her song, whereas a father was constrained to sing a religious tune.[28]

Lullabies that have been recorded over the last century reveal that mothers expressed in their songs their desire to hush the baby to sleep, their fears and frustrations, as well as their hopes for the baby's future. Alternatively, mothers let their tunes drift into a dream or a familiar ballad, carrying their thoughts away from worry.

Women also sang to their infants about the tensions that ensued from living with in-laws. In one well-known lullaby, Iraqi Jews sang of an evil sister-in-law who makes the new mother's life a misery, and part of the lullaby is in the form of a dialogue between the young woman and her brother, asking for help. Jewish women in Bombay sang to their babies of their hope that their own mothers would come to help. The folk songs of Iraqi Jews have also included the opportunity for a mother to sing about her older children. In one song, the mother expressed her worries about the child's acceptance in the games of other children, but she could always improvise new words and express another, more pressing worry to the same well-known tune.[29]

Another popular lullaby sung by Iraqi Jews tells of the mother going up to the roof of her house on a hot and windy evening to look at the view. Up there she escapes the burdens of her life to take a flight into fantasy. Her son appears in her dream, riding on a bright-eyed mare, while his enemy rides on a dog with clipped ears. The dream meanders through many verses, encompassing her hopes and fears for her son.[30]

A Yiddish lullaby implies that a baby girl's crying irritates her father and implores the infant to go to sleep. A second bemoans social injustice: When the child grows up, the mother sang, he or she will see the luxurious palaces that poor men build for the rich to live in, while the poor suffer sicknesses in their damp cellar homes. A third Yiddish lullaby asks the infant to ignore mother's tears, shed for father who was dragged away and murdered. And in one more, the mother notices that the sky is a cloudy gray, just like her heart. A Jewish servant girl in Bessarabia sang an even sadder tune, ending with the thought that it is better to be dead than alive in this ugly world.[31]

By Releasing Emotion

Wedding songs, lullabies, and dirges may have a cathartic effect in releasing pent-up emotion. By expressing emotion through these forms of music, Jews have regained their inner harmony. Some Yiddish lullabies known today were actually written by men in the late nineteenth or early twentieth century to express communal fears and insecurity in this harsh world, as well as the national dreams of the Jewish people. Similarly, during the Second World War, some Jewish prisoners chose the lullaby, the age-old antidote for infant distress, to cope with their own distress in the face of the Nazi horrors. For example, in a song written by Leah Rudnitsky, a stranger rocks a baby to sleep in its cradle, in the field, as its parents had been killed at Ponar, near Vilna. In Shmerl Kaczerginsky's lullaby, a mother tells her orphaned child to be still, since graves grow here; "planted by the enemy, they blossom to the sky." He managed to find some optimism for his closing verse, recalling the well-known refrain, "Father will return with freedom. Sleep, my child, be still. . . ." However, in Isaiah Shpigl's lullaby, sung in the Lodz Ghetto theater to a tango-like tune, the father will never come home; the child lies in an open field, his parents' house burned to the ground. Shpigl was almost deported by the Judenrat for expressing such pessimism. When his daughter died, he wrote another equally pessimistic song, "No More Raisins, No More Almonds," a negative version of the well-known lullaby "Rhozhinkes mit Mandeln," with a different tune.[32]

Jews under Nazi terror sang primitive lyrics that faced their concerns. They set these lyrics to well-known tunes that evoked shared memories of a better world. For example, a poet in the Kovno Ghetto took the tune of a popular song evoking the warmed heder, the classroom where the rabbi taught little boys the alphabet. The imprisoned poet replaced the little children of the well-known song with a little commandant in his green uniform, the terror of the ghetto who takes everything away. This poet also adopted the riddle format of the well-known *Tumbala, tumbala* song to ask, in the same tune, why some Jews ascended to power in the Judenrat and Jewish police, at the expense of other Jews.[33]

A Jew in the Vilna Ghetto chose to sing a happy, popular wedding tune whose original lyrics mentioned dancing in stockinged feet. The Vilna version was about dancing with torn shoes and ripped garments in the icy cold Siberian wind when marrying whoever has a yellow pass, the pass that enabled survival in the ghetto instead of death in the woods of Ponar. In the Lodz Ghetto, Yankele Hershkowitz composed songs with piquant words and refrains that his audience picked up quickly and sang with him. For example, "Do not worry and don't fret / Someday things will be good . . . / So everyone sing with me the refrain / Oy, oy, oy." Another ghetto Jew adapted Abraham Goldfaden's "Song of the Abandoned Orphan" so that the child, named Izzy (Israel) and orphaned by the Nazis, represented the Jewish people as a whole. These traditional tunes linked Jews to their communal past and stimulated them to feel, share, and release emotion.[34]

By singing the songs of happier times, these Jews may have been seeking consciously or unconsciously to regain the worry-free harmony of past moments. Freud did not discuss music in particular, but considered all forms of art to be socially acceptable ways of fleeing from reality. Prisoners might well have preferred a song that helped them to flee from reality, but their adapted songs admitted reality very clearly. As people struggled to survive in the Nazi hell, they became emotionally numb. The tunes they sang aroused feelings of nostalgia and memories of happy times; they allowed emotions to flow.[35]

However, we do not have to experience captivity to discover that a melody can affect us privately, stimulate personal memories, and allow us to regain brief access to feelings that we have forgotten. Music can carry our souls to ugly moments when we have suffered, moments that we may have forgotten or want to forget. Theodor Reik (1888–1970), a Viennese psychoanalyst, noticed that the impressions that music once made on a person revive as a tune is recalled, eliciting images and emotions.[36] Few Israelis can hear the song of peace that thousands sang in the hope of peace in a large square in central Tel Aviv in November 1995 without their memories jolting back to the murder of Prime Minister Rabin on that fateful night. A tune may access our feelings and release distressing emotion.

By Elevating the Soul

Music can be enchanting; the word "enchant" is derived from the Latin words *in + cantare*, to sing. Music can put us under a spell so that we lose awareness of the world about us. It can alter our state of consciousness. Music can send us to sleep, induce ecstasy, or lead us "upward out of the valley of depravity into the heart of God," as we saw at the beginning of this chapter.

The musicians who played to the prophets in antiquity elevated the souls of the prophets to access divine revelations. Many pietists later sought to travel the same path with the help of music, either to induce a vision or merely to attain ecstasy by elevating their souls to the divine realm. Music can transport the soul out of the abyss of anxiety to the divine world, to the world of fantasy, or merely down memory lane, to a time and place we visited long ago.

In antiquity, some pietists may have chanted psalms in meditation to elevate their souls to reach the Divine and gain enlightenment. The Talmud explains that those psalms beginning with *mizmor le-david*, "A psalm of David," enabled David to reach up to the Divine Spirit. Some medieval mystics assumed that Moses recited or sang certain psalms to gain divine revelations. One Spanish kabbalist wrote (c. 1300) that all the psalms clear the mind of mundane worries.[37]

The *merkavah* mystics sang special hymns to induce a revelation like Ezekiel's. The language of these songs is rich in word-music and vocal harmony; they may have been sung in short, repetitive, melodic phrases to induce a sort of hypnotic state conducive to the seeing of visions.[38]

We have already seen (in chapter 4) that Abraham Abulafia and his followers played music and sang to elevate their souls to the divine realm for a special vision that could reduce their worries. In the early seventeenth century, the musical Rabbi Leone of Modena pointed out that the sages had recognized long ago that "through music and song, the soul awakens to be elevated and lifted from matter to the heavenly dwelling place of its Creator." Some Jews who elevated their souls with music believed they were continuing a long-established tradition.[39]

The false messiah Shabbetai Zevi similarly attained a prophetic, ecstatic trance while listening to music. Some of those in his circle induced prophesy with music. For example, an account from Gallipoli in 1666 tells that a group of his followers sang him hymns of praise to the accompaniment of musical instruments until one of those present began to prophesy in a trance.[40]

In the eighteenth century, kabbalists in a Sephardic congregation in Jerusalem elevated their souls with song. It is told that when their Yemenite-born leader, Shalom Sharabi (1720–1777), sang the *Shema* prayer, the music of his voice washed away all worries and transported even the uninitiated into the realms of thought where they commune with God.[41]

Hasidic Jews tell that Shmelke of Nikolsburg (d. 1778) sang new melodies that no human ear had ever heard before. He did not know what tune he sang because when he sang his soul was in the divine realm. They also tell that Shneur Zalman of Liadi composed a tune when he was imprisoned in the fortress of St. Petersburg in 1799. The melody begins slowly and leisurely, at the tempo of relaxed breathing, representing "the pouring forth of the soul." The tune then gains speed, leading to spiritual awakening, enthusiasm, and communion with God. Finally, at the tempo of the heartbeat, the singer attains spiritual ecstasy, when the soul has become disembodied from the material body and fuses with the heavenly flame.[42]

Max Graf (1873–1958), an early member of Freud's psychoanalytic circle and a music critic, stressed music's function in lifting a person out of the world of worries to an idealized spiritual world of beauty and truth, even to connect with or approach God. Sometimes music created as a work of art can indeed appear divine, or at least promote a sense of wonder at the existence of beauty.[43]

By Drawing Power and Giving Strength

We have already seen that music may have tremendous power to move the heart and the soul. Its ability to move us confirms our vitality and can make us feel that life is worth living. Martin Buber believed that the power of music could prevent a person from "falling into the abyss." And indeed, Ludwig Wittgenstein (another philosopher) recorded that more than once the slow movement of a certain Brahms quartet pulled him back from the brink of suicide.[44]

We have also seen that Jews have used tune to give power to their prayers. They have sought to pray in tuneful voices, believing that a chorus of voices has more power than a lone prayer and is better able to reach up to God. Worried people demonstrating to stop war or depose a government also sing together to show their power and find extra strength in the invisible bonds generated by collective singing.

In the late twelfth century, in a violent aftermath of a blood libel, the Jews of Blois went to their deaths singing about God's supremacy and their messianic hope. They sang in a soul-stirring melody, at first subdued, but rising into a mighty crescendo. The crescendo revealed the rising of their spirits as they sang. The song aroused them all together, giving each Jew the knowledge that he or she was not alone. The crescendo probably also revealed to the murderers the psychological power of the group. The Jews could not have been afraid if they sang with such fervor. Their song was the *Aleinu le-shabbe'aḥ* prayer, which the early mystics sang to gain access to the divine realm. The song provided an escape from the cruel world; it transported their souls away from worry to joy, a joy that they could only reach through music. Did these poor people believe that their song would open the gates to heaven? We cannot know.[45]

While interned in Theresienstadt, Victor Ullman (1898–1944) composed an opera that parodied well-known strains of German music. However, its performance was banned as soon as the German guards noticed the powerful effect it had on the audience at the dress rehearsal. The opera gave them strength and transformed their worry into defiance against the Nazis.[46]

Downtrodden Jews have often sung when their spirits were threatened, to show and persuade themselves that they were unbroken. In the past, Jews sang as they were burned at the stake and when they were marched to their deaths. Incarcerated in the Lodz Ghetto during the Second World War, David Beygelman declared his song "full of soul and emotions / It brings comfort to the Jew /. . . Only a Yiddish song has so much power / Especially when a fiddle plays / It soothes a sick heart. . . ." One Holocaust survivor commented: "The Nazis could take everything away from us, but they could not take singing from us. This remained our only human expression." Leah Hochberg, who was also interned in the Lodz Ghetto, recently recalled that singing "was one of the things that helped us to survive. . . . There is no doubt that singing helped." It helped because it had the power to affirm their vitality. Eli Wiesel, who survived the Auschwitz and Buchenwald concentration camps, wrote "a Jew is he—or she—whose song cannot be muted."[47]

Dov Gruner (1912–1947), a member of a Jewish underground brigade who was caught attacking a British police station in 1946, sang the "Hatikvah" ("The Hope," the anthem of the Zionist movement and eventually the Israeli national anthem) as he was led out to be shot by the British. In 1947, the refugees on board the *Exodus* sang the same song when forced to return from Haifa to the displaced persons camp from where they had come. This song was physically and mentally arousing, promoting vitality and psychological strength.[48]

However, we do not have to be facing death for music to energize us and promote our inner strength. Most of us have at some time come away from a concert invigorated by the music that had just been performed. Yet Jewish mystics have sung to draw a different sort of power. They have sung in the hope of drawing down divine power that would bring a blessing and make their worries vanish.

Some medieval Spanish Jews believed that the melodic compositions of King Solomon and the singing and playing of the Temple musicians of antiquity drew down divine blessings. These Jews believed that music gave Solomon and the High Priest the power to draw down these blessings for the good of the people. Spanish and later kabbalists imagined that vocal and instrumental music influences the divine music of the angels, the stars, and the trees in the Garden of Eden, in fact the whole divine world, so that God showers blessings on those living down on Earth.[49]

The spiritual leader of the Safed kabbalists, Rabbi Isaac Luria (1534–1572), believed that through song, he and his comrades might bring about the ultimate blessing, the coming of the Messiah, which would put an end to all human worries. One Friday afternoon, when the sun was low in the sky, he took his disciples to a meadow just outside the town to welcome the holy Sabbath with songs. As they were singing Psalm 92, "A Song for the Sabbath Day," to a particularly moving melody, Luria suddenly turned to his companions and invited them to join him in Jerusalem (a long way from Safed) before the Sabbath began, to spend the holy day there. Some of the disciples readily agreed, not pausing to think about how they could possibly reach the sacred city in time for the Sabbath. However, the others hesitated, saying they would have to ask their wives. When he heard the worried husbands hesitate, Luria threw up his hands in dismay. "Woe to us all," he grieved, "if only you had all joyously agreed and not worried, the Messiah would have come for all Israel."[50]

If they could only have shed their worries, the story teaches, their wonderful singing would have transported them to Jerusalem. Their destination was, of course, the metaphorical Jerusalem, as there was no way in those days that they could have reached the town built of stone, one hundred and fifty miles away, in time for the Sabbath. In Jewish tradition, the metaphorical Jerusalem is the rebuilt city where all the exiles will finally come to rest, a place of holiness at the gateway to heaven. In this story, the melody offered the possibility of permanent escape from worry by drawing blessings for all Israel.

The eastern European Hasid Levi-Itzhak of Berditchev (c. 1740–1810) thought that the righteous who can sing the song of the angels can draw down divine blessings. This rabbi knew how to meditate, as described in chapter 4, and believed that this enabled his soul to reach its divine source. Up there, he believed, it could learn the song of the angels and influence them to do whatever he wanted. This experience gave him the feeling that he could draw down divine blessings. It is told that Levi-Itzhak was indeed a wonderful singer. At one point in his life, however, he became frightened, could no longer fulfill his duties, and lay reading from a small book for hours on end. Some thought the angels had taken their revenge; the Berditchev rabbi had pushed his quest of the divine realm too far. Now he had lost his power and was overcome by anxiety. But one day he suddenly left his bed and addressed God melodiously, in Yiddish, in the midst of his prayers. He took God to task, calling on God to forgive and to answer the prayers of the Jews. He had lost the powerful feeling that he could draw down divine blessings, but perhaps, he thought, he could yet persuade God to send some blessings after all.[51]

Max Graf wrote about music's "narcissistic" function to intensify emotion and provide an experience of omnipotent power. Had he heard the story of the Berditchev rabbi, Graf would not have been surprised by this man's belief that he could draw goodness for the Jews using his wonderful voice.

By Promoting Understanding

Some Jews have played music when they wanted to gain a divine revelation that might improve their understanding of a situation, or an insight that could put an end to their worries. The Bible gives two examples. In one, three kings set out to conquer Moab, but soon run out of water in the desert. Fearing that they and their men will all perish, they call the prophet Elisha to find out what God has in store for them. Elisha requires a musician to induce his prophecy. When the musician plays, "the hand of the Lord came upon him," and he prophesies that they will find water and conquer Moab, which they did (2 Kings 3:9–27). Similarly, the Bible tells that Saul met a group of prophets who could prophesy with the aid of musicians, and when Saul joined this group, he too, gained this ability (although, as we have seen, he later lost it when God withdrew divine favor). The musicians apparently enabled the biblical prophets to gain enlightenment. Although the age of prophecy ended, worried Jews sometimes attempted to revive the ancient skill of using music to gain desired knowledge.[52]

In medieval times, some Jews believed that, in order to attain prophecy, they had to strengthen their intellectual powers and that music could do just that. Music might help induce prophecy by preparing the intellect for reception of divine revelation, they thought. Thus, for example, the thirteenth-century kabbalist Itzhak ibn Latif wrote that music improves a man's state of mind as well as his understanding of some of "the higher intellectual principles." The Zohar taught that the worthy people who "raise up" their hearts in song gain divine understanding and can discern what has been and what will be. According to the Zohar, Solomon and David were worthy of gaining such understanding, but Solomon was more gifted and wrote many proverbs and a book, the Song of Songs, which is "the song containing all mysteries of Torah and of Divine wisdom; the song wherein is power to penetrate into things that were and things that will be." Abulafia, who sang and played music to induce prophecy and joy, also recognized that while worries drag down the intellect, music—instrumental and vocal—frees it from this undesirable state and sharpens understanding.[53]

Leone of Modena was convinced that art music, music created with an aesthetic purpose, in particular, can lead us to a knowledge of "higher things" about God's ways and intentions. These "higher things" are order, relation, proportion, sweetness (beauty), understanding, and wisdom. Furthermore, Modena hoped to achieve a world of harmony through such music, a new era of peace and prosperity, but, as we have mentioned, his efforts met with rabbinic opposition and were not long-lasting.[54]

The Hasidim tell that one day, as Shneur Zalman of Liadi discoursed about communing with God, he noticed an old man in the audience who appeared not to understand his words. The old man looked troubled and was not following the lesson. Shneur Zalman stopped talking, but sang him a wordless melody. The old man closed his eyes and listened. The Hasidic rabbi watched as the old man relaxed: Now, at last, he understood the rabbi's lesson about how to trust and long for God. After that day, the rabbi always sang his wordless melody in every discourse.[55]

In modern times, the anthropologist Claude Lévi-Strauss and the psychiatrist Anthony Storr became convinced that music can promote our intellectual understanding. Lévi-Strauss compared music to myth since both music and myth give meaning to humanity's primitive worries and lead us to understand our own lives better. Lévi-Strauss believed that music can lead to inspiration and a widened vision. Storr has also argued that music can help us to make sense out of chaos, by ordering our minds and thereby enhancing our memory and understanding.[56]

Nowadays, music fills our environment in recorded forms. Electronic music fills the air in shops, elevators, and waiting rooms to provide a stimulating atmosphere (for example, to promote shopping), a relaxing atmosphere, or merely to prevent our being left alone with our worries. Often such music is annoying and does not have any of the beneficial effects we have mentioned above.

Music Therapy

Therapy is a "treatment intended to relieve or heal a disorder." We have just seen that, since antiquity, Jews have used music to relieve or heal disordered emotion.

Music therapy, according to the definition of the American Music Therapy Association, is "the prescribed use of music by a qualified person to effect positive changes in the psychological, physical, cognitive or social functioning of individuals with health or educational problems." This organization adds, notably, that healthy people can use music, by actively making music or merely listening to it, to reduce stress.[57]

Since 1917, some hospitals have used music as a sedative and to relieve patients' suffering. Some hospitals used music therapy to help veterans from both world wars who were suffering from nervous syndromes. Music was played to patients on the assumption that it might relieve mental stress.[58]

Since the 1960s, there has been considerable experimentation on the therapeutic use of music with many different categories of patients, such as psychiatric, neurological, and cancer patients. Some psychoanalysts have used musical improvisations during therapy sessions. Some therapists have employed musical stimuli to elicit emotions or stories. Ongoing research is assessing how music therapy works on the neuro-endocrine and immune systems in the hope of eventually revealing how, why, or which music can make people feel better.[59]

Jews have long known, however, that we do not need a trained music therapist, nor do we have to be a patient in order to use music to relieve our worries. In 1997, in Rehovot, Israel, twenty-five third-graders were stuck in an elevator with their teacher. The teacher panicked, the children screamed in fear and pressed all the buttons on the control panel to no avail. When an electrician arrived on the scene, he immediately offered the first line of a well-known tune and told all the class to sing as he worked to free them from the elevator. The children and teacher sang happily until they could go home.

Unlike King Saul and Moses ibn Ezra, we do not necessarily have to call on someone else to provide music that will help to calm our worries. Today we can obtain a recording of almost any music that we choose and listen to it almost whenever we want. A favorite old song may still affect us by making us tap our fingers, or get up and dance and forget all our worries, or relax and go to sleep. We can emulate our foremothers and sing to express our worries, or hum a cheerful tune to improve our mood. A new experience of sound combinations and progressions may arouse us, raise our spirits, or heighten our awareness. Alternatively, it may transport us only once and unforgettably to a special state of awareness, intensify our feeling of being, and increase our psychological strength. The effect of music is intensely personal.

8 ～ Humor

In his book *Souls on Fire,* Elie Wiesel paints a scene with words. He depicts a country that encompasses all the countries of the world. In that country, there is a town, the town of all towns. In the town, there is a street, the universal street, and within that street is a house, the archetype of all houses. Inside the house is a room, and there stands a man who laughs and laughs.[1]

Who is the laughing man, Wiesel wonders? Does he represent you and me, all men and all women? And why is the person laughing? Has he gone mad? Is he merely happy and joyous at being alive? Or is he laughing because he is worried about his terrible aloneness in the universe? Is he laughing to banish his anxiety or because he faces it and wants to show his strength? Is this the Jew who laughs off worry?

Wiesel's scene comes, he tells us, from Nahman of Bratzlav. Let us go back to the tale that was written down by Nahman's scribe. As we have seen in the previous chapter, the Hasid wanted Jews to interpret his tales just as they interpret Torah, to discover their deeper meaning. Indeed, this is exactly what Wiesel attempted to do, retelling the scene and asking questions. This is what the rabbi's scribe wrote:

"Toward morning, the sound of very, very great laughter was heard throughout the forest. The sound of the laughter spread throughout the forest because it was very, very great. The tree shook and swayed from the sound. And [the man sitting in the tree] was very, very scared and frightened by this." As the story continues, we are told that the laughter occurs at the end of every night, as dawn approaches. The spirit of the forest explains that this is the laughter of the day. The day laughs at the night, the night disappears, and day breaks.[2]

This scene occurs in the same story as that quoted in the previous chapter, about two men who were lost in the forest and found happiness through music. It is the same forest and the same spirit of the forest that explains the sounds. The forest could be the room in the house anywhere in Wiesel's universe; it represents the lost Jewish soul anywhere in the world. It represents the anxiety of the man who has lost his way in life, who does not know who or where he is. The night is the dark side of the soul, the instinctual side of ourselves that fills us with fear. The tree where the lost man takes refuge is the archetypal tree, giving knowledge and life. The laughter is the rejoicing of the day at conquering the night. Laughter conquers fear and brings relief and happiness.

Nahman of Bratzlav told stories to teach people how to serve God. He believed that laughter liberates the mind of worry, making room for holy thoughts. He believed, moreover, that human joy brings harmony and joy to the divine realm. So he pulled out of his melancholy by laughing, clowning, mocking, and joking, but his joy was short-lived; when his good humor subsided, he was again afraid and insecure.[3]

Rabbi Akiva also laughed. He laughed when others wept at how bad things were in the world. Why did he laugh, his companions wondered? He rejoiced that God would reward them in the world to come for their present suffering. The sages taught that God laughs with the wicked in this world, but with the righteous in the world to come.[4] Does God laugh with the wicked because God is worried? If God has indeed a sense of humor, then perhaps it is God who is laughing in Wiesel's scene. Perhaps his little sketch represents the divine world, where God is laughing.

Laughter is one way of coping with worry, especially among Jews today. As the French novelist Romain Gary noted, "If [fear of] Death didn't exist, life would lose its comic aspect."[5] Clearly, humor and laughter have other functions too, but this chapter is concerned with why, when, and how humor can help us to cope with worry. First, though, we will look at some of the characteristics of Jewish humor.

What Is Jewish Humor?

Jewish humor, some say, is humor that a non-Jew does not understand. A Jewish joke is a joke that a Jew has already heard and, what's more, can tell much better than the person who just told it. Jewish humor is a way of yelling, according to Romain Gary. Yet, Jewish humor is simply the humor created and enjoyed by Jews.[6]

Humor is a state of mind and an inclination, rather like worry, and as we will see, it can both express and relieve worry. We can be "out of humor" when we are worried; alternatively, we can draw on our "sense of humor" and perceive or express humor to relieve anxiety. Humor is therefore also a way of seeing things, in a depressing way if we are out of humor, or in an amusing way if we have a sense of humor. In this chapter, we notice the ability of Jews to see the funny side of a worrying situation, to find the ludicrous and laugh at it.

Humor is a universal phenomenon, yet culture-bound and subjective. All peoples laugh, but they cannot laugh at the same jokes. What one person finds funny, another may not find at all amusing. A non-Jew may not appreciate a Jewish joke because it refers to an aspect of Jewish life or a word that is unfamiliar to the non-Jew. Similarly, an Ashkenazic Jew may not laugh at a joke told by a Sephardic Jew, because their language and culture differ. Humor depends on associations, experience, and expectations.

Jewish humor—like any other humor—includes joking, facetiousness, and appreciating the comic aspects of a situation. It can be verbal or nonverbal, or both at once. Satire and irony are verbal forms of humor. But parody, comedy, ridicule, and jest may be verbal or nonverbal. Children, especially, and jesters whose job it is to generate laughter, enjoy fooling and buffoonery, often using mimicry and caricature to draw a response from others. Jews have used all of these forms of humor, at different times, in different places.

However, Jewish humor is most often an intellectual humor that flaunts the mental strength of the Jew. This humor reveals an ability to use the tongue and the pen as a weapon of attack, to render absurd an unpleasant reality, or as a shield for self-defense in moments of insecurity.

For years, Freud collected Jewish jokes, including examples of self-disparaging humor, witty word play, and comic mimicry. "I don't know whether there are many other instances of a people making fun to such a degree of its own character [like the Jews]," he wrote, in 1905, in *Jokes and Their Relation to the Unconscious*. He thought that jokes have "deep significance" and concluded that humor is a defense against unpleasantness.[7]

Theodor Reik (1888–1970), a Viennese-born Jewish psychoanalyst who studied the proverbs and jokes of German-speaking Jews, concluded that Jewish humor oscillates between masochistic self-humiliation and paranoid feelings of superiority.[8] The admission of our own weaknesses in a show of mental strength is characteristic of Ashkenazic Jewish humor. Generally, Sephardic Jewish humor is less aggressive and does not involve self-humiliation.

Why Does Humor Help Us Cope with Worry?

Humor helps us to change negative feeling into positive feeling: "Look, I'm laughing at all my problems and at the stupid world that causes them!" By taking a bravado attitude and treating a danger or other problem as a laughing matter, Jews have persuaded themselves and others that their worry is not serious. Jews often joke about their worries, facing them with humor, banishing them with humor, and converting their anxieties into more positive emotions.

Humor shows us suddenly how we can see the world in a new, unexpected way. The Ba'al Shem Tov, in the eighteenth century, realized that when we laugh "a breath of gentleness wafts through the world. What was rigid thaws, and what was a burden becomes light."

When we see the funny side of a situation, the burden of worry lessens, even if the worry stays inside, hidden and unexpressed.[9]

Shared humor connects people. By telling jokes and humorous tales in worrying times, Jews have bonded with fellow Jews and been comforted by the feeling that they are not alone. Humor can promote love and the approval of others, which adds to the worrier's feeling of security. However, humor can, of course, fall on deaf ears and remain unappreciated, or worse, offend and bring trouble. The schoolboy's wisecrack in front of his class, when his teacher catches him copying during a test, may win him laughing admiration from his buddies, but angry punishment from his teacher.

"Laughter protects one's honor," said Rabbi Akiva.[10] We may use humor to retaliate against offense, to reduce the dignity and authority of an opponent or oppressor and inflate our own feeling of strength. In addition, humor allows us to hide our fear and protect our own self-esteem.

By joking in times of danger, Jews have kept their spirits alive and confirmed their own and others' vitality and strength. In the most difficult situations, Jews have used humor as a tool for survival. It is told that one day, the Hasid Simha Bunam of Pshiskhe (1762–1827), noticed a man drowning in the Gulf of Danzig. He could see the man was giving up hope and shouted to him, "Give my greetings to the Leviathan!" The drowning man smiled at the joke, and realized he had not gone down yet. He managed to keep himself afloat until he was rescued. Bunam taught that some jokes come from heaven. He had a wonderful sense of humor that prevented him from worrying until his dying day. Even on that day, apparently, he was not afraid.[11]

Laughter does not make a worry disappear, however. On the contrary, we may remain preoccupied with it or unable to escape from the problem that we joke about: "The heart may ache even in laughter, and joy may end in grief" (Prov. 14:13). But humor serves to release the worrier's tension and distress. In the past, the poor Jew joked about the Rothschilds, the concentration camp inmate joked about the Nazis and death, and the refusenik joked about the KGB.

Today, middle-aged men spin tall tales about Viagra, and Israelis somehow dig up a laugh even in the grimmest moments.

Freud thought that humor protects the ego from suffering by diverting embarrassing sexual and aggressive energy into socially acceptable humor. People tell jokes, he reasoned, because they find it difficult to express their sexuality and aggression directly and have a "psychoneurotic constitution," although he admitted he had insufficient evidence to prove his hypothesis. He thought that those who tell sexual jokes have a concealed inclination to exhibitionism, whereas those who tell aggressive jokes are sadistically inclined people who are inhibited from fulfilling their wishes. Humor helps to convert their unconquered emotion, such as guilt, fear, and anger, into laughter that is socially acceptable. Like Freud, Reik believed that humor acts as a shield, protecting the mind from dangers lurking in the unconscious, such as guilt feelings over forbidden impulses. He believed also that Jews have used humor to reduce their considerable guilt-induced anxiety because in this way they gain admiration from others.[12]

Modern humor research does not support Freud's psychoneurotic view of humor. For example, an Israeli study done in 1986 investigated the incidence of psychological problems, including nightmares, in children in border settlements, who often needed to take shelter from rocket attacks. Those who were with a friend with a sense of humor during the attacks revealed fewer problems compared to those without such a friend. The study concluded that humor helped the children cope with stress and proved to be an adaptive, not a neurotic, behavior. A variety of recent psychological experiments have shown that humor contributes to stress reduction, social cohesiveness, and better communication. People who have a sense of humor are more optimistic and enjoy life more than those without. Humor reveals an ability to think originally and therefore to interpret a worrying situation in unusual ways. Humor may also help us to tolerate pain and unpleasantness; worry is usually unpleasant, if not actually painful.[13]

When Have Jews Used Humor to Cope with Worry?

The writer of Ecclesiastes was wary of merriment, but admitted that there is a time for laughter, just as there is a time for weeping. There are times in life when a Jew should laugh and be joyous, for example, at Purim and at wedding celebrations. Another time for laughter is when we are worried but want to hide it and instead show our strength. In addition, when our companions are anxious, we can banish disturbing thoughts with a joke and raise their morale.[14]

The Time to Laugh

Many rabbis have disapproved of levity and foolish merriment, associating these with lewdness and sin. However, Purim, in the Jewish month of Adar, is the time for rejoicing over the Jews' victory over Haman, the descendent of Agag, king of Amalek. On Purim, observant Jews remember Amalek, the grandson of Esau, who represents evil, defilement, and hatred for Israel. The Bible commands: "Remember what Amalek did to you . . . after you left Egypt. . . . Therefore, when the Lord your God grants you safety from all your enemies around you . . . you shall blot out the memory of Amalek from under heaven. Do not forget!" (Deut. 25:17–19). We must remember the force of hatred and evil until we can be sure of God's protection. On Purim, we remember by reading the story of the victory of Queen Esther and Mordecai over Haman, and rejoice over the downfall of the wicked by drinking, dressing up, and laughing. We cannot blot out the memory of Amalek as we are not yet free from worry; the winds of evil and anti-Semitic hatred come and go all over the world, taking innocent lives over and over again. On Purim, however, laughing is permitted and professional jesters have often helped Jews to feel joyous.[15]

The fourteenth-century Provençal translator Kalonymus ben Kalonymus wrote a witty debate on food and drunkenness to cheer people on Purim, when Jews should laugh and be happy. It was a parody of rabbinic disputation. He declared that his treatise was like a book of medicine, which could benefit the body and would not harm the soul. It would surely make people laugh, reduce the melancholic humor of the black bile, and blot out worries. Some rabbis, however, thought his parody unjustifiably sacrilegious and wanted it burned. But the text survived the ages and set a precedent for ridiculing rabbis and parodying their texts. Similarly, in 1728 the rabbis of Hamburg banned the Purim-*shpil,* the Purim play that gave license to vulgar jokes and promoted joy and laughter. However, some Jews have continued to include an amusing *shpil* in their Purim festivities.[16]

Professional jesters have created a joyous atmosphere at weddings, too, which (as we have seen) have often been worrying as well as joyful occasions. It is told that the breaking of a glass at the wedding ceremony is a way to remind merrymakers to become serious again. In twentieth-century Morocco, the women's "song of curses" at a wedding ceremony made fun of specific worries; for example, it made fun of old men who seek to marry young women, either as a first wife, or to replace an older wife. In Salonika, Greece, Sephardic Jews sang humorous prenuptial songs to help the bride face her worries about leaving her parent's home or about marrying an old man.[17]

The prospect of living with in-laws could be daunting. "Why did Adam and Eve live so long?" asks the Yiddish-speaking entertainer. "Because their lives were not shortened by *machotanim* [in-laws]." Eastern European Jews employed itinerant entertainers to create a joyful atmosphere when needed, especially at weddings. In the early seventeenth century, a rabbi in Poland condemned their irreverent jesting at marriage ceremonies, but the tradition nevertheless flourished. The Jewish jester addressed the bride's worries in humorous verse before the wedding ceremony, as she sat under her veil, surrounded by all the wedding guests. A wedding, still today, is often a time of both anxiety and joy.[18]

The birth of a child is another time in the life cycle when joy is mixed with worry. Jewish jesters in medieval Spain and southern France performed comic acts and adapted the words of well-known songs to entertain people after the birth of a child. In seventeenth-century Italy, Jews gathered in the home of the newborn on the night before a circumcision to make merry. A traveler to North Africa in the late seventeenth century noted that here too Jewish women visited a new mother on the eve of her newborn son's circumcision and passed the whole night together in laughter. On this night the new mother was especially worried that the newborn would be harmed by a demon. Laughter allowed the mother to forget her worry, while the merry women's noise had the added advantage of frightening away the evil spirits.[19]

When We Want to Appear and Feel Strong

Jews have used their wits to belittle their worries or to hide them, when they want to appear strong. They have satirized, parodied, caricatured, and mimicked to degrade the source of their worry and gain a temporary feeling of fortitude and control when there was nothing else they could do to improve a dismal situation. They have used such humor, for example, when they have been unable to conquer injustice or oppression.

In antiquity, Elijah scoffed at the prophets of Baal who invoked their god to no avail. The pagans had knives and spears and there were so many of them. What would happen to Elijah if God remained silent, or if the pagans believed that their god had somehow responded? Perhaps their god was busy talking, away on a journey, or asleep, Elijah mocked. He surely laughed at the pagans because he was worried during the long morning's contest. The Psalmist noticed that the righteous laugh at the wicked out of fear.[20]

Jews have frequently used their tongues, as Elijah did, in aggressive humor to reduce the authority of an opponent and reveal their own superiority. The sages were not happy about Elijah's example, however. They permitted sneering and scoffing at idols, but in no other situation: scoffing brings suffering and destruction, they warned.[21]

In the early fourth century, Rabbi Jeremiah used his sense of humor to diffuse rabbinical arguments, but was thrown out of the study house for his impudence. Similarly, the satiric wit of Hershele

Ostropoler (1770–1810), a ritual slaughterer in the small town of Ostropol, Poland, offended the communal leaders and led to his dis-
missal. Destitute, he wandered from inn to inn, where the common
folk appreciated his jokes about Jewish life, especially those about
religious hypocrites, rich misers, and pretenders to wisdom. He
gained strength through his humor in worrying situations. For example, when he could not pay the rent for his room, and the landlord
threatened to evict him and look for another lodger, he quipped:
"That would be silly. You mustn't do that." "Oh no? My decision
doesn't suit you?" replied the landlord. "It won't suit you, either," explained the Jew. "Why look for a new lodger, whose ability to pay
may be uncertain? With me, at least you know where I stand."[22]

As the Enlightenment reached eastern European Jews, some used
such humor to rebel against and attack the limiting world of the rabbis, Torah studies, and the *shtetl* community. A young married man,
the son of a rabbi, was forced by his traditionalist father-in-law to divorce his new wife when he became interested in the Western intellectual movement. In 1824, the outcast wrote a witty parody of the
sixteenth-century code of Jewish law, wielding his humor against
Jewish tradition as he struggled with his own Jewish identity crisis.
His text offended the rabbis of Vilna, who banned and burned it.
Other Jews, too, laughed at the Jewish tradition that they rejected
and parodied Jewish texts to hide their lingering anxiety and to show
their own superiority.[23]

It is told that a Rumanian Jewish prisoner, exhausted by the Nazis,
turned his humor toward God: "Dear God, for five thousand years
we have been Your chosen people. Enough! Choose another one
now!"[24] Of course, this prayer is not in the Jewish prayer book and
the liturgy is not the place to look for Jewish humor. In addition,
when someone else tells this tale, the author of the prayer may not be
the Rumanian prisoner, but another Jew in another hopeless situation. It is a popular story whose aim is to give strength. It teaches
that if you think your situation is upsetting, look, here is a Jew who
did not accept things meekly, but argued with God for a change.

Maurice Sendak converted his childhood fears into illustrated stories full of devilish humor that may help children to face anxiety and feel and become strong. He knows that all children worry. "Will Mama and Papa go away and never come back? Will I die?" These were his own boyhood worries. Every time his hungry aunts and uncles, with hairy nostrils and blackened teeth, came for lunch, he worried that they might eat him up. In addition, the vacuum cleaner and school triggered floods of apprehension. In *Where the Wild Things Are*, Max dares to tell his mother that he will eat her up and conquer frightening monsters who have terrible roars, terrible teeth, terrible eyes, and terrible claws.[25]

On board the hijacked plane that crashed in Pennsylvania on September 11, 2001, Jeremy Glick joked with his wife that at least he had kept his plastic butter knife from breakfast as a weapon to fight the terrorists. We can imagine that such gallows humor gave him strength. As two girls head for home in different directions after their day at school in a Jewish settlement on the West Bank, they part with the usual joke: "So when shall we meet again? At your funeral or mine?" Teenage children of Jewish settlers have developed their own particular black humor to help them express their worry that they could be the next victims of terrorism and win out by turning it into a laughing matter.[26]

When We Want to Raise Morale

Moroccan Jews advise: "Laughter calms worries." "For one who has many worries, it is best to laugh" means that laughter is the best medicine for worry. A Yiddish proverb counsels ridiculously: "Don't be afraid when you have no other choice." These folk sayings remind us that Jews have long used humor to raise morale when anxiety threatens to take over and win out.[27]

The Talmud teaches that jesters who raise people's morale have a place in the world to come. Legend tells that one day Hershele Ostropoler was called to the Hasidic court of Medzibezh to cure with his humor the Ba'al Shem Tov's grandson, who suffered from melancholy. Yakov Itzhak, the Seer of Lublin, also employed a jester, Reb Mordecai Rakover, to improve his mood. Nahman of Bratzlav taught that we are duty-bound to share good humor and cheer a worried person with it. He knew that laughter is contagious.[28]

When interned at Auschwitz, Viktor Frankl, the Austrian psychiatrist, nurtured a sense of humor in his friend. Together, they tried to invent amusing stories about life after their liberation, to maintain their hopes that their nightmare would end, and to keep their spirits alive. Another survivor recalled how he and another friend often joked together at the absurdity of their ordeal. He thought that their shared sense of humor had given them strength to survive the war.[29]

Humor thrives today in the Israeli army, among the young fighters in combat units, on the front line, just as it did among the tough Jewish fighters for Israel's independence, half a century ago. This humor keeps morale high and gives the impression of psychological strength. Two soldiers, who had been well trained for an attack on a refugee camp in the West Bank, in April 2002, joked together in the dead of night, just minutes before their dangerous mission began. "Shall we phone home to say good-bye—this may be our last chance," said one to the other with a hint of worry in his voice. "Why disturb their sleep, why get them panicky," his friend replied. "If my mother knew I were here, she'd come running straight over in her nightgown to take my place."[30]

Each crisis that threatens Israel's unity produces a fresh set of jokes and cartoons, so that Israelis can laugh and feel strong, instead of giving in to pessimistic anxiety. Bus drivers open their radios at full volume so that all travelers can chuckle over the humor of Israeli comedians, "*Ha-gashash ha-ḥiver*," who caricature the trials and tribulations of Israeli daily life. An evening meeting with friends in an Israeli home on a Friday night is a time for exchanging the latest political jokes that concern the national worry of the day. Instead of moaning, like Akiva's colleagues, Israelis face their worries with laughter, like Akiva himself.

How Has Humor Helped Jews Cope with Worry?

Jews have used humor as a weapon to fight their feelings of insecurity and turn their vulnerability into a joyful show of strength. They have also wielded their humor as a shield to protect themselves from threats from without as well as from within themselves. They have banished the feeling of worry with a distracting joke or ridiculous fantasy to gain a shared smile, a laugh, or an amused shrug. But they have also flaunted their weakness humorously and won admiration. They have converted the energy of worry into humor, with cathartic effect. They have, in addition, reinterpreted a worrying situation by finding a new, funny way of looking at it.

By Serving As a Weapon

Humor has often been the only weapon available to Jews to fight worries that have no apparent solutions. Natan (Anatoly) Sharansky, who was accused of treason on trumped-up charges and spent nine years in Soviet prisons (including more than four hundred days in isolation), said: "In freedom, humor is a mere luxury. In prison, it's the only weapon. The moment you can laugh at them [your oppressors] you are free."[31]

The Jews living in the Soviet Union under the oppression of Communist rule told anti-establishment jokes and laughed disrespectfully between themselves at the fear-inspiring KGB, the hostile bureaucracy, and the pervasive anti-Semitism. By facing their worries with humor, usually allowing the stereotyped Jew—Rabinovich, Shapiro, or the wise rabbi—to win out, they felt strong: Shapiro phones the KGB to declare that his neighbor—Rabinovich, why not?—is hiding illegal dollars in his firewood. The KGB thugs descend on Rabinovich, find the shed with the firewood, and break up all the wood. They threaten, kick, and leave empty-handed. Soon, Shapiro pokes his head through Rabinovich's window: "Nu, did they chop your firewood? Now it's your turn, my cabbage patch needs turning over."[32]

Soviet Jews worried about neighbors reporting them to the KGB as well as the possibility that one day these thugs would barge in on them and wreak their dreaded havoc on their lives. There was nothing they could do to make the worrying KGB disappear, so why not find a way of benefiting from them? Soviet Jews had a large repertoire of jokes; they had a witty quip for almost every worrying situation. The shared joke ridiculed common worries, allowing those who could laugh to feel fortified. In addition, shared jokes strengthened the bonds of friendship and raised morale.

By Acting As a Shield

Humor allows us to hide a worry and escape from unpleasantness and, at the same time, to show our psychological strength. The Bible tells us that Sarah was an old, withered woman of about ninety when some visitors arrived and told her husband that within a year she would bear him a son. She laughed! This was absurd, nonsensical, a joke! It was a mean joke, as she had suffered so much from her barrenness. God noticed her laughter, however, and accused her of lacking faith in the Lord's wondrous powers. Sarah's humor was skeptical and cynical; in laughing she revealed her doubt. She laughed to escape from the unpleasantness of the truth; she knew she could not have the promised child. Her distress did not disappear, but she revealed courage; by laughing, she showed that her spirit was strong in spite of her sad situation. (She did, of course, give birth as predicted, to Itzhak [Isaac], whose name derives from the Hebrew root for laughter, tz-ḥ-k.) Sarah was the first person in the Bible to reveal a sense of humor.[33]

The German poet Heinrich Heine remained anxious about his Jewishness, even after converting to Christianity in 1825, at the age of twenty-six, in order to be accepted into non-Jewish society. This act brought him no advantages and he worried about it. "It is extremely difficult for a Jew to be converted to the religion of Jesus, for how can one Jew believe in the divinity of another?" he quipped. His last laugh was on his deathbed: When a priest reminded him of God's mercy and that God might pardon his sins, Heine again showed he had the upper hand: "Of course He'll forgive me, that's His job."[34]

At the close of the nineteenth century, Freud loved to tell *shnorrer* jokes, in which a poor man treats the rich man's money impudently. We have already mentioned that Freud believed that jokes have "deep significance." These jokes surely touched his sensitive memory of his own shnorring when he was an impecunious student, as well as his debts to rich men whom he later avoided. Similarly, Freud was fond of the anti-religious witticisms of Heine and Moritz Saphir, who both converted from Judaism. He himself did not convert, but struggled, like them, to come to terms with his Jewish identity as he strove for success in the non-Jewish world. He remained an anxious Jew with a sense of humor that helped him shield his worries. Rather than admit the relevance of these jokes to his personal concerns, Freud generalized that the indignation that such jokes created was directed against "highly oppressive" Jewish law. In this way he hid his insecurity, expressed his hostility to his Jewish heritage, and felt strong and superior.[35]

By Banishing Worry

We have already seen, in chapter 2, that the oldest therapeutic advice for worry is found in the Bible: "If there is anxiety in a man's mind let him quash it, and turn it into joy with a good word" (Prov. 12:25). Jews have cracked a joke or performed a comic act, even made a funny face to distract another person from worrying. Unexpected or incongruous behavior can produce laughter that makes worry disappear. Once, when my family was on holiday, we lost our way in a forest on a steep mountain. Our worry increased when the drizzle turned into a downpour, thunder boomed, and the lightning broke up the sky above the trees. Suddenly my daughter cupped her hands, caught the raindrops, and shouted, "Honey, this is *great* coffee!" We burst into laughter and ran onward, no longer flustered, determined to reach the village safely.

A Hasid, Rabbi Naftali of Ropshitz (1760–1827), was a joker as a boy. As a young man, he jested at a wedding; guests said they laughed so hard that the angels laughed, the holy souls in paradise interrupted their studies and laughed, and God, too, laughed. Naftali poked fun at the sages and mimicked his teacher leaning on his cane, frowning, and distributing blessings. But one day Naftali went into seclusion. He stopped joking, turned away all those who visited him, and sat in silence, refusing to speak even to his own son. On his deathbed, the son tried once again to discover what had happened. He pleaded that it was the last chance to find out. The old man stared for a long time and then in a terrible whisper he said, "I . . . am . . . afraid. Do you understand? Do you understand. . . ? I Am Afraid." We do not know why he suddenly lost his ability to laugh away his anxiety.[36]

The Ropshitz rabbi may have feared "the last day," the certainty of death, but the exemplary woman of valor "laughs at the last day" (Prov. 31:25, in accordance with the literal meaning of the text). Her laughter banishes her fear of death and shows everyone her strength.

By Winning Admiration

Humor, like prophecy, needs an audience. When laughing about their worries with friends, Jews have often taken the approach of Rabbi Assi, who encouraged facing, expressing, and sharing worry. By sharing worry with friends in an amusing way, Jews have won love, or at least social approval, and raised morale.

The Yiddish writer Sholom Aleichem (1859–1916) did not deny people's worries; he showed them how to admit them and laugh. He sought the comic in the irrational. One of his characters wrote from the scene of a pogrom to a relative in the New World: "We're not in the least afraid of a pogrom. We've already had one, along with two encores . . . No one from our family was hurt, except Lipa, who was killed along with his two sons, and Noah and Melekh, two workers with golden hands . . . You asked about Hershele. Don't worry about him. For the past six months, he's been unemployed, sitting in solitary confinement in prison." He ends the family news report by commenting that "Mendel did a smart thing: he simply died. Some say from weakness, some say from hunger. I personally think he died from both. Really, I don't know what else to write, except that cholera is spreading like wildfire."[37]

Woody Allen craves to be loved and fears dying. In his writing and films, he wants us to laugh with him about his being so obviously Jewish. The alienated, neurotic, and unsuccessful Jew is the target of his humor. He laughs at sex, death, and Jewish tradition. He converts anxiety into humor in a speech to undergraduates: "More than any other time in history, mankind faces a crossroads. One path leads to despair and utter hopelessness. The other, to total extinction. Let us pray we have the wisdom to choose correctly."[38]

Many other Jewish comedians, such as Lenny Bruce (1925–1966), the Marx Brothers—Chico, Groucho, Gummo, Harpo, and Zeppo (b. between 1891 and 1901)—and Fanny Brice (1891–1951), won admiration through their humor, which, like the Jewish humor on the Internet today, focused on the common worries associated with being Jewish, family relations, money, sex, and the fear of death.[39]

By Converting or Diverting Worry into Laughter

Jews use humor to convert undesired, pent-up emotion, including worry, into a smile or a laugh. Instead of yelling or crying, humor can help us cope with unpleasant reality. Abraham ibn Ezra, a philosopher and physician in medieval Spain, laughed at his penury: if he were a dealer in shrouds, no one would die as long as he lived, and if he were to deal in candles, the sun would never set. His quip about dealing in candles eventually turned into a Yiddish proverb that helped people convert unpleasant reality into amusing fantasy.[40]

Jews have often diverted worry with a good story. They have a huge repertoire of humorous tales that help them to smile in worrying situations. For example, in the early twentieth century, when the Sephardic Jews in Jerusalem regularly walked through the dirty alleys of the Old City to pray at the Western Wall, they feared the Arabs who sometimes terrorized them on their way or urinated on them from above. These Jews relieved their fear by laughing at a well-known tale in which a saintly rabbi uttered a phrase that caused all the Arabs to freeze on the spot. The peeing urchins were left standing with their trousers dropped and the armed men stood petrified, cocking their guns throughout the night, until the rabbi was persuaded to lift his spell.[41]

Jews today still tell stories that were popular a century or two ago, about Moshiko or Joha, the simpleton loved by Sephardic Jews, and the "wise men" of Chelm, to convert anxiety into laughter. These innocent fools worry over their problems and come up with unbelievably stupid solutions, which provoke laughter. For example, the Chelm Jews look for a lost coin in the dry ground outside of town instead of in the muddy synagogue courtyard where it was lost, as it is easier to search for a lost coin on dry ground. When an Israeli mother worried that her son would not be able to change his flight home from India recently, due to some "misunderstanding" with Air India, the travel agent reminded her that there are Chelmites all over the world. Mentioning Chelm was enough—there was no need for a folktale. She diffused the woman's worry about her son's return and solved the problem with good humor.[42]

In a similar vein, Joha is foolish but often unexpectedly witty, winning out over those who mean to harm him. When he brings his landlord some figs and the landlord throws them in his face, Joha thanks God that he had brought figs and not beets that would surely have knocked off his head. On another occasion, Joha brings seven camels to market, but when he arrives he counts them and finds only six. He tells a sage who points out that he has not counted the camel that he is sitting on. The sage's words have turned into a Sephardic proverb about a shortsighted fool who turns small problems into large ones.[43]

In the mid-twentieth century, Mel Brooks joked at his problems in becoming a real American. This second-generation Jew admitted that his humor came from his feeling that he did not fit and would never fit into mainstream American society. This feeling, which he converted to laughter in stand-up comedy, was a mixture of fear, insecurity, anger, and resentment. Joan Rivers, also an American child of immigrant parents, has wielded comedy in a similar way, to cover her insecurity and gain the love, admiration, and attention that she has craved. The Hungarian-born satirist George Mikes (1912–1987) laughed at the British who made him feel alien.[44]

Jokes about Arabs allow a release from the constant worry of yet another suicide bomb, Israeli humorists admitted in a discussion on politically incorrect humor in August 2001. Thus, for example, jokes and cartoons allowing people to laugh at bearded martyrs counting virgins in heaven were permissible.[45]

By Changing Perspective

Rabbi Akiva set another example of how it is possible to cope with worry by looking at a situation from an unusual angle, humorously. After the destruction of the Temple, Akiva and his colleagues arrived in Jerusalem. They reached the Temple mount just as a jackal ran out of the ruined Holy of Holies. The friends began to weep, all except Akiva, who laughed. They wept, we are told, for witnessing the fulfillment of the biblical verse, about "Mount Zion, which lies desolate, jackals prowl over it" (Lam. 5:18). But Akiva laughed, rejoicing in the fulfillment of another verse, which declares Uriah and Zechariah "reliable witnesses" (Isa. 8:2). Because the words of Uriah— "Jerusalem shall become a heap of ruins" (Jer. 26:18)—had come true, Akiva realized that Zechariah's prophecy ("the squares of the city shall be crowded with boys and girls playing" [Zech. 8:5]) would also come true. He laughed as he imagined the unlikely scene of a beautiful city rising again on this desolate site; he imagined young children happily skipping about in its little squares. But for Akiva's mirth, the miserable sages would have gone home crying their hearts out. He distracted his friends by laughing and helped them to think positively. They could return home with raised morale.[46]

Jews have been quick to convert or divert worry with ridiculous fantasy, with a ludicrous tale that distracts, entertains, and shows that there might be a clever solution, all at the same time. In a Sephardic tale, a hotel manager overcharges Salomon and Rivka on their honeymoon. Over and above the price of bed and breakfast, the bill included extras.

"It includes the use of the ballroom, the tennis court, the Turk-ish baths, and the smoking room," explained the manager.

"But we did not dance, play, bathe, smoke, or even enter any of these areas," protested the newly wed.

"You could have done all these activities," retorted the hote-lier, and held out the bill for paying.

"Last night you lay with my beautiful wife and that will cost *you* 30,000 pounds!" said Salomon, suddenly.

"I certainly did not!"

"But you could have done so," said Salomon and left without paying for the extras.[47]

Salomon worries over the unexpectedly high bill for his honey-moon, but quickly finds an alternative way of viewing his problem. His solution makes us smile, although his bride may not have appre-ciated the joke. His sudden change of perspective avoids undesirable emotion. It would not go down well, though, if a woman who found herself seriously overcharged for renting a car, for example, were to offer the clerk on the other side of the counter a night with her hus-band. The woman worried about being overcharged would have to solve the problem differently. The tale, whether midrashic or folk-loric, like some of the short, pithy Jewish proverbs, is not meant to be taken literally; it merely encourages us to seek new ways of viewing our worries.

In late antiquity, if you worried about what others were saying about you, a proverb offered you humorous advice: "If one person says you are a donkey, don't pay any attention; but if two people say this, go and buy yourself a saddle" (Genesis Rabbah 45:7). The proverb invited you to introspect and change your ways.

A fifteenth-century poet named Solomon Bonafed fled Saragossa during anti-Semitic massacres and wrote to a friend who had lost his fortune: "See how horses streak through the sea like lightning bolts, and ships sail through the market-place. A thread of linen splinters a bar of iron, and water blazes like wood. Leopards flee before kids and foxes give chase to lions." He encouraged his friend to look at the world differently, change his assumptions and expectations about the rules of nature, and laugh at the instability and uncertainty that worried them.[48]

Bulgarian Jews tell the story of Perla, who notices her husband tossing and turning sleeplessly in bed next to her. "What is bothering you?" she asks. He does not want to share his worries with her. But eventually she presses him to talk and he reveals that he must repay a debt but does not have the money to do so. Perla gets up, dresses, and rushes out, even though it is past midnight. She goes to the lender's house and calls through his closed shutters not to expect the money from her husband: "My husband will not pay you tomorrow!" She returns to her bed and reassures her husband. Now the lender can worry and lose sleep over the loan while her husband rests peacefully all night.[49]

Some Jewish prisoners locked in the ghettos and Nazi death camps managed to mock and ridicule their tragic plight. Jews in the Lodz Ghetto called deportation notices "wedding invitations." In the Sobibor death camp, a prisoner painted "Road to Heaven" on a street sign.[50]

Elie Wiesel describes one Jew who laughed with all his heart as his guard took him to be hanged.

> "Have you gone crazy?"
> "No, of course not."
> "Aren't you afraid?"
> "Scared to bits!"
> "So why are you laughing?"
> "Today, I am Mordecai the water-carrier, but tomorrow I'll be Mordecai the Martyr, Mordecai the Saint, and him you'll never hang, never!"[51]

Recent psychological research supports the idea that humor helps people to cope with worry by bringing about a change in attitude. The feeling of "I am worried" is challenged by the message that humor elicits, that "this is an amusing situation" and leads to the conclusion that "as this is amusing, I need not worry."[52]

Can We Acquire a Sense of Humor?

Some people have a sense of humor, and others are not so lucky. The American comedian Mel Brooks said that "you are either blessed with humor, or it escapes you." If you are not born with a sense of humor, according to this comedian, you can never acquire this gift. But if you are born with this gift, you may lose it one day, as Naftali of Ropshitz has shown us.[53]

Perhaps we are all born with this gift, but some of us lose it in childhood. Two influential eighteenth-century Hasidic rabbis, Dov Baer, the Maggid of Mezritch, and the Seer of Lublin, noticed that infants know how to laugh but lose the ability as they grow up. We have to learn this skill from infants, said the one; we must learn to laugh while weeping, like a child, said the other. It would appear that they believed that we are born with the gift of humor, but we lose it, sooner or later, for one reason or another, and need to learn to develop it and make use of it. We can imagine that most Jews who grew up in late eighteenth-century Poland lost their carefree childhood laughter as they took on the burdens of adult life.[54]

Freud also noticed that children naturally enjoy comic situations, mimicry, and word play. He thought that these forms of humor evoke in adults the mood of childhood. As he did not believe in God, he could not consider humor to be a divine gift. Nevertheless, Freud came to think of humor as a gift for coping with suffering. He supposed that humor comes from the unconscious and is formed from thought processes that developed in early childhood. He proposed that humor employs a regressive mode of thinking: by reverting to infantile thought processes, we escape from threat and uncertainty and regain childish sources of pleasure. He believed that we develop or fail to develop our sense of humor unconsciously.[55]

Are some unlucky souls born straight-faced without the possibility of ever developing a sense of humor? More than anyone else, Sholom Aleichem taught Yiddish-speaking Jews to laugh over their worries. His readers laughed with his characters; they laughed through their tears. His characters, like his readers, were the fiddler on the roof, the traveling salesmen, and market women. In addition, his matchmakers, fathers and mothers, and sons and daughters used their skillful tongues to fight and to shield themselves from harm. He invented humorous nuances in Yiddish, Hebrew, and a smattering of other languages too, which Jews turned into weapons against the dangers confronting them. He joked about the *shtetl* running scared at the news of impending disaster, but at the same time was fully aware of the real dangers facing the Jews. Sholom Aleichem's humorous stories reflect the worries that accompanied the breakdown of tradition and the difficulty of the old Jew in adjusting to new realities. He showed Jews how to retain their dignity in a cruel world. In 1911, he wrote: "I tell you it is an ugly and mean world and only to spite it one mustn't weep! . . . Not to cry out of spite! Only to laugh out of spite, *only to laugh.*"[56]

Sephardic Jews and the Jews who lived in Arab lands traditionally acquired their humor through their folktales and proverbs. Except for the very Orthodox, who distance themselves from the secular world, most Jews today acquire their humor, like non-Jews, mostly from the media, and not from ancestral culture. We know that humor depends on associations, experience, and expectations, and therefore it is, to a large extent, a product of learning. We can seek to reinterpret situations, and attempt to look at them from a new angle. By reinterpreting a threat as a joke, we can often diffuse tension through laughter instead of through stress and tears.

Viktor Frankl showed that if we do not develop humor naturally as we grow up and mature, we may still learn to see the funny side of anxiety. Frankl, who resorted to humor to keep his spirit alive in the concentration camps, assumed that people can acquire a sense of humor and can learn to distance anxiety by laughing at their fears. This psychiatrist managed to teach his neurotic patients to use humor deliberately to overcome their fears. His method, which he called "paradoxical intention," demands that the patient should desire and intend to happen exactly what he or she fears.[57]

Our grandparents' sayings and folktales are fading like old clothes; they are hardly of interest or relevance to our modern daily lives. Humor, like fashion, changes from one generation to the next. Whereas Sholem Aleichem, Mel Brooks, and Woody Allen taught some of us funny ways of seeing familiar situations, today there are many other sources for acquiring humor. Television comedy, comics and cartoons, videos, and computerized games are only some of the influences—subliminal or conscious—on the humor that we use.

We can acquire a humorous way of looking at and responding to our environment as we grow up or as we find our place in society, without our realizing that this learning process is taking place. We can also make a conscious effort to seek humor in a worrying situation. We can learn to make humor a part of our lives. When we catch ourselves worrying, we can remind ourselves of the Moroccan Jewish adage—"For one who has many worries, it is best to laugh"—or of the Yiddish proverb—"Don't be afraid when you have no other choice." We can learn to look for the funny side of a worrying situation. Often we can be sure that we will be able to laugh at ourselves later, when the worry is over and we tell the story of our distressing adventure to friends or family. Why wait until later? Why not laugh now, instead of worrying? But remember, it is always safer to laugh at ourselves than to laugh at others. Scorn, sarcasm, and ridicule can hurt. If the listener does not have the same sense of humor, that person could become hostile and create new worries for the joker.

9 ～ Worry: For Better or for Worse?

In Genesis 22, we are told that "God put Abraham to the test" by telling him to take his son Isaac and sacrifice him as a burnt offering. Father and son set out to the land of Moriah. "Where is the sheep for the burnt offering?" wonders Isaac, who is carrying the firewood. Isaac is bound and laid on the altar, on top of the wood. Surely both the father and the son are worried, but the Bible does not tell us this; we must remember that in the Bible the experience of worry is associated with iniquity. Instead, the message of this famous story is that psychological strength stems from faith, faith gives courage, and brings reward. We hear no word of protest from Isaac, and in fact he disappears from the story after Genesis 22:10, to reappear only two chapters later, when he meets Rebekah. The story of the sacrifice casts the spotlight on Abraham's love and fear of God, not Isaac's thoughts and feelings.

The Bible excludes any sign of worry. Even if we believe that Abraham's faith was so strong that he did not worry, it is hard to imagine that young Isaac did not fear for his life when he was bound and put on the altar. But this story, which depicts an archetypal worrying situation, does not recognize the existence of worry. It does not allow the expression of worry. Does it assume that, ideally, we can and should not worry?

When I began writing this book, I thought that my concluding chapter would guide the reader to banish worry and attain peace of mind. Abraham, with his exemplary faith, accepted that human life is bestowed and reclaimed by God, and apparently did not worry about sacrificing his son. And if Isaac worried, there was evidently no point in acknowledging his feeling. We should learn from the Bible, I presumed.

But should we always conquer our worry? Some two thousand years ago, Hillel taught that we must worry about our own well-being as well as that of others. Other great Jewish thinkers, including Sa'adia Gaon, Maimonides, and Rabbi Kook, similarly taught that on occasion worry is necessary. We conclude therefore that although we should sometimes conquer our tendency to worry, at other times we might be well advised to engage in worrying. We should make every effort to banish this process when it leads nowhere. But we should worry, face up to and deal with worrying thoughts, when this behavior can motivate us to save life, or improve our deeds, our relationships, or our environment. We should talk about our worries if this can lead to our making the world a better place. However, we must place limits on our tendency to worry, just as we place limits on our other impulses, and not allow the emotion of worry to harm us or hurt anyone else.

In antiquity, Ben Sira noticed that the workman's worry improves his performance. In 1908 (almost two millennia later), Robert M. Yerkes and J. D. Dodson showed in their laboratory at Harvard University that electric shocks promoted a mouse's performance at a learning task, but only up to a certain intensity. Beyond that crucial intensity, the mouse's performance deteriorated. Yerkes and Dodson's inverted U-curve applies to human behavior as well. It shows that as our anxiety increases, our performance increases up to a point, after which (as anxiety increases further) performance declines until the anxiety is so great that we cannot cope at all.[1] For example, if we do not worry about a forthcoming exam, we may not prepare for it and may fail it. If we do worry about the exam, our anxiety may push us to study for it, so that we pass it. But if we worry too much, our distress may prevent us from performing properly and we may fail it. Thus a certain amount of worry may serve us well, whereas not worrying at all or worrying greatly are both likely to be maladaptive.

We will see below that human relationships also follow the inverted U-curve pattern, where a middling amount of worrying sets the right balance for a loving relationship. If we do not worry at all, we appear unloving and uncaring. But if we worry too much, we harm our relationships with others, for example, by inducing guilt, anger, and suffering in those we care about. Worry that falls within the golden mean, however, may serve a relationship well. Unfortunately, we have no Richter scale of worry that will turn on a red light when our worrying reaches the danger level, when it becomes counterproductive to our fulfilling our goals in life. It is usually other people, our family or friends, who notice that we have reached the point where worrying is no longer fruitful, and they tell us to stop. Worrying can be good, useful, and necessary, although when misplaced or exaggerated, it can be harmful.

We will first look at the harmful consequences of worrying and end with the beneficial effects of this behavior. After examining the abuse of worrying, we shall explore the significance and purposes of this mental activity for the individual and for humanity. Can worrying assist humanity? Or does this behavior serve only our own personal, egotistical goals? How can we use this human tendency creatively for the better?

How Do We Worry Destructively?

We have seen that a certain amount of worrying can be useful, but too little or too much can be counterproductive, or even harmful. Just as we can desire sex without necessarily performing the procreative act, we can also worry without taking action. Just as we can desire a piece of chocolate without feeling hungry, we can worry when there is no threat to survival, morality, or to our relationships. Such worrying is egotistical and serves only ourselves. And just as some people indulge in sexual abuse and others abuse the need to eat, so too some of us worry inappropriately, sometimes to an abusive extent, so that we harm ourselves or others.

Jews have observed that worrying can lead to bodily sickness and can have an adverse affect on our work and our relationships. They have also observed that a worry may become a self-fulfilling prophecy, so that what we worry about actually comes true. In addition, a sixteenth-century rabbi went so far as to declare that worry that does not serve God is idolatry.[2]

When Worry Leads to Sickness

Moses warned his people that they would fear the anxiety in the *levav*—the heart or mind, the inner site where worry is felt—if they did not obey God's commandments (Deut. 28:67). In biblical times people did not distinguish between mind and body, but Jews continued to think of the *levav*, or *lev*, as the place where we feel fear. Nowadays we usually call this the heart, and indeed we feel a constriction in the heart and an increase in pulse when we become particularly worried.[3]

Ben Sira observed that worrying causes insomnia and "brings on old age before its time." The early rabbis realized that the process of worrying affects the functioning of the body in other ways too. It depletes our energy, can delay a woman's menstruation, and reduce a man's libido. The sages' observations that "the body is strong, but fear breaks it" could refer to a man's loss of virility, as well as to his overall physical deterioration.[4]

Maimonides noticed that brooding and thoughts of anxiety weaken and diminish body strength; constant worrying causes a loss of muscle and fat. In addition, such disturbed emotion can cause a "dissolution of [life] spirits," referring to respiratory difficulty.[5]

Of course, one did not have to be a doctor or a rabbi to notice the physical effects of severe or chronic worrying. For example, a medieval Jewish government official who had been dismissed from his job, plunging his family into poverty, wrote, "Because of my distress, I contracted a dry tumor and my skin is falling off my bones." The letter of another unemployed man in the Middle Ages tells that "this state of . . . suffering losses has constrained my chest and turned my mind upside down." Yet another medieval Jew, an Indian trader, bemoaned civil war, the cost of living, and the death of a rabbi, all of which greatly disturbed his mind. His body and soul did not enjoy good health, he wrote, and he lacked energy.[6]

In Prague, in 1619, at the beginning of the Thirty Years War, a Jewish woman, Sarel, described the physical effects of her worry in a letter to her husband, from whom she had not received news for seven weeks. "Honestly," she wrote, "I do not know how I live in my great distress; the Lord, be He praised, knows how I feel. I do not eat, I do not drink, I do not sleep, my life is no life for me." We all know how she felt. Who has not, on occasion, found a meal taste-less and tossed sleeplessly from side to side all night out of worry?[7]

At about the same time, Abraham Yagel, a physician and kabbalist in northern Italy, noted the physical complaints of severely anxious patients. A twenty-one-year-old man became acutely frightened when he was studying alone after midnight and suddenly heard a noise. Terrified, he took to his bed, and for weeks he cried a lot and refused to eat. Yagel also treated a young woman who refused to consum-mate her marriage "because of a fear she has of dying. She is stricken with spasms and trembling."[8]

Jacob Zahalon (1630–1693), a physician and rabbi of Rome and Ferrara, noted a change in pulse in clearly troubled patients. In Con-stantinople, the Polish-born physician Tobias Cohn (1652–1729) rec-ognized that the heart of an anxious person trembles or "jumps" and a fearful woman may faint or suffer menstrual dysfunction.[9]

Freud described the somatic symptoms of chronic worriers and of patients with severe anxiety disorders. His long list of symptoms included sweating, nausea, tremor, diarrhea, and decrease in sexual interest.[10]

By the late twentieth century, doctors attributed many physical symptoms to excessive worry.[11] Eruptions on the skin (such as psori-asis), digestive disorders (not only diarrhea, but also constipation and ulcers), and migraines are only some of the complaints associated with acute or chronic worry. Excessive worry could be behind a child's bed-wetting or poor performance at school. Many people bite their nails or smoke when worried.

When Worry Leads to Impaired Function

Habitual worriers become progressively more anxious as they worry and cannot cope with their worrying. Whereas constructive worrying often leads to the reduction of anxiety, as insight is gained, a problem is solved, or a new perspective is found, destructive worrying leads to increased anxiety. Destructive worriers might become depressed, phobic, obsessive-compulsive, or give in to a panic attack.[12]

"Worry stops me from thinking straight." "Worry obscures my thoughts." "Worry makes me focus on the wrong things." These are common complaints. Worry may swamp the mind so that it no longer works properly or efficiently. When worry stops us from living for a while and assumes a stranglehold over us, it is destructive. When we become incapable of decisive action and feel we are not coping, it is maladaptive. When worry prevents us from reasoning and performing our daily tasks, it is unproductive and sometimes noxious. Severe worriers report that their habit impairs their ability to work and socialize. They also complain of suffering from indecision and doubt. They are unable to solve a problem, seek information, or take control of the situation. They give in to it and hope it will just somehow disappear.

A psychological study among healthy people, mainly college students, revealed that most normal worrying is related to current concerns and to real rather than imaginary problems. The students worried about concerns that they believed had a moderate likelihood of actually occurring. The students who worried constructively were able to terminate their worrying within a few minutes by problem solving, gathering information, or distraction. In contrast, the destructive worrier broods on imaginary problems and engages in flights of dramatic and unrealistic fantasy. This person does not pause to think whether or not the imaginary problem could realistically become fact. Such a worrier also does not think about whether the imaginary problem could realistically be solved. He or she cannot close down the imagination and does not accept evidence that the concern is indeed imaginary. The worrier's reality-testing abilities do not function and the worrier falls into a self-created abyss.[13]

When Worry Harms Relationships

"What's the difference between a Jewish parent and a rottweiler?" The answer: "Eventually the rottweiler lets go." This Jewish joke is about worry and usually has the Jewish mother as its butt. However, the Jewish father can also be an aggressive worrier and therefore I have used the term "parent." The Jewish parent's worry can be aggressive and manipulative. Reflecting insecurity, mistrust, and lack of faith, a parent's admission of worry nevertheless requires the child's attention. However, often there is nothing the child can do to remove the parent's worry.

A Jewish mother is worrying about her son away at college as she walks around the shopping mall. Will he have enough to eat? Will he have enough money? Will he be warm enough? Will he pass his exams? Will he find a nice girl? She notices some warm shirts and buys him two, which she mails him with all her love. When he comes home at the end of term, he is wearing one of her shirts, to please her. His mother welcomes him home with a huge hug: "I am extremely happy to see you! And you are even wearing one of the shirts I sent you! But tell me, didn't you like the other one?"

The son can of course reason with and console his mother. In this way, he gives her love and attention, positive reinforcement for her worry. She will continue to worry and the game will go on. Alternatively, he may feel guilty. He has upset her and made her worry again. He thinks he should have worn the other shirt, or both shirts at once, to please her. He might start worrying about causing his mother's anguish. He may become a neurotic worrier like his mother. Philip Roth has parodied such destructive parental worrying in *Portnoy's Complaint*.[14]

"How many Jewish mothers does it take to change a light bulb?" The answer: "Not a single one. It's okay, I'll sit here in the dark." This joke is also about worry. But this time the Jewish mother is not going to worry. She wants you to worry instead and to feel guilty for not helping her.

Worry can be a person's tool, an implement of manipulation, aggression, and destruction. It can be as dangerous as a rottweiler. It can reduce another person to guilt and despair.

Self-Fulfilling Prophecy

There is no security in life; no one can promise or know that tragedy will not strike tomorrow. But by imagining and dwelling on misfortune, we may actually help to induce it. In sixteenth-century Prague, Maharal realized that "whoever persistently fears something ultimately comes to experience the fear as reality. . . . When a person persistently fears poverty, that person actually becomes poor." Four hundred years later, Rabbi Kook taught that the more we are afraid, the more we fall, and when we are frightened, the fright itself makes us stumble. Viktor Frankl drew the same conclusion in the twentieth century. "Fear always tends to bring about precisely that which is feared," he observed.[15]

As we worry, we imagine and fantasize. Sometimes, as we have seen in chapter 4, imagination and fantasy become reality in a person's mind. A girl may worry about walking in the street at night. As she imagines the assault that she fears, every dark alley, shadow, and male passerby becomes dangerous.

The tendency to pump up a worry into a possible catastrophe is linked with negative mood. Worriers who catastrophize may use their pessimism to confirm their view that their problem is unsolved and therefore may not put an end to their worrying. While anticipatory worry can be a useful mental preparation for facing risk and challenge, there is a danger that anticipatory catastrophizing may lead to prolonged anxiety, unhappiness, and inescapable misery.[16]

Sinful, Self-Serving Worry

"Adam's real sin is that he worried about the morrow," according to Yitzhak of Worke (1779–1858), a Hasidic master. The ancient Jewish sources teach that worry may result from transgression, as we saw in chapter 1, but Maharal and some of his Hasidic followers believed that self-centered worry leads to transgression. Such worry alienates a Jew from God, they thought, and prevents that Jew from cleaving to God. Such anxiety is equivalent to "having other gods in God's face," and is therefore idolatrous. When we use our intellect to see a multitude of possibilities, when we notice all that could go wrong, and when we think of all the different ways that we could behave in a certain situation, taught Rabbi Menaham Mendel of Vitebsk, we lack faith. Faith enables us to perceive wholeness, as it is at a higher level than the intellect. Thus by giving in to self-centered worry, we allow our intellect to take precedence over our faith, we lose faith, and we end up sinning.[17]

Self-serving worries over wealth, power, and social status may lead a person to transgress. Although Nahman of Bratzlav worried about losing leadership, he thought such worrying was a sign of pride and egocentricity.[18]

What Are the Purposes of Worrying?

Worry arouses. The feeling of worry can arouse us to do something that will promote human survival and help us to live productively in a peaceful, moral, cooperative society. When some British students (in the study referred to above) were asked to say how worry helped them, the most common response was that worrying arouses, stimulates, and motivates a person to act: "Worrying challenges and motivates me. Without this [worrying] I would not achieve much in life." The students believed that worrying increases their adrenaline levels, their awareness, and their performance.[19]

Just as sexual intercourse has a biological function for the reproduction of the species, although we engage in this behavior not only to procreate, so too worry has a biological function in promoting survival, even though we do not always worry only in order to promote survival. Worry may help us to think ahead, anticipate danger, and rehearse ways of avoiding the danger. The feeling of worry associated with guilt and inner conflict can arouse us to avoid antisocial or immoral behavior, or to improve our ways. Worry can help us think of different ways of solving a problem and mastering a situation. In addition, worry can help us to develop social responsibility and work ethics.

Do we need to worry, however, if we can think ahead and reason with possibilities? Do we need to worry if we can solve a problem through rational thinking? Do we need to worry if we can repent and make a new resolution to improve ourselves or behave better next time the same situation arises? And do we need to worry if we have no control over a situation? The answer to all these questions is probably "no." At the same time, we could ask if joy, sadness, and anger are necessary emotions. Again, the rationalist may answer "no," although the artist would protest. Emotion—joy, sadness, and the emotion generated by worrying—gives color to our lives. Without emotion, our lives would be dull and tasteless. Some people may feel at times that they would like to reduce the volume and frequency of the emotion of worry, but few would want to live without emotion. Emotion enriches us, although it can also threaten our well-being. Historically, most Jews have not aspired to the pietist ideal of equanimity. Most Jews have wanted to serve God with emotion—with joy and through their tears, with worry and through their fears. The happiness that comes with the successful resolution of a period of worry is sweet indeed.

Emotion is only one dimension of the experience of worry, of course. The imagination is another dimension. Some people may want to change the content and frequency of their nightmares, but few of us would want to live without dreams. The imagination allows us pleasant fantasies as well as troublesome worries. The imagination allows us to think creatively. Life without the imagination would be unimaginable!

The combination of pessimistic imagination and stressful emotion activates the motivational dimension of the experience of worry. It is here, in the motivation that comes out of the worry behavior, that we find the purpose of worry. Worry may push us to act. We may get up and do something adaptive, such as seek knowledge or change perspective. Alternatively, we may do something that is maladaptive, such as stop eating or start crying. If we do nothing, we just go on worrying until something happens to distract us.

How Does Worry Serve Humanity?

"Do not harden your heart and shut your hand against your needy kinsman," commands Deuteronomy 15:7. We must worry about the needy and give them charity. A woman of valor, the Proverbist observes, is not worried for her household because she sews and keeps her family warm; she worries, however, about the poor and needy. As she sees to the needs of her own family, she is aware that others lack what her family has, and she worries about them, opening her arms to help those who are less fortunate.[20]

The ancient sages formalized the communal and personal need to worry about the hungry and destitute. They set up communal charity funds and demanded that individual Jews give money every year as well as a loaf of bread or "requirements for the night" to a traveling beggar.[21]

We should worry about the well-being of the underprivileged, but not necessarily about the morality of others, the sages taught. We should worry about others' behavior only when our own is exemplary. In a discussion about land ownership, the Talmud instructs about the removal of straw. One should first remove the straw on one's own land before worrying about the neighbor's straw. Jews have applied this teaching to other situations too. We should first make sure that we are behaving properly, and only then begin to worry about what someone else is doing.[22]

The well-being of a Jew is tied up with the physical and moral well-being of other Jews. We need to worry about others, not only about ourselves, taught Hillel, as we have already mentioned. Legend tells that one day a poor man came to Rabbi Shmelke's door. Shmelke was a penniless Hasid, but he gave the poor man a ring that had a precious stone embedded in it. As the rabbi closed the door, his wife realized what he had done and protested at his giving away this valuable jewelry. The rabbi rushed out and called after the poor man,

"The ring is worth a lot of money; be sure to receive its full value when you sell it!"[23]

The rabbi worries about the poor. "If I am only for myself, what am I?" he thinks as he attends to the needs of others. However difficult the circumstances, Jews have maintained a collective responsibility to help those worse off than themselves, doing their best to reduce the worries of the stranger as well as the poor in their communities and to help Jews elsewhere in distress or in danger. Shmelke is a righteous Jew, giving his last treasured possession to a person who is worse off than he is. He is a man who does not worry about his own needs, but only about other people. His wife, however, worries about herself and her family's well-being. If he gives away the precious ring, she has no guarantee that she and her penniless family will have food for dinner. With her feet planted firmly on the ground, she thinks, "If I am not for myself, who will be for me?" Whereas the rabbi wins the punch line of the story, her worry, caused by her realistic appraisal of her predicament, has a purpose. Both the rabbi and his wife teach us that worry serves humanity. It motivates us to preserve human life and to improve the lot of other people.

Worry Can Help Us Preserve Human Life   The Hasidim tell a story about two saintly men who lived around 1800. Rabbi Menahem Mendel of Kosov was a worrier, but his brother-in-law, Rabbi Uri of Strelisk, did not worry. The first felt responsible for the well-being of his people and drew down divine blessings for them. The second was a spiritual man who spent his days in the joys and ecstasies of prayer and service to God.

When the rabbi of Kosov came to visit his brother-in-law, he was shocked at the poverty of the Strelisk community. He saw bony bodies in tattered clothes living in run-down houses. "Why do you allow this?" he protested angrily. The rabbi of Strelisk was also very thin and lived in poverty among his people, but this did not bother him at all. "My people do not feel any want. They are all happy," he replied.

When all the people of Strelisk gathered to meet their visitor, Rabbi Menahem Mendel asked them what wish they most wanted fulfilled.

He worried about these poor people and wanted to better their miserable lot. The Jews of Strelisk wanted to be able to pray like their rabbi and become a saint like him, but none of them said this out loud. They stood in silence. So Rabbi Mendel suggested that they might want sustenance—hot, wholesome food—and good dowries for their daughters. Yes, why not? They agreed. Rabbi Menahem Mendel promised, "Tomorrow, whatever you pray for will be fulfilled."

That night the Jews of Strelisk thought about the prayer for sustenance that they would utter in the company of the rabbi of Kosov the next day. They began to dream about things they had never dreamed of before and they were all excited when they gathered the next morning for their communal prayer. Then Rabbi Uri strode in, the way he always strode in, and roared *Adon Olam* (a prayer beginning "Lord of the Universe"). The Jews joined his prayer in loud voices. Together they sang and prayed, and in doing so they opened the gates of heaven. Together their souls rose to the divine realm and eventually returned at the end of the morning prayer. The Strelisk Jews were very happy. Only then, when they put away their prayer shawls, did they notice Rabbi Menahem Mendel and remember what he had said.[24]

For the Jews of Strelisk, the true reality was the Divine Presence, and the material world of human life, including hunger and cold, was only illusion. Rabbi Menahem Mendel, however, was conscious of the reality of the material world and believed that people could not serve God properly if they were hungry and cold. While he worried about sustenance, Rabbi Uri did not worry and swept his people with him, out of the world of illusion and worry, to the divine realm. Rabbi Uri is the hero of the tale. The Hasidim tell this tale to teach us how to find happiness in God and not worry. They will not tell us that the Strelisk rabbi and his people soon died of hunger. If pressed, the storyteller might explain that their souls went straight to heaven. The early sages and many later rabbis taught that the earthly world is like a vestibule where one prepares oneself for entering the banqueting hall of the world to come. For these men, the only purpose of worrying was to find the way to enter this supernal hall. The life of the soul was more important than the life of the body.[25]

Yet worry is a natural response to life; it derives from our love of life and confirms our desire to live. One who never worries cannot value human life. The Jewish pietists, including Rabbi Uri, whose goal in life was to merge their souls with God, have not worried about preserving human life on Earth or improving the material existence of other Jews. They have worried instead about purifying their souls and about the fate of their souls in the world to come. However, these Jews have always been a small minority of the Jewish people.

Hunger and cold may be illusory, but Rabbi Mendel knew that for many people hunger and cold are very real. We can die from malnutrition and hypothermia. Worry helps us promote bodily survival. It can arouse us to perceive the threat of hunger and cold before these become life threatening and make us look for a way of finding food and warmth. Whereas animalistic fear enables a creature to flee from or to fight an enemy in the face of danger, the human imagination enables us to prepare for or avoid the possibility of danger through worry. Worry can mobilize us for action long before any sign of danger, even in the absence of any sign of danger. Since antiquity, rabbis have ruled repeatedly that we must not rely on miracles or providence, but must do all we can to maintain health and life, which are God-given. Alerting oneself or others to possible danger and taking action (to prevent what we pessimistically imagine could occur) is part of this process.[26]

Worry Can Help Us Improve Society Jews have believed that worry is necessary to improve the ethical and social fabric of society. Abraham, Moses, and the prophets possessed a social and a moral conscience. They worried about the physical and moral well-being of their people. The Bible reveals that Abraham argued with God in the hope of saving the innocent from destruction in the immoral cities of Sodom and Gomorrah. Moses also argued with God in the hope of saving the Israelites after the incident of the Golden Calf. Both Abraham and Moses knew that God's promise of numerous offspring depended on their creating a moral society. The prophets warned their people of imminent destruction if they did not mend their ways.[27]

Rabbis have long taught people to improve their ways for love of God. But rabbis have also realized that people might be more likely to improve their ways if they are made to worry about the consequences of their transgressions. Love of God is more abstract and elusive than fear of punishment and therefore rabbis have sometimes chosen to instill the latter emotion in order to motivate people to behave ethically and improve society. Still today there are a few desperate rabbis who preach that tragedies that have fallen upon the Jews, during the Holocaust as well as from the terrorist bombs in Israel more recently, have resulted from their immorality. These are statements made by worried men who want to improve the moral fabric of Jewish society. However, such comments breed resentment and anger and do not improve society in any way.[28]

In the sixteenth century, the Safed kabbalist Isaac Luria gave Jews a reason for worrying about other people's moral well-being. He taught that it is the task of the Jews to "mend" (tikkun) their souls through their religious behavior in order to mend the world and bring about final redemption. Each sin and each bad thought nourishes the force of evil, he believed. Jews can restore the world to its pristine cosmic state by observing all of the commandments, performing acts of penitence to expiate their sins and purify their souls, and undertaking mystical meditations to strengthen divine blessing and weaken the forces of evil. Luria taught that we have to improve our own behavior and help others to improve theirs because this affects the eventual well-being of the whole world.[29]

By the eighteenth century, many Jews—including kabbalists, the followers of Shabbetai Zevi, and the Hasidim—had accepted the Lurianic idea of tikkun and worried about repairing the world for sthe good of all. Some Hasidim believed that only a few saintly men—the tzaddikim—could do this for their whole generation.[30]

Jewish concerns over the physical well-being of others began to change under the influence of the Enlightenment. Jewish community associations for helping the sick, the handicapped, and the homeless were overtaken by bigger and better state-provided health services. Poor boys who once found an apprenticeship within the Jewish community began instead to attend trade schools in the city; and new immigrants and refugees were soon looked after by national and international agencies. A co-religionist's worries are no longer necessarily our own when officials outside the community take over this responsibility. For secular Jews, giving charity is no longer seen as the fulfillment of a religious duty, but as a matter of personal conscience. However, secular as well as religious Jews continue to maintain a high sense of social responsibility and civic duty. Their formidable presence in the medical profession, in government, and in philanthropy continues to reflect the traditional Jewish concern for the physical and moral well-being of humanity.

How Does Worry Serve Our Own Personal Goals?

Worry may help us examine possibilities before taking a decision or acting. It may help us to think ahead, face risks, and prepare for a challenge. It may help us to perfect ourselves and to perfect our work. Worry may also prepare us for coping with misfortune.

Moreover, worry can improve the quality of our relationships with other people. It can make us aware of our need for love and our desire to love. It can make us aware of the importance in our lives of those whom we love. It can lead us to appreciate that which we may have taken for granted.

Problem Solving and Creative Thinking   Worry is a sort of dream involving pessimistic fantasies. While we may have little control over our night visions, we should be able to play with our daydreams and will ourselves to convert pessimistic fantasies into optimistic dreams. For example, when a twenty-year-old son does not come home at the expected time on a dark and stormy night, his parents could fantasize that a lovely girl whom he has just met is the cause of his delay, instead of imagining that he has drowned in an enormous puddle. When we worry constructively, we think creatively. We invent, imagine scenarios, and elaborate. We fabricate possibilities and create fictions. We convert these fictions into hypotheses about reality. We accept what we find useful and reject what is useless. We analyze these hypotheses and seek information to put an end to the activity of worrying.

The above-mentioned psychological study of worry supports the idea that a purpose of this cognitive activity is to solve problems. Almost half of all the respondents suggested this. The majority (some 83 percent) of respondents said that worrying "sometimes" or "definitely" resulted in a "reasonable" solution to a problem. One person explained that "worrying gives me the opportunity to analyze situations and work out the pros and cons." Worrying motivates us to find alternative approaches to problem solving. Only one in four respondents admitted to sometimes worrying about insoluble problems, and then only rarely. The authors of this study propose that one of the main differences between "normal" and "pathological" worriers is that the former group of people can solve problems through worrying, but that the latter group cannot. They also propose that "normal" worriers are better able to switch and control their thoughts than "pathological" worriers, who have difficulty with this mental work and with putting an end to their worrying.[31]

By Helping Us Strive for Perfection   Worry can help us strive for perfection in our deeds (including our work) and in our character. Rabbis have repeatedly taught that we must examine our every act and thought, and repent and correct when we find a deed or thought that is unethical. Jews have often introspected and repented through prayer (see chapter 3), worrying about their thoughts and conduct in their efforts to improve themselves.[32]

Some Jewish thinkers have believed that our goal in life should be to perfect ourselves ethically. For example, the medieval pietist Eleazar of Worms reasoned that God did not wish to create a world where everyone is as good as angels, and therefore created a world with much evil in it so that people might prove their righteousness. Since no righteous people emerged, God destroyed that world. God then decided to create another world where the righteous could find a way to use the divinely provided Good Inclination to overcome the Evil Inclination. Eleazar, who witnessed anti-Semitic massacres in which he was wounded and his wife and two children were killed, was acutely aware of the human capacity for evil, yet he believed that God has given us the possibility to choose good.[33]

Worry can help us solve the ongoing, never-ending conflict between good and evil. Worry lurks at the interface between our conflicting inclinations and allows us to imagine the consequences of our behavior. As we worry, we consider our possibilities and we see where our inclinations can lead us. In this way, worry may help us choose the good path.

For Nahman of Bratzlav, too, the battle against his evil urges was an important occupation and objective in life. The more a person struggles with these urges, he thought, the stronger that person's moral character becomes, but he knew from his own experience that the battle never ends.[34] It is not enough merely to worry about morality, however; we have to use this worry as a motivating force to correct and perfect our behavior and ourselves. Some people give up the struggle and allow their worries free rein.

By Helping Us Cope with Risks and Challenges Worry can prepare us for the eventuality that we fear, in case one day that event comes to be. When we worry, we think of possible scenes. Such thinking may prepare us for action should one of these be realized. Such thinking may also lead us to take precautions to prevent the realization of the imagined scenario.

We have to take risks in life. Marriage is a risk; for example, one partner might fall out of love. Conception is a risk; pregnancy can miscarry or harm the mother's health. Investing money is a risk; the stock market could crash. Going to work is a risk; we may be involved in a car accident, or be mugged, or trip and break a leg. Admittedly some risks are greater than others. It is also true that some risks have to be taken, while others are unnecessary. A life without risks would have to be lived in a bubble and few of us would choose such an existence. Risks are part of life, and thinking about them may be a way of coping with them. If we worry about some possible unfortunate outcomes, we may end up doing something (such as taking precautions or changing plans) to reduce their likelihood of happening.

In the mid–eighteenth century, a Lithuanian kabbalist, Alexander Susskind, believed that Jews should think about their readiness to suffer torture and death for the sake of God so that they would be prepared when the time for such suffering came. To Westerners today, this may seem an unnecessary preparation, but he reached this conclusion after visiting a Jew in prison who had been condemned to death for a trumped-up charge of ritual murder. The prisoner had been offered reprieve on condition that he apostatize. Susskind urged him not to abandon his faith and taught him the martyr's prayer to recite in his last minutes. The kabbalist must have said "Amen" with a heavy heart to the man's prayer as the death sentence was carried out. He was probably convinced that the Jew would have been killed anyway, as happened in a previous case of blood libel.

Susskind proposed that we practice imagining ourselves standing on the edge of a high tower, ordered by our enemy to apostatize or be thrown over the edge. We should visualize the scene in our minds carried through to its bitter end; we must imagine ourselves being thrown off the parapet and suffering terribly. He prescribed contemplating other ways of dying too; we should imagine all the details of how we might be stoned to death, burned, decapitated, or strangled—methods of capital punishment meted out by the court in the Mishnah. We should also imagine the possibility of our dying by having molten lead poured down our throats. We may well wonder whether such morbid mental exercises really helped the kabbalist and his students.[35]

Susskind believed that anticipatory catastrophizing might help us to cope with the ultimate challenge of our own mortality. But we do not have to take his teaching literally. He assumed that we can prepare ourselves to face a painful challenge. Indeed, if we worry about failing a driving test and then fail it, we have prepared ourselves for the failure and can probably cope better with the disappointment than if we had not worried about it. In such a case, anticipatory worry may serve us well. Unfortunately, we cannot always foresee all the challenges that we are likely to meet. Also, as mentioned above, anticipatory anxiety can sometimes turn into a self-fulfilling prophecy or lead to prolonged anxiety and unhappiness.

We feel courageous and brave when we face our anxiety and overcome it. Worry can teach us about our own vulnerability, perseverance, and the meaning of courage. One who does not fear does not feel vulnerable and cannot experience courage. One who does not worry cannot know what it means to be brave.[36]

By Making Us Aware of Love   God said, "It is not good for man to be alone" (Gen. 2:18). Worry makes us aware of our divinely decreed—or genetically programmed—need for others. Worry can reveal our love for another, but also our fear of finding ourselves alone, abandoned by the one we love. Worry highlights our social bonds.

A friend once declared that her worry about her children's welfare as they were growing up was one way in which she could let them know that she loved them. Her worry taught them about environmental risks and behavioral limits, as well as about love and consideration for other people's feelings. Her children grew up knowing they are loved, which gave them psychological strength, she insisted. She feels that now that her children are grown up, she is reaping the benefits of all the worry that she invested in them. They do not take unnecessary risks and they phone her once a week, she said proudly. She believes that her worry as a mother has contributed to the good relationship she has with her children and to their sense of responsibility and independence. She concluded that her worrying had helped her fulfill her goal in raising her children to become loving, independent adults.

Yet the next day she told me that she realized that her worrying over her children was somewhat egocentric. She knew that she worried because she was attached to her children and would be devastated if something terrible happened to them. She understood that her worry was partly for their own good, but was also largely the result of her own attachment to them and her inability to control their lives or to guarantee their safety. She knew that she would always worry about her children even now that they are grown and no longer living at home.

Three hundred years ago, Glückl of Hameln reached the same conclusion. She worried about her children, much as my friend did. She pointed out in her memoir that many animals look after their young until they can fend for themselves, but we human beings worry about our children not only when they are young, but for as long as they live, even after they have left home and are independent adults.

She told a fable about a father bird and his three fledglings to illustrate her thinking. They lived by the seashore, but one day there was a terrific storm and the bird decided that he had to fly his family to another land. He picked up the first baby bird in his claws and flew over the tumultuous sea. Halfway across, he said to the little one, "How I suffer and risk my life for you now. When I am old, will you look after me?"

The little one replied, "Dear father, just take me to dry land now, and when you are old, I will do all that you ask of me."

"What a selfish liar," thought the father and dropped him into the sea.

The big bird flew back for the second fledgling. Halfway across the sea, the father asked the same question of this second one. The little bird gave the same answer as his sibling and met the same fate.

When the father had flown halfway across the raging sea with the third, he again repeated his question. This little bird acknowledged the great risk and care his father was undertaking on his behalf as well as his duty as a son to repay his father, but said that he could not promise to care for his parent in old age. What he could promise, however, was that he would care and risk his life for his own young, in the same way as his father had done for him. The father carried this clever little bird across to dry land.

Aging and lonely, Glückl knew that for a mother to worry about her children was natural—this was how she tried to ensure their survival—but she could not take for granted that her children would worry about her in her old age.

"People should love one another, for it is said, 'Thou shalt love thy neighbor' [Lev. 19:18]" she continued, commenting bitterly that very seldom did a person love another wholeheartedly in her day. What was she thinking when she added this comment? We can guess that the widow was feeling lonely and upset that no one was worrying about her. One of the many ways that we show our love is through our worry. Our aging parents may not be sure of our continued love for them unless they see that we worry about them.

Having worried about us for so long, they may want us to worry about them, just like the father bird in Glückl's story.[37]

The younger generation, though, may not see parental worry as an expression of love; a son or daughter may interpret parental worry as mistrust, or the refusal to give a child independence and desired learning opportunities. As my friend realized, parental worry may indeed become egocentric, serving the parent's attachment needs and hindering the child's opportunity to explore the world alone.

In 1952, the Israeli poet Yehuda Amichai wrote an autobiographical poem that began with the following lines:

My father built over me a worry big as a shipyard
And once I left it and before I was finished
And he remained there with his big, empty worry.
And my mother—like a tree on the shore between her arms that
    stretched out after me.

Now, the poet continues, his father's face had become like the lamp on the end of a train disappearing into the distance, while his mother had closed all the many clouds into her brown cupboard.[38]

When the poet was a child, his father's worry was "big as a shipyard." The boy could run around in this huge, protective worry. He was able to feel safe in view of his mother's ever-present outstretched arms. But when he grew up and no longer needed or wanted the large and spacious worry of his father, or the security of his mother's arms, his parents' worry nevertheless remained. It was still big, but now empty. Children usually outgrow their parents' worries, but parents do not necessarily stop worrying about their children. Parents carry their worry on their fading faces (like the lamp on the end of the train in the distance), or keep them hidden (in the brown cupboard) as they remain attached to their children.

These examples focus on the parent-child relationship, but worry has a similar role in the expression of love in the marital relationship and in other interpersonal relationships. Worry may be a way of loving, needing, and appreciating another person. When that person goes away, does not phone, or is late in coming, our own worry may make us realize how much we value that person.

Worry: For Better, Not for Worse

We can use worry destructively or constructively, for better or for worse. When we use worry destructively, we enter a vicious circle where pessimistic thoughts chase round and round in our heads and there is no way out. Thoughts become blacker and blacker, and we become more and more anxious. Such worry leads to depression, insomnia, and the inability to function properly in everyday life. Yet, when we worry constructively, we manage to take a precaution that will save us from unpleasantness or danger, we solve a problem, or we gain information that makes us understand what we have previously not understood. In this case, we end up reducing our anxiety; we feel relieved or successful. We laugh or we think "aha! now I understand!"

Children know that life is an adventure. They enjoy exploring new places and ideas and discovering new possibilities. They are curious. The unknown is interesting and exciting. The environment is a mystery. They learn to master their environment by experimenting, sometimes by hurting themselves. They choose the highest slide in the playground and long to jump off the highest diving board at the swimming pool. There is much that parents teach their children, but there are many things that children have to learn for themselves by facing uncertainty and overcoming it. Some people remain children all their lives; they continue to seek adventure, take pleasure in mystery, and enjoy exploring the unknown. They are willing to face uncertainty even though they may worry about each step. But many of us lose this joie de vivre. We seek security and shun whatever is beyond our understanding and control. We are frightened to leave the well-beaten track through life that is familiar and predictable. When something happens and we face a hurdle, we suffer worry passively instead of seeking and looking forward to its denouement.

With all our insurance policies today, we still cannot take precautions against all the risks that we will meet in life. Life is an unpredictable adventure with no guarantees. We have to find ways of living with uncertainty, of accepting the unknown, of marveling at mystery. We have to take some risks and live hopefully. We do not have to understand everything. Indeed, we cannot. We do not have to know everything in advance, and of course we cannot. We do not have to control everything that happens in our world; again, we cannot. But each day we face choices. According to Deuteronomy 30:19, God puts before us life and death, blessing and curse, and tells us to "choose life." We often make our choice without thinking that we are in fact making a choice. We usually take our lives and our blessings for granted and do not actively "choose life" on the spur of the moment or on a daily basis. Most of the time, we choose life unconsciously. When we realize that our choice is threatened, however, we worry. Worry can teach us to appreciate our blessings. Worry can remind us that we have choices and it can motivate us to look for, consider, and explore them.

Of course, on occasion, we face a hurdle that we have not encountered before, or we receive terrible news. We realize that the choice for life is no longer ours to make. In this case, the work of worry may be harder than usual. We may spend more time worrying and find ourselves becoming anxious and depressed. At these times, we may need to invest more effort in finding a suitable coping strategy. If we do not find a coping strategy, our worrying is likely to gain the upper hand and become destructive.

In the introduction to this book we proposed that worry is a pregnancy. A seed of uncertainty enters the imagination and begins to mature within us. We have looked at some of the ways that Jews have aborted this seed, for example, by thinking of God, escaping into fantasy, or joking. We have also seen that Jews have sometimes nurtured the seed of worry to build the future expectantly, even though it will always be uncertain, and to give birth to new ideas and understanding.

Glossary

aggadah (lit. "narrative"): The stories and chronicles, the sayings of the wise, and moral instructions; the rabbinic teaching that is not concerned with halakhah, the religious laws and regulations in the literature of the Oral Law (Mishnah).

Akedah (lit. "binding" [of Isaac]): This word refers to the narrative in Gen. 22:1–19 that describes God's command to Abraham to offer his son Isaac as a sacrifice. Abraham takes Isaac to the place of sacrifice and binds him on the altar. The angel of the Lord then tells him not to carry out the task and a ram appears that Abraham can use for sacrifice instead of his son. The *Akedah* is the supreme example of faith in God. Through the ages, Jews have used it as a symbol of Jewish martyrdom.

alef and *beit:* The first two letters of the Hebrew alphabet.

Ashkenaz, Ashkenazim: A name applied since medieval times to Germany and the German Jews. After the Crusades, some of these Jews migrated to Eastern Europe.

ba'al shem (lit. "master of the Name"): Title attributed since the Middle Ages to a Jew, usually a kabbalist or Hasid, who knows the esoteric names to gain divine action. While the earlier masters were scholars, this title was later applied to Jews who worked wonders using kabbalistic methods.

Ba'al Shem Tov: Israel ben Eliezer (1700–1760), the founder of the eastern European Hasidic movement.

Chabad (an acrostic for *hokhmah, binah,* and *da'at,* three different types of knowledge used in finding and cleaving to God): The name used for a specific Hasidic movement, founded by Shneur Zalman of Liadi in White Russia, in the early nineteenth century. Chabad Hasidim stress the importance of fulfillment of the commandments and study of Torah, which leads (they believe) to true cleaving to God and surrender of the soul to God.

crown: Translation of the Aramaic word *"tag,"* referring to the special designs resembling crowns placed by a scribe on the upper left-hand corner of some of the Hebrew letters in a Torah, tefillin, or mezuzzah scroll. This is also the translation of the Hebrew word *"keter,"* referring to a crown-shaped Torah ornament and, in Kabbalah, to the highest divine emanation. The "Terrible Crown," *keter nora*, was a potent magical formula used by Rabbi Ishmael.

devekut (lit. "cleaving"): Attachment or adhesion to God, the binding of one's soul to God, communion with God, intense love of God.

Gaon, gaonic (lit. "eminence"): The title of the heads of rabbinic academies, especially in Babylonia. The gaonic period was from the sixth to the eleventh centuries.

Gehenna *(Geihinnom):* A name derived from the valley of the sons of Hinnom, south of Jerusalem, where (according to the Bible) children were once burned by a cult. This name is used by Jews to refer to a place of torment reserved for the wicked after death.

genizah (lit. "storing"): Depository of sacred books. The best known was discovered in the synagogue of Fostat, old Cairo.

halakhah: Jewish law.

Hanukkah: The eight-day festival of lights commemorating the rededication of the Temple in Jerusalem in 165 B.C.E. after its desecration.

Hasid (lit. "fervent, pious"): In the Psalms, Hasid (pl. Hasidim) denotes the "faithful," the lover of God. In the Mishnah, the Hasid is described as one who is slow to anger and quick to relent. The Talmud identifies a Hasid as one "who even before he prays, turns his heart to God: for at least one hour." In the thirteenth century, the Hasidei Ashkenaz, who lived in the Rhineland, stressed silent piety, prayer, and asceticism that culminate in total fear and love of God. The mystical, religious movement, Hasidism, emerged in eighteenth-century southeastern Poland and had a massive following, especially among poor Jews.

hatavat ḥalom (lit. "turning a dream to good"): A ritual to bring about a good solution for a bad dream, which helps a person transmute the worry created by that dream.

Judenrat (lit. "Jewish council"): The German term for the council of Jews appointed by the Nazis during World War II to enforce Nazi orders affecting the Jews and to administrate the affairs of the Jewish community.

Kabbalah (lit. "tradition"): An esoteric form of mysticism that allegedly denotes an oral tradition handed down alongside the Written Law, giving a secret interpretation to every word and letter of Torah. It involves both communion with God and a particular understanding of the concepts of God, creation, and good and evil. Kabbalists have sought the hidden mysteries of God and the relationship between divine emanations, human life, and the creation of the universe. Kabbalah was given a new direction in the late sixteenth century by the mystical theories and practices of Isaac Luria (see Lurianic Kabbalah, below) and his circle of mystics in Safed, Israel.

Lurianic Kabbalah: The Lurianic theory of the drama of creation proposed that God originally contracted to create a space where the world could exist. The divine light that flowed into this new space proved too strong, however, and shattered the "vessels" or divine emanations, mixing light with darkness, the spiritual with the material, and in this moment evil entered the world. Isaac Luria taught that Jews must release the holy sparks that are scattered about by observing and studying Torah, atoning, and meditating, thus bringing about *tikkun*, the restoration of the cosmic harmony that was originally shattered.

Magen David (lit. "shield of David"): Mystical symbol consisting of two superimposed triangles forming a hexagram, today regarded as a Jewish symbol. In ancient and medieval times it was a predominantly non-Jewish decorative motif and was sometimes used in magic. In the eighteenth century, Shabbateans, the followers of the messianic movement that was begun by Shabbetai Zevi, used the hexagram as the shield of the son of David, the Messiah. Its use as a Jewish symbol became widespread only in the last few centuries.

maggid: A popular preacher; also a divine spirit that speaks to a kabbalist.

menorah: A candelabrum; the seven-branched oil lamp used in the Tabernacle and Temple.

merkavah (lit. "chariot"): The mystical practice associated with Ezekiel's vision of the divine throne-chariot (Ezek. 1). The *merkavah* mystics used meditative techniques to ascend through worlds and heavens until they reached the point where they beheld the radiance of the divine presence and the divine throne.

mezuzzah (pl. *mezuzzot,* lit. "doorpost"): The parchment inscribed with Deut. 6:4–9 and 11:13–21 on one side, and *Shaddai* (a Name for God) on the other, which is affixed in a small tubular case to the right doorpost of the Jewish home.

Midrash (lit. "exposition, interpretation"): Homiletic exegesis of the Bible, rich in legends, parables, similes, and sayings.

mikveh: Ritual bath; a pool of clean water in which a Jew immerses for ritual purification.

mi she-berakh (lit. "may the One who blessed"): A blessing. The original version, the Aramaic *yekum purkan* (may salvation arise) prayer, was recited in the Babylonian academies for the welfare of the heads of the academies, the rabbis, and students. Later, when these academies declined, a second version was added for the welfare of each individual person. It was to be recited only in the presence of a congregation and was translated into Hebrew for the benefit of those who could not understand Aramaic.

Mishnah (lit. "study"): The compendium of laws and tradition compiled in Palestine c. 200 C.E.

mitzvah: A duty or commandment; a good deed.

Musar movement (*musar,* lit. "ethics"): The movement, founded by Rabbi Israel of Salant in nineteenth-century Lithuania, that encouraged ethical perfection by studying traditional ethical literature (*musar*) and engaging in self-criticism.

Purim: The festival celebrated on the fourteenth of the month of Adar, which commemorates the rescue of Persian Jewry through the mediation of Esther from the annihilation engineered by Haman as related in the biblical Book of Esther.

shnorrer (Yiddish): A scrounger.

Sepharad, Sephardim: In the Middle Ages, the Jews of Spain, Sepharad, were called Sephardim. At the end of the fifteenth century, all the Jews were expelled from Spain, but the emigrants and their descendants are still called Sephardim, wherever they reside.

Shabbat: The Sabbath, the day of rest observed from sundown on Friday until nightfall on Saturday.

Shaddai : Name of God found frequently in the Bible and commonly translated "Almighty."

she'elat ḥalom (lit. "the questioning of a dream"): The process of inducing a dream that will answer a person's question.

Shekhinah: The divine presence. Rabbinic sages used this term to mean the presence of God, whereas medieval Jewish philosophers used it to refer to the glory of God, which was an intermediary between God and humankind. Kabbalists have used this term to refer to the feminine principle in the divine world, the last principle in the divine hierarchy. Lurianic kabbalists imagined her exiled from the rest of the divine whole and taught that Jews should fulfill commandments to reunite her with the Holy One.

Shema (lit. "hear"): The *Shema* prayer, beginning "Hear O Israel" (Deut. 6:4), which is recited daily at morning and evening services. It expresses Israel's ardent faith and love of God.

shofar: A ram's horn, blown on set occasions in Temple and synagogue worship.

shtetl (Yiddish): A small Jewish town or village in Eastern Europe.

Shulḥan Arukh: The code of Jewish law compiled in the sixteenth century by Joseph Karo.

siddur (lit. "order"): The volume containing the daily prayers.

Talmud (lit. "learning"): A compilation of rabbinic commentaries on the Mishnah produced in rabbinical academies from c. 200–500 c.e. A compilation was done both in Babylonia and in the Land of Israel during this era. Discussion in the Talmud attempts to apply mishnaic teaching to the daily life of the people and also addresses many questions that are purely theoretical.

tefillin: Phylacteries. These are two leather cases containing parchments with specific biblical verses. These cases have straps attached to them so that they can be bound to the forehead and the left arm.

teshuvah (lit. "going back, returning"): Return to the correct path; return to God.

Tetragrammaton: YHVH, the holy Name of God.

tikkun (lit. "mending, restitution"): This is a mystical term used in Lurianic Kabbalah to denote the restoration of the right order, unity, and harmony after the cosmic destruction (the "breaking of the vessels") that occurred at the beginning of time, when God created the world.

Torah (lit. "teaching"): This word can refer to the Pentateuch or to all of Scripture, or to all revelation (written or oral) in Judaism.

tzaddik (lit. "righteous man"): A righteous and pious man of faith. In Hasidism, the *tzaddik* became a spiritual ideal. The Hasidic *tzaddik* is a man whose special holiness enables him to act as an intermediary between God and man, who can pray on behalf of his people, bring them blessings, and perhaps even prophesy.

tzaraf (lit. "refined" or "combined"): The word used for the jeweler's refining of metal and the mystic's combining of letters to draw divine blessing.

urim and thummim: Sacred means of divination used only until about the tenth century B.C.E. which permitted choosing between two possibilities and was used only to answer questions relating to the nation or its rulers.

yeshivah (pl. yeshivot): Jewish traditional school devoted primarily to the study of the Talmud and rabbinic literature.

Zohar (lit. "splendor"): The Book of Zohar is the principal work of Kabbalah, an esoteric commentary on the Pentateuch attributed to Shimon bar Yohai, but written by Moses de Leon at the end of the thirteenth century.

Notes ⟞

Introduction

1. M. Buber, *Ten Rungs: Hasidic Sayings* (New York: Schocken, 1970), 43. M. S. Kleinman, ed., *Or yesharim* (Piotrkow: 1924), 9.
2. T. D. Borkovec, E. Robinson, T. Pruzinsky, and J. A. DePree, "Preliminary Exploration of Worry: Some Characteristics and Processes," *Behavior Research and Therapy* 21 (1983): 10.

Chapter One

1. Jedayah Bedersi (Ha-penini), *Beḥinot olam,* trans. Tobias Goodman (London: 1806), chapter 13. See also chapters 15, 18, and 19 on worry, fear, and anxiety.
2. B. Spinoza, *The Ethics,* ed. S. Feldman, trans. S. Shirley (Indianapolis: Hackett Publishing Company, 1992), part 3, prop. 18, p. 115 and def. 13, p. 143.
3. G. C. L. Davey, and F. Tallis, *Worrying: Perspectives on Theory, Assessment, and Treatment* (Chichester: John Wiley and Sons, 1994), xi, 40. The term "work of worry" was coined by Irving Janis in the 1950s and refers to the worrying that enables us to cope more effectively in the long run with a situation of painful reality.
4. B. *Sanhedrin* 106b.
5. The Tanakh uses the words *pahad, haradah, eymah, hat, aratz, yagor, be'atah, balahah, de'agah, tzar, dehilah and behalah* to refer to various feelings of anxiety, worry, and fear. Thus, for example, it uses *pahad* to refer to fear of an enemy (Ps. 64:2), fear of night (Ps. 91:5), fear of evil (Prov.

1:33), fear in the heart (Deut. 28:67), and sudden fear (Prov. 3:25, Job 22:10). *Haradah* indicates the anxiety felt by Joseph's brothers (Gen. 42:28), care and concern (2 Kings 4:13), and worry (Ezek. 32:10). *Eymah* is used in fear of darkness (Gen. 15:12) and terror in the heart (Deut. 32:25, Isa. 33:18). *Hat* signifies fear (Deut. 1:21, 31:8) and *aratz* means to be afraid (Josh. 1:9). *Yagor* is used to refer to fear of other men (Jer. 39:18). *Ba'at,* is the root of the word used for Saul's emotion when the evil spirit "troubled" him, David's terror of the sword of the angel of the Lord, and Haman's fear before the king (1 Sam. 16:14, Esther 7:6 and 1 Chron. 21:30). *Belahah* denotes terror of death (Lev. 26:16, Ps. 78:33, and Job 24:17). *De'agah* refers to heartfelt concern (Prov. 12:25), worry over children's behavior (Josh. 22:24, 1 Sam. 9:5, 10:2), concern for the Jews who fell in battle, fear of famine, and worry like the [restless] sea (Jer. 38:19, 42:16, 49:23). *Dehilah* and *behalah* both signify a fearful and alarming dream (Dan. 4:2).

6. Deut. 6:13, Lev. 19:3, Gen. 3:10 (Adam), 18:15 (Sarah), 19:30 (Lot), 26:7 (Isaac), 31:31, 32:8, 32:12 (Jacob), 42:35 (Joseph).

7. For examples of the use of two words together, see *hared ve-haradah* (Gen. 27:33 and Ezek. 26:16), *eymata* and *pahad* (Exod. 15:16), *yirah* and *hat* (Deut. 1:21, 31:8, Josh. 1:9, 8:1, 10:25, and Jer. 1:17, 30:10, 46:27), *yirah* and *hared* (Judg. 7:3), *yirah* and *aratz* (Deut. 1:29 and Isa. 8:12), *hared* and *pahad* (Isa. 19:16, Jer. 30:5–6), *tzarah* and *tzukah* (Isa. 30:6), *yirah* and *de'agah* (Isa. 57:11 and Jer. 17: 8), and *yirah* and *pahad* (Ps. 91:5).

8. God worries (*do'eg*), B. *Sanhedrin* 106b. Worry (*de'agah*) in the heart of man is mentioned in B. *Sotah* 42b and B. *Sanhedrin* 100b. The same Hebrew word is used for worry about bad breath or coughing, B. *Berakhot* 40a, and the worry of one who is punished every day, B. *Sukkah* 29a. For a person who is feared (*hitit*) by others, see B. *Rosh Hashanah* 17a. Fear (*pahad*) in the night is mentioned in J. *Ta'anit* 4:1; the same word is used for a father's worry about his daughter in B. *Sanhedrin* 100b, for the fear that breaks the body, B. *Baba Batra* 10a; and the fear that breaks man's energy, B. *Gittin* 70a. Apprehension (*hashash*) lest something bad happen is used in B. *Yoma* 83b and J. *Avodah zarah* 2:3 (41a). Worry (*davai*) can damage one's health and great men had actually died from worry (*davai*), B. *Sanhedrin* 100b. Thoughts that weigh on the heart (*hirhurei lev*) can surface in dreams at night, B. *Berakhot* 55b. A sigh (*anahah*) breaks the body, B. *Berakhot* 58b. In addition, anxiety (*haradah*) prevents regular menstruation, M. *Niddah* 4:7. Worry (*tirda*) over performing the marital act with a virgin and worry over the food supply are referred to in B. *Berakhot* 16b, 35b, and worry over a religious matter in B. *Sukkah* 25a. Worry (*ba'at*) over a long delay is discussed in M. *Yoma* 5:1.

9. Yehudah ibn Tibbon used the words *de'agot* and *mahshavot matridot,* worries and disturbing thoughts, in 1161, when he translated Bahya ibn Paquda's ethical treatise into Hebrew: Bahya ibn Paquda, *Hovot ha-levavot* 8:3 (Tel Aviv: *Hotza'at mahbarot le-safrut,* 1964), 470–471. Maimonides' medical aphorisms were translated into Hebrew seventy years after he wrote them, mostly using the words *de'agah* for worry, as well as *pahad* and *haradah:* M. Maimonides, *The Medical Aphorisms of Moses Maimonides,* ed. S. Muntner (Jerusalem: Mossad Harav Kook, 1959). Jonah ben Abraham of Gerona, *The Gates of Repentance,* trans. S. Silverstein (Jerusalem: Feldheim, 1967), chapters 16–18 uses *de'agah. De'agot matridot* appears in Judah ben Samuel the Pious, *Sefer Hasidim,* ed. R. Margoliyot (Jerusalem: Mossad Harav Kook, 1957), no. 527. Jacob ben Asher, *Arba'ah ha-turim* (Vilna: 1900), *Orah hayyim* 98 mentions *mahshavot tordot. Pahad* and *de'agah* are used in Meir Aldabi, *Shevilei emunah* (Warsaw: 1887), part 5, section 9. The term *mahshavot zarot* appears in *Sha'arei tzedek,* which was written by a Jew from the Abulafian school, and in Moses Cordovero's teaching: M. Idel, *Hasidism: Between Ecstasy and Magic* (Albany: State University of New York Press, 1995), 350. *Tirdot ha-lev* and *nidnud de'agah* are referred to in Y. M. Epstein, *Kitzur shnei luhot ha-brit* (Amsterdam: 1707), 72b. *Pahadim mele'im dimyonot* and *behalah* appear in T. Cohn, *Ma'aseh Tuvya* (Venice: 1707), vol. 1, *Olam ha-katan* 75b; vol. 2, *Bayit hadash* 114b, and vol. 3, *Gan na'ul* p. 135a. For the use of *mahshavot zarot* in eastern European Hasidic literature, see L. Jacobs, *Hasidic Prayer* (London: Littman Library of Jewish Civilization, 1993), chapter 9.

10. R. Ben-Simhon, *Yahadut Marocco* (Lod: Orot Yahadut ha-magreb, 1994), 304ff. S. Ben-Amri, *Ha-shed tintal* (Herzliya: published by the author, 1987), 19ff. A. Ben-Yakov, *Otzar ha-segullot* (Jerusalem: 1991), 130. Amulets 27.12.6 and 27.12.3 from the Gross family collection use many different words for anxiety, worry, and fear. Miriam, an eighty-five-year-old Yemenite folk healer in Rehovot, Israel, explained the Yemenite terms, June 2000.

11. Glückl of Hameln's words; personal communication, Professor Chava Turniansky. These Yiddish words also appear in Yiddish personal supplicatory prayers and remedy books.

12. R. May, *The Meaning of Anxiety* (New York: The Ronald Press Company, 1950). R. J. Edelman, *Anxiety: Theory, Research, and Intervention in Clinical and Health Psychology* (Chichester: Wiley, 1995). S. Rachman, *Anxiety* (Hove: Psychology Press Ltd., 1998). K. P. Lesch et al., "Association of Anxiety-Related Traits with a Polymorphism in the Serotonin Transporter Gene Regulatory Region," *Science* 274 (Nov. 29, 1996): 1527–31. Chromosome 17 carries a gene that regulates the serotonin in the brain. Lesch et al. found that people with a shorter version of the gene

admitted more to worrying than those with the long form. Doctors administer a serotonin-enhancing drug, such as Prozac or Zoloft, to help some patients reduce their anxiety: E. M. Hallowell, *Worry* (New York: Ballantine, 1997), 61, 114, 261, 290–91.

13. M. Buber, *The Way of Man* (London: Routledge and Kegan Paul, 1950), 125. M. Buber, *The Knowledge of Man,* ed. and trans. Maurice Friedman (Atlantic Highlands, N.J.: Humanities Press International, 1988), 116–26, a reprint of Buber's lecture "Guilt and Guilt Feelings," delivered in 1957 and published in *Psychiatry* 20, no. 2 (May 1957). Gen. 3:10.

14. Moses assures his people that they must not worry (*yirah*) as God will not fail them (Deut. 1:29ff). God puts fear and dread into the hearts of enemies, and the Israelites have no cause for fear (Deut. 2:4,25; 3:2,22; 11:25).

15. Isa. 33:14; Ps. 14:3–5, 53:5–6; B. *Pesaḥim* 112a; *Pesikta de-Rav Kahana,* trans. W. G. Braude and I. J. Kapstein (Philadelphia: Jewish Publication Society, 1975), 94–96, paragraph 5:3. Also, "He who takes upon himself the yoke of Torah will have the yoke of worldly care removed from him; but he who casts off the yoke of Torah will have the yoke of worldly care placed upon him," *Pirkei Avot* 3:5. Zohar 1:202a–202b: "[Joseph's] brothers were afraid on account of their sin . . . for had they not sinned they would not have had any cause to fear; for it is only a man's sins that break his courage," and "whoever is burdened by sins is constantly in fear." Later kabbalists, too, such as Joseph Karo and Abraham Yagel (who both lived during the sixteenth century), believed that transgression may be the hidden cause of anxiety. See R. J. Z. Werblowsky, *Joseph Karo: Lawyer and Mystic* (Oxford: Oxford University Press, 1962), 150–56; and D. B. Ruderman, *Kabbalah, Magic, and Science* (Cambridge, Mass.: Harvard University Press, 1988), 29.

16. M. A. Morgan, ed., *Sefer ha-razim: The Book of Mysteries* (Chico, Calif: Society of Biblical Literature, 1983), 43. Eleazar of Worms, *Hokhmat ha-nefesh* (Lemberg, 1876, and Safed, 1907), 6c, 26c–d, 27d. J. Dan, "'Sefer malakhim' le-Rabbi Yehudah ha-Ḥasid" *Da'at* 2–3 (1979): 99–120 Zohar 1:149a–149b; 2:183a–183b, 199b–200a; 3:222a–222b, 277a. M. Idel, *Studies in Ecstatic Kabbalah* (Albany: State University of New York Press, 1988), 38ff. (regarding Abraham Abulafia), and 74–82 on Isaac of Acre's idea of a world of illusory imagination, where images and forms that confuse and frighten are generated. Werblowsky, *Joseph Karo,* 155. Manasseh ben Israel, *Sefer nishmat ḥayyim* (Leipzig: 1862, reprinted Tel Aviv, 1968), part 3, chapters 4, 9, pp. 63a–b and 67a assume that a spirit, but not necessarily an evil spirit, causes anxiety. For the extensive literature on demon possession, see G. Nigal, *Magic, Mysticism, and Hasidism* (Northvale, N.J.: Jason Aronson, 1994).

17. M. Klein, *A Time to Be Born: Customs and Folklore of Jewish Birth* (Philadelphia: Jewish Publication Society, 1998), chapters 1 and 2.

18. *Wisdom of ben Sirach* in *The Apocrypha*, trans. E. J. Goodspeed (New York: Vintage Books, 1959), 38:26ff.

19. "A person who has bread in his basket yet worries about food for the next day has little faith," B. *Sotah* 48b. See also B. *Yevamot* 63b and H. L. Ansbacher, and R. R. Ansbacher, eds., *The Individual Psychology of Alfred Adler* (London: George Allen and Unwin Ltd., 1958), 226.

20. V. E. Frankl, *The Doctor and the Soul* (Harmondsworth: Penguin, 1965), introduction and 171ff.

21. 1 Sam. 10:2. Solomon ibn Gabirol, *The Improvement of the Moral Qualities*, trans. S. Wise (New York: Columbia University Press, 1901), 78–80, 100.

22. A. J. Heschel, *Man Is Not Alone* (New York: Farrar, Strauss, and Young, 1951), 69, 193. Also A. J. Heschel, *God in Search of Man* (London: Calder, 1956), 101. Cf. Alfred Adler's *The Need for Affection* (1908), reprinted in Ansbacher and Ansbacher, *Individual Psychology*, 39ff.

23. H. J. Ayalti, , ed., *Yiddish Proverbs* (New York: Schocken, 1976), 83, 85, 41, and 34.

24. E. Fromm, *The Sane Society* (London: Routledge and Kegan Paul, 1963), 68, 196–204. E. Fromm, *Fear of Freedom* (London: Routledge and Kegan Paul, 1966), 15, 23–29. E. Fromm, *The Revision of Psychoanalysis*, ed. R. Funk (Boulder, Colo.: Westview Press, 1992), 20. Also, E. Fromm, *The Art of Loving* (New York: Bantam Books, 1956), 7.

25. *Wisdom of ben Sirach* 40:1–10.

26. Sa'adia Gaon, *The Book of Beliefs and Opinions*, ed. and trans. S. Rosenblatt (New Haven: Yale University Press, 1951), treatise 10, 357ff.

27. Maimonides, *The Medical Aphorisms*, seventh treatise. Gershom ben Shlomo of Arles, *The Gate of Heaven*, trans. F. S. Bodenheimer (Jerusalem: Kiryat Sefer, 1953), 302–11. M. Maimonides, *The Eight Chapters of Maimonides on Ethics*, trans. J. I. Gorfinkle (New York: Columbia University Press, 1912), chapter 5, p. 86. Ruderman, *Kabbalah*, 40. Cohn, *Ma'aseh*, see note 9 above. Pinhas Eliyahu (Horowitz) of Vilna, *Sefer ha-brit ha-shalem* (Jerusalem: Kreuss, 1990; first published Bruenn, 1797), part 1, chapters 9–13, pp. 284ff.

28. M. Maimonides, *The Guide of the Perplexed*, trans. S. Pines (Chicago: The University of Chicago Press, 1963), part 1, chapter 73 (under discussion of tenth proposition). Maimonides, *Eight Chapters*, chapter 1.

29. For example, Isaac of Acre's views on the illusory imagination: Idel, *Studies in Ecstatic Kabbalah*, 74ff.

30. B. Safran, "Maharal and Early Hasidism," in *Hasidism: Continuity or Innovation?*, ed. B. Safran (Cambridge, Mass.: Harvard University Press, 1988), 64. S. H. Bergman, "On Death and Immortality," in *Essays on the*

Thought and Philosophy of Rabbi Kook, ed. E. Gellman (New York: Herzl Press, 1991), 63, citing from Kook's *Orot ha-kodesh* (Jerusalem: Mossad Harav Kook, 1981).

31. Ecclesiastes Rabbah 7:1 para 4.
32. Maimonides, *Eight Chapters,* 58. Ibn Gabirol, *The Improvement,* 78–80, 100.
33. S. Freud, "Inhibitions, Symptoms, and Anxiety," in *On Psychopathology,* ed. A. Richards and J. Strachey, trans. J. Strachey, Penguin Freud Library (Harmondsworth: Penguin, 1993), 10: 324–26. See also, for example, H. S. Sullivan, *Conceptions of Modern Psychiatry* (New York: Norton, 1953), 19ff.
34. J. Bowlby, *Attachment and Loss* (London: Hogarth Press, 1969). E. H. Erikson, *Childhood and Society* (Harmondsworth: Penguin, 1975), 239ff. J. Dunn, *Distress and Comfort* (London: Fontana, Open Books, 1977), chapter 5. M. Rutter, *Maternal Deprivation Reassessed* (Harmondsworth: Penguin, 1972). M. S. Mahler, , F. Pine, and A. Bergman, *The Psychological Birth of the Human Infant* (London: Hutchinson, 1975).
35. Bahya ibn Paquda, *The Duties of the Heart,* trans. Y. Feldman (Northvale, Jason Aronson 1996), gate 5, chapter 4, p. 242–63.
36. J. Dan, ed., *The Early Kabbalah* (Mahwah, N.J.: Paulist Press, 1986), 30, 50–51, 165ff., citing the thirteenth-century kabbalists. F. Lachower and I. Tishby, *The Wisdom of the Zohar* (Oxford: Oxford University Press,1989), 2:509ff. Zohar 2:161b; 3:41b–42a; 5:43a. P. Giller, *The Enlightened Will Shine* (Albany: State University of New York Press, 1993), 48. S. Shokek, *Jewish Ethics and Jewish Mysticism in Sefer ha-yashar* (London: Edwin Mellen Press, 1991), 140–41.
37. This is the teaching of Shneur Zalman, founder of Chabad Hasidism: R. Schatz-Uffenheimer, *Hasidism As Mysticism* (Princeton and Jerusalem: Princeton University Press and Magnes Press, 1993), 271ff. R. Elior, *The Paradoxical Ascent to God,* ed. trans. J. M. Green (New York: State University of New York, 1993), 108ff. Concerning Nahman of Bratzlav, see A. Steinsaltz, *Beggars and Prayers* (New York: Basic Books, 1985), 44–72.
38. I. Etkes, *Rabbi Israel Salanter and the Mussar Movement* (Philadelphia: Jewish Publication Society, 1993), 98 and 304ff.
39. B. *Sanhedrin* 64a. Freud's first major discussion of anxiety, first published in 1895, was "On the Grounds for Detaching a Particular Syndrome from Neurasthenia under the Description 'Anxiety Neurosis'" in *Case Histories II,* ed. A. Richards, trans. J. Strachey, Penguin Freud Library 9 (Harmondsworth: Penguin, 1991), 9:433–46. S. Freud, *Introductory Lectures on Psychoanalysis,* ed. J. Strachey and A. Richards, trans. J. Strachey, Penguin Freud Library 1 (Harmondsworth: Penguin, 1974), chapter 25. This chapter on anxiety was written in 1916–1917.

40. Freud, "Inhibition, Symptoms, and Anxiety," 227ff. Freud wrote his last paper on anxiety in 1932; see lecture 32 in *New Introductory Lectures on Psychoanalysis*, ed. A. Richards, trans. J. Strachey, Penguin Freud Library 2 (Harmondsworth: Penguin, 1991), 113ff.
41. J. D. Soloveitchik, "The Lonely Man of Faith," in *Studies in Judaica*, ed. L. D. Stitskin (New York: Ktav and Yeshiva University, 1974), originally published in *Tradition* 7, no. 2 (summer 1965).
42. A. Eban, *Heritage* (New York: Summit Books, 1984), 261.
43. H. Arendt, *Rahel Varnhagen: The Life of a Jewess* (John Hopkins University Press, 1999). *Encyclopedia Judaica* (Jerusalem: Keter, 1972), 8:272. See K. Lewin, *Field Theory in Social Science* (New York: Harper and Row, 1951), 142–43 on marginality.
44. Women are of unstable temperament: B. *Shabbat* 33b.
45. Girls were found to worry more than boys in some studies of children's worrying behavior, but no gender difference was found in studies of geriatric worriers: Davey and Tallis, *Worrying*, 188, 250–51.
46. Eccles. 12:5. Sa'adia Gaon, *Book of Beliefs*, treatise 10, chapter 11, p. 386.
47. Maimonides, *Guide of the Perplexed*, part 3, chapter 51, p. 628.
48. Davey and Tallis, *Worrying*, chapter 10.
49. Freud, *Introductory Lectures*, 454ff.

Chapter Two

1. I. Y. Yuval, *"Autobiographia ashkenazit me-ha-me'ah ha-arba'esreh,"* *Tarbitz* 55, no. (4) (1986): 541–66.
2. B. *Sanhedrin* 100b, B. *Sotah* 42b, B. *Yoma* 75a.
3. B. *Berakhot* 5b and *Encyclopedia Judaica*, 10:144–47.
4. B. *Berakhot* 5a, B. *Kiddushin* 30a–b, B. *Baba Batra* 16a.
5. Maimonides, *Eight Chapters*, chapter 5, p. 70. Similar advice was given by Nahman of Bratzlav, *Likkutei etzot* (Jerusalem: *Agudat meshekh ha-nahal*, undated), *hitbodedut*, 12, p. 56 and *neginah*, 11, p. 137. Jacob Zahalon, *Otzar ha-hayyim* (Venice, 1683), chapters 1 and 7. Division 13 of this book, on mental diseases that are like physical diseases, was never published.
6. M. Buber, *Tales of the Hasidim: Early Masters* (New York: Schocken, 1972), 108–9. Also L. Jacobs, *Jewish Mystical Testimonies* (New York: Schocken, 1977), 218 for the same idea of seeking to attain the spiritual.
7. Shneur Zalman, *Liqqutei amarim*, trans. N. Mindel (Brooklyn: Kehot, 1962), chapter 28.
8. M. Buber, *Tales of the Hasidim: Later Masters* (New York: Schocken, 1948), 306–7. The meaning of this phrase is the performance of good deeds and worship of God.

9. L. I. Newman, *The Hasidic Anthology* (New York: Schocken, 1963), 127. See also E. Bin-Gorion, *Me-makor Israel* (Bloomington: Indiana University Press, 1976), vol. 3, no. 91, Shem Tov Falaquera on not to worry.

10. For retellings of the *Akedah,* see S. Spiegel, *The Last Trial* (Woodstock, Vt.: Jewish Lights Publishing, 1993).

11. For the woman and her seven sons, B. *Gittin* 57b, *Seder Eliyahu Rabba,* chapter 28, and G. D. Cohen, "The Story of Hannah and her Seven Sons in Hebrew Literature" in *Mordecai M. Kaplan Jubilee Volume,* ed. M. Davis (New York: Jewish Theological Seminary of America, 1953), Hebrew section p. 109ff. For Akiva's death, see J. *Berakhot* 9:5; Adolph Jellinek, ed., "*Eileh ezkerah,*" in *Beit ha-midrash,* 3d ed. (Jerusalem: Wahrmann, 1967), 2:64–72. Also, D. G. Roskies, ed., *The Literature of Destruction* (Philadelphia: Jewish Publication Society, 1988), 42, 48. E. Wiesel, *Four Hasidic Masters and Their Struggle Against Melancholy* (Notre Dame: University of Notre Dame Press, 1978), 7.

12. D. G. Roskies, *Against the Apocalypse* (Cambridge, Mass.: Harvard University Press, 1984), 43ff. H. M. Sachar, *Farewell España* (New York: Alfred J. Knopf, 1994), 341.

13. B. *Ta'anit* 21b. God deals death and gives life and no one can deliver from God's hand: Deut. 32:39. Also Newman, *Hasidic Anthology,* 127 citing Joshua, the Belz Hasid, giving the same talmudic advice to the Hasidim. V. E. Frankl, *Man's Search for Meaning* (New York: Touchstone, Simon and Schuster, 1984), 137ff.

14. Ezek., chapters 34ff. Sachar, *Farewell España,* 67. Y. Liebes, "Mysticism and Reality: Towards a Portrait of the Martyr and Kabbalist, R. Samson Ostropoler" in *Jewish Thought in the Seventeenth Century,* ed. I. Twersky and B. Septimus (Cambridge, Mass.: Harvard University Press, 1987), 243ff.

15. Safran, "Maharal and Early Hasidism," 66ff. and 75ff.

16. Etkes, "Rabbi Israel Salanter," 304ff.

17. P. Sadeh, *Jewish Folktales* (New York: Doubleday, 1989), 326. For parallel tales from other Jewish communities, see R. Haboucha, *Types and Motifs of the Judeo-Spanish Folktales* (New York: Garland, 1992), 604.

18. R. Alter, *Defenses of the Imagination* (Philadelphia: Jewish Publication Society, 1977), 156.

19. *Wisdom of Ben Sirach* 38:26–39:5, 22:16.

20. Sa'adia Gaon, *Book of Beliefs,* treatise 10, p. 357ff.

21. Maimonides, *Eight Chapters,* chapter 4. M. Maimonides, *Mishneh Torah, Sefer ha-madda: Hilkhot de'ot* 1:5 and 1:7, *Hilkhot t'shuvah* 5:1 and 7:1.

22. Maimonides, *Hilkhot de'ot* 1:5 and 1:7, also *Eight Chapters,* chapter 4. J. Wolpe, *The Practice of Behavioral Therapy,* 3d ed. (New York: Pergamon Press, 1982). O. H. Mowrer, *Learning Theory and Behavior* (New York:

Wiley, 1960), and H. J. Eysenck, and S. Rachman, *The Causes and Cures of Neurosis* (London: Routledge and Kegan Paul, 1965).

23. H. N. Kranzler, "Maimonides' Concept of Mental Illness and Mental Health," in *Moses Maimonides: Physician, Scientist, Philosopher,* ed. F. Rosner and S. S. Kottek (Northvale, N.J.: Aronson, 1993), 53ff. Maimonides, *Guide of the Perplexed,* part 3, chapter 48. M. Idel, *The Mystical Experience in Abraham Abulafia* (Albany: State University of New York Press, 1988), 143. Nahman of Bratzlav, *Likkutei etzot, mahshavot ve-hirhurim,* p.16. The thirteenth-century *Sefer ha-hinnukh* (Jerusalem: Eshkol, 1958) *mitzvah* 416 similarly taught that we can restrain our thoughts and control the heart.

24. Buber, *Later Masters,* 249–50, 263–65. The quotations on the pockets are from *Sanhedrin* 4:5 and Gen. 18:27. See also Soloveitchik, "The Lonely Man of Faith," on the tension between majesty and humility.

25. Abraham Isaac Kook, *The Lights of Penitence, The Moral Principles, Lights of Holiness, Essays, Letters, and Poems,* trans., and intro., B. Z. Bokser (London: SPCK, 1979), 166, citing from Kook's "The Moral Principles" (Fear of God, no. 7) and his poetry on p. 379–80. See also B. Ish-Shalom, *Rav Avraham Itzhak Hacohen Kook,* trans. O. Wiskind-Elper (New York: State University of New York Press, 1993), 220.

26. For drugs used in treatment of anxiety, see Hallowell, *Worry,* chapter 25.

27. H. Schwartz, *Elijah's Violin and Other Jewish Fairy Tales* (New York: Harper and Row, 1985), 89–93.

28. Spinoza, *The Ethics,* part 5, prop. 10, p. 207–9.

29. B. *Sanhedrin* 101a.

30. R. P. Bulka, *Work, Love, Suffering, Death: A Jewish Psychological Perspective through Logotherapy* (Northvale, N.J.: Jason Aronson, 1998). For positive psychology, see E. De Bono, *Future Positive* (Harmondsworth: Penguin, 1990) and http://psych.upenn.edu/seligman/apintro.htm.

31. T. Reik, *Jewish Wit* (New York: Gamut Press, 1962), 177.

32. Assi left Babylon for the land of Israel to escape from his demanding mother. When he heard that she was on her way to visit him, he wanted to return to Babylon. He consulted one rabbi when he worried that another was angry with him. He taught that the Evil Inclination, which begins as fragile as a spider's web, becomes as tough as a cart rope: his bodily appetites probably tormented him. He apparently knew something about the pains of earning a living as he said that these are twice as hard as those of childbirth. See B. *Kiddushin* 31b; B. *Sukkah* 52a, Genesis Rabbah 20:9. Also, B. *Eruvin* 65b suggests he was a worrier.

33. Buber, *Later Masters,* 206–7.

34. J. Weiss, *Studies in Eastern European Jewish Mysticism,* ed. D. Goldstein (Oxford: Oxford University Press, 1985), 165–66 on the "Talk Hasidim," a group associated with Rabbi Abraham Kalisker, a disciple of

Menaham Mendel of Vitebsk. H. S. Kushner, *When Bad Things Happen to Good People* (New York: Avon Books, 1983), 120.

35. Newman, *Hasidic Anthology,* 213.

36. For psychoanalysis, see Freud, *Introductory Lectures.* For Gestalt therapy, see E. Polster, and M. Polster, *Gestalt Therapy Integrated* (New York: Random House, 1974). For Frankl's "logotherapy," see Frankl, *The Doctor and the Soul* and Frankl, *Man's Search for Meaning.*

37. Frankl, *The Doctor and the Soul,* introduction and pp. 171ff.

38. O. Wiskind-Elper, *Tradition and Fantasy in the Tales of Reb Nahman of Bratslav* (Albany: State University of New York Press, 1998), citing Nahman's *Likkutei moharan* 4:8.

39. Solomon ibn Gabirol, *Mekor ḥayyim,* 1:1, 2:1, 5:43, summarized in R. Loewe, *Ibn Gabirol* (London: Peter Halban, 1989), 44–53 and in I. Heinemann, "The Purpose of Human Existence As Seen by Greek-Roman Antiquity and the Jewish Middle Ages," in *Studies in Jewish Thought,* ed. A. Jospe (Detroit: Wayne State University Press, 1981), 130ff. The same idea appears in Gabirol's poetry, for example, T. Carmi, ed. and trans., *The Penguin Book of Hebrew Verse* (Harmondsworth: Penguin, 1981), 305. Maimonides, *Guide of the Perplexed,* part 3, chapter 51.

40. *Encyclopedia Judaica,* 7:125–31 on free will. R. S. Lazarus, *Emotion and Adaptation* (New York and Oxford: Oxford University Press, 1991), 136 on the assumption, in contemporary psychology, that the feeling of personal control helps us to cope.

41. Maimonides, *Eight Chapters,* chapter 8. Spinoza, *The Ethics,* 15 and part 3, propositions 2–3, p. 104ff., and end of part 3, p. 150; also part 4, prop. 7, p. 158 and prop. 47, p. 181.

42. Ansbacher and Ansbacher, *Individual Psychology,* 111.

43. S. Freud, *The Origins of Religion,* Penguin Freud Library 13 (Harmondsworth: Penguin, 1990), 367ff. This paper was written in 1934–1938 and first published in 1939.

44. M. C. Seligman, C. Peterson, and S. Maier, *Learned Helplessness* (Oxford: Oxford University Press, 1993).

45. M. White, *Selected Papers* (Adelaide, Australia: Dulwich Centre Publications, 1989), 115–24. Also M. White, and D. Epston, *Narrative Means to Therapeutic Ends* (New York: Norton, 1990).

46. Deut. 27:1. For example, S. J. Halberstam-Bielitz, "*Takkanot kadmoniyot,*" in *Jubelschrift zum siebzigsten Geburtstage des Prof. Dr. H. Graetz* (Breslau: 1887), 53–64 includes rulings from Italian Jewish communities about dress, moving around in the street, celebrations, and gambling. I. Halperin, *The Records of the Council of the Four Lands, 1580–1792,* vol. 1 (Jerusalem: The Bialik Institute, 1990), especially about relations with Polish non-Jews. S. Dubnow, *Pinkas ha-medinah* (Berlin: 1925) concerns the Jews of Lithuania in the seventeenth and

eighteenth centuries. I. Halpern, *Takkanot medinat mehrin* (Jerusalem: Mekitzei Nirdamim, 1951) concerns the Jews of Moravia. See also *Encyclopedia Judaica*, 15:712–737 on *takkanot* and *takkanot ha-kahal*

47. A. Phillips, *Houdini's Box: The Art of Escape* (London: Faber and Faber, 2001).

48. L. Appignanesi and J. Forrester, *Freud's Women* (Harmondsworth: Penguin, 2000), 153. The dream has more details, but the extra details and Freud's analysis are irrelevant here.

49. E. Yassif, *The Hebrew Folktale* (Indiana University Press: Bloomington and Indianapolis, 1999), for example, p. 411 on the recent resurgence of folktales to help Jews cope with anxieties. M. Saperstein, ed., *Jewish Preaching: 1200–1800* (New Haven: Yale University Press, 1989); see examples listed under index entry "stories in sermons."

50. B. *Shabbat* 33b, B. *Nedarim* 50a. G. Scholem, *Kabbalah* (New York: Meridian, 1978), 43, 69, 253, 412, and 422. G. Scholem, *On the Kabbalah and Its Symbolism* (New York: Schocken, 1996), 19ff. D. Ben-Amos, *In Praise of the Baal Shem Tov*, ed. and trans. J. R. Mintz (Bloomington: Indiana University Press, 1972), nos. 3 and 29. I. Klapholz, *Stories of Elijah the Prophet* (Jerusalem: Philipp Feldheim, 1970). Buber, *Early Masters*, 56–59. I. Ben-Ami, *Ha'aratzat ha-kedoshim* (Jerusalem: Magnes Press, 1984).

51. H. Bar-Itzhak, and A. Shenhar, *Jewish Moroccan Folk Narratives from Israel* (Detroit: Wayne State University Press, 1993), 18–22. T. Alexander, and D. Noy, *Otzaro shel abba* (Jerusalem Center for Research of Sephardic and Oriental Culture, 1989), vi.

52. H. Schwartz, *Reimagining the Bible* (New York and Oxford: Oxford University Press, 1998). Hans Vaihinger, in his *Philosophy of "As If"* (London: Routledge and Kegan Paul, 1935, first published in German in 1911) proposed that creating false fictions that do not need to be verified is a way of living peacefully in an irrational world. Ansbacher and Ansbacher, *Individual Psychology*, 77ff. B. Bettelheim, *The Uses of Enchantment* (London: Penguin, 1991).

53. "Let us search and examine our ways, and turn back to the Lord" (Lam. 3:40). B. *Avodah zarah* 9a. For examples from medieval philosophy, see Bahya ibn Paquda, *Duties of the Heart*, gates 7 and 8 on repentance and introspection. Maimonides, *Guide of the Perplexed*, part 3, chapter 54. For examples in Kabbalah, see Zohar 1:235a, 2:150a; see Lachower and Tishby, *The Wisdom of the Zohar*, 748 and 834–35, and M. Cordovero, *Tomer Devorah*, chapters 7, 9 in *Anthology of Jewish Mysticism*, trans. R. Ben Zion (New York: Judaica Press, 1981), 67, 72ff. In Hasidism, see for example, M. M. Faierstein, "Personal Redemption in Hasidism," in *Hasidism Reappraised*, ed. A. Rapoport-Albert (London: Littman Library of Jewish Civilization, 1996), 214–24. See also M. H. Luzzato, *Path of*

the *Upright, Mesillat yesharim*, trans. M. M. Kaplan (Northvale, N.J.: Aronson, 1995), chapter 1.

54. B. Z. Abrahams, ed. and trans., *The Life of Glückl of Hameln* (London: Horowitz Publ. Co., 1962) 19.

55. For example, in Gestalt therapy, see note 36 above. Rik Isensee practices psychotherapy with gay people in San Francisco: R. Isensee, *Reclaiming Your life: The Gay Man's Guide to Love, Self-Acceptance, and Trust* (Los Angeles: Alyson Books, 1997).

Chapter Three

1. M. Buber, *Later Masters,* 280.
2. Newman, *Hasidic Anthology,* 341.
3. *Encyclopedia Judaica,* 13:978–84, "prayer." E. Klein, *Jewish Prayer* (Columbus, Ohio: Alpha Publishing Co., 1986). S. H. Dresner, *Prayer, Humility, and Compassion* (Philadelphia: Jewish Publication Society, 1957). A. Z. Idelsohn, *Jewish Liturgy and Its Development* (New York: Schocken, 1967).
4. B. *Yoma* 86a–b.
5. A. Steinsaltz, *The Thirteen-Petalled Rose* (New York: Basic Books, 1980), 125ff. Jonah ben Abraham of Gerona, *The Gates of Repentance,*13–69, listing worry about sin as one of the twenty steps to repentance. A. B. Z. Metzger, "Rabbi Kook's Philosophy of Repentance," in *Studies in Judaica,* ed. L. D. Stitskin (New York: Ktav and Yeshiva University, 1974), 8:13; 14:11–13,15; 15:4. See also M. Buber, "The Way of Man," in *Judaism and Modern Man* (Atlantic Highlands, N.J.: Humanities Press International, 1988), 127.
6. Judah Halevi, *The Kuzari,* trans. N. D. Korobkin (Northvale, N.J.: Jason Aronson, 1998), 3:5.
7. J. D. Soloveitchik, "Majesty and Humility," *Tradition* 17, no. 2 (spring 1978): 33.
8. Gen. 18:23–33, 24:12–14, 32:10–13; 1 Sam. 1:10. Also Exod. 32:31–32; Josh. 7:6–9. Idelsohn, *Jewish Liturgy,* 16–17.
9. M. *Ta'anit* 2:4.
10. Aaron Berekhiah ben Moses of Modena, *Ma'avar yabok* (Vienna: 1857; first published Venice: 1626), 22a.
11. B. *Berakhot* 32b, 55a, although J. *Ta'anit* 4:1 teaches that whoever prays abundantly is answered. Judah ben Samuel of Regensburg (Judah the Pious), *Sefer Ḥasidim,* ed. Judah Hacohen Wistinetzki, 2d ed. (Frankfurt: 1924) nos. 1575, 1582–85, 1590. Zohar 1:202a, 2:15a. J. Albo, *Sefer ha-ikkarim,* trans. I. Husik (Philadelphia: Jewish Publication Society, 1946), book 4, chapter 16, p. 145. L. Jacobs, "Hasidic Prayer" in

Essential Papers on Hasidism, ed. G. D. Hundert (New York: New York University Press, 1991), 338.

12. Ibn Paquda, *The Duties of the Heart,* gates 9, 7, and 8, pp. 429, 365, and 387.

13. N. Tarnor, *A Book of Jewish Women's Prayers* (Northvale, N.J.: Jason Aronson, 1995), 20–22, citing from *Freger teḥinno* (Lemberg: Israel David Suss, 1897), 5ff.

14. R. N. Remen, *Kitchen Table Wisdom* (London: Pan, 1997), 270–71. Cf. A. J. Heschel, who said that "prayer is a way to master what is inferior in us" and disregard our personal concerns: Klein, *Jewish Prayer,* 9–10.

15. M. *Berakhot* 4:1; J. *Berakhot* 9:1; B. *Shabbat* 32a–b; M. *Ta'anit* 2:1–5.

16. *The Fathers According to Rabbi Nathan,* trans. J. Goldin (New Haven: Yale University Press, 1955) chapter 15. B. *Sanhedrin* 44b; B. *Berakhot* 5a, 60b. E. E. Urbach, *The Sages,* trans. I. Abrahams (Jerusalem: Magnes Press, 1979), 1: 471 and n. 8.

17. S. Buber, ed., *Pesikta Kahana* (Lyck, 1868), 157a–b, *shuvah.*

18. Leviticus Rabbah 10:5.

19. Yahya Yosef Tzalah, *Siddur tikhlal: minhag kehillot Teiman,* (Sana'a, Jerusalem: S. H. Zuckerman, 1894), 84b prayer before setting out on business *(eizeh esek).*

20. M. *Berakhot* 4:4; B. *Menaḥot* 53b. See also Fromm, *Revision of Psychoanalysis,* 43–52, on the prayers of the distressed.

21. Maimonides, *Guide of the Perplexed,* part 3: chapter 36. Also M. Maimonides, *Mishneh Torah, Sefer ha-madda: Hilkhot t'shuvah* 7:2; *Sefer ahavah: Hilkhot tefillah* 4:16; and *Sefer z'manim: Hilkhot ta'ani'ot* 1:2–3.

22. M. *Ta'anit* 2:4ff. J. B. Soloveitchik, and A. R. Besdin, *Reflections of the Rav* (Jerusalem: Department for Torah Education and Culture in the Diaspora of the World Zionist Organization, 1979), 88, citing from Nahmanides, *Sefer ha-middot* 5.

23. Liebes, "Mysticism and Reality," 243ff. and notes 20–21. The rabbi of Polnoye at the time was Samson Ostropoler. The description appears in N. N. Hannover's book, *Yeven ha-metzulah* (Venice: 1653), 6b. See B. *Berakhot* 61b for Rabbi Akiva.

24. See references in previous note.

25. J. R. Marcus, *Communal Sick-Care in the German Ghetto* (Cincinnati: Hebrew Union College Press, 1947), 218–19.

26. F. Neuda, *Hours of Devotion,* trans. M. Mayer, 5th ed. (New York: Werblowsky, 1866), 78–79. This is a translation of F. Neuda, *Stunden der Andacht* (Prague: 1857).

27. According to Rabbis Yohanan and Eleazar: M. *Berakhot* 5:1 and B. *Berakhot* 10b, 33a, and 61b for Akiva. *Sefer Yetzirah,* ed. A. Kaplan (York Beach, Maine: Weiser, 1997), chapter 1:8, *"b'lom . . . levkha me-leharher."*

28. *Avot* 3:13 on tradition as a fence to Torah.

29. Deut. 4:4; Gen. 2:24, 34:3; 1 Kings 11:2; Ps. 102:6; Job 19:20, 29:10; B. *Sanhedrin* 64a; B. *Ketubbot* 111b; and Genesis Rabbah 80:7.
30. Ibn Paquda, *The Duties of the Heart,* gate 8, p. 362–63.
31. Maimonides, *Hilkhot tefillah* 4:15–16. Maimonides, *Guide of the Perplexed,* part 3: chapter 51, p. 622.
32. G. Scholem, "The Concept of Kavvanah in the Early Kabbalah," in *Studies in Jewish Thought,* ed. A. Jospe (Detroit: Wayne State University Press, 1981), 162–80 citing also *Sefer ha-bahir* on sacrifice as unification. Lachower and Tishby, *The Wisdom of the Zohar,* 947, citing David ben Judah Hasid, grandson of Nahmanides, and 982, citing Rabbi Ezra: "'Worship' signifies the elimination of thoughts that are preoccupied with the affairs of the world and subjugating them to concentration in prayer (*kavvanah*)."
33. Werblowsky, *Joseph Karo,* 57–66, 157ff.
34. Jacobs, "Hasidic Prayer," 335ff. R. A. Foxbrunner, *Habad: The Hasidism of R. Shneor Zalman of Lyady* (Tuscaloosa and London: University of Alabama Press, 1992), 110–16, 186–91. Zalman, *Liqqutei amarim,* chapter 28. Schatz-Uffenheimer, *Hasidism As Mysticism,* 277. Weiss, *Studies in Jewish Mysticism,* ed., 126–30. M. Hallamish, "R. Menahem Mendel of Vitebsk," in *Hasidism Reappraised,* ed. A. Rapoport-Albert (London: Littman Library of Jewish Civilization, 1996), 275ff.
35. Hallamish, "Mendel of Vitebsk," 274ff. In contrast, one who worries must have little faith: B. *Sotah* 48b.
36. B. *Berakhot* 30b; B. *Eruvin* 65a.
37. Maimonides, *Guide of the Perplexed,* part 3, chapter 51. Judah ben Samuel, *Sefer Ḥasidim,* Wistinetzki, ed., nos. 11, 440, 445, and 451 based on B. *Berakhot* 30b, and also nos. 1575, 1582, 1583, 1584, 1585, 1590, and 1602. I. G. Marcus, "The Devotional Ideals of Ashkenazic Pietism," in *Jewish Spirituality: From the Bible through the Middle Ages,* ed. A. Green (New York: Crossroad, 1994), 1:356–66.
38. Zohar 1:155b, 167b–168a, 243b–244a; 2:56b–57a, 63a–63b, 133a, 161a; 3:226a, 255a; in English, Lachower and Tishby, *The Wisdom of the Zohar,* 1400–1403, 1042, 1045, and 1049. The instruction to praise God first and then petition comes from B. *Berakhot* 32a.
39. Werblowsky, *Joseph Karo,* 155ff., citing from *Maggid Mesharim.* Hayyim of Volozhin, the disciple of the Vilna Gaon, promoted Karo's views on suppressing distracting thoughts during prayer; Idel, *Hasidism,*151.
40. P. Katzenellenbogen, *Yesh manḥilin* (Jerusalem: Makhon Hatam Sofer, 1986), signs 34 and 48.
41. A. Green, *Tormented Master: A Life of Rabbi Nahman of Bratslav* (University of Alabama Press, 1979), 62: Nahman was concerned with the uplifting of disturbing thoughts until 1798. After this, he came to believe

that only the *tzaddik* of the generation, a man with rare spiritual abilities, could uplift disturbing thoughts and everyone else should banish worries and not try to uplift them.

42. M. *Berakhot* 4:4, 9:3. J. *Berakhot* 9:5, T. *Berakhot* 3:7.
43. Isaiah Horowitz, "The Martyr's Prayer," in *Language of Faith,* ed. N. N. Glatzer (New York: Schocken, 1975), 75. The original was printed in Isaiah Horowitz, *Shnei luhot ha-brit* (Amsterdam: 1649).
44. A. Rapoport-Albert, "God and Zaddik," in *Essential Papers in Hasidism,* 310. Safran, "Maharal and Early Hasidism," 81; Jacobs, L., *Hasidic Prayer* (London: Littman Library of Jewish Civilization, 1993), chapter 9.
45. Jacobs, *Hasidic* (1993), chapter 9.
46. Etkes, "Rabbi Israel Salanter," 101ff. and 289ff.
47. E. M. Umansky, and D. Ashton, *Four Centuries of Jewish Women's Spirituality* (Boston: Beacon Press, 1992), 97–8.
48. For example, ibid., part IV and S. Rothschild, and S. Sheridan, eds., *Taking up the Timbrel* (London: SCM Press, 2000).
49. J. D. Soloveitchik, "Catharsis," *Tradition* 17, no. 2 (spring 1978), 38–54.
50. B. *Ta'anit* 22b; M. *Berakhot* 9:3; Zohar 1:111b. J. Reimer, *Likrat Shabbat,* ed. J. D. Levine, trans. S. Greenberg Media Judaica Inc., Prayer Book Press, 1981). Reprinted in Kushner, *When Bad Things Happen,* 118.
51. Ibn Paquda, *The Duties of the Heart,* gate 7 (Gate of Repentance) and gate 8 (Gate of Introspection), pp. 305ff. Jonah ben Abraham of Gerona, *The Gates of Repentance.* I. G. Marcus, "Hasidei Ashkenaz Private Penitentials: An Introduction and Descriptive Catalogue of Their Manuscripts and Early Editions," in *Studies in Jewish Mysticism,* ed. J. Dan, and F. Talmage (Cambridge, Mass.: Association for Jewish Studies, 1982), 57–83.
52. *Tehinnot banot jeschrun* (Sulzbach: S. Arnstein and Söhne, 1832).
53. Ps. 71: 9 "Do not cast me off in old age; when my strength fails, do not forsake me!" quoted in all the *selihot* of Elul as well as (in the plural) on Yom Kippur before the opening of the ark. Tarnor, *Book of Jewish Women's Prayers,* 58–59 and 93–95.
54. Sam. 1:10–11, 1 Kings 18:37.
55. M. *Berakhot* 4:4; B. *Berakhot* 16b–17a, 28b, 29b; B. *Shabbat* 30b. In talmudic times, people inserted their petitions in the last of the intermediate benedictions of the *Amidah.* The *Tahanun* was originally a private supplication and confessional prayer with no fixed form; today's format dates from the sixteenth century. Idelsohn, *Jewish Liturgy,* xv, 92ff., 110ff., and 257–58 with reference to special editions of private devotions in the different languages spoken by Jews in everyday life. M. Nulman, *Encyclopedia of Jewish Prayer* (Northvale, N.J.: Jason Aronson, 1993), "tefillat ha-derekh." J. *Berakhot* 4:4; T. *Berakhot* 3:7.

56. Maimonides, *Hilkhot tefillah* 4:15. Zohar 1:132a–b, 168b, 223a, 249b; 2:20a, 245b. Lachower and Tishby, *The Wisdom of the Zohar,* 1047.

57. M. Buber, *For the Sake of Heaven* (Philadelphia: Jewish Publication Society, 1945), 17. See also Newman, *Hasidic Anthology,* 330, no. 5, attributed to Rabbi Bunim, that the prayer of the brokenhearted is answered at once.

58. Umansky and Ashton, *Four Centuries,* 98.

59. Neuda, *Hours of Devotion.* Also see note 52 above for the Sulzbach prayer book. Also *Tehinnot banot yeshurun* (Fürth: 1842) and Meir Halevi Letteris, *Tahnunei bat yehudah* (Prague: 1851). For Yiddish personal supplicatory prayers, see C. Weissler, "The Traditional Piety of Ashkenazic Women," in *Jewish Spirituality:From the Sixteenth Century Revival to the Present,* ed. A. Green (New York: Crossroad, 1987), 2:245–75; T. G. Klirs, comp., *The Merit of Our Mothers: A Bilingual Anthology of Jewish Women's Prayers* (Cincinnati: Hebrew Union College Press, 1993); and Tarnor, *Book of Jewish Women's Prayers.* N. B. Cardin, *Out of the Depths I Call to You: A Book of Prayers for the Married Jewish Woman* (Northvale, N.J.: Jason Aronson, 1992) in Hebrew and Italian.

60. E. Wiesel, *Souls on Fire, and Somewhere a Master* (Harmondsworth: Penguin, 1987), 87–90.

61. Gen. 24:63. B. *Berakhot* 26b. Nahman of Bratslav, *Likkutei moharan* no. 99, *Likkutei etzot, hitbodedut* 12, 16, 19, *tefillah* 18. For English translations, see A. Kaplan, *Meditation and the Bible* (York Beach, Maine: Samuel Weiser, 1992), 312 and Wiskind-Elper, *Tradition and Fantasy,* 88, 98.

62. J. Heinemann, *Prayer in the Talmud* (Berlin, New York: Walter de Gruyter, 1977), 178ff. Rabbi Yohanan warned that praying for one's needs in the vernacular is pointless; B. *Sotah* 33a; B. *Shabbat* 12b. However, medieval Jewish law stated that this applies only to individual prayers and not to group prayers for the collective welfare that are recited in the congregation; Karo, J., *Beit Yosef, Tur, Orhot Hayyim* 101. See for example Klirs, *The Merit of Our Mothers,* 112ff. and Cardin, *Out of the Depths,* 78–85. See R. Ben-Simhon, *Yahadut Marocco,* 41–42 for a Judeo-Arabic prayer.

63. D. G. Roskies, *The Literature of Destruction* (Philadelphia: Jewish Publication Society, 1989), 492–93.

64. The Aramaic medieval prayer, from *Tikkunei Zohar,* appears in Hebrew translation in Shmuel ben Yehoshua Zelig, *Sha'arei dimah* (Jerusalem: 1884), 6bff. See also B. A. Halevi, *A Modern Guide to the Jewish Holy Places* (Jerusalem: Posner and Sons, Ltd., 1982), 63–64.

65. B. *Ta'anit* 47a. J. Trachtenberg, *Jewish Magic and Superstition* (New York: Atheneum, 1982), 64. L. Fine, "The Contemplative Practice of Yihudim in Lurianic Kabbalah," in *Jewish Spirituality,* ed. Green, 2:79ff. I. Ben-Ami, *Ha'aratzat ha-kedoshim* (Jerusalem: Magnes Press, 1984).

Y. Bergman, "Ha-refu'ah ha-ammamit," *Edot* 1 (1945–1946): 199ff. Y. Avishur, *Women's Folk Songs in Judeo-Arabic from Jews in Iraq* (Tel Aviv: Iraqi Jews Traditional Culture Center Publication, 1987), 163ff.

66. Zelig, *Sha'arei dimah*, 5b–6b.

67. Simeon ben Israel Judah Frankfort, *Sefer ha-ḥayyim* (Amsterdam: 1703) in Hebrew and Yiddish. *Sefer refu'at ha-nefesh* (Amsterdam: 1692). *Refu'at neshamah* (Frankfort an der Oder: 1704). *Ḥesed ve-emet* (Berlin: 1746). *Sefer divrei emet* (Prague: 1805). See also Marcus, *Communal Sick-Care*, 228–31. M. Klein, "Infertility and the Religious Pilgrimage," *Journal of Psychology and Judaism*, in press.

68. Buber, *Later Masters*, 282.

69. B. *Berakhot* 16b–17a, 30a.

70. *Zohar* 1:160b, 167b; 2:246a.

71. L. Fine, ed. and trans., *Safed Spirituality* (Mahwah, N.J.: Paulist Press, 1984), 66.

72. The Italian woman's prayer appears in handwritten personal prayer books; Cardin, *Out of the Depths*, 78–85, and *Kol teḥinnah* (Trieste: 1824, in Sir Isaac Wolfson Museum, Jerusalem), f.12, taken from Isaiah Horowitz, *Sha'ar ha-shamayim* (Amsterdam: 1717), which was published almost a century after Horowitz's death. The same prayer appears in Epstein, *Kitzur shnei luḥot ha-brit*, 112 (an abbreviation of Horowitz's opus) and in Y. M. Epstein, *Seder tefillah derekh yesharah* (Frankfort an der Oder: 1703), 11b–12a. Other private prayers were taken from the kabbalistic prayerbook, *Sha'arei tziyyon* of Nathan Nata Hannover (d. 1683), such as the prayer for a child's first day in school (ḥeder); Tarnor, *Book of Jewish Women's Prayers*, 23, no. 28. See also Weissler, "Traditional Piety," 250.

73. Y. Eliach, *Hasidic Tales of the Holocaust* (New York: Vintage Books, 1988), 13–15.

74. The quote is from Genesis Rabbah 53:14. B. *Berakhot* 29b–30a; B. *Shabbat* 12b; B. *Baba Kamma* 92a; B. *Ketubbot* 8b.

75. A. Yaari, "Tefillot mi she-berakh, hishtalshelutan, minhageihen ve-nusha'oteihen," *Kiryat Sefer* 33 (1958): 118–30. Also Nulman, *Encyclopedia of Jewish Prayer*, "Mi shebayrakh" and "Yekum purkan." The *mi she-berakh* is also often recited as a blessing, for example, during life-cycle rituals and to honor a special guest in the congregation.

76. Moses argues on behalf of his people after the episode of the Golden Calf (Exod. 32:31–32) and intercedes for his people (Num. 11:10). Abraham argues with the Lord for the sake of the people of Sodom (Gen. 18:23–33). Solomon asks God to hear the prayers of his people when they are afflicted and answer them (1 Kings 8:12–53). See also 2 Kings 19:2ff., Jer. 14:7–9 and Amos 7:2ff. Ps. 90 is also a supplication for the people.

77. B. *Berakhot* 34b; B. *Baba Bathra* 116a.
78. B. *Ta'anit* 23a–25b. Over the centuries, Jews added verses to Akiva's *Avinu Melkenu* prayer to address their particular concerns. They recited this prayer on certain fast days, and eventually also on Rosh Hashanah, Yom Kippur, and the intervening penitential days, which is the custom today. Today, for example, the Sephardic ritual has twenty-nine verses, the Yemenite tradition has twenty-seven, the Salonican has fifty-three, and the Polish, which a British prayer book also uses, has forty-four. This prayer, and other penitential prayers that Jews added to the liturgy over the centuries, came to be recited at fixed times and places, in fixed format, and usually in a public place with other Jews. Once standardized, they were not necessarily personal, heartfelt communications with God, unless recited with full mental intention, *kavvanah*. I. Elbogen, *Jewish Liturgy: A Comprehensive Literature* (Philadelphia: Jewish Publication Society, 1993), 177ff. Nulman, *Encyclopedia of Jewish Prayer,* "Avinu malkenu."
79. Gen. 6:9, Hab. 2:4; Ps. 11:31; B. *Sanhedrin* 65b, 97b, 108a; B. *Mo'ed Katan* 16b; B. *Yevamot* 64a; B. *Hagigah* 12b; B. *Sukkah* 45b.
80. Nigal, *Magic, Mysticism, and Hasidism,* 171ff. and 7ff. shows how some rabbis disseminated miraculous stories about themselves to inflate their reputations. For wondrous tales about Akiva, see L. Finkelstein, *Akiba: Scholar, Saint, and Martyr* (New York and Philadelphia: Meridian, 1962), 130ff.; about Luria in M. Benayahu, ed., *Toldot ha-Ari* (Jerusalem: Ben-Zvi Institute, 1967) and about the Besht in Ben-Amos, *Baal Shem Tov.* See also Martin Buber's and Elie Wiesel's collections of Hasidic tales. Idel, *Hasidism,* 169, 189ff., 203.
81. Y. Sabar, *The Folk Literature of the Kurdistani Jews* (New Haven: Yale University Press, 1982), 115–16.
82. S. H. Dresner, *The Zaddik* (Northvale, N.J.: Jason Aronson, 1994). A. Green, "Typologies of Leadership and the Hasidic Zaddik," in *Jewish Spirituality,* ed. Green, 2:131. Rapoport-Albert, "God and Zaddik," 326 n. 44. Idel, *Hasidism,* 189, 352 n. 137. The idea of a *maggid* drawing down divine influx was mentioned by Todros Abulafia in the thirteenth century. Wiesel, *Souls on Fire,* 326. Buber, *Early Masters,* 22.
83. T. Alexander, and D. Noy, *Otzaro shel abba* (Jerusalem: Center for Research of Sephardi and Oriental Culture, 1989), nos. 4, 8, and 24. H. Bar Itzhak, and A. Shenhar, *Jewish Moroccan Folk Narratives from Israel* (Detroit: Wayne State University Press, 1993), 55, 116. Ben-Amos, *Baal Shem Tov,* no. 107, p. 132. S. Poll, *The Hasidic Community of Williamsburg* (New York: Schocken, 1969), 118. North African Jews in Israel flocked to the Baba Sali, Israel Abuhatzeira (1890–1984), to ask him to pray for them, just as many Jews today seek out Rav Kadouri, the aged Iraqi-born Jerusalem *tzaddik.*

84. Exod. 18:18. Dresner, *The Zaddik,* 125ff., Idel, *Hasidism,* 204.

85. Schatz-Uffenheimer, *Hasidism As Mysticism,* 273. Foxbrunner, *Habad,* 124, citing *Igerot kodesh,* p. 55, no. 24. Buber, *Later Masters,* 193, 310. Rabbi Mendel of Kotzk also tired of praying for others and appointed someone else to do the job; see also ibid., 287, "Those Who Cannot Pray." Wiesel, *Souls on Fire,* 337. The Seer of Lublin also broke down under the weight of hearing everyone's worries; Wiesel, *Four Hasidic Masters,* 91.

86. Freud, *Introductory Lectures,* 494. Also R. D. Hinshelwood, *A Dictionary of Kleinian Thought* (London: Free Association Books, 1991), 231–36, 246–53.

87. Hallowell, *Worry,* 298. Dr. Hallowell says that "prayer and/or meditation can effectively change the state of your brain. . . . If you are religious, talk to God when you get worried" (p. 265). Hallowell claims that "there is lots of evidence that people who pray and have religious faith worry less and live longer . . ." (p. 31) but does not cite empirical studies to back this sweeping statement.

Chapter Four

1. Earlier versions in J. *Hagigah* 77b, *Tosefta Hagigah* 2:3–4. Song of Songs Rabbah 1:4. D. J. Halperin, *The Faces of the Chariot* (Tübingen: J. C. B. Mohr [Paul Siebeck], 1988), 31ff. and 199ff., and D. R. Blumenthal, *Understanding Jewish Mysticism* (New York: Ktav, 1978), 56ff. G. Scholem, *Jewish Gnosticism, Merkabah Mysticism, and Talmudic Tradition* (New York: Jewish Theological Seminary, 1965), 14–19.

2. For the link between meditative technique and the methods of the ancient prophets and sages, see for example P. B. Fenton, "Abraham Maimonides (1186–1237): Founding a Mystical Dynasty," in M. Idel, and M. Ostow, eds., *Jewish Mystical Leaders and Leadership in the Thirteenth Century* (Northvale, N.J.: Jason Aronson, 1998), 144. Werblowsky, *Joseph Karo* 63–64. M. Idel, *Studies in Ecstatic Kabbalah* (Albany: State University of New York Press, 1988), 8–11, and Idel, *Hasidism,* 56 and 59. The inspiration for this imagery comes from the association of the cherubs in Ezekiel's vision (Ezek. 10:1ff.) with the word *merkavah* (1 Chron. 28:18).

3. http://www.rebgoldie.com/ is the website of Rabbi Goldie Milgram who teaches Jewish meditation; she cites other Jewish women who can teach this practice, such as Melinda Ribner, founder of the Jewish Meditation Circle.

4. E. R. Valentine, and P. L. G. Sweet, "Meditation and Attention: A Comparison of the Effects of Concentrative and Mindfulness Meditation on

Sustained Attention," *Mental Health, Religion, and Culture* 2, no. 1 (1999): 59–70.

5. M. *Berakhot* 5:1. D. Winston, "Philo and the Contemplative Life," in *Jewish Spirituality,* ed. Green, (1:219–20, 225–26).

6. M. Ostow, ed., *Ultimate Intimacy* (London: Karnac Books, 1995), 133, 137. See also D. W. Winnicott, *Playing and Reality* (Harmondsworth: Penguin, 1985), chapter 1 on illusion.

7. Halperin, *The Faces of the Chariot,* 30ff. and 440–52. See also R. M. Lesses, *Ritual Practices to Gain Power,* Harvard Theological Series (Harrisburg, Pa.: Trinity Press International, 1998).

8. A. Kaplan, *Meditation and Kabbalah* (York Beach, Maine: Samuel Weiser, 1982), 113, citing from Albotini's *Sulam ha-aliyah* 9, p. 16a–16b and B. *Ketubbot* 111a.

9. D. R. Blumenthal, *Understanding Jewish Mysticism* (New York: Ktav, 1982), 2:42ff.

10. An earlier Spanish kabbalist, Bahya ben Asher (thirteenth century), assumed that Moses drew down divine power in his prayer. Isaac of Acre (late thirteenth to mid-fourteenth century) assumed that Moses had united his soul with the Divine Nothing: M. Idel, *Kabbalah: New Perspectives* (New Haven: Yale University Press, 1988), 68, 163, and 204. M. Idel, "Hitbodedut As Concentration in Ecstatic Kabbalah," in *Jewish Spirituality,* ed. Green, 1:427ff. Kaplan, *Meditation and Kabbalah,* 170 and 299ff. Idel, *Hasidism,* 119.

11. Idel, *Kabbalah,* 95.

12. Zohar 1:99b. Joseph Gikatilla (1248–1323) stressed that we should not meditate for our own uses, but only at a time of an evil decree or for the purpose of sanctifying God. Abraham ben Eliezer Halevi of Jerusalem (d. c. 1530) advised those who are tortured on account of their faith (a common occurrence during the Spanish Inquisition) to meditate: G. Scholem, *Major Trends in Jewish Mysticism* (New York: Schocken, 1974), 146. Yohanan Alemanno (1435–c. 1504) tried to use meditation to work miracles: M. Idel, "The Magical and Neoplatonic Interpretations of the Kabbalah in the Renaissance," in *Essential Papers on Jewish Culture in Renaissance and Baroque Italy,* ed. D. Ruderman (New York: New York University Press, 1992), 119. H. Vital, *Sefer ha-ḥizyonot,* ed. A. Z. Aeshcoli (Jerusalem: Mossad ha-rav Kook, 1954), 54–55. Werblowsky, *Joseph Karo,* 154ff. Joshua Heshel Tzoref (seventeenth century) also meditated to gain prophecy, and to gain insight into the worrying political situation in his day: Scholem, *Kabbalah,* 276 and 453.

13. I. Gawler, *Peace of Mind* (Melbourne: Hill of Content, 1987). J. Kabat-Zinn et al., "Effectiveness of a Meditation-Based Stress Reduction Program in the Treatment of Anxiety Disorders," *American Journal of Psychiatry* 149 (1992): 936–43.

14. Schatz-Uffenheimer, *Hasidism As Mysticism,* chapter 7. Jacobs, *Hasidic Prayer,* chapter 7.

15. Blumenthal, *Understanding Jewish Mysticism,* chapter 15ff. A. Kuyt, *The "Descent" to the Chariot* (Tübingen: J. C. B. Mohr [Paul Siebeck], 1995), 127ff.

16. Kaplan, *Meditation and Kabbalah,* 173–74. Sachar, *Farewell España,* 165.

17. Liebes, "Mysticism and Reality," 221–55.

18. Jacobs, *Jewish Mystical Testimonies,* chapter 13.

19. Fenton, "Abraham Maimonides," 152, citing this view of Obadyah Maimonides (1228–1265, grandson of Maimonides). The imagery is taken from Sufi mysticism. See also D. C. Matt, "*Ayin:* The Concept of Nothingness in Jewish Mysticism," in *The Problem of Pure Consciousness,* ed. R. K. C. Forman (Oxford: Oxford University Press, 1990), 135.

20. Num. 19, for biblical purification ritual. B. *Niddah* 6b. Scholem, *Major Trends,* 49. B. M. Lewin, *Otzar ha-geonim* (Jerusalem: 1931), vol. 4, *masekhet Hagigah,* 14 on Hai Gaon's preparations. Lesses, *Ritual Practices,* 99. Fine, "The Contemplative Practice of Yihudim in Lurianic Kabbalah," 70ff. Blumenthal, *Understanding Jewish Mysticism,* 57 on *heikhalot* preparations. Blumenthal, *Understanding Jewish Mysticism 2,* 70–72 on Albotini's preparations for meditation.

21. Num. 15:38–39. B. *Hullin* 89a. Kaplan, *Meditation and Kabbalah,* 96, citing Abulafia on wearing white, and p. 312. *Sefer ha-bahir,* ed. Daniel Abrams (Los Angeles: Cherub Press, 1994), no. 65 on the blue in the prayer shawl. See also Marcus, "The Devotional Ideals of Ashkenazic Pietism," 362.

22. In 1 Sam. 10:5 and 2 Kings 3:15 the prophet used music to attain divine revelation. Idel, *The Mystical Experience,* 61ff. Blumenthal, *Understanding Jewish Mysticism 2:72* for a translation of chapter 10 of Albotini's *Sullam ha-aliyah.*

23. Judah Löw ben Bezalel, *Ner Mitzvah* (Bnei Brak: 1972), 21. Ben-Amos, *Baal Shem Tov,* tales 51 and 104.

24. B. *Kiddushin* 71a; B. *Ta'anit* 25b; B. *Yoma* 23a; B. *Megillah* 28a. Akiva and Nehunya ben ha-Kana are cited as examples of such a person. Also Winston, "Philo," 219, 225–26.

25. Blumenthal, *Understanding Jewish Mysticism 2:71–72.* Also Idel, "Hitbodedut," 425.

26. Werblowsky, *Joseph Karo,* 161 quoting from *Maggid Mesharim* 16b.

27. Idel, "Hitbodedut," 433, quoting Azikri on Ps. 16:8. Matt, "Ayin," 134–35. Kaplan, *Meditation and Kabbalah,* 145 translates the Ba'al Shem Tov's *Tzva'at ha-ribash* 2. In note 85, Kaplan offers parallel references in *Or torah* on Ps. 16:8, *Keter shem tov* 220, and *Likkutum yekarim* no. 179. Hallamish, "Mendel of Vitebsk," 285.

28. See notes 35 and 55 below concerning warnings about the danger of meditating alone. M. *Berakhot* 5:1 and Judah ben Samuel, *Sefer Ḥasidim*, ed. Wistinetzki, no. 451. Also Kaplan, *Meditation and Kabbalah*, 20 and 122 quoting from a medieval kabbalistic text.

29. Ibn Paquda, *The Duties of the Heart*, gates 6 and 10, chapters 1 and 6, pp. 267ff., 441–42, and 453–54. Maimonides, *Guide of the Perplexed*, part 3, chapter 51.

30. Judah ben Samuel, *Sefer Ḥasidim*, Wistinetzki, ed., nos. 1582 and 1584. For translation, see. Marcus, "Devotional Ideals," 362. Fenton, "Abraham Maimonides," 149–152.

31. Gershonides, *Milḥamot ha-shem* 2:6, Levi ben Gershom, *Wars of the Lord*, trans. S. Feldman (Philadelphia: Jewish Publication Society, 1987), 62. Idel, "*Hitbodedut*," 417–420.

32. Fine, *Safed Spirituality*, 141. Werblowsky, *Joseph Karo*, 58ff., and p. 69, and p. 75 on Vital's similar desire for seclusion. See also Idel, "*Studies in Ecstatic Kabbalah*, 128, and Idel, "*Hitbodedut*," 435–36 on Vital's seclusion.

33. Ben-Amos, *Baal Shem Tov*, 12. M. Buber, *The Legend of the Baal-Shem* (New York: Schocken, 1969), 56–63. Matt, "Ayin," 139–140. Schatz-Uffenheimer, *Hasidism As Mysticism*, 172. Kaplan, *Meditation and Kabbalah*, 275–305. See also Elimelekh of Lizhensk, *Noam Elimelekh* (Jerusalem: 1960), 39a and 40b.

34. Nahman of Bratzlav, *Likkutei etzot, hitbodedut*, 55ff. Wiskind-Elper, *Tradition and Fantasy*, 135.

35. Idel, *The Mystical Experience*, 122–23 on Abulafia's warnings. Idel, "*Hitbodedut*," 415 on Rabbi Isaac of Acre's warning. Werblowsky, *Joseph Karo*, 67 on Vital's warnings. Idel, *Hasidism*, 131 quotes from the son of the Maggid of Koznitz, and 324, note 185 quotes Jacob ben Sheshet, a thirteenth-century kabbalist of Gerona, who also spoke of this danger. See also Matt, "*Ayin*," 135–36 on the warning of Ezra of Gerona of this mortal danger; and Jacobs, *Jewish Mystical Testimonies*, 223 on Elimelekh of Lizhensk's precaution. See more examples in note 55 below.

36. Blumenthal, *Understanding Jewish Mysticism*, 56ff. Kuyt, *The "Descent" to the Chariot*, 127ff. Idel, *The Mystical Experience*, 14. The primary source in all these is *Heikhalot Rabbati*, chapter 16. See also Lesses, *Ritual Practices*, 114 and 414. Kaplan, *Meditation and Kabbalah*, 45.

37. Idel, *The Mystical Experience*, 17. L. Fine, "Recitation of Mishnah As a Vehicle for Mystical Inspiration: A Contemplative Technique Taught by Hayyim Vital," *Revue des Etudes Juives* 141, no. 1–2 (1982): 194–95. Werblowsky, *Joseph Karo*, 260ff.

38. Fine, "Recitation of Mishnah," 183–99. Fine, "The Contemplative Practice," 83ff. Vital, *Sefer ha-ḥizyonot*, 55, for example. Here the two instances he cites refer to his interest in having inherited the soul of a talmudic *tzaddik*.

39. Liebes, "Mysticism and Reality," 234–37. The rabbi says that he would recite the chosen biblical verse before going to sleep at night and immediately the *maggid* would come to him. Liebes deduces from this that the *maggid* came in his dream, "through a sort of 'dream question,'" but it may well be that the rabbi meditated, received his revelations, and made a note of them at night before going to sleep.

40. Etkes, "Rabbi Israel Salanter and His Psychology of Mussar," in *Jewish Spirituality*, ed. Green. 2:240, citing from *Kitvei Rabbi Israel Salanter,* 148.

41. Marcus, "Devotional Ideals," 361. Idel, *The Mystical Experience,* 23.

42. B. *Berakhot* 55a. *Sefer Yetzirah* 6:4, translated in Kaplan, *Meditation and Kabbalah,* 76. For the "lore of combination of letters" in the Zohar and in *Sefer ha-peliyah,* a fourteenth-century text, see Idel, *Hasidism,* 56. Idel, *The Mystical Experience,* 20ff. Idel, "*Hitbodedut*," 409–13.

43. Idel, "*Hitbodedut*," 414ff., concerning Isaac of Acre, Shem Tov ibn Gaon (late thirteenth- to early fourteenth-century Safed), and Judah Albotini. Kaplan, *Meditation and Kabbalah,* 137ff., 107–14.

44. Kaplan, *Meditation and Kabbalah,* 119 followed Professor Scholem in stating that the author of this text, *Sha'ar ha-kavvanah,* was probably Azriel of Gerona, but Professor Moshe Idel thinks the author was a late thirteenth-century kabbalist; Idel, *Hasidism,* 275, n. 53. On the concept of the Divine Nothing, see Matt, "*Ayin,*".

45. G. Scholem, "*Ha-maggid shel R. Yosef Taitatzak,*" *Sefunot* 11 (1971–1978): 69–109.

46. Kaplan, *Meditation and Kabbalah,* 158–66.

47. Idel, Hasidism, 67–69 quoting from *Pardes rimmonim,* gate 10, the gate of colors. At the end of the eighteenth century, a Hasid wrote in the name of the Ba'al Shem Tov about the righteous man who performs a unification (*yihud*) to reach God and draw down a divine flow of blessings, but many of his Hasidic followers did not adopt this method of contemplation. Idel, *Hasidism,* 105 and Schatz-Uffenheimer, *Hasidism As Mysticism,* chapter 10.

48. Idel, "*Hitbodedut*," 433–34, citing from Azikri's mystical diary (Jewish Theological Seminary, New York, Ms. 809) and *Sefer Haredim,* 43. J. Tirshom, *Shoshan Yesod Olam,* Sassoon Ms. 290, f. 648, microfilm no. samekh 9273 at the Erna and Jacob Michael Microfilm Center, Jewish National University Library, Jerusalem.

49. Idel, "*Hitbodedut*," 417–18.

50. Scholem, *On the Kabbalah,* 107–8. Werblowsky, *Joseph Karo,* 51–52.

51. The following rabbis reportedly induced an angel (*maggid*) that revealed desired information, but not all of these did so through meditation: Joseph Taitatzak (c. 1490), Joseph Karo (1488–1575), Menahem Azaryah (1548–1620) of Fano in Italy, Moses Zacuto (1625–1697), Aaron Berakhia of Modena (d. 1639), David Habillo (d. 1661), Sam-

son of Ostropol (d. 1648), various Shabbateans in Adrianople in 1668 and in Modena between 1675 and 1691, Moses Hayyim Luzzatto (1707–1744 or 1747), and Elijah ben Solomon Zalman, the gaon of Vilna (1720–1797). See Werblowsky, *Joseph Karo*, 76, 78, 80, appendix F, and 13ff.; and G. Scholem, *Sabbetai Sevi* (London: Routledge, Kegan Paul, 1973), 736, 896, 918–20, citing the *maggidim* of Nathan of Gaza, Jacob ben Isaac of Tsirojon, Joseph ben Tzur, and Abraham Rovigo, all in the second half of the seventeenth century.

52. A. Maslow, *Religions, Values, and Peak Experiences* (Harmondsworth: Penguin Books, 1970). Also A. Maslow, *The Farther Reaches of Human Nature* (London: Penguin, Arkana, 1993), part 3. A. Maslow, *Toward a Psychology of Being* (New York: Van Nostrand, 1968).

53. K. Cornish, *The Jew of Linz* (London: Arrow Books, 1999), 122ff. Valentine and Sweet "Meditation and Attention," 62 cite the study involving Zen masters, as well as other studies on the effect of meditation on the brain.

54. D. Concar, "You Are Feeling Very, Very Sleepy . . . ," *New Scientist*, 159, no. 2141 (1998), 26ff.

55. Blumenthal, *Understanding Jewish Mysticism*, 61 on Ishmael's warnings. See also M. D. Swartz, *Scholastic Magic* (Princeton: Princeton University Press, 1996), 170–71 on the cloth used to end the meditation of Ishmael's teacher, Rabbi Nehuniyah. See Blumenthal, *Understanding Jewish Mysticism*, 2:74 on Albotini's warnings. See the *Likkutim yekarim* (Jerusalem: 1974), no. #13, translated in Kaplan, *Meditation and Kabbalah,* 275, on the warning given by the Ba'al Shem Tov.

56. 2 Kings 9:11; Jeremiah 29:26. Kaplan, *Meditation and the Bible*, 138, citing Isaac Abravanel's commentary to 2 Kings 9:11.

57. Abulafia's followers were Shem Tov ibn Gaon (late thirteenth- to early fourteenth-century) in Safed; the anonymous author of *Sha'arei Tziyyon,* in Hebron, c. 1295, Albotini in Jerusalem, and Cordovero and Vital in sixteenth-century Safed. Kaplan, *Meditation and Kabbalah,* 58.

58. Scholem, *Sabbetai Sevi*, chapters 4 and 5. Sachar, *Farewell España,* 140–41. Joshua Heshel Tzoref (seventeenth century) also came to believe that he, Tzoref, was the Messiah: Scholem, *Kabbalah*, 452.

59. Green, *Tormented Master,* 115, 172–73 and chapter 5. Wiskind-Elper, *Tradition and Fantasy,* 19, 38–39, 129, 235–36, notes 91 and 92 (citing *Keter shem tov* 28b:217). Y. Liebes, *Studies in Jewish Myth and Jewish Messianism,* trans. B. Stein (Albany: State University of New York Press, 1993), chapter 5.

60. S. C. Heilman and E. Witztum, "All in Faith: Religion As the Idiom and Means of Coping with Distress," *Mental Health, Religion, and Culture* 3, no. 2 (2000): 115–24.

61. B. A. Maher, *Principles of Psychopathology* (London: McGraw-Hill, 1970), 70, 301, 306, 416. A. Crowcroft, *The Psychotic* (Harmondsworth: Penguin Books, 1967), 57.

62. Kaplan, *Meditation and Kabbalah.* Kaplan, *Meditation and the Bible.* A. Davis (ed.) *Meditation from the Heart of Judaism: Today's Teachers Share Their Practices, Techniques and Faith* (Woodstock, Vt: Jewish Lights, 1997). M. Ribner, *Everyday Kabbalah: A Practical Guide to Jewish Meditation, Healing, and Personal Growth* (Secaucus, N.J.: Citadel Press, 1998). *Chochmat ha-lev,* San Francisco Bay Area, http://www.chochmat.org; Elat Chayyim, Accord, N.Y., http://www.elatchayyim.org; *Makom Ohr Shalom,* Woodland Hills, Ca.; Devekut, Los Angeles, http://www.devekut.com; *Metivta,* a Jewish meditation center in Los Angeles, http://www.metivta.org; C-Deep, http://rabbishefagold.com; and *Yakar* in Jerusalem. G. A. Yorston, "Mania Precipitated by Meditation: A Case Report and Literature Review," *Mental Health, Religion, and Culture* 4, no. 2 (2001): 209–13.

Chapter Five

1. H. Schwartz, *Gabriel's Palace* (Oxford: Oxford University Press, 1993), 175ff.

2. A. Stevens, *Private Myths: Dreams and Dreaming* (Harmondsworth: Penguin, 1996). Chapter 3 provides a good overview of dream theories from Freud, through Jung and many others, to Charles Rycroft's ideas on dreams as expressions of the imagination during sleep, which he proposed in his book, *The Innocence of Dreams* (London: Hogarth Press, 1979).

3. Eccles. 5:2. See also B. *Berakhot* 57b and Genesis Rabbah 17:5. S. Kumove, *Words Like Arrows: A Collection of Yiddish Folk Sayings* (New York: Schocken, 1985), 76.

4. Another version replaces the emperor with the third-century Persian King Shapur. B. *Berakhot* 56a. See also a folktale version, P. Sadeh, *Jewish Folktales* (New York: Doubleday, 1989), 329.

5. Sabar, *Folk Literature of Kurdistani Jews,* 205, no. 44.

6. J. Dan, "*Torat ha-halom shel Hasidei Ashkenaz,*" *Sinai* 68 (1971): 288–93. Zohar 1:83a, 130a–130b, 2:200a, and 3:25a. Kumove, *Words Like Arrows,* 76.

7. Num. 12:6. Zech, 1:8ff. God spoke plainly, not in riddles, to Solomon; 1 Kings 3:5–15.

8. Jer. 23: 25ff., 29:8–9.

9. B. *Berakhot* 55b. Dan, *"Torat ha-ḥalom,"* 288–93. Lachower and Tishby, *The Wisdom of the Zohar,* 2:811–13. Zohar 1:130a. Menasseh ben Israel, *Nishmat ḥayyim,* part 3, chapter 5, p. 64.

10. Joseph (Joslein) ben Moses, *Leket yosher* (Berlin: 1903), 1:41. Manasseh ben Israel, *Nishmat ḥayyim,* 3:5, p. 63ff. See also the dreams of Leon of Modena, *Ḥayyei Yehudah,* ed. A. Kahana (Kiev: 1911), 21, 24, 28, 35, and 36.

11. Ben-Amos, *Baal Shem Tov,* no. 75. Ben-Ami, *Ha'aratzat ha-kedoshim,* 565.

12. M. H. Spero, *Judaism and Psychology: Halakhic Perspectives* (New York: Ktav, 1986), 106.0

13. S. Freud, *The Interpretation of Dreams,* ed. and trans. James Strachey (New York: Avon Books, 1965), 194, 588ff., and 612ff. Isa. 29:7–8.

14. Abimelekh's in Genesis 20, Laban's in Gen. 31:24, and apparently Jacob's in Gen. 32:26; Maimonides says that *Ish* in the Torah refers to a dream vision. More dreams appear in Gen. 28:12–15, 40:9ff., and chapter 41. See also Philo on dreams: F. H. Colson, and G. H. Whitaker, *Philo* (Cambridge, Mass.: Harvard University Press; and London: W. Heinemann, 1949), 5:285ff.

15. B. *Horayot* 13b. H. Malter, "Dreams As a Cause of Literary Compositions," *Studies in Jewish Literature Issued in Honor of Prof. Kaufmann Kohler* (Berlin: 1913, reprinted, Arno Press, 1980), 199–203. More examples are included in Trachtenberg, *Jewish Magic and Superstition,* 231. See also Zadok Hacohen of Lublin, *Resisei laylah* (Bnei Brak: 1967), 181ff., *kontras divrei ha-halomot,* and G. Scholem, *Ḥalomotav shel ha-shabbeta'i R. Mordecai Ashkenazi* (Leipzig: Schocken, 1938).

16. B. *Berakhot* 55a. Buber, *Early Masters,* 134.

17. Freud, *The Interpretation of Dreams,* 194, 270, 301, and 622.

18. Ansbacher and Ansbacher, *Individual Psychology,* 359–361.

19. E. Hartmann, "Outline for a Theory on the Nature and Functions of Dreaming," *Dreaming,* 6, no. 2 (1996), 147–70 reproduced on www.ASDreams.org.

20. A. Revonsuo, "The Reinterpretation of Dreams: An Evolutionary Hypothesis of the Function of Dreaming," *Behavioral and Brain Sciences* 23 (2000): 793–1121.

21. Gen. 40:8, 41:16; Daniel 2, 4, 7, and 8. B. *Berakhot* 55b. A medieval pietist compared a dream that is divinely inspired to a verse of Torah as both can be understood in a number of ways; Judah ben Samuel, *Sefer Ḥasidim,* Wistinetzki ed., no. 1522 and M. Harris, "Dreams in Sefer Hasidim," *Proceedings of the American Academy for Jewish Research,* 31 (1963): 62.

22. B. *Berakhot* 56a.

23. Genesis Rabbah, *Mikketz,* 89:8, retold in English in J. Covitz, *Visions of the Night* (Boston: Shambhala, 1990), 51. Also Ben-Ami, *Ha'aratzat ha-kedoshim,* 79ff. and index, *ḥalom,* for similar beliefs among Moroccan Jews today.

24. T. Alexander-Frizer, *Ma'aseh ehov va-hetzi* (Jerusalem: Magnes, 1999), 436–37.

25. S. Almoli, *Mefaresh halomin* (Salonika: 1515), gate 6. This book was republished under the name *Pitron halomot* (Constantinople: 1518) and many times subsequently; see, for example, S. Almoli, *Pitron halomot* (Jerusalem, 1989). In 1694, a Yiddish edition was published in Amsterdam and in Brooklyn. The dream interpretation manual was copied into J. Emden, *Siddur beit Yakov* (Budapest: Schlesinger, Jos., 1894). For a study of Almoli's work by a Jungian analyst, see Covitz, *Visions of the Night*. For the Jewish tradition of interpreting dreams, see Eleazar of Worms, *Hokhmat ha-nefesh* (Lemberg: 1876), 6, *pitron halomot*. Fifteenth-century manuscripts of *Sefer Daniel ish hamudot*, literally, "The Book of Daniel the Pleasant," on the interpretation of dreams, as Daniel interpreted for Nebuchadnezzar: Bayerische Staatsbibliothek Heb. 418, and Moscow, Guenzburg 1733/5. H. Isaacs, *Medical and Paramedical Manuscripts in the Cambridge Genizah Collection* (Cambridge: Cambridge University Press, 1994) TS. Ar. 11.17, 30.310v., 43.95, 43.134, and TS. NS. 164.163 (medieval Judeo-Arabic dream interpretation manuals) and TS.K.14.29 (a Hebrew manual). R. Patai, *The Alchemists* (Princeton: Princeton University Press, 1995), 368 cites the JTS manuscript (no. 2,556) with the dream interpretations of Ravad of Posquières, f. 11a. For Yemenite Jewish dream interpretation manual, see Y. Ratzhabi, "Pitronei halomot," *Edot* 2 (1947): 121–25. See also Trachtenberg, *Jewish Magic and Superstition*, 238–39. Covitz, *Visions of the Night*, 39.

26. Zohar 1:183a–b, 200a. Judah ben Samuel, *Sefer Hasidim*, Wistinetzki ed.), nos. 325 and 386: *Sefer Hasidim* ed. R. Margoliyot (Jerusalem: Mossad harav Kook, 1957), no. 447. Simeon ben Tzemah Duran, *Magen avot* (Livorno: 1785), 73a. Almoli, *Pitron halomot*, gate 7, chapter 3. Pinhas Eliyahu (Horowitz) of Vilna, *Sefer ha-brit ha-shalem* (Bruenn: 1797, reprinted Jerusalem: Kreuss, 1990), 1 chapter 13.

27. Freud, *Introductory Lectures*, 250ff., and 509.

28. Isa. 29:7–8. Kumove, *Words Like Arrows*, 76.

29. Eliach, *Hasidic Tales*, 38.

30. Ibid., 126.

31. Y. Bilu, "*Demut ha-oyev be-halomot yeladim mishnei evrei ha-kav ha-yarok*," *Mishkofayim* 26 (1996): 50–53. The research for this study was done in 1980–1981, before the Intifada began. A repeat study now would surely produce the same predominance of violent dreams, some with happy endings, fulfilling the wishes of the anxious dreamers. For a more recent study of the dreams of children living in traumatic conditions in Gaza, see R. L. Punamäki, "Determinants and Mental Health Effects of Dream Recall Among Children Living in Traumatic Conditions," *Dreaming* 7, no. 4 (1997) 235–63.

32. Sadeh, *Jewish Folktales,* 287, a Jewish Iranian version of a tale in Arabian Nights. See also P. Schram, *Jewish Stories One Generation Tells Another* (Northvale, N.J.: Jason Aronson, 1989), 284ff.
33. Buber, *Judaism and Modern Man,* 162–65. E. Wiesel, *Souls on Fire* (London: Weidenfeld and Nicolson, 1972), 203–5. For another dream folktale, see Sadeh, *Jewish Folktales,* 181, told also in M. Gaster, *The Exempla of the Rabbis* (London: The Asia Publishing Co., 1924), no. 435.
34. Green, *Tormented Master,* 165ff. I. Lewin, D. Schlezinger, and D. Derby, "The Personality of R' Nahman of Bratzlav: Comparing Dream Content Analysis and Biography," *Journal of Psychology and Judaism* 22, no. 1 (1998): 33–50.
35. Ben-Ami, *Ha'aratzat ha-kedoshim,* 79ff. and see index, *halom.*
36. Ben-Ami, *Ha'aratzat ha-kedoshim,* 333. Schram, *Jewish Stories,* 194ff. on a woman's role as dream interpreter.
37. Judah ben Samuel, *Sefer Hasidim,* Wistinetzki, ed., no. 1138. See also T. Alexander-Frizer, *The Pious Sinner* (Tübingen: J. C. B. Mohr [Paul Siebeck], 1991), 60, and Harris, "Dreams in Sefer Hasidim," 51–79.
38. Vital, *Sefer ha-hizyonot,* 42–47, 62.
39. A magical handbook written in the early talmudic period names the angels in charge of dreaming: Morgan, ed., *Sepher ha-razim,* 40–41. Later, Jews merely addressed the Prince or Master of Dreams. However, Shimon bar Yohai, Judah the Pious of Regensburg, Moses Cordovero, Isaac Luria, David ibn Zimra, Moshe Hayyim Luzzatto, the Ba'al Shem Tov, Elimelekh of Lizhensk, and other Hasidic rabbis believed they received divine revelations from Elijah. I. Klapholz, *Stories of Elijah the Prophet* (New York and Jerusalem: Feldheim, 1970). M. Friedman, *Seder Eliahu Rabba ve-Seder Eliahu Zuta* (Jerusalem: 1960), 32–40. Hayyim Vital received divine revelations from Luria and Joseph Karo.
40. Lewin, ed., *Otzar ha-geonim,* vol. 4, *masekhet Hagigah,* 17, 24–25, translated in Lesses, *Ritual Practices,* 236–37.
41. Jacob of Marvège, *She'elot ve-t'shuvot min ha-shamayim,* ed. R. Margolis (Jerusalem: 1957), para. 5, p. 52. See also Malter, "Dreams," D. Abrambs, "Jacob ben Jacob ha-kohen, *Sefer ha-orah,*" (Ph.D. diss., Tel Aviv University, 1993). More examples can be found in R. Elior, "Messianic Expectations and Spiritualization of Religious Life in the Sixteenth Century," in *Essential Papers in Renaissance and Baroque Italy,* ed. D. Ruderman (New York: New York University Press, 1992), 291, citing *Galia raza.* Also Trachtenberg, *Jewish Magic and Superstition,* 230.
42. Alexander-Frizer, *The Pious Sinner,* 87ff.
43. *Sefer Hasidim,* Wistinetzki ed., no. 1456. Vital, *Sefer ha-hizyonot,* 41, 42.
44. Leone of Modena, *Hayyei Yehudah,* 21. M. R. Cohen, *The Autobiography of a Seventeenth Century Venetian Rabbi* (Princeton: Princeton University Press, 1988), 90–91.

45. Scholem, Ḥalomotav, 11–12, 22.
46. The extracts from the supplication are drawn from the English translation in Lesses, *Ritual Practices*, 396–397, of Hekahlot Rabbati, no. 504 in P. Schäfer, *Synopse zur Hekhalot-Literatur* (Tübingen: Mohr, 1981). See similar advice in the early talmudic *Sepher ha-razim*: Morgan, *Sepher ha-razim*, 41–42.
47. *Shimmush tehillim* (Crakow: 1648). P. Schäfer and S. Shaked, *Magische Texte aus der Kairoer Geniza* (Tübingen: J. C. B. Mohr [Paul Siebeck], 1994), 1:136, a transcript from Geniza fragment T.S. K 1.28. Lesses, *Ritual Practices*, 235–36.
48. Ibn Ezra, Abraham *The Commentary of Abraham ibn Ezra on the Pentateuch*, trans. and annot. H. N. Strickman and A. M. Silver (New York: Menorah Publishing Co., 1996), commentary on Exod. 14:19. *Sefer Razi'el* (Amsterdam: 1701), 3a–b, 33b, 40a–b reprinted as *Sefer Razi'el ha-malakh* (Israel: Meirav, undated), 114, also 137. Similar suggestions for dream induction exist in Tirshom, *Shoshan yesod olam*, Sassoon ms. 290, f. 230, transcribed and translated in Lesses, *Ritual Practices*, 249ff. and 404–5. See also Trachtenberg, *Jewish Magic and Superstition*, 243 on dream induction formulas in *Sefer gematriot*, f. 68a, 75a.
49. A. Hamoi, *Ha'aḥ nafshenu* (Izmir: 1870), 36b. Itzhak ben Eliezer, *Refu'ah ve-ḥayyim me-Yerushalayim* (Jerusalem: Bakall, 1974), 17, and see other formulas on 40 and 47. M. Bernstein, ed., "Two Remedy Books in Yiddish from 1474 and 1508," in *Studies in Biblical and Jewish Folklore*, ed. R. Patai, F. L. Utley, and D. Noy (Bloomington: Indiana University Press, 1960), 299, no. 1037.
50. A. Hamoi, *Devek me'aḥ* (Jerusalem: Bakall, 1980), 196–200. Hamoi's source was the notoriously unreliable Spanish kabbalist Moshe Botaril (late fourteenth to early fifteenth century).
51. B. *Sanhedrin* 65b and B. *Baba Metzia* 107b.
52. *Sefer Ḥasidim*, Wistinetzki ed., no. 1556.
53. Maimonides, *Guide of the Perplexed*, part III, chapter 37, p. 543. *Sefer Ḥasidim*, Margoliyot ed., nos. 205, 528, and 1072. Jacob Anatoli, a thirteenth-century physician and translator, also denounced the practice of asking dream questions: *Encyclopedia Judaica*, 2:929. See also Manasseh ben Israel, *Nishmat ḥayyim*, 3:16, p.85 on dream divination. For a modern instruction for asking a dream question, see for example, Covitz, *Visions of the Night*, 140–41.
54. B. *Berakhot* 60b. Solomon ben Isaac, *Siddur rashi*, ed. S. Buber (Berlin: Mekitzei Nirdamim: 1910–1911), no. 429, p. 214. Simhah ben Samuel, *Maḥzor vitry*, ed. S. Hurvitz (Nürnberg: J. Bulka, 1923), no. 78, p. 47. Moses ben Abraham Mat, *Matteh Moshe* (London: 1958), no. 398–401. Yehiel Mikhal Epstein, *Kitzur shnei luḥot ha-brit* (Amsterdam: 1707),

massekhet shabbat, dinei ta'anit halom, p. 72a. *Siddur otzar ha-tefillot* (Jerusalem: 1950), Sephardic ed., 1:563. *The Authorised Daily Prayer Book*, trans. S. Singer, 2d rev. ed. I. Brodie (London: 1962), 391, *seder kiryat shema al ha-mitah.*

55. Gross family collection: bowl 27.24.1. Amulet in *Genizah* collection, e.g., T.S. K 1.28 (Cambridge University Library). Amulet for wife and child against bad dreams; *Encyclopedia Judaica* 2:907, fig. 1b. Amulet for a woman (Italy, twentieth century) in E. Davis, and D. A. Frenkel, *Ha-kame'a ha-ivri* (Jerusalem: Institute for Jewish studies, 1995), 140, no. 312, from the Glazer collection, Jerusalem. Abraham Ibn Ezra, *The Commentary on the Pentateuch*, on Exod. 28:9. Later treatises on gemstones and remedy books do not include this wisdom.

56. J. O. Leibowitz, and S. Marcus, *Sefer haNisyonot, the Book of Medical Experiences Attributed to Abraham Ibn Ezra* (Jerusalem: The Magnes Press, 1984), 158–61.

57. Isaacs, *Medical and Paramedical Manuscripts*, TS-NS.164.194. Also TS. Ar. 43.114 bears a recipe for wet dreams. For ideas about the cause and the natural occurrence of wet dreams, see M. Aldabi, *Shevilei emunah* (Amsterdam: 1708), part 5, section 6.

58. B. *Ta'anit* 12b. B. *Shabbat* 11a.

59. Maimonides, *Mishneh torah, Sefer z'manim, Hilkhot ta'aniyot* 1:12. *Sefer Hasidim*, Wistinetzki ed., no. 1525 and Margoliyot ed., nos. 66, 226, 229, and 349. Simhah ben Samuel, *Mahzor vitry*, no. 79, p. 48. Pinhas Eliyahu of Vilna, *Sefer ha-brit ha-shalem*, 1:13 against fasting after a bad dream.

60. Manasseh ben Israel, *Nishmat hayyim*, 3:5, p.85. Rabbi Mordecai Ashkenazi and Rabbi Abraham Rovigo also reported undertaking dream fasts (late seventeenth century): Scholem, *Halomotav*, 20.

61. Trachtenberg, *Jewish Magic and Superstition*, 246, citing the twelfth-century Rabbi Kalonymos and Maharil (Moellin) who both objected to fasting on Shabbat. Horowitz, *Shnei luhot ha-brit*, 2:7b, *masekhet shabbat.* See also Mat, *Matteh Moshe*, nos. 759–63, and Yosef Yuspa Hahn, *Yosef ometz* (Jerusalem: 1965), no. 944, p. 210.

62. J. Karo, *Shulkhan Arukh* (Jerusalem: El ha-mekorot, 1955), *Orah hayyim* 288:5. See also Werblowsky, *Joseph Karo*, 181–83. Freud, *The Interpretation of Dreams*, 422, n. 1, for example. E. Hoffman, *The Way of Splendor: Jewish Mysticism and Modern Psychology* (Northvale N.J.: Jason Aronson, 1989), 149. Moses Mat (c. 1551–c. 1606), a Galician rabbi just a little older than Karo, attributes the origin of this wisdom to Hai Gaon, the early eleventh-century Babylonian halakhist: Mat, *Matteh Moshe*, no. 760.

63. After J. *Berakhot* 5:1. Biblical verses are then recited: Ps. 30:11–12, Deut. 23:5, and Jer. 31:12.
64. B. *Berakhot* 55b. The biblical verses recited in the ritual are Ps. 30:12, 55:19; Jer. 31:12; Isa. 35:10, 57:19; 1 Sam. 14:45, 25:6; 1 Chron. 12:18; and Deut. 23:6.
65. A. I. Sperling, *Ta'amei ha-minhagim ve-makor ha-dinim* (Jerusalem: Eshkol, 1961), 298–99.
66. *Hatavat ḥalom* is omitted in the codes of Alfasi and Maimonides but noted in others (Rosh, *Berakhot* 55b; Tur, *Shulkhan Arukh, Orah ḥayyim* 220:1). *Hatavat ḥalom* was observed, however, by Meir of Rothenburg and Israel Isserlein (see Trachtenberg, *Jewish Magic and Superstition,* 245), and instructions for this are given in Simhah ben Samuel, *Maḥzor vitry,* no. 79, p. 48. Zohar 2:200a.
67. Eleazar of Worms, *Ḥokhmat ha-nefesh,* 8b, cited in Trachtenberg, *Jewish Magic and Superstition,* 244–45.
68. M. Cazés, *Voices from Jewish Salonika* (Jerusalem and Thessaloniki: Misgav Yerushalayim, The National Authority for Ladino Culture, and The Ets Ahaim Foundation of Thessaloniki, 1999), 21.
69. Manuscripts of the *Siddur minhag Roma le-khol ha-shanah* (Parma nos. 3499, 2884, 2405, and 3008) include the *hatavat ḥalom* ritual. For a fifteenth-century miniature illustration of "*hatavat ḥalom*" in a northern Italian liturgical manuscript; Garrett Ms. 26, Firestone Library, Princeton. For a Yiddish version of *hatavat ḥalom,* see prayer book Parma no. 1912. Almoli, *Pitron ḥalomot,* gate 3, chapter 2. Also, *Siddur,* Ashkenazic ed. (Venice: 1549) at the end of *Shaharit.* Epstein, *Seder tefillah derekh yesharah,* 71ff., and Epstein, *Kitzur shnei luḥot ha-brit,* 72ff. offer a lengthened version following Isaac Luria's formula, including both the ancient ritual and the prayer. *Siddur tefillot mekhol ha-shanah,* Isaac Luria's edition, edited by Shneur Zalman of Liadi (Vilna: 1849), 37 (end of *Shaharit*). *Siddur ḥibat Zion* (Jerusalem: Eshkol, undated), Sephardic ed., p. 308 has a shortened version. *Siddur tefillah ha-shalem* (Tel Aviv: Beit Rafael, undated), Ashkenazic ed., p. 610. Mat, *Matteh Moshe,* no. 397 proposes recitation of Song of Songs 3:7 ("each with sword on thigh because of terror by night") and the Priestly Blessing. The Sephardic *Siddur* (Venice, 1601) and the British prayer book *Ha-siddur ha-metzuyan* ("The Standard Siddur-Prayer Book") compiled by Rabbi S. Schonfeld (London: 1976) both reproduce longer versions of the prayer from the Talmud of the Land of Israel for recitation during the Priestly Blessing of the morning liturgy. Most prayer books published in Israel today include the *hatavat ḥalom* ritual, often in an abridged format, rather than the ancient prayer.

Chapter Six

1. Judah Halevi, *The Kuzari,* trans. N. D. Korobkin (Northvale, N.J.: Jason Aronson, 1998), 1:79; 3:23. Maimonides, *Guide of the Perplexed,* part 3, chapter 37, p. 543. Also Maimonides, *Mishneh Torah, Hilkhot akkum* 11:11–12. Y. M. Hillel, *Tamim tiheyeh* (Jerusalem: Ahavat Shalom, 1986) denounces Jewish magic today.
2. Idel, *Hasidism,* 29, 31, and 67. Ashkenazic pietists Samuel and his son Judah, and Eleazar of Worms, as well as some of the Spanish and Safed kabbalists knew how to use the Divine Name for magical purposes. Ephraim Reischer (late seventeenth century to early eighteenth century) was also a *ba'al shem.* Hasidic masters, the Ba'al Shem Tov, Elimelekh of Lizhensk, Nahum of Tchernobil, Israel of Koznitz and his grandson Hayyim Meir Yehiel of Mogielnica, Isakhar Baer of Radoshitz, and Shalom Roke'ah of Belz were wonder-workers. Nigal, *Magic, Mysticism, and Hasidism,* chapter 1.
3. Abbaye (278–338), who headed a rabbinic academy in Babylon, valued the expert knowledge of his foster-mother (nurse), since he quotes her advice in the Talmud. B. *Shabbat* 134a, 66b. See also Klein, *A Time to Be Born,* chapter 7. Magical healing potions often relied on the principle of sympathy, where like produces like; a material is thought to act on a person by virtue of a secret sympathy, imitation, or resemblance. Other magical potions relied on the principle of contagion, where things that have once been in contact continue to act on each other at a distance.
4. Idel, *Hasidism,* 156ff.
5. Exod. 22:17. Judah Leib of Prossnitz (c. 1670–1730) was one of these rare exceptions. He was an uneducated peddler who taught himself kabbalistic mysteries. He believed he was visited by the spirits of Isaac Luria and Shabbetai Zevi, gained a reputation as a sorcerer who attempted to overcome Samael, king of the forces of evil, and sacrificed a chicken as a bribe to these forces. *Encyclopedia Judaica,* 13:1241.
6. J. Preuss, *Biblical and Talmudic Medicine,* 2d ed. (Brooklyn: Hebrew Publication Company, 1983), chapter 3. H. J. Zimmels, *Magicians, Theologians, and Doctors* (London: Edward Goldston and Sons, 1952), chapter 5. Trachtenberg, *Jewish Magic and Superstition.* G. Sternberg, *Stefanesti: Portrait of a Romanian Shtetl* (Oxford: Pergamon Press, 1984), 83. Ben-Amri, *Ha-shed tintal,* 19ff. N. Stillman, "Women on Folk Medicine: Judaeo-Arabic Texts from Sefrou," *Journal of the American Oriental Society* 103, no. 3 (1983): 485–93. Ben-Simhon, *Yahadut Marocco,* 278 and 308ff. Rabbi Abraham Azulai (c. 1660–c. 1741) wrote amulets for sick people in Morocco, and Jerusalem-born kabbalist Rabbi Hayyim Yoseph David Azulai (1724–1806) brought magical remedies to Jews all over

the Ottoman Empire. *Encyclopedia Judaica,* 3:1018, 1020, 14:1215. See also T. Schrire, *Hebrew Amulets* (London: Routledge, Kegan and Paul, 1966), 83.

7. B. *Sanhedrin* 67a–68a. See also note 18 below.

8. Y. Ratzhabi, *"Darda'im,"* Edot 1 (1945–1946): 165–80. Nigal, *Magic, Mysticism, and Hasidism,* 95–96. Ben-Yakov, *Otzar ha-segullot,* 180 and 198: Rabbi Petayah's main informant about demonic afflictions was Rosa, a woman.

9. 1 Samuel 28.

10. Exod. 28:30; Num. 27:21; 1 Sam. 28:6. B. *Yoma* 7a–7b, 73b. Rashi's commentary on Exod. 28:30 in *Chumash with Targum Onkelos, Haphtaroth and Rashi's Commentary,* trans. A. M. Silbermann and M. Rosenbaum (Jerusalem: Silbermann, 1984), and B. *Yoma* 73b in most Hebrew editions of the Babylonian Talmud. Zohar 2:234b. Idel, *The Mystical Experience,* 105–8 and notes.

11. I. Jakobovits, *Jewish Medical Ethics* (New York: Bloch, 1975), chapters 1 and 2. K. Thomas, *Religion and the Decline of Magic* (Harmondsworth: Penguin, 1985). B. *Berakhot* 54b. A. Portaleone, *Shilte ha-gibborim* (Mantua: 1612). Ruderman, *Kabbalah.* M. Benayahu, *"Inyanei refu'ah be-k'tav-yad lo yadu'a shel rabbi Hayyim Vital,"* Korot 9, no. 3–4 (1986): 3–17. I. Barzilay, *Yoseph Shlomo Delmedigo (Yashar of Candia)* (Leiden: E. J. Brill, 1974): Yoseph Solomon Delmedigo (1591–1655), a rabbi and physician, admitted that he studied Kabbalah to find in it solutions that were unavailable in the other intellectual disciplines. Another physician, Joseph Tzayyah, also used magical remedies: J. Tzayyah, *Even ha-shoham,* 1538 (Jewish National University Library, ms. 416). For yet another example, see Trachtenberg, *Jewish Magic and Superstition,* 194.

12. Swartz, *Scholastic Magic,* 178–80. The magical text is *Shimmushei Torah. Sefer Razi'el,* 146. J. Naveh, and S. Shaked, *Magic Spells and Formulae* (Jerusalem: Magnes Press, 1993), 133 for an amulet printed in Warsaw (1867) bearing a protection against the plague attributed to Eliezer of Worms, and protection for the home attributed to Isaac Luria. Idel, *The Mystical Experience,* 17, and Ruderman, *Kabbalah,* 109, 112, and 118 document the belief that Jewish magic, especially permutations of Hebrew letters to form magic names, could be traced back to Abraham, the patriarch. In fifteenth-century Italy, the philosopher Isaac Abrabanel and kabbalist Johanan Alemanno both traced Jewish magical practices to King Solomon. Idel, "Magical and Neoplatonic Interpretations," 115, 126–28, 134–35. Moses Zacuto, *Shorshei ha-shemot,* Jewish National University Library, $8^0$2454, attributes a magic square to Ibn Ezra (see Davis and Frenkel, *Ha-kame'a*

ha-ivri, 31). Tirshom, *Yesod Shoshan Olam,* item 566 cites the authority of Judah the Pious.

13. B. *Baba Metzia* 59b.
14. Maimonides, *Guide of the Perplexed,* part 3, chapter 37, p. 543. Also Maimonides, *Hilkhot akkum* 11:11–12.
15. Buber, *Early Masters,* 13. D. W. Winnicott, *Playing and Reality* (Harmondsworth: Penguin, 1985).
16. B. *Sanhedrin* 101a.
17. Klein, *A Time to Be Born,* 153 and 190. F. Raphael, and R. Weyl, *Juifs en Alsace* Toulouse: Collection France-Judaica, 1977), 234–35, citing examples from Ashkenazic Jews since the sixteenth century. Trachtenberg, *Jewish Magic and Superstition,* 121, 160, 169, and 174. Scholem, *On the Kabbalah and Its Symbolism,* 154–55.
18. For example, B. *Berakhot* 58a; B. *Yevamot* 45a, 106a; B. *Shabbat* 34a; B. *Baba Batra* 75a; B. *Baba Metzia* 59b, 85a; B. *Baba Kamma* 117a–117b. See also R. Ulmer, *The Evil Eye in the Bible and in Rabbinic Literature* (Hoboken, N.J.: Ktav, 1994), chapter 7.
19. *Encyclopedia Judaica,* 11:601. Luzzatto is the author of *Mesillat yesharim: Path of the Upright,* trans. M. M. Kaplan (Northvale, N.J.: Aronson, 1995). Wiesel, *Souls on Fire, and Somewhere a Master,* 110. Buber *Early Masters,* 33.
20. Swartz, *Scholastic Magic,* 44–45. Also, *Yesod Shoshan Olam,* 184ff., 264, 279, 462, 493, 506, and 526. Bernstein, "Two Remedy Books," 293ff. Ben-Yakov, *Otzar ha-segullot,* chapter 11 has charms for love, winning a court case, and harming an unpleasant neighbor.
21. *Encyclopedia Judaica,* 15:904.
22. In the Mishnah, *kame'ot* (amulets) and tefillin are mentioned together in *Shabbat* 6:2, 8:3, *Mikva'ot* 10:2, and *Shekalim* 3:2.
23. Minor tractates of the Talmud: *Tefillin* and *Mezuzzot.* B. *Avodah zarah* 11a. M. *Mikva'ot* 10:3. M. *Menahot* 3:7, 4:1, B. *Menahot* 31b–34a. Maimonides, *Mishneh Torah, Sefer ahavah, Hilkhot tefillin u-mezuzzah ve-sefer Torah* 6:13.
24. J. *Pe'ah* 1:1; the king was Artaban (d. 227). B. *Shabbat* 32b compares the failure to affix a mezuzzah to failure to study Torah; B. *Menahot* 43b.
25. B. *Erubin* 96a. J. *Berakhot* 2:2. Michal's story appears in 1 Sam. 14:49, 2 Sam, 6:23.
26. V. Aptowitzer, "Les Noms de Dieu et des Anges dans la Mezouza," *Revue des études juives* 60 (1910): 38–52. V. Aptowitzer, "Noms de Dieu et des Anges," *Revue des études juives* 65, no. 129 (1913): 55–60. F. Landsberger, "The Origin of the Decorated Mezzuzah," *Hebrew Union College Annual* 31 (1960): 149–66. *Jewish Encyclopedia* (New York and London: Funk and Wagnalls, 1904), 7:532ff.

27. Trachtenberg, *Jewish Magic and Superstition*, 146ff.
28. Ibid., p. 4. The rabbi was Jacob ben Moses Moellin. Jews should not leave their *mezzuzot* for possession by non-Jews: Karo, *Shulkhan Arukh, Yoreh De'ah* 291:2.
29. Maimonides, *Hilkhot mezuzzah* 5:4. Idel, "Magical and Neoplatonic Interpretations," 132.
30. Nigal, *Magic, Mysticism, and Hasidism*, 88.
31. Z. Baharav, *Shishim sippurei am* (Haifa: Israel Folk Archives, 1964, reprinted in Israel by Ya'ad, 1977), 212–13. Trachtenberg, *Jewish Magic and Superstition*, 147.
32. M. *Sanhedrin* 10:1. J. *Pe'ah* 1:1. B. *Kiddushin* 71a. Trachtenberg, *Jewish Magic and Superstition*, chapter 7. Schrire, *Hebrew Amulets*, chapter 17.
33. *Avot* 1:13; *The Fathers According to Rabbi Nathan*, end of chapter 12.
34. *Encyclopedia Judaica*, 3:25. The Zohar, too, written in thirteenth-century Spain, was attributed to Shimon bar Yohai. Pseudoepigraphy gave weight to the writings of the Spanish kabbalists.
35. M. Idel, "Jewish Magic from the Renaissance Period to Early Hasidism," in *Religion, Science, and Magic*, ed. J. Neusner, E. C. Frerichs, and P. V. McCracken Flesher (New York: Oxford University Press, 1989), 95ff. Sadeh, *Jewish Folktales*, 233, gives a version detailing Della Reina's battle with Samael, which the Jew loses and apostatizes in his grief.
36. Liebes, "Mysticism and Reality," 221–55. The Ostropoler named all the evil spirits, so that the redeeming angels whose names had equivalent numerical values could negate the evil spirits.
37. M. Benayahu, "*Inyanei refu'ah. Tirshom, Shoshan Yesod Olam*. Nigal, *Magic, Mysticism, and Hasidism*, chapter 1. Idel, *The Mystical Experience*, chapter 1. Idel, *Hasidism*, 65ff. Zacuto, *Shorshei ha-shemot*. See note 2 above concerning the pietists, kabbalists, and Hasidim who knew how to use the Divine Name for magical purposes.
38. Naveh and Shaked, *Magic Spells and Formulae*, 25–27. *Sefer Raziel ha-malakh*, 141, an incantation against spirits causing worry and fear, includes the Priestly Blessing.
39. *Seder R. Amram gaon* (Warsaw: 1865), 1:54. R. O'Hana *Mareh ha-yeladim* (Jerusalem: 1901, reprinted Jerusalem, 1990), 237, *pahad*, advises reciting Ps. 91 forward and backward as well as Ps. 20:10 three times.
40. B. *Shevu'ot* 16b. J. *Shabbat* 6:8b. B. *Berakhot* 55b; B. *Baba Batra* 118a–b; B. *Baba Metzia* 84a. Genesis Rabbah 78:10, 97:3, 99:2. Zohar 1:14b, 47b–48a. See also Trachtenberg, *Jewish Magic and Superstition*, 112ff. on the magical uses of Ps. 91.
41. Naveh and Shaked, *Magic Spells and Formulae*, 149 transcribes and translates the medieval amulet. *Sefer Razi'el*, p. 147. Bernstein, "Two

Remedy Books," 295, citing from manuscript H.B. XI/17, Württemberg National Library, Stuttgart, item 1001. B. Binesh, *Amtaḥat Binyamin* (Wilmersdorf: 1716), 18b. A. I. Sperling, *Ta'amei*, 567–68. *Shoshan Yesod Olam*, item 651. Hamoi, *Ha'aḥ nafshenu.* Y. Y. Rozenberg, *Rafael ha-malakh* (Piotrkow, 1911), *makshah leyaled.* Cardin, *Out of the Depths*, 96–97. Ben-Yakov, *Otzar ha-segullot*, chapter 10, part 6. I. Itzḥaki, *Laḥash ve-kame'a* (Tel Aviv: Shakked, 1976), 135. Hayyim Vital's remedy book, with repeated recommendations to use variations of the word *puk* to ease delivery, is in the Moussaief collection, Jerusalem, f. 69a, 69b, and 110b.

42. Scholem, *Kabbalah*, 366.
43. J. Naveh, and S. Shaked, *Magic Bowls and Amulets* (Jerusalem: Magnes, 1985), 189–97, plates 28 and 29. L. H. Schiffman, "A Forty-two Letter Divine Name in the Aramaic Magic Bowls," *Bulletin of the Institute of Jewish Studies* 1 (1973): 97ff.
44. L. H. Schiffman, and M. D. Swartz, *Hebrew and Aramaic Incantation Texts from the Cairo Geniza* (Sheffield: Sheffield Academic Press, 1992), 99ff. For other amulets in the Genizah, see also S. D. Goitein, *A Mediterranean Society* (Berkeley: University of California, 1978), 4:218–19. Naveh and Shaked, *Magic Bowls and Amulets*, transcribes and translates eight Genizah amulets. Naveh and Shaked, *Magic Spells and Formulae*, 162ff. transcribes and translates TS K1 19, an amulet with an incantation "for one who is fearful and trembling," as well as twenty other amulets and amuletic formulas from magic books. Schiffman and Swartz, *Incantation Texts*, 77 and 78. See Isaacs, *Medical and Paramedical Manuscripts* for quasi-medical manuscripts bearing amuletic and other magical formulas for remedial and protective purposes; for example, TS AR. 44.44, a Judeo-Arabic manuscript with amulets with names of angels and diagrams, to protect against fear.
45. *Sefer Razi'el ha-malakh*, 150–51. This book contains formulas for amulets to protect a woman in childbirth, to promote success in business, and to win a woman's love.
46. Eliahu ben Moshe Luntz, *Toldot Adam* (Zolkiew: 1720), no. 158.
47. B. *Avodah zarah* 18a–b. E. Bin-Gorion, *Me-makor Israel* (Bloomington: Indiana University Press, 1976), vol. 2, no. 33. Davis and Frenkel, *Ha-kame'a ha-ivri*, no. 295; Gross collection amulets 27.12.3, 27.12.24.
48. Idel, *Hasidism*, 76–78, 289 n. 187: Israel of Ruzhin reasoned that this wonder-worker's amulets worked through the divine power of the Hebrew letters.
49. Ben-Simhon, *Yahadut Marocco*, 278.
50. R. Arbel, and L. Magal, eds., *In the Land of the Golden Fleece* (Tel Aviv: Ministry of Defence Publishing House, 1992), 103.
51. Davis and Frenkel, *Ha-kame'a ha-ivri*, 140, nos. 312, 313, and 314.

52. Raphael and Weyl, *Juifs en Alsace,* 234-35.

53. Scholem, *Kabbalah,* 362–68. B. *Gittin* 68a–b. Ben-Simhon, *Yahadut Marocco,* 294 and 349. The seal of Asmodeus drawn in a formula in *Shoshan Yesod Olam,* f. 238, sixteenth century, Damascus, appears also on amulet 776, Feuchtwanger, Israel Museum, nineteenth century, labeled Iraq or Israel, and on an amulet in the collection of the Gross family, no. 27.12.6. Gross 27.12.3 and 23, and Lehmann foundation MS K 98 depict the seal of Solomon.

54. Scholem, *Kabbalah,* 362–64. Davis and Frenkel, *Ha-kame'a ha-ivri,* 23–24 lists some twenty amulets bearing a *Magen David* with an inscription in it. Amulets Gross 27.12.4, 6, and 24.

55. Davis and Frenkel, *Ha-kame'a ha-ivri,* amulets 246, 249, and 300 carry the three-by-three magic square; see p. 30 for the four-by-four square, and p. 32 for the Eybeshutz story. Schrire, *Hebrew Amulets,* chapter 11.

56. M. Franklin, and M. Bor, *Sir Moses Montefiore* (London: A. Blond, 1984), diary entry for 26 November, 1827.

57. For example, Reuven ben Avraham, *Sefer segullot* (Munkacs: 1906), no. 79. This is a book of charms from Jerusalem.

58. Klein, *A Time to Be Born,* p. 121 documents these customs and provides primary sources. See also ibid., 117 concerning the *etrog.*

59. Z. Hanegbi and B. Yaniv, *Afghanistan: Beit ha-k'nesset ve-ha-bayit ha-yehudi* (Jerusalem: Hebrew University and Center for Jewish Studies, 1991), 81–82. Ben-Ami, *Ha'aratzat ha-kedoshim,* 59 and 522.

60. E. Shiller, *Kever Raḥel* (Jerusalem: Ariel, 1977), 16. Y. Zlotnik, Y. (J. L. Elzet), "Me-minhagei Israel," *Reshumot* 1 (1918):366. Bergman, "Ha-refu'ah ha-ammamit," 207.

61. Gen. 44:5, 15. B. *Sotah* 36b. Schiffman and Swartz, *Incantation Texts,* 40, on verses in amulet TS K1.168.26. See Morgan, *Sepher ha-razim* for adjurations to angels to reveal information. This magical text dates from the early talmudic period.

62. Trachtenberg, *Jewish Magic and Superstition,* 219ff. Such divination was also practiced in medieval Europe: R. Kieckhefer, *Magic in the Middle Ages* (Cambridge: Cambridge University Press, 1990) 158.

63. Lesses, *Ritual Practices,* 101, 206ff., and 412ff., citing from the Heikhalot literature. A magical treatise dating from late antiquity, *Sheva de-Eliyahu,* uses these formulas for mastering threatening spirits: P. S. Alexander, "Incantations and Books of Magic," in *The History of the Jewish People in the Age of Jesus Christ, 175 B.C.–A.D. 135,* ed. E. Schürer, trans. and ed. G. Vermes, F. Millar, and M. Goodman (1st ed. 1885, rev. ed. Edinburgh: T. & T. Clark Ltd., 1986), III, i: 362–63. Suriel, a heavenly angel, spoke to Rabbi Ishmael; the angel of death gave Joshua ben Levi useful advice on what to do in certain worrying situations, B. *Berakhot* 51a.

64. S. Muntner, *Introduction to Sefer Asaf ha-rofe* (Jerusalem: Genizah Publishers, 1958), 147–49 on the angel Raphael. M. Gaster, "The Sword of Moses," in *Studies and Texts* (New York: Ktav, 1971).

65. B. *Sanhedrin* 101a and Rashi's commentary on B. *Sanhedrin* 101a.; Rashi on B. *Sanhedrin* 65b and 67b; J. Dan, *Inyanim be-safrut Hasidei ashkenaz* (Tel Aviv: Massada, 1975), 34–43; Manasseh ben Israel, *Nishmat hayyim* 3, chapter 19. Vital, *Sefer ha-hizyonot,* 3, no. 5. Rabbi Moses ben Joav of Florence (d. after 1530), a poet, harshly condemned those who caused the descent of spirits.

66. Josephus Flavius, *Antiqua* 8:2, 5 p. 45–49. Gaster, "The Sword of Moses," 320 (35), nos. 3 and 5. The rod of Moses appears in Exod. 17:5. Naveh and Shaked, *Magic Spells and Formulae,* 93. Also Gross family collection, amulets 27.12.3, 27.12.23. In Kabbalah the rod of Moses is associated with the Ten Commandments, the Ten Plagues, and the ten worlds in the creation of the world: Idel, *Kabbalah,* 115.

67. *Rosh Hashanah* 16b: blowing on the shofar confuses Satan. Zohar 1:114a–114b, 2: 184a–184b. The shofar arouses a similar sound above and moves God to show mercy: Zohar 3:98b–100b. Judah the Pious, *Sefer Hasidim,* Margaliyot ed.,nos. 205–206, 1153. Also *Sefer Hasidim,* Wistinetzki ed., nos. 129, 239, 534, 939, and 1462–67. Zimmels, *Magicians, Theologians, and Doctors,* 82ff. on treatment, such as with incense and sweetmeats, of mental and physical disturbances caused by demons.

68. Nigal, *Magic, Mysticism, and Hasidism,* chapter 4. Manasseh ben Israel, *Nishmat hayyim,* 3: chapter 10.

69. Sadeh, *Jewish Folktales,* 245–46, taken from Joseph Shabtai Farhi's *Oseh Pele* (Livorno, nineteenth century).

70. Scholem, *Sabbetai Sevi,* 422. Cohn, *Ma'aseh Tuvya,* Part 1, chapter 6 and Part 3, chapter 8. Nigal, *Magic, Mysticism, and Hasidism,* 100–1 includes a survey of seventy-five tales; the second revised Hebrew edition of Nigal's *Dybbuk Tales in Jewish Literature* (Jerusalem: Rubin Mass, 1994) includes ninety tales.

71. Pinhas Eliyahu, *Sefer ha-brit ha-shalem,* I, chapter 15, p. 292–94

72. Sadeh, *Jewish Folktales,* 345, taken from Ben-Amos, *Baal Shem Tov,* 159–60, and from Mordecai ben Yehezkel's *Sefer ha-ma'asiyot* (Tel Aviv: 1928). See also Nigal, *Magic, Mysticism, and Hasidism,* 112–14 on Jewish exorcisers, including the Hasidim Dov of Radoshitz, Elimelekh of Lizenskh, Nahum of Tchernobil, Israel of Koznitz, Hayyim Meir Yehiel of Mogielnica, Isakhar Baer of Radoshitz, and Shalom Roke'ah of Belz, and several working in Baghdad at the beginning of the twentieth century.

73. Ben-Amri, *Ha-shed tintal,* 19–22. Nigal, *Magic, Mysticism, and Hasidism,* 86, 95ff. *Shoshan Yesod Olam,* f. 225. Ben-Simhon, *Yahadut Marocco,* 304ff. Ben-Yakov, *Otzar ha-segullot,* 198.

74. Nigal, *Magic, Mysticism, and Hasidism,* 71–72 on the satire of Isaac Arter, the pamphlet about the *dybbuk* by Pinhas Ruderman and others. Anski's play, *The Dybbuk* was performed only after his death.
75. S. Freud, *The Origins of Religion,* Penguin Freud Library 13, ed. A. Dickson (London: Penguin, 1985), 78ff. "Totem and Taboo."
76. H. Shapiro, *The Jerusalem Post,* April 27, 1999, and C. Ben David, *The Jerusalem Post,* April 30, 1999. *Ha'aretz* weekend supplement May, 7, 1999.
77. Y. Bar-Moha, *Ha'aretz,* English ed., December 22–24, 1999.
78. Gen. 12:3, Ps. 10:7. J. *Yoma* 3:8; B. *Sanhedrin* 49a and Rashi's commentary; B. *Baba Kamma* 93a.
79. E. Sprinzak, "Israel's Radical Right and the Countdown to the Rabin Assassination," in *The Assassination of Itzhak Rabin,* ed. Y. Peri (Stanford: Stanford University Press, 2000), 120. B. *Baba Metzia* 85a: *pulsa de-nura* (sixty fiery lashes) is a punishment from heaven. By giving their curse this name, the worried Jews were asking that Rabin die through divine punishment. By portraying the curse as a secret, unwritten, kabbalistic formula, Jews legitimized the behavior within the boundaries of Jewish tradition. See http://faculty.biu.ac.il/~barilm/segen.html on alleged use of curses in the twentieth century.
80. *Siddur minhag Roma* (Venice: 1546), 3:40, *seder hatarat ha-kelalot.* Y. M. Epstein, *Kitzur shnei luhot ha-brit* (Warsaw: 1874), 202 *(seder hatarat kelalot),* translated in Trachtenberg, *Jewish Magic and Superstition,* 60.
81. Nigal, *Magic, Mysticism, and Hasidism,* 22ff.
82. Wiesel, *Souls on Fire, and Somewhere a Master,* 131.
83. Ibid.
84. http://www.chabad.org.

Chapter Seven

1. B. *Berakhot* 57b.
2. B. *Pesahim* 118a. Zohar 1:230b–232a, 2:19a. See also A. Shiloah, *Music Subjects in the Zohar: Texts and Indices* (Jerusalem: Magnes, 1977) and A. Shiloah, *Jewish Musical Traditions* (Detroit: Wayne State University Press, 1992), 141. G. Steiner, *Errata* (London: Phoenix, 1998), 75.
3. M. Proust, *Remembrance of Things Past,* vol. 3, *The Captive,* trans. C. K. Scott Moncrieff, T. Kilmartin, and A. Mayor (London: Chatto and Windus, 1981), 260. A. Storr, *Music and the Mind* (London: Harper Collins Publishers, 1997), 71. C. Lévi-Strauss, *The Raw and the Cooked,* trans. J. Weightman and D. Weightman (London: Cape, 1970), 18. Also P. Noy, "How Music Conveys Emotion" in *Psychoanalytic Explorations in Music,* Second Series, ed. S. Feder, R. L. Karmel, and G. H. Pollock (Madison,

Conn.: International Universities Press, 1993), 136, arguing that music permits regression to the paradise of infancy, allowing communication at a preverbal phase. Also M. Buber, *Between Man and Man* (London: Collins, Fontana Library, 1973), 245–46; a song promotes a relationship, even a fleeting meeting, a nonverbal dialogue between two or more people listening or singing at the same moment, making participants feel essentially human.

4. Nahman of Bratzlav, *Sippurei ma'asiyot* (Jerusalem: *Keren R. Israel Dov Odser*, 1995), 171.

5. See interpretations in Steinsaltz, *Beggars and Prayers*, 44ff. and in H. Schwartz, *Miriam's Tambourine* (Oxford: Oxford University Press, 1988), 384–85. Wiskind-Elper, *Tradition and Fantasy*, 92–99, 101. The idea of the nighttime singing of the angels comes from the Zohar 1:40a–b. The animals of the forest that sing at night are the forces of the Other Side that rule at night, according to Zohar 1:34b, 92a.

6. Nahman of Bratzlav, *Sippurei ma'asiyot*, 303ff. Steinsaltz, *Beggars and Prayers*, 161ff. For the zoharic idea of the ten categories of the pulse beat, associating music and medicine, and the ten types of hymns created by David, see Shiloah, *Music Subjects in the Zohar*, nos. 178, 190–91, citing from *Tikkunei ha-zohar* and Zohar 1:71a.

7. Nahman of Bratzlav, *Likkkutei moharan* (Jerusalem: *Keren R. Israel Dov Odser*, 1995), section 54.

8. D. Silverman, *Legends of Safed* (Safed: Ha'Ari Safed, 1984), 44.

9. M. *Ta'anit* 1:5, 2:5, 3:1–8

10. B. *Shabbat* 30b; B. *Arakhin* 11a, 12a; B. *Sotah* 48a; B. *Kiddushim* 82b. The *Ge'onim* Rabbi Moses Gaon and Rabbi Hai Gaon prohibited instrumental music, and Rabbi Isaac Alfasi incorporated this ruling into his code of Jewish law: B. Cohen, "The Responsum of Maimonides Concerning Music," *Jewish Music Journal* 2, no. 2 (1935): 4.

11. D. Harrán, "Tradition and Innovation in Jewish Music of the Later Renaissance," in *Essential Papers on Jewish Culture in Renaissance and Baroque Italy*, ed. D. Ruderman (New York: New York University Press, 1992). E. Horowitz, "The Eve of Circumcision: A Chapter in the History of Jewish Night Life," *Journal of Social History* 23, no. 1 (1989): 54. This is reprinted in D. Ruderman, ed., *Essential Papers on Jewish Culture in Renaissance and Baroque Italy* (New York: New York University Press, 1992), 554–88. By the close of the eighteenth century, rabbis succeeded in abolishing the group singing on the night before circumcision. Musical instruments have been kept out of the Orthodox synagogue to this day. The art music that entered the synagogue in the eighteenth century in Prague and Frankfort, and the choirs and organs introduced into Reform synagogues in the late nineteenth and early twentieth centuries, conformed to non-Jewish customs. Such

music was not intended to help Jews banish their worries and make room for God. *Encyclopedia Judaica,* 12:615, 628 and Shiloah, *Jewish Musical Traditions,* 84. In the 1860s Rabbi Meir Auerbach banned instrumental music at weddings in Jerusalem, and his successor, Rabbi Diskin, continued this ban: Y. Mazor, and M. Taube, "A Hassidic Ritual Dance: The *mitsve tants* in Jerusalemite weddings," *Yuval* 6 (1994): 165.

12. Sa'adia Gaon, *Book of Beliefs,* 402–4. Sa'adia mainly followed the teachings of Al-kindi (d. c. 874). H. G. Farmer, *Sa'adyah Gaon on the Influence of Music* (London: A. Probsthain 1943), 32. Confucius (551–479 B.C.E.) taught that music can portray the emotions. He also taught that great music is in harmony with the universe, can restore order to the physical world through harmony, and therefore a ruler must understand music. Plato (428–348/7 B.C.E.) and Aristotle (384–322 B.C.E.) were also convinced of the power of music to mold a person's character and promote individual and national happiness.

13. A. Shiloah, "The Musical Passage in Ibn Ezra's Book of the Garden," *Yuval* 4 (1982): 211–24. Shem Tov Falaquera also proposed the same ideas on the relationship between the strings of the instrument and the humors, see Shiloah, *Jewish Musical Traditions,* 57. Both he and Ibn Ezra relied on an earlier Arabic source; these ideas were not their own. The *Zohar Hadash* proposed that the world was created in song, in harmony; Shiloah, *Jewish Musical Traditions,* 144–45.

14. H. Brody, ed., *Selected Poems of Moses Ibn Ezra,* trans. S. Solis-Cohen (Philadelphia: Jewish Publication Society, 1934).

15. The writings on the therapeutic power of music by Joseph ben Judah Aknin, Isaac ibn Ghiyyat, and Profiat Duran are printed in I. Adler, *Hebrew Writings Concerning Music in Manuscripts and Printed Books, from Geonic Times up to 1800* (Munich: G. Henle Verlag, 1975), 157, 169, and 128. See also *Encyclopedia Judaica,* 6:300 and Horden, ed., *Music As Medicine* (Burlington, Vermont: Ashgate, 2000).

16. Idel, *The Mystical Experience,* 53 and 61ff.

17. Sachar, *Farewell España,* 73.

18. Eliach, *Hasidic Tales,* 185–87.

19. Wiesel, *Souls on Fire,* and *Somewhere a Master,* 336.

20. Judah ben Samuel, *Sefer Ḥasidim,* Wistinetzki, ed., no. 11, pp. 8–9 also forbids singing prayer like musicians in a tavern. The attitude of Hasidei Ashkenaz to music spread to other communities through the writings of Eleazar ben Judah of Worms. Extended tunes, or long melodies, are referred to by Israel Isserlein (c. 1394–1460) and his contemporary Moses Mintz, Joseph Karo, Abraham ben Shabbetai Hurwitz, and others: H. Avenary, "The Cantorial Fantasia of the Eighteenth and Nineteenth Centuries," *Yuval* 1 (1968): 83.

21. D. Harrán, *"Dum Recordaremur Sion"*: Music As Practiced and Theorized by the Venetian Rabbi Leon Modena (1571–1648)," *AJS Review* 23, no. 1 (1998): 17–62. Harrán, "Tradition and Innovation in Jewish Music."

22. Etkes, "Rabbi Israel Salanter and His Psychology of Mussar," 2:213–14.

23. Shiloah, *Jewish Musical Traditions,* 174–75. Cazés, *Voices from Jewish Salonika,* 168–78. Dr. I. Ben-Ami has recorded many of the folk songs of Moroccan Jews, but these are as yet unpublished: personal communication, 13 February 2002.

24. M. Grunwald, *"Shirei ḥatunah ve-leidah shel yehudei Sefarad,"* *Folklore Research Center Studies* 6 (1982): 202–5. Cazés, *Voices from Jewish Salonika,* 168–78.

25. Avishur, *Women's Folk Songs,* no. 53.

26. Y. Ratzhabi, *"Shirei ahavah al nashot Tsana'a,"* *Folklore Research Center Studies* 4 (1974): 80ff.

27. M. Noy, "The Cancelled Wedding Motif in Yiddish Folk-Song: A Bibliographical Survey," *Folklore Research Center Studies* 4 (1974): 53–68 (Hebrew with English summary).

28. Judah ben Samuel, *Sefer Ḥasidim,* Margoliyot ed., no. 238, p. 211.

29. Avishur, *Women's Folk Songs,* part 1 and p. 59ff. H. S. Kehimkar, *The History of the Bnei Israel of India* (Tel Aviv: Dayag, 1937), 120–22. See also S. G. Armistead and J. H. Silverman, ed., "Judeo-Spanish Ballad Chapbooks of Y. A. Yona," in *Folk Literature of the Sephardic Jews* (Berkeley: University of California, 1971), 1:185ff.; and S. Weich-Shakak, *"Shirim sephardi'im yehudi'im le-brit milah,"* *Doḥan* (1989): 172.

30. Avishur, *Women's Folk Songs,* 35ff. Eight versions of this fantasy on the roof are recorded, some in nineteenth-century manuscripts, others in recent times from Iraqi and Indian Jews.

31. N. Ausubel, ed., *A Treasury of Jewish Folklore* (New York: Crown, 1948), 684, 682, 678; E. G. Mlotek, and J. Mlotek, comp., *Pearls of Yiddish Song* (New York: Ed. Dept. of Workman's Circle, 1988), 4–5, a lullaby by Moyshe Oysher (1906–1958); the Bessarabian song is cited in Sternberg, *Stefanesti: Portrait of a Romanian Shtetl,* 177–78. Also R. Bromberg, *The Yiddish Lullaby: Its Musical-Literary Qualities and Its Social Function* (M.A. thesis, Bar Ilan University, Department of Musicology, 1995 [in Hebrew]).

32. Roskies, *The Literature of Destruction,* 466, 478–482. G. Flam, *Singing for Survival: Songs of the Lodz Ghetto* (Urbana and Chicago: University of Illinois Press, 1992), 148–50.

33. Avrom Akselrod's song was to the tune of Mark Varshavsky's, *Oifn pripitshek;* Roskies, *The Literature of Destruction,* 465ff.

34. Flam, *Singing for Survival,* 60. Roskies, *Against the Apocalypse,* 204–5.

35. Freud, *Introductory Lectures*, 138. Freud, *The Interpretation of Dreams*, 418 (footnote added in 1909) and 497. He gave an example of how a neurotic patient distorted a song to serve her unconscious fantasies.

36. T. Reik, *The Haunting Melody: Psychoanalytic Experiences in Life and Music* (New York: Grove Press, 1960), 3–4.

37. Kaplan, *Meditation and the Bible*, 139–40. The Spanish kabbalist was Joseph Gikatilla.

38. Halperin, *The Faces of the Chariot*. Kuyt, *The "Descent" to the Chariot*. The primary source in all these is *Heikhalot Rabbati*.

39. Leone of Modena, *Beit Yehudah* (Venice: Bendramin, 1635), 44b; and Harrán, "Dum Recordaremur Sion," 28.

40. Scholem, *Major Trends*, 293. Also Scholem, *Sabbetai Sevi*, 217 and 436 on the musically induced prophesying of Nathan of Gaza and of Moses Suriel.

41. Jacobs, *Jewish Mystical Testimonies*, 161.

42. Buber, *Early Masters*, 182 and 272. Also A. Z. Idelsohn, *Jewish Music* (New York: Schocken, 1967), 419 and Table 33, 5.

43. D. M. Abrams, "Freud and Max Graf: On the Psychoanalysis of Music," and Noy, "How Music Conveys Emotion," both in *Psychoanalytic Explorations in Music*, 288ff.

44. Buber, *Between Man and Man*, 245–46. Steiner, *Errata*, 76.

45. A. Soltes, *Off the Willows* (New York: Bloch, 1970), 35–36.

46. N. Ben Zeev, "Rak le-rega, be-ḥazarah ha-generalit, shavat ha-mavet me-malakhto," *Ha'aretz*, October, 15, 1999, p. 10b.

47. Flam, *Singing for Survival*, 180. Flam quotes Miriam Harel on the first page of the introduction and Leah Hochberg on p. 156. Wiesel, *Four Hasidic Masters*, 95.

48. Soltes, *Off the Willows*, 30–31.

49. Idel, *The Mystical Experience*, 58–63, citing kabbalist Isaac ben Jacob Ha-kohen. Adler, *Hebrew Writings Concerning Music*, 139–42. M. Idel, "Ha-perush ha-magi ve-ha-ti'urgi shel ha-musikah be-textim yehudi'im me-tekufat ha-Renaissance ve-ad ha-Ḥasidut," *Yuval* 4 (1982): 37–45. P. Fenton, "A Jewish Sufi on the Influence of Music," *Yuval* 4 (1982): 126, n. 8. Abulafia's follower Yohanan Alemanno (1435–c. 1504) also believed in the power of music to draw down emanations. M. Cordovero, *Shi'ur komah* (Warsaw, 1885), 30d; and Hayyim Vital, quoted in Idel, "Hit-bodedut," 429–30. The Safed mystics taught, however, that the sins of people block the channels through which human music rises up to the divine realm.

50. Sadeh, *Jewish Folktales*, 237–38, citing from *Shivḥei ha-ari*.

51. Idel, "Ha-perush ha-magi," 61; Wiesel, *Souls on Fire*, and *Somewhere a Master*, 74–91; Idelsohn, *Jewish Liturgy*, 212.

52. 1 Sam. 10:5.

53. Idel, *The Mystical Experience*, 57ff. and n. 28. Zohar 2:18b.
54. Harrán, "*Dum Recordaremur Sion*," 60–61.
55. Newman, *Hasidic Anthology*, 283.
56. C. Lévi-Strauss, *Myth and Meaning* (New York: Schocken, 1979), 50–54, and *Mythologiques: Le Cru et Le Cuit* (Paris: Plon, 1964), 22–40. Storr, *Music and the Mind*, 41 and 123.
57. www.musictherapy.org.
58. D. Soibelman, *Therapeutic and Industrial Uses of Music* (New York: Columbia University Press, 1948).
59. L. Bunt, "Music Therapy: An Introduction," *Psychology of Music* 16 (1988): 3–9. Music therapists have improved the feelings and behavior of children with learning disabilities. Deaf, blind, geriatric, and brain-damaged adults have also responded well. J. Alvin, *Music Therapy* (London: Stainer and Bell, 1998). For recent research on the effect of music on the immune system, see for example www.heartmath.org/research-Papers/soh_30.html

Chapter Eight

1. Wiesel, *Souls on Fire*, and *Somewhere a Master*, 154.
2. Nahman of Bratzlav, *Sippurei ma'asiyot*, 165.
3. Green, *Tormented Master*, 244; Wiesel, *Souls on Fire*, and *Somewhere a Master*, 153–55; Newman, *Hasidic Anthology*, 205 and 259.
4. B. *Sanhedrin* 101a; B. *Shabbat* 30b.
5. R. Gary, *The Dance of Genghis Cohn* (New York: The World Publishing Company, 1968), 139.
6. Ibid., 141. I. Howe, and E. Greenberg, eds., *A Treasury of Yiddish Stories* (Greenwich, Conn.: Fawcett Publications, 1968), 33 on telling a joke better.
7. S. Freud, *Jokes and Their Relation to the Unconscious*, Penguin Freud Library 6, ed. A. Richards, trans. J. Strachey (Harmondsworth: Penguin, 1991) 157, 299–301.
8. Reik, *Jewish Wit*, 27, 168–70, and 228–33.
9. Buber, *Early Masters*, 109–10.
10. *Avot de-Rabbi Natan* 1:26, p. 41b.
11. Newman, *Hasidic Anthology*, 213. Wiesel, *Souls on Fire*, and *Somewhere a Master*, 171ff. Buber, *Later Masters*, 248.
12. Freud, *Jokes*, 157, 299–301. Reik, *Jewish Wit*.
13. Prof. A. Ziv, personal communication, October, 11, 2002. A. Ziv, "Humor's Role in Married Life," *Humor* 1, no. 3 (1988): 223–29. T. Lundell, "An Exploration of Why Men and Women Laugh," *Humor* 6, no. 3 (1993): 299–317. D. E. Berlyne, *Conflict, Arousal, and Curiosity*

(New York: McGraw-Hill Book Company, 1960), 255–61 studies the relationship between humor and fear with respect to cortical arousal. T. J. Schaff, *Catharsis in Healing, Ritual, and Drama* (Berkeley: University of California Press, 1979), 184ff. on humor and tension levels. M. R. Chandler, "Healthy Irreverence: Humor in Stories of Illness," *Humor* 1, no. 3 (1988), 299–305. W. Ruch, "Current Issues in Psychological Humor Research," *Humor* 6, no. 1 (1993): 6–7 and the experiments of Nevo, Keinan, and Teshimovsky-Arditi in the same volume. For beneficial effects of humor on the mind and body, also www.canceronline.org/humor/research and www.healthy.net.

14. Eccles. 1:18–2:2, 3:4, 7:3–4.

15. *Avot* 3:13; B. *Berakhot* 30b–31a; B. *Baba Kamma* 117a–b; B. *Sanhedrin* 63b; B. *Shabbat* 30b; B. *Eruvin* 65b; B. *Megillah* 25b (ridiculing idolaters is permitted); B. *Nedarim* 51a. Also J. *Berakhot* 2:5c. B. *Ta'anit* 29a. In fact, the Talmud depicts the whole month of Adar as a time for joy as it was on specific days in this month that Jews were victorious over the Syrian ruler Nicanor and the evil Haman and Honi's prayer brought rain. E. Kitov, *The Book of our Heritage* (Jerusalem and New York: Feldheim, 1968), chapters 1–4.

16. J. Chotzner, *Hebrew Humour and Other Essays* (London: Luzac and Co., 1905), 106. J. Chotzner, "Kalonymos ben Kalonymos, a Thirteenth-Century Satirist," *Jewish Quarterly Review* 13 (1901): 128–46. *Encyclopedia Judaica* 13:1396–1404. There are many examples of the Purim *shpil* (sometimes spelt *shpiel*) on the Internet.

17. B. *Berakhot* 30b–31a; B. *Ketubot* 17a. M. Zborowski and E. Herzog, *Life Is with People* (New York: Schocken, 1962), 279–82. Shiloah, *Jewish Musical Traditions*, 175. See also, I. Ben-Ami, *Yahadut Marocco* (Jerusalem: Reuven, Mass, 1975), 127ff., and 225 ff. on the humor of Moroccan Jews. Cazés, *Voices from Jewish Salonika*, 175–76.

18. S. Liptzin, *A History of Yiddish Literature* (New York: Jonathan David Publishers, 1985), 20. Idelsohn, *Jewish Music*, 435ff. A. Zajdman, "The Transactional Implications of the Jewish Marriage Jokes," in A. Ziv and A. Zajdman, *Semites and Stereotypes* (Westport, Conn.: Greenwood press, 1993) 143–61.

19. Klein, *A Time to Be Born*, 179ff. Horowitz, "The Eve of Circumcision," 554–88.

20. 1 Kings 18:27. Ps. 52:8. Rabbi Isaac (middle of the second century) also noticed that some people mock and scoff at those they dislike and concluded that the righteous indeed laugh at the wicked whom they fear; B. *Sanhedrin* 106b.

21. B. *Niddah* 23a.

22. B. *Baba Batra* 23b. Howe and Greenberg, *A Treasury of Yiddish Stories* 499. The Italian poet Immanuel of Rome (c. 1261–c. 1332) used

sarcastic, aggressive humor to hide his distress when a man robbed his clothes: "He has a foreskin, but for fear of wearing it out he would rather use his neighbor's when he copulates." T. Carmi, ed. and trans., *The Penguin Book of Hebrew Verse* (Harmondsworth: Penguin, 1981), 425. Chotzner, *Hebrew Humour,* 96–97 gives other examples.

23. *Sefer ha-kundas* (1824) by Abraham Isaac, son of Rabbi Hayyim Landa. Tobias Feder, a Polish Jew, parodied the Zohar; Tsvi Hirsch Sommerhausen parodied the Haggadah; Isaac Erter, N. Goldberg, and Abraham Gottlober each chose to parody the Hasidim. Judah Leib Gordon (1831–1892) satirized Elijah tales and Joseph Brill (1839–1919) parodied Jewish educators, literary types, and wrote a satire on those who assimilated.

24. S. Lipman, *Laughter in Hell: The Use of Humor During the Holocaust* (Northvale: Jason Aronson, 1991), 140, n. 26. Some Hasidic rabbis, such as Levi-Itzhak of Berditchev, also communed with God in their own words, with humor, to cope with worry.

25. M. Sendak, *Where the Wild Things Are* (San Francisco: HarperCollins, 1984) and "Where the Wild Things Began," *The New York Times Book Review*, May 17, 1987, p. 1. Some modern Israeli writers, such as A. Hillel, E. Sidon, and Yehudah Atlas, have similarly written humorous verse that can help children confront fears and gain strength by laughing at them.

26. NBC news, September, 14, 2001. The settler joke was told to me in October 2002 by a mother living in the settlement of Eilon Moreh.

27. A. Bendelac, "Humor and Affectivity in Jaquetia, the Judeo-Spanish Language of Northern Morocco," *Humor* 1, no. 2 (1988): 177–86. H. Dahan, *Otzar ha-pitgamim shel yehudei Marocco* (Tel Aviv: Stavit, 1983), e.g., nos. 1360 and 1372. H. J. Ayalti, ed., *Yiddish Proverbs* (New York: Schocken, 1976), no. 328. Jewish proverbs address all the worrying aspects of Jewish social and religious life. Proverbs about women address the fears and tensions associated with family life: seducers, shrews, gossips, mothers, mothers-in-law, brides, wives, and daughters. Many address the fear of misfortune and the fear of death. Some proverbs relate to God, sin, charity, and the world to come. Some comment on hypocrisy and relations with the gentiles. And some laugh at anxiety, plain and simple. For proverbs as jokes, see Reik, *Jewish Wit,* 166ff. H. V. Sephiha, "L'Humour des Proverbes Judeo-Espagnols," in *Humoresques: L'Humour Juif,* ed. J. Stora-Sandor (Nice: Z'éditions, 1990), 37. See also Y. Moskunah, *P'ninei sefarad: alpayim pitgamim me-otzar ha-hokhmah shel yehudei sefarad,* ed. and trans. Moshe-Giora Elimelekh (Tel Aviv: Sifryat Ma'ariv, 1981); Y. Avishur, *Folk Proverbs of the Jews of Iraq* (Haifa: University of Haifa, 1997). Sabar, *Folk Literature of Kurdistani Jews,* 203ff. A. Ratzabi, "Ha-humor shel yehudei teiman," in *Judaeo-Yemenite Studies,* Proceedings of the

Second International Congress, ed. E. Isaac and Y. Tobi (Princeton and Haifa: Institute of Semitic Studies, 1999), 61ff.

28. B. *Ta'anit* 22a. Wiesel, *Four Hasidic Masters,* 54 and 89. M. Buber, *Ten Rungs: Hasidic Sayings* (New York: Schocken, 1970), 44–45.

29. Frankl, *Man's Search for Meaning,* 54–55. M. Gilbert, *The Boys: Triumph over Adversity* (London: Weidenfeld and Nicholson, 1996), 179 and 198.

30. R. Leshem, "*Tzanhanim be-tofet shel Balata,*" *Yediot Aharonot,* April, 2, 2002, *Pessah Magazine,* p. 2ff. R. Michaeli, "*Ha-girsah ha-tzahalit le-teksei ha-shevet,*" *Ha'aretz,* May, 29, 1997, p. d1–2, reporting on a study done by Hebrew University researcher Leora Shion. See also, E. Oring, *Jokes and Their Relations* (Lexington, Ky.: University Press of Kentucky, 1992), 42–51, about the humor of the Palmah in Israel's War of Independence; A. Ziv, "Humor in Israel," in *National Styles of Humor,* ed. A. Ziv (New York: Greenwood Press, 1988), 122–29 on the development of Israeli humor during forty years.

31. Lipman, *Laughter in Hell,* 134, citing from Lipman's interview of Sharansky. Cf. Joan Rivers says "The only weapon more formidable than humor is a gun." www.joanrivers.com.

32. D. A. Harris, and I. Rabinovich, *The Jokes of Oppression: The Humor of Soviet Jews* (Northvale, N.J.: Jason Aronson, 1988). Professor Ed Trifonov was active in the Jewish dissident movement in the U.S.S.R. in the mid-seventies. When he eventually reached Israel, his home was a meeting place for past refuseniks, and a treasure house of jokes.

33. Gen. 18:12ff. For humor in the Bible, see Y. T. Radday, and A. Brenner, eds., *On Humor and the Comic in the Hebrew Bible* (Sheffield: The Almond Press, 1990).

34. C. Bermant, *What's the Joke? A Study of Jewish Humour Through the Ages* (London: Weidenfeld and Nicolson, 1986), 47ff. Freud, *Jokes,* 72, 79, 160, and index for other Heine jokes.

35. A. Ziv, *Personality and Sense of Humor* (New York: Springer, 1984), chapter 4. Freud, *Jokes,* 299. S. Freud, "Humour," in *Art and Literature,* Penguin Freud Library 14, ed. A. Richards and A. Dickson (Harmondsworth: Penguin, 1988), 433. For the analysis of Freud's jokes, see Oring, *Jokes and Their Relations,* chapter 8.

36. Wiesel, *Souls on Fire,* and *Somewhere a Master,* 337–38. See also p. 314 for another Hasidic tale using humor.

37. Roskies, *Against the Apocalypse,* chapter 7. Liptzin, *A History of Yiddish Literature,* 66–72. C. Madison, *Yiddish Literature* (New York: Schocken, 1971), 96. I. Howe, and R. R. Wisse, ed., *The Best of Sholom Aleichem* (New York: Simon and Schuster, Touchstone, 1980). The long quotation is from "Otherwise, There's Nothing New," in *Sholom Aleichem: Some Laughter, Some Tears,* trans. Curt Leviant (New York: G. P. Putnam's Sons, 1968), 239ff.

38. W. Allen, *Side Effects* (New York: Random House, 1980), 57.

39. S. S. Janus, "The Great Comedians: Personality and Other Factors," *American Journal of Psychoanalysis* 35 (1975): 169–74. B. W. Grossman, *Funny Woman: The Life and Times of Fanny Brice* (Bloomington: Indiana University Press, 1991).

40. Carmi, *Hebrew Verse*, 353. J. Schirmann, "The Hebrew Poet in Medieval Spain," *Jewish Social Studies* 16 (1954): 235–52.

41. Alexander-Frizer, *Ma'aseh ehov va-hetzi*.

42. Howe, and Greenberg, *A Treasury of Yiddish Stories*, 504ff.

43. M. Grunwald, "Tales, Songs, and Folkways of Sephardic Jews," *Folklore Research Center Studies* 6 (1982): xxxiv–xxxv; tales 61–70 are all Joha tales. Also Alexander-Frizer, *Ma'aseh ehov va-hetzi*, chapter 11.

44. Quoted in J. Dorinson, "The Jew As Comic: Lenny Bruce, Mel Brooks, Woody Allen," in A. Ziv, ed., *Jewish Humor* (Tel Aviv: Papyrus, 1986), 37–38. www.joanrivers.com. G. Mikes, *How to Be an Alien* (London: A. Deutsch, 1946).

45. O. Shavit, *"Al zeh lo tzohakim,"* *Ha'aretz*, Weekend supplement, 10 August 2001, 43.

46. Midrash on Lamentations, see Roskies, *The Literature of Destruction*, 59–60.

47. Alexander-Frizer, *Ma'aseh ehov va-hetzi*, 379.

48. Carmi, *Hebrew Verse*, 430.

49. R. Haboucha, *Types and Motifs of the Judeo-Spanish Folktales* (New York: Garland, 1992), 577.

50. Lipman, *Laughter in Hell*, 146 n. 49, 18 n. 45, 145 n. 42.

51. E. Wiesel, *One Generation After* (New York: Pocket Books, 1970), 92. For another example of the last laugh, see Lipman, *Laughter in Hell*, 21.

52. G. Galloway, and A. Cropley, "Benefits of Humor for Mental Health: Empirical Findings and Directions for Further Research," *Humor* vol. 12, no. 3 (1999): 301–14.

53. http://www.geocities.com/Hollywood/Studio/1382/Who.html

54. Wiesel, *Souls on Fire*, and *Somewhere a Master*, 62; Newman, *Hasidic Anthology*, 213. Babies start to laugh when they are about ten weeks old and by the time they are four months old they laugh frequently in their waking hours. Many people lose their childhood ability to laugh frequently as they grow up and "get serious."

55. Freud, *Jokes*, 287–92, 299, 302. Freud, "Humour," 433 refers to humor as a gift. Also Reik, *Jewish Wit*, 234.

56. Ziv, *Jewish Humor*, 54, citing from a letter quoted in C. A. Madison, *Yiddish Literature: Its Scope and Major Writers* (New York: Garden, 1968).

57. Frankl, *Man's Search for Meaning*, 127 ff., citing examples as well as the theory. Also V. E. Frankl, *The Unheard Cry for Meaning: Psychotherapy and Humanism* (London: Hodder and Stoughton, 1978), 120ff. Cf. O. Nevo,

H. Aharonson, and A. Klingman, "The Development of a Systematic Program for Improving Sense of Humor," in W. Ruch, ed., *The Sense of Humor* (Berlin and New York: Mouton de Gruyter, 1998), 385–404.

Chapter Nine

1. *The Wisdom of Ben Sirach* 38:26–39:5. R. M. Yerkes, and J. D. Dodson, "The Relation of Strength of Stimulus to Rapidity of Habit Formation," *Journal of Comparative Neurology and Psychology* 18 (1908): 459–82.
2. The rabbi was Judah Löw ben Bezalel of Prague: Safran, "Maharal and Early Hasidism," 66–67.
3. Maimonides, *Eight Chapters,* chapter 1. Aldabi, *Shevilei emunah,* part 5, section 9.
4. *The Wisdom of Ben Sirach* 30:24, 31:1. B. *Gittin* 70a; M. *Niddah* 4:7; B. *Baba Batra* 10a; B. *Berakhot* 58b.
5. Maimonides, *The Medical Aphorisms,* seventh treatise, nos. 2, 4, and 12.
6. S. D. Goitein, *A Mediterranean Society* (Berkeley: University of California, 1978), 5:242–44.
7. Umansky, and Ashton, *Four Centuries,* 41.
8. Ruderman, *Kabbalah,* 38–41.
9. Jacob Zahalon, *Otzar ha-ḥayyim* (Venice: 1683), chapters 1 and 7. Cohn, *Ma'aseh,* vol. 1, *Olam ha-katan,* 75b; vol. 2, *Bayit ḥadash,* 114b; vol. 3, *Gan na'ul,* 135a.
10. S. Freud, *Collected Papers* (London: Hogarth Press, 1957), 1:76–106.
11. R. J. Edelman, *Anxiety: Theory, Research, and Intervention in Clinical and Health Psychology* (Chichester: Wiley, 1995), chapter 11.
12. Davey, and Tallis, *Worrying,* 38ff. and 81ff.
13. Davey and Tallis, *Worrying,* 75, 77, and 80ff.
14. P. Roth, *Portnoy's Complaint* (New York: Vintage Books, 1994).
15. Safran, "Maharal and Early Hasidism," 64. Rabbi Kook on *paḥdanut* in his treatise on moral principles, translated in Kook, *The Lights of Penitence,* 178. Frankl, *The Unheard Cry for Meaning,* 115.
16. H. Startup, "Stop Rules for Catastrophic Worrying," *Proceedings of the British Psychological Society* 7, no. 2 (1999): 139.
17. Newman, *Hasidic Anthology,* 95. Safran, "Maharal and Early Hasidism," 78–79.
18. Exodus Rabbah 31:5. "*Iggeret Mussar* of Nahmanides" in I. Abrahams, *Hebrew Ethical Wills* (Philadelphia: Jewish Publication Society, 1926), 1:97–98. Newman, *Hasidic Anthology,* 486, 453 no. 5, and 353 nos. 3 and 5. Also I. Lewin, D. Schlezinger, and D. Derby, "The Personality of R' Nahman of Bratslav: Comparing Dream Content Analysis and Biography," *Journal of Psychology and Judaism* 22, no. 1 (1998): 33–50.

19. Davey and Tallis, *Worrying,* 77.
20. Prov. 31:20. See Ezek. 16:49: not worrying about the poor and needy is a sin.
21. B. *Baba Batra* 9a. Also B. *Sukkah* 49b; J. *Pe'ah* 1:1 on the importance of charity.
22. B. *Baba Metzia* 107b: "*hitkosheshu va-koshu*" was explained by Resh Lakish "Decorate yourself, and then decorate others."
23. Buber, *Early Masters,* 190.
24. D. R. Blumenthal, *Understanding Jewish Mysticism* (New York: Ktav, 1982), 2:89–92, citing from A. J. Heschel's *The Earth Is the Lord's.*
25. Jedayah Bedersi Ha-penini (fourteenth century) believed that true reality is not to be found in the material world, and therefore there is no point in worrying: "In Dream and in Waking" in Bin-Gorion, *Me-makor Israel,* 3:136, no. 78. *Pirkei Avot* 3:16, B. *Shabbat* 152b.
26. B. *Shabbat* 32b, *Ta'anit* 20b. Maimonides, *Mishneh Torah, Hilkhot nedarim* 4:4 and 6:8. Karo, *Shulhan Arukh, Yoreh de'ah* 116:5.
27. Gen. 18:23ff. and Exod. 32:11ff., for example, and Jer. 3ff. and Ezek. 18.
28. Deut. 10:12. B. *Berakhot* 33b. Ibn Paquda, *The Duties of the Heart,* gate 6. Jonah ben Abraham of Gerona, *The Gates of Repentance,* 21ff. Etkes, "Rabbi Israel Salanter," 215ff. B. Z. Bokser, *Abraham Isaac Kook* (London: SPCK, 1979), 162ff. See Newman, *Hasidic Anthology,* p. 134ff. on fear and love of God. See also Rabbi Ovadia Yosef's heavily reported pronouncements, for example, in his Saturday night sermon on August 5, 2000.
29. Scholem, *Sabbetai Sevi,* 28, 37–42, and 49–50. Scholem, *Kabbalah,* 140–44 and 162–65. Scholem, *On the Kabbalah and Its Symbolism,* 113–17 and 127. J. Dan, *Jewish Mysticism and Jewish Ethics* (Northvale, N.J.: Jason Aronson, 1996), 107–10.
30. Scholem, *Sabbetai Sevi,* 63. Dresner, *The Zaddik,* 154–55 and 194. Liebes, *Studies in Jewish Myth,* chapter 5.
31. Davey and Tallis, *Worrying,* 38ff. and 76ff.
32. Ibn Paquda, *The Duties of the Heart.* Maimonides, *Guide of the Perplexed,* part 3, chapter 54. Jonah ben Abraham of Gerona, *The Gates of Repentance.* Uri, "Salanter," 245–46. Ish-Shalom, *Rav Avraham Itzhak Hacohen Kook.* J. D. Soloveitchik, *On Repentance,* trans. P. H. Peli (Northvale, N.J.: Jason Aronson, 1996).
33. Eleazar of Worms, *Hokhmat ha-nefesh* (Lemberg, 1876), 10c–d, or 12c–d, translated and commented on in Dan, J., "Samael, Lilith, and the Concept of Evil in Early Kabbalah," *Association for Jewish Studies Review* 5 (1980): 17–40, 33–35 and I. Marcus, *Piety and Society: The Jewish Pietists of Medieval Germany* (Leiden: E. J. Brill, 1981), 30–33 and 157 n. 44. The early kabbalist Isaac ben Jacob Ha-Cohen in Spain (the

second half of the thirteenth century) cites the similar myth that God had created and destroyed worlds before ours where only the Evil Inclination existed (and not the Good), and he was undoubtedly influenced by Eleazar's ideas.

34. Newman, *Hasidic Anthology,* 453 no. 5, and 353 nos. 3 and 5. Also Lewin, Schlezinger, and Derby, "The Personality of R' Naḥman of Bratzlav," 33–50. "The more profoundly he is in anxiety, the greater is the man," wrote Kierkegaard, expressing a similar idea: S. Kierkegaard, *The Concept of Anxiety,* ed. and trans. R. Thomte and A. B. Anderson (Princeton: Princeton University Press, 1980), 155.

35. Jacobs, *Jewish Mystical Testimonies,* 177–80. The mishnaic capital punishments appear in M. *Sanhedrin* 7:1. Ritual murder charges continued in Germany and farther east to Bulgaria and Russia in the nineteenth and early twentieth centuries. More recently, Jews in the Soviet Union, in Iran, and in some Arab lands have had to face the threat of death posed by trumped-up charges.

36. Toward the middle of the eleventh century, Solomon ibn Gabirol wrote *The Improvement of the Moral Qualities.* He assumed that courage and cowardice are the two opposite ends of the same personality trait. Cowardice occurs in those whose spirits are abject, downcast, and wretched, he observed, while the spirits of the courageous are high and enviable. Similarly, Ibn Gabirol believed that anxiety and joy are the two opposite ends of another personality trait. When we stop worrying, we become happy. The apprehensive, anxious person can improve, he believed, and become joyful and courageous. Solomon ibn Gabirol, *The Improvement of the Moral Qualities,* trans. S. Wise (New York: Columbia University Press, 1901), 78–80, 100.

37. Abrahams, *The Life of Glückel,* 8–9.

38. Y. Amichai, *Shirim: mish'nat 1948 ad 1968* (Tel Aviv: 1969), 15, "*Autobiographia, be-shanat 1952.*" An inadequate translation appears in C. Bloch, and S. Mitchell, *The Selected Poetry of Yehuda Amichai* (New York: Harper Perennial, 1992), 2, "Autobiography, 1952."

Index

A

Abraham, 59, 237–238, 250
  faith of, 30–31, 68
  as intercessor, 55, 57, 81
  and magic, 153, 172, 299 n. 12
  and meditation technique, 98, 99
Abraham ibn Ezra. see Ibn Ezra, Abraham
Abuhatzeira, Israel (Baba Sali), 181, 284 n. 83
Abulafia, Abraham, 9, 33, 95, 100, 108
  and music, 193, 204, 209
action, 37, 43–44, 73, 246, 250
  see also passivity, coping strategies
Adam, 12
  creation of, 17
  and sin, 8, 47, 244
  worries, 6
Adler, Alfred, 10, 44, 50, 120
Afghanistan, 170
  see also tales
age, 22–23
aggression, 17
Akedah, 29, 30, 237
Akiva, 30–31, 49, 166, 172
  and the "garden," 85, 87, 90
  humor of, 37–38, 214, 217, 231
  prayer of, 62, 65, 81
Aknin, Joseph ben Judah, 193
Albo, Joseph, 58
Albotini, Judah, 89, 95, 96, 107
Aleichem, Sholom (Sholom Rabinowitz), 228, 234

Alemanno, Yohanan, 89
Allen, Woody, 22, 229
Almoli, Solomon, 124
Amalek, 219
Amichai, Yehuda, 258
Ammi, 27, 39, 65
amulet, 45, 46, 138, 150, 151
  bowls, 140, 165
  expert, 164
  protective, 113, 140, 147, 153, 155–169, 174, 179
  recommended, 152, 164
  to secure gain, 157, 181
angel, 16, 59, 147, 149, 160
  of death, 199, 303 n. 63
  and dreams, 117, 133, 135–136, 294 n. 39
  invoking of, 42, 45, 149–150, 171–172
  and performance, 238–239, 245
  protective, 45, 49, 167
  and revelation, 98–99, 101, 109, 110, 150, 289 n. 51
  see also dreams, Prince of; Gabriel; Raphael; Razi'el; Samael; song
An-ski, S. (Solomon Zainwil Rapaport), 175
anticipation, 255
  see worry, causes of
Antiochus IV, 30
anxiety
  and depression, 5, 20, 46
  disorder, 7, 23, 175, 241
  distinguished from fear, 14

meditation on, 89–90, 98, 100–102, 137
reciting 100, 134, 148, 158
theurgical use of, 149–150, 179
see also Ba'al Shem
divine service, 16, 17, 26, 31, 33, 96, 214
and prayer, 7, 55, 64, 70, 248–249
Dodson, J. D., 238
Dora. *see* Bauer, Ida
Dov Baer, Maggid of Mezritch, 28, 67, 97, 234
dread. *see* worry
dream question, 132–136, 289 n. 39, 295 n. 53
dreams, 7, 19, 49, 113–144
anxiety, 113–115, 118, 127, 129, 139–144
emotion in, 120–121
and fasting, 132, 136, 140–142
and Freud, 48, 118, 120, 125, 142
hatavat halom, 142–144
interpretation of, 114, 121–125, 132, 135
nature of, 114–118
Prince of, 133, 136, 137
problem-solving in, 119–120, 125–130
recurring, 113, 115, 126
revelation in, 50, 51, 116–119, 125, 128–139
and seeking knowledge, 132–139
wet, 129, 140, 296 n. 57
wish fulfillment in, 118, 123, 125, 130
see also daydream; divination; Joseph; prayer; prayer, specific; prophecy; strength; Zohar
Duran, Profiat, 193
dybbuk. see demonic possession

E

Eban, Abba, 18
Ecclesiastes, 22, 43, 116, 219
Ego, 17, 218
Eleazar, (Rabbi), 60, 68, 123
Eleazar ben Judah of Worms, 72, 116, 143, 153, 253, 299 n. 12
on meditation, 98, 100
Eliezer, (Rabbi), 37, 60, 70
Eliezer ben Hyrcanus, 89, 154

Elijah, 49–50, 73, 77, 170, 221
in dream, 50, 129, 133
Elijah de Vidas, 102
Elisha, 155, 208
Elisha ben Avuya, 85, 107, 166
Eliyahu Ba'al Shem of Chelm, 163
emotion, 12, 13, 33
and bodily sensations, 12, 19, 240–241
control, 83, 96
intense, 32, 57
and music, 183–185, 190, 201–203, 205–206
in prayer, 64, 73–75
unpleasant, 3, 19, 26, 37, 73, 175
see also catharsis; projection; transference; transformation; dreams; worry, nature of
equanimity, 87, 95–96
Erikson, Erik H., 15
Esau, 6, 57
Essingen, Samuel, 180
Esther, 219
ethical
improvement, 16, 31, 99, 253
study, 71, 99
trial, 16
Europe, 75, 77, 140
Eastern, 75, 161, 174, 199
pogroms, 89, 92
see also Ashkenazic Jews; Cossacks; France; Germany; Hasidim; Italy; Poland
Eve, 8, 12, 17
evil, 251
see also spirit
Evil Eye, 150
protect against, 152, 156, 157, 163, 165
Evil Inclination, 15–16, 64, 130, 168, 253, 275 n. 32
see also inclinations
Exodus
Book of, 83, 164
from Egypt, 164
ship, 206
exorcism, 173–177, 304 n. 72
Eybeschutz, Jonathan, 169, 180
Ezekiel, 31, 78, 89, 203
Book of, 137
and *merkavah*, 87
Ezra, 78

F

faith, 17, 54, 76, 125, 150, 161
   act of, 146, 149
   affirm, 55, 69, 79
   benefits of, 10, 31, 37, 68
   exemplary, 30–31, 37
   gain, 49, 53, 66, 73, 75, 109, 147
   loss of, 85, 126, 174, 226, 245
   maintain, 80, 84
faith healer, 45, 147, 154, 179
fantasy
   escape into, 48–50
   force of, 12, 42
   women's ability for, 21
   see also imagination; tales
fasting, 90, 110, 138, 148
   see also meditation, preparation for;
     dreams
father, 237, 243, 257–258
fear, 3, 6, 40, 81
   of darkness, 7, 23, 41, 163
   of death, 6, 41, 63, 81, 149, 214,
     228
   definition of, 14
   of God, 6, 51, 237
   of punishment, 9–10, 71, 133, 251
   remedy for, 28, 59, 62, 149–150,
     165
   of suffering, 6, 41
   vocabulary of, 7
   see also phobia
France, 133, 160, 205, 220
Frankl, Viktor E., 30, 38, 41, 244
   on goal in life, 10, 40
   and humor, 224, 235
free will, 43
Freud, Sigmund, 40, 45, 84, 202, 241
   on anxiety, 14–15, 16–17, 23, 120,
     125
   on demons, 176
   on humor, 216, 218, 234
   see also dreams
Fromm, Erich, 12

G

Gabriel, 167, 171
Gary Romain, 214, 215
gender, xviii, 21–22, 50, 139, 149–150,
   273 n. 45
   see also meditation

Genesis, 8, 10, 15, 17, 78, 256
Genizah, 165
Georgia, Republic of, 167
Germany, 18, 25, 160, 168, 205
Gershom ben Shlomo, 12
Gikatilla, Joseph, 153, 309 n. 37
Glückl of Hameln, 52, 256–257
God
   cleaving to, 55, 86, 95. see also de-
     vekut; meditation, purposes of
   communion with, 54–55, 57, 67,
     74, 81, 204, 210
   dream of seeing, 129
   and evil, 253
   faith in, 17, 31, 35–37
   laughs, 214, 227
   worries, 5
   see also divine blessing; Divine
     Names; divine service; revela-
     tion, divine; evil spirit; fear; love;
     power; prayer, general; soul;
     strength; thought
Goldfaden, Abraham, 202
Graf, Max, 204, 208
Greece, 143, 220
Gruner, Dov, 206
guilt, 4, 6, 9, 114, 218, 246

H

Ha-gashash ha-hiver, 224
Hai ben Sherira Gaon, 133, 138
hallucination, 109–110
Halperin, D. J., 88
Haman, 219
Haninah ben Dosa, 81
Hannah, 30, 57, 73
harmony, 183–185, 186–187, 192–193,
   203, 209, 214
Hartmann, Ernest, 120
Hasidim, xxiii, 7, 16, 26, 39, 83, 176,
   251
   Lubavitch, 31, 181
   and meditation, 90, 96
   messianic, 31, 157
   and prayer, 70–71, 82
   see also tzaddik; melody; tales; and
     individual rabbis
Heilman, S. C., 109
Heine, Heinrich, 18, 226, 227
helplessness, 12, 17, 43, 45–46, 61, 63,
   115, 151

Hershkowitz, Yankele, 202
Heschel, Abraham Joshua, 11
Hillel, 10–11, 34, 161, 238, 247
Hisda, 41, 120, 121
historical paradigms, 29–30
Hochberg, Leah, 206, 309 n. 47
Honi, 145–146, 149, 154, 180
Horowitz, Isaiah, 70, 141
Houdini, Harry (Erik Weisz), 47
humor, 37–38, 40, 46, 117, 213–236
    acquiring, 234–236
    and banishing worry, 216, 219,
        227–228
    effects of, 216–218, 221–224
    and fighting worry, 225–227, 235
    forms of, 215–216
    functions of, 225–233
    rabbinic views on, 219–220, 221
    time for, 219–225
    and transmuting worry, 216, 218,
        229–231
    see also jester; joke; catharsis; dan-
        ger; Israel; strength
humors, bodily, 12, 13, 192, 307 n. 13
hypnosis, 104–106, 203

I

Ibn Ezra, Abraham, 76, 137, 140, 153,
    229, 299 n. 12
Ibn Ezra, Moses, 185, 192–193
Ibn Gabirol, Solomon, 11, 14, 42
Ibn Latif, Itzhak, 209
Ibn Paquda, Bahya, 15–16, 59, 66, 72,
    97
Id, 16
imagination
    activity of, 9, 13, 14, 19, 45, 50,
        116, 242, 250
    control over, 4, 19, 20, 21, 32,
        33–34, 45
    disturbance of, 7, 12, 173, 174
    erroneous, 9, 13–14, 16
    and meditation, 100–103, 106
    sources of, 13, 16, 152
    see also danger
impulse, 3
    control over, 94
    forbidden, 15, 17, 31, 69, 218
    innate, 8, 33, 192
    see also appetite
incantation, 29, 143, 157, 174, 175

protective, 45, 46, 140, 149, 162,
    163
    remedial, 150, 155, 163
inclinations, 15, 31, 103, 254
    see also Evil Inclination
intellect, 12, 13, 22, 29, 33
    and music, 193, 209–210
intercessors, 38, 55, 80–83
interpretation
    of dreams, 42
    of gestures, 11
Iraq, 7, 78, 150, 175
    see also proverbs
Isaac, 6, 29, 30, 29, 237–238
    and meditation, 76, 98
    see also Abraham
Isaac ben Solomon Luria. see Luria,
    Isaac ben Solomon
Isaac Meir of Gur, 83
Isaac of Acre, 97, 100, 102
Isaac Yehudah Yehiel Safrin, 90
Isaiah, 118, 125
Ishmael ben Elisha, 89, 91, 98, 107,
    162, 166, 172
Israel, 44–45, 77, 78, 126, 167
    humor in, 218, 223, 224, 231
    see also Jerusalem; Safed
Israel ben Eliezer. see Ba'al Shem Tov
Israel Hapstein, Maggid of Koznitz, 82
Israel Lipkin of Salant, 16, 31, 71, 99,
    196
Israel of Ruzhin, 180–181
Isserlein, Israel, 117
Isserles, Moses, 77
Italy, 62, 135, 191, 221, 276 n. 46
    prayer book, 75, 144
    remedy book, 173

J

Jacob, 6, 57, 163
Jacob of Marvège, 133
Jehu, 107
Jeremiah (Prophet), 74
Jeremiah (Rabbi), 221
Jerusalem
    destruction of, 89
    exorcism in, 176–177
    kabbalists, 89, 101, 129–130, 147,
        181, 204
    metaphorical, 26, 207
    remedies from, 137, 167

tale from, 229
jester, 220, 223–224, 227
Job, 74
Joel Ba'al Shem Tov of Zamosc, 163, 166
Joha, 230
joke, 21, 52, 215–233
Jonah, 78
Jonah ben Abraham of Gerona, 72
Joseph, 6, 92, 122, 163
    and divination, 171
    dreams, 114, 130–132
Joseph ben Tirshom, 162
Joseph ben Yehudah Aknin. *see* Aknin, Joseph ben Yehudah
Josephus Flavius, 173
Judah ben Samuel the Pious of Regensburg, 68, 134, 139, 153
    on prayer, 72, 100, 195
Judah Halevi, 56, 147
Judah Löw, "Maharal," 77, 95
    tale, 113–114, 116
    on worry, 14, 31, 244, 245

K

Kaczerinski, Shmerke, 201
Kadouri, Itzhak, 181, 284 n. 83
Kalonymus ben Kalonymus, 219
Karo, Joseph, 69, 142, 307 n. 20
    and meditation, 90, 96, 98, 110
Katzenellenbogen, Pinhas, 69
knowledge, 16, 87, 88, 94, 153
    divine, 86–93, 101, 107
    esoteric, 85, 149. *see also* Moses
    of future, 41, 43, 92–93, 100, 150–152
    and meaning, 40–43
    tree of, 8, 214
    and understanding, 87, 91, 208–210
    see also dreams, revelation in; dreams, interpretation of; revelation
Kook, Abraham Isaac, 14, 34, 238, 244
Kushner, Harold, S., 40

L

laughter. *see* humor
Leone of Modena, 134–135, 191, 196, 204, 209
Lesser, Miriam, 125
Levi ben Gershom, 97

Levi-Itzhak of Berditchev, 75, 208, 312 n. 24
Levin, Rachel (Varnagen von Ense), 18
Lévi-Strauss, Claude, 185, 210
liturgy, 30, 54, 56, 65, 68, 73
loneliness, 11, 12, 63, 98, 213
Lot, 6
love, 11, 70, 217, 252, 256–259, 300 n. 20
    of God, 29, 158, 195, 237, 251
    of life, 250
    see also worries, causes of
lullaby, 197, 198, 199–201
Luria, Isaac, 79, 153, 207, 251
Luzzatto, Moshe Hayyim, 157, 173

M

Magen David, 164, 167, 168
magic, 50, 89, 145–182
    definition of, 148–149
    prohibitions against, 146, 149, 171
    and publicity, 179–182
    reasons for using, 150–156
    tools of, 149, 158–173, 179–182
    see also amulet; biblical verses; Divine Names; divination; dreams, *hatavat halom*; *Magen David*; necromancy; Solomon, seal of
magic circle, 145–146, 149, 156
    on amulet, 158, 167, 168
magic square, 101, 158, 168–169
Maharal. *see* Judah Löw
Maharil. *see* Moellin, Jacob Segal
Maimonides, Moses, 33, 42, 138, 143, 238
    on anxiety, 12, 14, 22–23, 28, 240
    on controlling thought, 13, 44, 68
    on dream fast, 141
    on imagination, 13, 33
    on magic, 138, 147, 154, 160
    on prayer, 61, 67, 74, 97
Manasseh ben Israel, 118, 141
martyr, 30, 62, 92, 93
Marx Brothers, 229
Maslow, Abraham, 104–105
meaning, 8, 31, 38, 50, 51
    of dreams, 114, 117, 121–125
    see also dreams, interpretation of; knowledge
meditation, 85–112, 148
    and banishing worry, 86, 95–100

relationships, 23, 49, 63, 75, 119, 198, 229
school, 23
self, 4, 6, 11, 23, 31, 38, 245, 248
sexuality, 52, 127, 229
status, 245
sustenance, 10, 249
transgression, 47, 64, 128, 138
travel, 95, 157, 166, 169
work, 10, 28, 32
world to come, 133
worry, acceptance of, 51–52
worry, causes of, 7–18
  anticipation of danger, 3, 4, 6, 14, 20, 33, 61–63, 165–170
  bitter experience, 4, 14–15, 22
  demonic force, 7, 9, 45, 101, 140, 152, 154, 165, 171
  dreams, 123, 127–128, 139–144
  guilt, 6, 246
  human nature, 3, 12, 17
  inner conflict, 11, 15–17, 246
  insecurity, 4, 10–12, 15, 18, 115, 214, 225, 230
  love, 11, 17, 47, 63
  morality, 47, 64, 247, 254
  needs and desires, 8, 10, 11–12, 17, 19, 118
  reason, failure of, 4, 13
  transgression, 6, 8–10, 64, 244
worry, definition of, xvii, 4. *see also* fear
worry, duration of, 20–21, 29, 65
worry, habitual, 20–21, 242
worry, harmful, 7, 20, 24, 26, 239–245
worry, nature of, 4–5, 18–23
  cognitive, 5, 7, 18–20, 253. *see also* imagination; perception; thought, disturbing
  emotional, 19, 22, 246. *see also* emotion
  physical, 13, 19, 22. *see also* arousal

worry, process of, 5, 18–23
  onset of, 4, 18–19
  termination of, 4, 20–21, 25, 27–51, 242, 252
  "work of worry" in, 5, 267 n. 3
  see also emotion; imagination; perception
worry, purposes of, 51–52, 245–259
  avoid danger, 32, 245, 250
  improvement, 246, 248, 253–254
  prepare for danger, 4, 13, 52, 121, 245, 250
  prepare for world to come, 249–250
  problem-solving, 20, 24, 37, 48, 121, 242, 252–253
worry, vocabulary of, xvi–xvii, 5–7, 267–269
  see also anxiety; evil spirit; fear

Y

Yagel, Abraham, 13, 134, 152, 241
Yakov Itzhak, "Seer of Lublin," 40, 157, 175, 224, 234, 285 n. 85
Yehiel Mikhal, Maggid of Zlotchov, 82
Yemen, 7, 50, 78, 150, 173, 175
Yerkes, Robert M., 238
Yiddish, 73, 75, 138, 220, 234–235
Yitzhak of Worke, 244
Yohanan, 185
Yohanan ben Nappaha, 27–28
Yom Kippur, 62, 75, 141, 142, 190
  Kol Nidrei, 196

Z

Zahalon, Jacob, 28, 241
Zohar, 16, 68–69, 74, 78, 162, 174
  on dreams, 116, 143
  on music, 185, 209, 306 n. 6